DOVER · THRIFT · EDITIONS

Four Great Russian Plays

Anton Chekhov, Nikolai Gogol,
Maxim Gorky and Ivan Turgenev

DOVER PUBLICATIONS, INC.
Mineola, New York

DOVER THRIFT EDITIONS

GENERAL EDITOR: PAUL NEGRI
EDITOR OF THIS VOLUME: T. N. R. ROGERS

Copyright

Theatrical Rights

Bibliographical Note

This Dover edition, first published in 2004, contains the unabridged texts of four Russian plays translated into English: *The Cherry Orchard,* from *The Works of Anton Chekhov: One Volume Edition,* Black's Readers Service Company, New York, n.d. (ca. 1929; translator not credited), republished as a Dover Thrift Edition in 1991; *The Inspector General* (translated as *The Inspector* by John Laurence Seymour and George Rapall Noyes) from *Masterpieces of the Russian Drama,* edited by George Rapall Noyes, D. Appleton and Company, New York, 1931, republished as a Dover Thrift Edition in 1995; *The Lower Depths* (translated by Jennie Covan) published by Brentano's Publishers, New York, in 1923, and republished as a Dover Thrift Edition in 2000; and *A Month in the Country* (translated by Constance Garnett) from a standard edition. The editor has supplied a new Introduction specially for this Dover edition.

Library of Congress Cataloging-in-Publication Data

Four great Russian plays / Anton Chekhov and others.
p. cm. — (Dover thrift editions)
First work originally published: New York : Dover, 1991. 2nd work originally published: New York : Dover, 1995. 3rd work originally published: Mineola, N.Y. : Dover, 2000. 4th work previously published; with new introd.
Contents: The cherry orchard / Anton Chekhov—The inspector general / Nikolai Gogol—The lower depths / Maxim Gorky—A month in the country / Ivan Turgenev.
ISBN 0-486-43472-9 (pbk.)
1. Russian drama—Translations into English. I. Chekhov, Anton Pavlovich, 1860–1904. Vishnevyi sad. English. II. Gogol', Nikolai Vasil'evich, 1809–1852. Revizor. English. III. Gorky, Maksim, 1868–1936. Na dne. English. IV. Turgenev, Ivan Sergeevich, 1818–1883. Mesiats v derevne. English. V. Series.

PG3245.F58 2004
491.72'308—dc22 2004043836

Manufactured in the United States of America
Dover Publications, Inc., 31 East 2nd Street, Mineola, N.Y. 11501

Introduction

FOUR GREAT PLAYS, four brilliant writers. The plays had their first productions between 1836 and 1904. The first of the authors was a friend of Pushkin's, and it is suspected that the last may have been poisoned on Stalin's order. Here are brief biographical notes, in order of their births:

Nikolay Vasilyevich Gogol (1809–1852) was born in Sorochintsy, Ukraine, and grew up on his parents' 200-serf country estate. His father, a talented amateur who wrote Ukrainian comedies in verse, died when he was sixteen. In 1828, after his graduation from the Nezhin boarding school, Gogol moved to Saint Petersburg where, through the help of a friend, he landed a minor governmental job. A couple of years later, the same year as the publication of the first volume of his story collection *Evenings on a Farm near Dikanka,* he met Aleksandr Pushkin, who was ten years his elder and is said to have had considerable influence on his writing; the two remained friends till the great poet's death in 1837. Like his contemporary Edgar Allen Poe (also born in 1809), Gogol was heavily influenced by the fantastic writings of E. T. A. Hoffmann (1776–1822)—as can be seen in such imaginative, hallucinatory stories as "The Nose," "Nevsky Prospect," "The Diary of a Madman," and "The Overcoat." (The last was so influential that Dostoyevsky is supposed to have said about his own generation of writers, "We have all come out from under Gogol's 'Overcoat.'"[1]) In 1836 (the same year as "The Nose") Gogol wrote his play *Revizor (The Inspector;* also translated as *The Inspector General)*—regarded by Vladimir Nabokov, among others, as the greatest play in the Russian language. But the production was not universally praised, and Gogol, upset, left Russia to travel in western Europe. In Rome he wrote *Dead Souls;* he also wrote reactionary essays defending the tsarist regime, which horrified his liberal friends and admirers. In 1848, after an unrewarding pilgrimage to Palestine, Gogol returned to Russia suffering from depression and a religious mania that was fed by a fanatical priest,

[1] Some people credit Turgenev with this remark.

Father Matvey Konstantinovsky. It has been suggested that Gogol was tortured all his life by homosexuality, and that he confessed this terrible fact to Father Matvey. Whatever the case, Father Matvey persuaded Gogol to cleanse his soul by fasting; he also convinced him that his writings were sinful and had to be destroyed. In February 1852 Gogol burned the manuscript he had been working on for ten years—a sequel to *Dead Souls*. Ten days later, after refusing to take any food, he died on the verge of madness.

Ivan Sergeyevitch Turgenev (1818–1883) passed an unhappy childhood in Oryol, 300 miles from Moscow. His mother was the owner of a huge estate, Spasskoye-Lutovinovo, where she ruled over her serfs and sons with a cruel despotism. Turgenev's father, who was to die when he was fifteen, was an impoverished cavalry officer who had married for money. The year his father died, Turgenev left Spasskoye to study in Moscow; he went on to the University of Saint Petersburg and the University of Berlin, and then entered the Russian civil service for a couple of years before quitting (bolstered by the success of two story poems) to devote himself to writing. He is best known for his novels and stories, but between 1843 and 1852 he also wrote ten plays—including *Mesyats v derevnye* (A *Month in the Country*, 1850). In this play, Eric Bentley wrote,[2] "Turgenev not only anticipated modern psychological drama, he also retained the ingenious plot and strict, intricate structure of the older theatre. How Ben Jonson or Molière would have enjoyed his version of the cuckold's discomfiture!" A *Month in the Country* was a precursor to the plays Chekhov wrote half a century later, and seems not to have been properly appreciated till its presentation by the Moscow Art Theater in 1909, after audiences had been trained to modern drama. Like many of Turgenev's works, the play was at least somewhat autobiographical. A gentle giant whose mistresses had included sisters of Tolstoy and of the anarchist Mikhail Bakunin, Turgenev never married. The shining star in his life was always to be Pauline Garcia Viardot (1821–1910), a Spanish opera singer he first met in 1843, when she was twenty-one—and, like Natalya Petrovna in A *Month in the Country*, already quite married (to the director of the Opéra Italien in Paris, who was twice her age). "Turgenev was her lifelong slave," wrote David Garnett.[3] "He first met her and, in all probability, became her lover when he somewhat resembled Beliayev, the young tutor in A *Month in the Country*. . . . Then, as the years went by, he came to occupy the painful position of Rakitin." Turgenev was so integral a part of the Viardot household that Pauline and her husband

[2] In *What is Theatre?*
[3] In his Introduction to *Three Famous Plays* by Turgenev. London: Duckworth, 1951.

even brought up Turgenev's daughter (by a Spasskoye seamstress), whom he called Paulinette, as part of the family.[4] After 1847 Turgenev lived mainly outside Russia, usually with the Viardots, though he returned to Spasskoye in the summers to write. He was the first nineteenth-century Russian writer to become well known in Europe, and his friends included George Sand, Emile Zola, Guy de Maupassant, George Eliot, and especially Gustave Flaubert. Henry James, another friend, called him "the most touching of writers, the most lovable of men" and said "I found him adorable."[5] (Dostoyevsky, on the other hand, did not like him, and Tolstoy sometimes found him boring and, after he had demonstrated a can-can for Tolstoy's children, a little pathetic.) It was at the Viardots' home near Paris that Turgenev died of cancer in 1883.

Anton Pavlovich Chekhov (1860–1904) was born in Taganrog, in the south of Russia, the third of six children. His father, the son of freed serfs, was a grocer who went bankrupt and fled town when Chekhov was sixteen. When Chekhov joined his family in Moscow in 1879, he took on himself the responsibility for their support; he began his writing career willy-nilly while still a medical student at the University of Moscow, dashing off short stories and comic sketches to earn money to help support them. His life thereafter was not a conventionally exciting one: first a balancing act between his medical practice and his writing, and later a struggle against tuberculosis and a struggle to get his writing done before he died. His first full-length play (an unnamed one, sometimes called *Platonov*, that was not discovered till after his death) was written in 1881. The first to be produced was *Ivanov* (1887), written three years after his 1884 graduation. His plays were not well received till the Moscow Art Theater in 1897 produced *The Sea Gull* (directed by the great Konstantin Stanislavsky)—a play that had gotten such a poor reception in its Saint Petersburg staging two years earlier that Chekhov had walked out during the second act and vowed never to write for the stage again. (Tolstoy, who admired some of the younger writer's short stories, famously advised Chekhov that his plays were "even worse than Shakespeare's.") After the Moscow success, Chekhov rewrote his flawed 1889 play *The Wood Demon* as *Uncle Vanya* (1899), and followed with *The Three Sisters* (1901) and *The Cherry Orchard* (*Vishnyovy sad*, 1904)—all three, after their Moscow Art Theater triumphs, recognized as masterpieces of the modern theater. Chekhov

[4] Charles Gounod (1818–1893), the French composer, also was in love with Mme Viardot, and also became part of the household. He wrote his 1850 opera *Sappho* with her in mind.

[5] In his 1903 memoir "Ivan Turgenev."

was wed in 1901 to the actress Olga Knipper (1870–1959), whom he had met when she played the lead in *The Sea Gull;* but by then, trying to recuperate from an 1897 lung hemorrhage, he was having to spend most of his time in Yalta while his wife pursued her career in Moscow. In the first presentation of *The Cherry Orchard*—which opened on Chekhov's final birthday, January 17, 1904—she took the role of Madame Ranevsky. (Stanislavsky himself played Gayev.) She was with him when, less than six months later, he died at the German health resort at Badenweiler.

Maxim Gorky (1868–1936) was born Aleksey Maksimovich Peshkov in Nizhny Novgorod (which the Soviets later renamed Gorky in his honor); his pen name comes from the Russian word *gorki,* meaning "bitter," which seems an appropriate description of his early life. His father died when he was five, and he was sent to live with his maternal grandparents. His grandmother treated him kindly; not so his grandfather, who sent him out to work at eight years old as (among other things) an assistant to a shoemaker, an icon-painter's assistant, and a dishwasher on a Volga steamer. On the steamer the cook taught him to read, and reading became Gorky's passion. At twelve he ran away from home and for years worked at small jobs where he was often beaten by his employers and often went hungry. For several years he worked in Kazan as a baker, a dock hand, and a night watchman—a dead-end sort of life that, when he was about twenty, led him to shoot himself in the chest in a failed suicide attempt. When he recovered, he left Kazan and for two years tramped through southern Russia, Ukraine, and Georgia—becoming acquainted with the hoboes, prostitutes, thieves, Gypsies, and other dregs of society who became fodder for his pen. His first published story appeared in a Tiflis (Tbilisi) newspaper in 1892. Gorky's stories introduced readers to characters who, though unquestionably alive, were unlike any they were used to seeing in fiction; they found a responsive audience, and Gorky became a kind of literary folk hero. When Chekhov introduced him to the Moscow Art Theater company in the spring of 1900, they persuaded him to give them a play. The second of his plays they produced was *The Lower Depths* (*Na dne;* literally, "At the bottom"), which opened in 1902. Gorky was a revolutionary at heart and donated to the Marxists much of the money earned by his plays. After a brief imprisonment (decried by the international community) following the abortive revolution of 1905, he went abroad, writing more plays and campaigning for revolution;[6] he returned to

[6] In New York in 1906 Gorky was fêted and the revolutionary cause championed by Mark Twain and others, but Americans turned against him when they found that he had been traveling with a woman who was not his wife.

Russia in 1913 and got to see the revolution firsthand. Nine years later, disillusioned with Soviet rule, he left again and spent the next six years in Italy. On his return to Russia in 1928 he was greeted as a hero. He died eight years later—whether from the tuberculosis treatment he was receiving or from poison administered on Stalin's order is unclear.

Contents

The Cherry Orchard

Cast of Characters

MME. RANEVSKY [Lyubov Andreyevna Ranevskaya], *a landowner*
ANYA, *her daughter, seventeen years old*
BARBARA [Varya], *her adopted daughter, twenty-four years old*
Leonid Andreyevich GAYEF, *Mme. Ranevsky's brother*
Yermolai Alexeyevich LOPAKHIN, *merchant*
Peter Sergeyevich TROPHIMOF, *student*
Boris Borisovich Simeonov-PISHTCHIK, *a landowner*
CHARLOTTE [Charlotta Ivanovna], *a governess*
EPHIKHODOF [Semyon Panteleyevich Epikhodov], *a clerk*
DUNYASHA, *a maidservant*
FIRS, *footman, eighty-seven years old*
YASHA, *a young footman*
TRAMP
STATIONMASTER
POSTMASTER
GUESTS

Act I

A room which is still called the nursery. One door leads to ANYA'S *room. Dawn, the sun will soon rise. It is already May, the cherry trees are in blossom, but it is cold in the garden and there is a morning frost. The windows are closed.*

Enter DUNYASHA *with a candle, and* LOPAKHIN *with a book in his hand.*

LOPAKHIN. Here's the train, thank heaven. What is the time?

DUNYASHA. Near two. [*Putting the candle out.*] It is light already.

LOPAKHIN. How late is the train? Two hours at least. [*Yawning and stretching.*] A fine mess I have made of it. I came to meet them at the station and then I went and fell asleep, as I sat in my chair. What trouble! Why did you not rouse me?

DUNYASHA. I thought that you had gone. [*She listens.*] I think they are coming.

LOPAKHIN [*listening*]. No; they have got to get the baggage and the rest. [*A pause.*] Madame Ranévsky has been five years abroad. I wonder what she is like now. What a fine character she is! So easy and simple. I remember when I was only fifteen my old father (he used to keep a shop here in the village then) struck me in the face with his fist and my nose bled. We were out in the courtyard, and he had been drinking. Madame Ranévsky, I remember it like yesterday, still a slender young girl, brought me to the wash-hand stand, here, in this very room, in the nursery. 'Don't cry, little peasant,' she said, 'it'll be all right for your wedding.' [*A pause.*] 'Little peasant!' . . . My father, it is true, was a peasant, and here am I in a white waistcoat and brown boots; a silk purse out of a sow's ear; just turned rich, with plenty of money, but still a peasant of the peasants. [*Turning over the pages of the book.*] Here's this book that I was reading without any attention and fell asleep.

DUNYASHA. The dogs never slept all night, they knew that their master and mistress were coming.
LOPAKHIN. What's the matter with you, Dunyásha? You're all . . .
DUNYASHA. My hands are trembling, I feel quite faint.
LOPAKHIN. You are too refined, Dunyásha, that's what it is. You dress yourself like a young lady, and look at your hair! You ought not to do it; you ought to remember your place.

[*Enter* EPHIKHODOF *with a nosegay. He is dressed in a short jacket and brightly polished boots which squeak noisily. As he comes in he drops the nosegay.*]

EPHIKHODOF [*picking it up*]. The gardener has sent this; he says it is to go in the dining-room. [*Handing it to* DUNYASHA.]
LOPAKHIN. And bring me some quass.
DUNYASHA. Yes, sir.

[*Exit* DUNYASHA.]

EPHIKHODOF. There's a frost this morning, three degrees, and the cherry trees all in blossom. I can't say I think much of our climate; [*sighing*] that is impossible. Our climate is not adapted to contribute; and I should like to add, with your permission, that only two days ago I bought myself a new pair of boots, and I venture to assure you they do squeak beyond all bearing. What am I to grease them with?
LOPAKHIN. Get out; I'm tired of you.
EPHIKHODOF. Every day some misfortune happens to me; but do I grumble? No; I am used to it; I can afford to smile. [*Enter* DUNYASHA, *and hands a glass of quass to* LOPAKHIN.] I must be going. [*He knocks against a chair, which falls to the ground.*] There you are! [*In a voice of triumph.*] You see, if I may venture on the expression, the sort of incidents *inter alia*. It really is astonishing!

[*Exit* EPHIKHODOF.]

DUNYASHA. To tell you the truth, Yermolái Alexéyitch, Ephikhódof has made me a proposal.
LOPAKHIN. Hmph!
DUNYASHA. I hardly know what to do. He is such a well-behaved young man, only so often when he talks one doesn't know what he means. It is all so nice and full of good feeling, but you can't make out what it means. I fancy I am rather fond of him. He adores me passionately. He is a most unfortunate man; every day something seems to happen to him. They call him 'Twenty-two misfortunes,' that's his nickname.
LOPAKHIN [*listening*]. There, surely that is them coming!

DUNYASHA. They're coming! Oh, what is the matter with me? I am all turning cold.
LOPAKHIN. Yes, there they are, and no mistake. Let's go and meet them. Will she know me again, I wonder? It is five years since we met.
DUNYASHA. I am going to faint! . . . I am going to faint!

[*Two carriages are heard driving up to the house.* LOPAKHIN *and* DUNYASHA *exeunt quickly. The stage remains empty. A hubbub begins in the neighbouring rooms.* FIRS *walks hastily across the stage, leaning on a walking-stick. He has been to meet them at the station. He is wearing an old-fashioned livery and a tall hat; he mumbles something to himself but not a word is audible. The noise behind the scenes grows louder and louder. A voice says: 'Let's go this way.'*

[*Enter* MADAME RANEVSKY, ANYA, CHARLOTTE, *leading a little dog on a chain, all dressed in travelling dresses;* BARBARA *in greatcoat with a kerchief over her head,* GAYEF, SIMEONOF-PISHTCHIK, LOPAKHIN, DUNYASHA, *carrying parcel and umbrella, servants with luggage, all cross the stage.*]

ANYA. Come through this way. Do you remember what room this is, mamma?
MADAME RANEVSKY [*joyfully through her tears*]. The nursery.
BARBARA. How cold it is. My hands are simply frozen. [*To* MADAME RANEVSKY.] Your two rooms, the white room and the violet room, are just the same as they were, mamma.
MADAME RANEVSKY. My nursery, my dear, beautiful nursery! This is where I used to sleep when I was a little girl. [*Crying.*] I am like a little girl still. [*Kissing* GAYEF *and* BARBARA *and then* GAYEF *again.*] Barbara has not altered a bit, she is just like a nun, and I knew Dunyásha at once. [*Kissing* DUNYASHA.]
GAYEF. Your train was two hours late. What do you think of that? There's punctuality for you!
CHARLOTTE [*to* SIMEONOF-PISHTCHIK]. My little dog eats nuts.
PISHTCHIK [*astonished*]. You don't say so! Well, I never!

[*Exeunt all but* ANYA *and* DUNYASHA.]

DUNYASHA. At last you've come!

[*She takes off* ANYA's *overcoat and hat.*]

ANYA. I have not slept for four nights on the journey. I am frozen to death.
DUNYASHA. It was Lent when you went away. There was snow on the ground, it was freezing; but now! Oh, my dear! [*Laughing and kissing*

her.] How I have waited for you, my joy, my light! Oh, I must tell you something at once, I cannot wait another minute.

ANYA [*without interest*]. What, again?

DUNYASHA. Ephikhódof, the clerk, proposed to me in Easter week.

ANYA. Same old story. . . . [*Putting her hair straight.*] All my hairpins have dropped out. [*She is very tired, staggering with fatigue.*]

DUNYASHA. I hardly know what to think of it. He loves me! oh, how he loves me!

ANYA [*looking into her bedroom, affectionately*]. My room, my windows, just as if I had never gone away! I am at home again! When I wake up in the morning I shall run out into the garden. . . . Oh, if only I could get to sleep! I have not slept the whole journey from Paris, I was so nervous and anxious.

DUNYASHA. Monsieur Trophímof arrived the day before yesterday.

ANYA [*joyfully*]. Peter?

DUNYASHA. He is sleeping outside in the bath-house; he is living there. He was afraid he might be in the way. [*Looking at her watch.*] I'd like to go and wake him, only Mamzelle Barbara told me not to. 'Mind you don't wake him,' she said.

[*Enter* BARBARA *with bunch of keys hanging from her girdle.*]

BARBARA. Dunyásha, go and get some coffee, quick. Mamma wants some coffee.

DUNYASHA. In a minute.

[*Exit* DUNYASHA.]

BARBARA. Well, thank heaven, you have come. Here you are at home again. [*Caressing her.*] My little darling is back! My pretty one is back!

ANYA. What I've had to go through!

BARBARA. I can believe you.

ANYA. I left here in Holy Week. How cold it was! Charlotte would talk the whole way and keep doing conjuring tricks. What on earth made you tie Charlotte round my neck?

BARBARA. Well, you couldn't travel alone, my pet. At seventeen!

ANYA. When we got to Paris, it was so cold! there was snow on the ground. I can't talk French a bit. Mamma was on the fifth floor of a big house. When I arrived there were a lot of Frenchmen with her, and ladies, and an old Catholic priest with a book, and it was very uncomfortable and full of tobacco smoke. I suddenly felt so sorry for mamma, oh, so sorry! I took her head in my arms and squeezed it and could not let it go, and then mamma kept kissing me and crying.

BARBARA [*crying*]. Don't go on, don't go on!

ANYA. She's sold her villa near Mentone already. She's nothing left, absolutely nothing; and I hadn't a farthing either. We only just managed to get home. And mamma won't understand! We get out at a station to have some dinner, and she asks for all the most expensive things and gives the waiters a florin each for a tip; and Charlotte does the same. And Yásha wanted his portion too. It was too awful! Yásha is mamma's new man-servant. We have brought him back with us.

BARBARA. I've seen the rascal.

ANYA. Come, tell me all about everything! Has the interest on the mortgage been paid?

BARBARA. How could it be?

ANYA. Oh dear! Oh dear!

BARBARA. The property will be sold in August.

ANYA. Oh dear! Oh dear!

LOPAKHIN [*looking in at the door and mooing like a cow*]. Moo-o.

[*He goes away again.*]

BARBARA [*laughing through her tears and shaking her fist at the door*]. Oh, I should like to give him one!

ANYA [*embracing* BARBARA *softly*]. Barbara, has he proposed to you? [BARBARA *shakes her head.*] And yet I am sure he loves you. Why don't you come to an understanding? What are you waiting for?

BARBARA. I don't think anything will come of it. He has so much to do; he can't be bothered with me; he hardly takes any notice. Confound the man, I can't bear to see him! Everyone talks about our marriage; everyone congratulates me, but, as a matter of fact, there is nothing in it; it's all a dream. [*Changing her tone.*] You've got on a brooch like a bee.

ANYA [*sadly*]. Mamma bought it for me. [*Going into her room, talking gaily, like a child.*] When I was in Paris, I went up in a balloon!

BARBARA. How glad I am you are back, my little pet! my pretty one! [DUNYASHA *has already returned with a coffee-pot and begins to prepare the coffee.*] [*Standing by the door.*] I trudge about all day looking after things, and I think and think. What are we to do? If only we could marry you to some rich man it would be a load off my mind. I would go into a retreat, and then to Kief, to Moscow; I would tramp about from one holy place to another, always tramping and tramping. What bliss!

ANYA. The birds are singing in the garden. What time is it now?

BARBARA. It must be past two. It is time to go to bed, my darling. [*Following* ANYA *into her room.*] What bliss!

[*Enter* YASHA *with a shawl and a travelling bag.*]

YASHA [*crossing the stage, delicately*]. May I pass this way, mademoiselle?
DUNYASHA. One would hardly know you, Yásha. How you've changed abroad!
YASHA. Ahem! and who may you be?
DUNYASHA. When you left here I was a little thing like that. [*Indicating with her hand.*] My name is Dunyásha, Theodore Kozoyédof's daughter. Don't you remember me?
YASHA. Ahem! You little cucumber!

[*He looks round cautiously, then embraces her. She screams and drops a saucer. Exit* YASHA, *hastily.*]

BARBARA [*in the doorway, crossly*]. What's all this?
DUNYASHA [*crying*]. I've broken a saucer.
BARBARA. Well, it brings luck.

[*Enter* ANYA *from her room.*]

ANYA. We must tell mamma that Peter's here.
BARBARA. I've told them not to wake him.
ANYA [*thoughtfully*]. It's just six years since papa died. And only a month afterwards poor little Grisha was drowned in the river; my pretty little brother, only seven years old! It was too much for mamma; she ran away, ran away without looking back. [*Shuddering.*] How well I can understand her, if only she knew! [A *pause.*] Peter Trophímof was Grisha's tutor; he might remind her.

[*Enter* FIRS *in long coat and white waistcoat.*]

FIRS [*going over to the coffee-pot, anxiously*]. My mistress is going to take coffee here. [*Putting on white gloves.*] Is the coffee ready? [*Sternly, to* DUNYASHA.] Here, girl, where's the cream?
DUNYASHA. Oh, dear! Oh dear!

[*Exit* DUNYASHA, *hastily.*]

FIRS [*bustling about the coffee-pot*]. Ah, you . . . job-lot! [*Mumbling to himself.*] She's come back from Paris. The master went to Paris once in a post-chaise. [*Laughing.*]
BARBARA. What is it, Firs?
FIRS. I beg your pardon? [*Joyfully.*] My mistress has come home; at last I've seen her. Now I'm ready to die.

[*He cries with joy. Enter* MADAME RANEVSKY, LOPAKHIN, GAYEF *and* PISHTCHIK; PISHTCHIK *in Russian breeches and coat of fine cloth.* GAYEF *as he enters makes gestures as if playing billiards.*]

MADAME RANEVSKY. What was the expression? Let me see. 'I'll put the red in the corner pocket; double into the middle——'
GAYEF. I'll chip the red in the right-hand top. Once upon a time. Lyuba, when we were children, we used to sleep here side by side in two little cots, and now I'm fifty-one, and can't bring myself to believe it.
LOPAKHIN. Yes; time flies.
GAYEF. Who's that?
LOPAKHIN. Time flies. I say.
GAYEF. There's a smell of patchouli!
ANYA. I am going to bed. Good-night, mamma. [*Kissing her mother.*]
MADAME RANEVSKY. My beloved little girl! [*Kissing her hands.*] Are you glad you're home again? I can't come to my right senses.
ANYA. Good-night, uncle.
GAYEF [*kissing her face and hands*]. God bless you, little Anya. How like your mother you are! [*To* MADAME RANEVSKY.] You were just such another girl at her age, Lyuba.

[ANYA *shakes hands with* LOPAKHIN *and* SIMEONOF-PISHTCHIK *and exit, shutting her bedroom door behind her.*]

MADAME RANEVSKY. She's very, very tired.
PISHTCHIK. It must have been a long journey.
BARBARA [*to* LOPAKHIN *and* PISHTCHIK]. Well, gentlemen, it's past two; time you were off.
MADAME RANEVSKY [*laughing*]. You haven't changed a bit, Barbara! [*Drawing her to herself and kissing her.*] I'll just finish my coffee, then we'll all go. [FIRS *puts a footstool under her feet.*] Thank you, friend. I'm used to my coffee. I drink it day and night. Thank you, you dear old man, [*Kissing* FIRS.]
BARBARA. I'll go and see if they've got all the luggage. [*Exit* BARBARA.]
MADAME RANEVSKY. Can it be me that's sitting here? [*Laughing.*] I want to jump and wave my arms about. [*Pausing and covering her face.*] Surely I must be dreaming! God knows I love my country. I love it tenderly. I couldn't see out of the window from the train, I was crying so. [*Crying.*] However, I must drink my coffee. Thank you, Firs; thank you, dear old man. I'm so glad to find you still alive.
FIRS. The day before yesterday.
GAYEF. He's hard of hearing.
LOPAKHIN. I've got to be off for Kharkof by the five o'clock train. Such a nuisance! I wanted to stay and look at you and talk to you. You're as splendid as you always were.
PISHTCHIK [*sighing heavily*]. Handsomer than ever and dressed like a Parisian . . . perish my waggon and all its wheels!

LOPAKHIN. Your brother, Leoníd Andréyitch, says I'm a snob, a money-grubber. He can say what he likes. I don't care a hang. Only I want you to believe in me as you used to; I want your wonderful, touching eyes to look at me as they used to. Merciful God in heaven! My father was your father's serf, and your grandfather's serf before him; but you, you did so much for me in the old days that I've forgotten everything, and I love you like a sister—more than a sister.

MADAME RANEVSKY. I can't sit still! I can't do it! [*Jumping up and walking about in great agitation.*] This happiness is more than I can bear. Laugh at me! I am a fool! [*Kissing a cupboard.*] My darling old cupboard! [*Caressing a table.*] My dear little table!

GAYEF. Nurse is dead since you went away.

MADAME RANEVSKY [*sitting down and drinking coffee*]. Yes, Heaven rest her soul. They wrote and told me.

GAYEF. And Anastási is dead. Squint-eyed Peter has left us and works in the town at the Police Inspector's now.

[GAYEF *takes out a box of sugar candy from his pocket, and begins to eat it.*]

PISHTCHIK. My daughter Dáshenka sent her compliments.

LOPAKHIN. I long to say something charming and delightful to you. [*Looking at his watch.*] I'm just off; there's no time to talk. Well, yes, I'll put it in two or three words. You know that your cherry orchard is going to be sold to pay the mortgage: the sale is fixed for the twenty-second of August; but don't you be uneasy, my dear lady; sleep peacefully; there's a way out of it. This is my plan. Listen to me carefully. Your property is only fifteen miles from the town; the railway runs close beside it; and if only you will cut up the cherry orchard and the land along the river into building lots and let it off on lease for villas, you will get at least two thousand five hundred pounds a year out of it.

GAYEF. Come, come! What rubbish you're talking!

MADAME RANEVSKY. I don't quite understand what you mean, Yermolái Alexéyitch.

LOPAKHIN. You will get a pound a year at least for every acre from the tenants, and if you advertise the thing at once, I am ready to bet whatever you like, by the autumn you won't have a clod of that earth left on your hands. It'll all be snapped up. In two words, I congratulate you; you are saved. It's a first-class site, with a good deep river. Only of course you will have to put it in order and clear the ground; you will have to pull down all the old buildings—this house, for instance, which is no longer fit for anything; you'll have to cut down the cherry orchard. . . .

MADAME RANEVSKY. Cut down the cherry orchard! Excuse me, but you don't know what you're talking about. If there is one thing that's interesting, remarkable in fact, in the whole province, it's our cherry orchard.

LOPAKHIN. There's nothing remarkable about the orchard except that it's a very big one. It only bears once every two years, and then you don't know what to do with the fruit. Nobody wants to buy it.

GAYEF. Our cherry orchard is mentioned in Andréyevsky's Encyclopaedia.

LOPAKHIN [*looking at his watch*]. If we don't make up our minds or think of any way, on the twenty-second of August the cherry orchard and the whole property will be sold by auction. Come, make up your mind! There's no other way out of it, I swear—absolutely none.

FIRS. In the old days, forty or fifty years ago, they used to dry the cherries and soak 'em and pickle 'em, and make jam of 'em; and the dried cherries . . .

GAYEF. Shut up, Firs.

FIRS. The dried cherries used to be sent in waggons to Moscow and Kharkof. A heap of money! The dried cherries were soft and juicy and sweet and sweet-smelling then. They knew some way in those days.

MADAME RANEVSKY. And why don't they do it now?

FIRS. They've forgotten. Nobody remembers how to do it.

PISHTCHIK [*to* MADAME RANEVSKY]. What about Paris? How did you get on? Did you eat frogs?

MADAME RANEVSKY. Crocodiles.

PISHTCHIK. You don't say so! Well, I never!

LOPAKHIN. Until a little while ago there was nothing but gentry and peasants in the villages; but now villa residents have made their appearance. All the towns, even the little ones, are surrounded by villas now. In another twenty years the villa resident will have multiplied like anything. At present he only sits and drinks tea on his verandah, but it is quite likely that he will soon take to cultivating his three acres of land, and then your old cherry orchard will become fruitful, rich and happy. . . .

GAYEF [*angry*]. What gibberish!

[*Enter* BARBARA *and* YASHA.]

BARBARA [*taking out a key and noisily unlocking an old-fashioned cupboard*]. There are two telegrams for you, mamma. Here they are.

MADAME RANEVSKY [*tearing them up without reading them*]. They're from Paris. I've done with Paris.

GAYEF. Do you know how old this cupboard is, Lyuba? A week ago I pulled out the bottom drawer and saw a date burnt in it. That cupboard was made exactly a hundred years ago. What do you think of that, eh? We might celebrate its jubilee. It's only an inanimate thing, but for all that it's a historic cupboard.

PISHTCHIK [*astonished*]. A hundred years? Well, I never!

GAYEF [*touching the cupboard*]. Yes, it's a wonderful thing. . . . Beloved and venerable cupboard; honour and glory to your existence, which for more than a hundred years has been directed to the noble ideals of justice and virtue. Your silent summons to profitable labour has never weakened in all these hundred years. [*Crying.*] You have upheld the courage of succeeding generations of our human kind; you have upheld faith in a better future and cherished in us ideals of goodness and social consciousness. [*A pause.*]

LOPAKHIN. Yes. . . .

MADAME RANEVSKY. You haven't changed, Leoníd.

GAYEF [*embarrassed*]. Off the white in the corner, chip the red in the middle pocket!

LOPAKHIN [*looking at his watch*]. Well, I must be off.

YASHA [*handing a box to* MADAME RANEVSKY]. Perhaps you'll take your pills now.

PISHTCHIK. You oughtn't to take medicine, dear lady. It does you neither good nor harm. Give them here, my friend. [*He empties all the pills into the palm of his hand, blows on them, puts them in his mouth and swallows them down with a draught of quass.*] There!

MADAME RANEVSKY [*alarmed*]. Have you gone off your head?

PISHTCHIK. I've taken all the pills.

LOPAKHIN. Greedy fellow! [*Everyone laughs.*]

FIRS [*mumbling*]. They were here in Easter week and finished off a gallon of pickled gherkins.

MADAME RANEVSKY. What's he talking about?

BARBARA. He's been mumbling like that these three years. We've got used to it.

YASHA. Advancing age.

[CHARLOTTE *crosses in a white frock, very thin, tightly laced, with a lorgnette at her waist.*]

LOPAKHIN. Excuse me, Charlotte Ivánovna, I've not paid my respects to you yet. [*He prepares to kiss her hand.*]

CHARLOTTE [*drawing her hand away*]. If one allows you to kiss one's hand, you will want to kiss one's elbow next, and then one's shoulder.

LOPAKHIN. I'm having no luck today. [*All laugh.*] Charlotte Ivánovna, do us a conjuring trick.

MADAME RANEVSKY. Charlotte, do do us a conjuring trick.

CHARLOTTE. No, thank you. I'm going to bed.

[*Exit* CHARLOTTE.]

LOPAKHIN. We shall meet again in three weeks. [*Kissing* MADAME RANEVSKY's *hand.*] Meanwhile, good-bye. I must be off. [*To* GAYEF.] So-long. [*Kissing* PISHTCHIK.] Ta-ta. [*Shaking hands with* BARBARA, *then with* FIRS *and* YASHA.] I hate having to go. [*To* MADAME RANEVSKY.] If you make up your mind about the villas, let me know, and I'll raise you five thousand pounds at once. Think it over seriously.

BARBARA [*angrily*]. For heaven's sake do go!

LOPAKHIN. I'm going, I'm going.

[*Exit* LOPAKHIN.]

GAYEF. Snob! . . . However, *pardon!* Barbara's going to marry him; he's Barbara's young man.

BARBARA. You talk too much, uncle.

MADAME RANEVSKY. Why, Barbara, I shall be very glad. He's a nice man.

PISHTCHIK. Not a doubt about it. . . . A most worthy individual. My Dáshenka, she says . . . oh, she says . . . lots of things. [*Snoring and waking up again at once.*] By the by, dear lady, can you lend me twenty-five pounds? I've got to pay the interest on my mortgage to-morrow.

BARBARA [*alarmed*]. We can't! we can't!

MADAME RANEVSKY. It really is a fact that I haven't any money.

PISHTCHIK. I'll find it somewhere. [*Laughing.*] I never lose hope. Last time I thought: 'Now I really am done for, I'm a ruined man,' when behold, they ran a railway over my land and paid me compensation. And so it'll be again; something will happen, if not today, then to-morrow. Dáshenka may win the twenty-thousand-pound prize; she's got a ticket in the lottery.

MADAME RANEVSKY. The coffee's finished. Let's go to bed.

FIRS [*brushing* GAYEF'S *clothes, admonishingly*]. You've put on the wrong trousers again. Whatever am I to do with you?

BARBARA [*softly*]. Anya is asleep. [*She opens the window quietly.*] The sun's up already; it isn't cold now. Look, mamma, how lovely the trees are. Heavens! what a sweet air! The starlings are singing!

GAYEF [*opening the other window*]. The orchard is all white. You've not forgotten it, Lyuba? This long avenue going straight on, straight on, like a ribbon between the trees? It shines like silver on moonlight nights. Do you remember? You've not forgotten?

MADAME RANEVSKY [*looking out into the garden*]. Oh, my childhood, my pure and happy childhood! I used to sleep in this nursery. I used to look out from here into the garden. Happiness awoke with me every morning! and the orchard was just the same then as it is now; nothing is altered. [*Laughing with joy.*] It is all white, all white! Oh, my cherry orchard! After the dark and stormy autumn and the frosts of winter you are young again and full of happiness; the angels of heaven have not abandoned you. Oh! if only I could free my neck and shoulders from the stone that weighs them down! If only I could forget my past!

GAYEF. Yes; and this orchard will be sold to pay our debts, however impossible it may seem. . . .

MADAME RANEVSKY. Look! There's mamma walking in the orchard . . . in a white frock! [*Laughing with joy.*] There she is!

GAYEF. Where?

BARBARA. Heaven help you!

MADAME RANEVSKY. There's no one there, really. It only looked like it; there on the right where the path turns down to the summer-house; there's a white tree that leans over and looks like a woman. [*Enter* TROPHIMOF *in a shabby student uniform and spectacles.*] What a wonderful orchard, with its white masses of blossom and the blue sky above!

TROPHIMOF. Lyubóf Andréyevna! [*She looks round at him.*] I only want to say, 'How do you do,' and go away at once. [*Kissing her hand eagerly.*] I was told to wait till the morning, but I hadn't the patience.

[MADAME RANEVSKY *looks at him in astonishment.*]

BARBARA [*crying*]. This is Peter Trophímof.

TROPHIMOF. Peter Trophímof; I was Grisha's tutor, you know. Have I really altered so much?

[MADAME RANEVSKY *embraces him and cries softly.*]

GAYEF. Come, come, that's enough, Lyuba!

BARBARA [*crying*]. I told you to wait till to-morrow, you know, Peter.

MADAME RANEVSKY. My little Grisha! My little boy! Grisha . . . my son. . . .

BARBARA. It can't be helped, mamma. It was the will of God.

TROPHIMOF [*gently, crying*]. There, there!

MADAME RANEVSKY [*crying*]. He was drowned. My little boy was drowned. Why? What was the use of that, my dear? [*In a softer voice.*] Anya's asleep in there, and I am speaking so loud, and making a noise. . . . But tell me, Peter, why have you grown so ugly? Why have you grown so old?

TROPHIMOF. An old woman in the train called me a 'mouldy gentleman.'

MADAME RANEVSKY. You were quite a boy then, a dear little student, and now your hair's going and you wear spectacles. Are you really still a student? [*Going towards the door.*]

TROPHIMOF. Yes, I expect I shall be a perpetual student.

MADAME RANEVSKY [*kissing her brother and then* BARBARA]. Well, go to bed. You've grown old too, Leoníd.

PISHTCHIK [*following her*]. Yes, yes; time for bed. Oh, oh, my gout! I'll stay the night here. Don't forget, Lyubóf Andréyevna, my angel, to-morrow morning . . . twenty-five.

GAYEF. He's still on the same string.

PISHTCHIK. Twenty-five . . . to pay the interest on my mortgage.

MADAME RANEVSKY. I haven't any money, my friend.

PISHTCHIK. I'll pay you back, dear lady. It's a trifling sum.

MADAME RANEVSKY. Well, well, Leoníd will give it to you. Let him have it, Leoníd.

GAYEF [*ironical*]. I'll give it him right enough! Hold your pocket wide!

MADAME RANEVSKY. It can't be helped. . . . He needs it. He'll pay it back.

[*Exeunt* MADAME RANEVSKY, TROPHIMOF, PISHTCHIK *and* FIRS. GAYEF, BARBARA *and* YASHA *remain.*]

GAYEF. My sister hasn't lost her old habit of scattering the money. [*To* YASHA.] Go away, my lad! You smell of chicken.

YASHA [*laughing*]. You're just the same as you always were, Leoníd Andréyevitch!

GAYEF. Who's that? [*To* BARBARA.] What does he say?

BARBARA [*to* YASHA]. Your mother's come up from the village. She's been waiting for you since yesterday in the servants' hall. She wants to see you.

YASHA. What a nuisance she is!

BARBARA. You wicked, unnatural son!

YASHA. Well, what do I want with her? She might just as well have waited till to-morrow.

[*Exit* YASHA.]

BARBARA. Mamma is just like she used to be; she hasn't changed a bit. If she had her way, she'd give away everything she has.

GAYEF. Yes. [A *pause.*] If people recommend very many cures for an illness, that means that the illness is incurable. I think and think, I batter my brains; I know of many remedies, very many, and that means really that there is none. How nice it would be to get a fortune left one by somebody! How nice it would be if Anya could marry a very rich man! How nice it would be to go to Yaroslav and try my luck with my aunt the Countess. My aunt is very, very rich, you know.

BARBARA [*crying softly*]. If only God would help us!

GAYEF. Don't howl! My aunt is very rich, but she does not like us. In the first place, my sister married a solicitor, not a nobleman. [ANYA *appears in the doorway.*] She married a man who was not a nobleman, and it's no good pretending that she has led a virtuous life. She's a dear, kind, charming creature, and I love her very much, but whatever mitigating circumstances one may find for her, there's no getting round it that she's a sinful woman. You can see it in her every gesture.

BARBARA [*whispering*]. Anya is standing in the door!

GAYEF. Who's that? [A *pause.*] It's very odd, something's got into my right eye. I can't see properly out of it. Last Thursday when I was down at the District Court . . .

[ANYA *comes down.*]

BARBARA. Why aren't you asleep, Anya?

ANYA. I can't sleep. It's no good trying.

GAYEF. My little pet! [*Kissing* ANYA'S *hands and face.*] My little girl! [*Crying.*] You're not my niece; you're my angel; you're my everything. Trust me, trust me. . . .

ANYA. I do trust you, uncle. Everyone loves you, everyone respects you; but dear, dear uncle, you ought to hold your tongue, only to hold your tongue. What were you saying just now about mamma? about your own sister? What was the good of saying that?

GAYEF. Yes, yes. [*Covering his face with her hand.*] You're quite right; it was awful of me! Lord, Lord! save me from myself! And a little while ago I made a speech over a cupboard. What a stupid thing to do! As soon as I had done it, I knew it was stupid.

BARBARA. Yes, really, uncle. You ought to hold your tongue. Say nothing; that's all that's wanted.

ANYA. If only you would hold your tongue, you'd be so much happier!

GAYEF. I will! I will! [*Kissing* ANYA'S *and* BARBARA'S *hands.*] I'll hold my tongue. But there's one thing I must say; it's business. Last Thursday, when I was down at the District Court, a lot of us were there together, we began to talk about this and that, one thing and another, and it seems I could arrange a loan on note of hand to pay the interest into the bank.

BARBARA. If only Heaven would help us!

GAYEF. I'll go on Tuesday and talk it over again. [*To* BARBARA.] Don't howl! [*To* ANYA.] Your mamma shall have a talk with Lopákhin. Of course he won't refuse her. And as soon as you are rested you must go to see your grandmother, the Countess, at Yaroslav. We'll operate from three points, and the trick is done. We'll pay the interest, I'm certain of it. [*Taking sugar candy.*] I swear on my honour, or whatever you will, the property shall not be sold. [*Excitedly.*] I swear by my hope of eternal happiness! There's my hand on it. Call me a base, dishonourable man if I let it go to auction. I swear by my whole being.

ANYA [*calm again and happy*]. What a dear you are, uncle, and how clever! [*Embraces him.*] Now I'm easy again. I'm easy again! I'm happy!

[*Enter* FIRS.]

FIRS [*reproachfully*]. Leoníd Andréyevitch, have you no fear of God? When are you going to bed?

GAYEF. I'm just off—just off. You get along, Firs. I'll undress myself all right. Come, children, bye-bye! Details to-morrow, but now let's go to bed. [*Kissing* ANYA *and* BARBARA.] I'm a good Liberal, a man of the eighties. People abuse the eighties, but I think that I may say I've suffered something for my convictions in my time. It's not for nothing that the peasants love me. We ought to know the peasants; we ought to know with what . . .

ANYA. You're at it again, uncle!

BARBARA. Why don't you hold your tongue, uncle?

FIRS [*angrily*]. Leoníd Andréyevitch!

GAYEF. I'm coming; I'm coming. Now go to bed. Off two cushions in the middle pocket! I start another life! . . .

[*Exit, with* FIRS *hobbling after him.*]

ANYA. Now my mind is at rest. I don't want to go to Yaroslav; I don't like grandmamma; but my mind is at rest, thanks to Uncle Leoníd. [*She sits down.*]

BARBARA. Time for bed. I'm off. Whilst you were away there's been a scandal. You know that nobody lives in the old servants' quarters except the old people, Ephim, Pauline, Evstignéy and old Karp. Well, they took to having in all sorts of queer fish to sleep there with them. I didn't say a word. But at last I heard they had spread a report that I had given orders that they were to have nothing but peas to eat; out of stinginess, you understand? It was all Evstignéy's doing. 'Very well,' I said to myself, 'you wait a bit.' So I sent for Evstignéy. [*Yawning.*] He comes. 'Now then, Evstignéy.' I said, 'you old imbecile, how do you dare . . .' [*Looking at* ANYA.] Anya, Anya! [*A pause.*] She's asleep. [*Taking* ANYA'S *arm.*] Let's go to bed. Come along. [*Leading her away.*] Sleep on, my little one! Come along; come along! [*They go towards* ANYA'S *room. In the distance beyond the orchard a shepherd plays his pipe.*

TROPHIMOF *crosses the stage and, seeing* BARBARA *and* ANYA, *stops.*]
'Sh! She's asleep, she's asleep! Come along, my love.

ANYA [*drowsily*]. I'm so tired! Listen to the bells! Uncle, dear uncle! Mamma! Uncle!

BARBARA. Come along, my love! Come along.

[*Exeunt* BARBARA *and* ANYA *to the bedroom.*]

TROPHIMOF [*with emotion*]. My sunshine! My spring!

CURTAIN

Act II

In the open fields; an old crooked half-ruined shrine. Near it a well; big stones, apparently old tombstones; an old bench. Road to the estate beyond. On one side rise dark poplar trees. Beyond them begins the cherry orchard. In the distance a row of telegraph poles, and, far away on the horizon, the dim outlines of a big town, visible only in fine, clear weather. It is near sunset.

CHARLOTTE, YASHA *and* DUNYASHA *sit on the bench.* EPHIKHODOF *stands by them and plays on a guitar; they meditate.* CHARLOTTE *wears an old peaked cap. She has taken a gun from off her shoulders and is mending the buckle of the strap.*

CHARLOTTE [*thoughtfully*]. I have no proper passport. I don't know how old I am; I always feel I am still young. When I was a little girl my father and mother used to go about from one country fair to another, giving performances, and very good ones too. I used to do the *salto mortale* and all sorts of tricks. When papa and mamma died an old German lady adopted me and educated me. Good! When I grew up I became a governess. But where I come from and who I am, I haven't a notion. Who my parents were—very likely they weren't married—I don't know. [*Taking a cucumber from her pocket and beginning to eat it.*] I don't know anything about it. [*A pause.*] I long to talk so, and I have no one to talk to, I have no friends or relations.

EPHIKHODOF [*playing on the guitar and singing*].

'What is the noisy world to me?
Oh, what are friends and foes?'

How sweet it is to play upon a mandoline!

DUNYASHA. That's a guitar, not a mandoline. [*She looks at herself in a hand-glass and powders her face.*]

EPHIKHODOF. For the madman who loves, it is a mandoline. [*Singing.*]

'Oh, that my heart were cheered
By the warmth of requited love.'

[YASHA *joins in.*]

CHARLOTTE. How badly these people do sing! Foo! Like jackals howling!

DUNYASHA [*to* YASHA]. What happiness it must be to live abroad!

YASHA. Of course it is; I quite agree with you. [*He yawns and lights a cigar.*]

EPHIKHODOF. It stands to reason. Everything abroad has attained a certain culmination.

YASHA. That's right.

EPHIKHODOF. I am a man of cultivation; I have studied various remarkable books, but I cannot fathom the direction of my preferences; do I want to live or do I want to shoot myself, so to speak? But in order to be ready for all contingencies, I always carry a revolver in my pocket. Here it is. [*Showing revolver.*]

CHARLOTTE. That's done. I'm off. [*Slinging the rifle over her shoulder.*] You're a clever fellow, Ephikhódof, and very alarming. Women must fall madly in love with you. Brrr! [*Going.*] These clever people are all so stupid; I have no one to talk to. I am always alone, always alone; I have no friends or relations, and who I am, or why I exist, is a mystery.

[*Exit slowly.*]

EPHIKHODOF. Strictly speaking, without touching upon other matters, I must protest *inter alia* that destiny treats me with the utmost rigour, as a tempest might treat a small ship. If I labour under a misapprehension, how is it that when I woke up this morning, behold, so to speak, I perceived sitting on my chest a spider of praeternatural dimensions, like that [*indicating with both hands*]? And if I go to take a draught of quass, I am sure to find something of the most indelicate character, in the nature of a cockroach. [*A pause.*] Have you read Buckle? [*A pause.*] [*To* DUNYASHA.] I should like to trouble you, Avdótya Fyódorovna, for a momentary interview.

DUNYASHA. Talk away.

EPHIKHODOF. I should prefer to conduct it *tête-à-tête*. [*Sighing.*]

DUNYASHA [*confused*]. Very well, only first please fetch me my cloak. It's by the cupboard. It's rather damp here.

EPHIKHODOF. Very well, mademoiselle. I will go and fetch it, mademoiselle. Now I know what to do with my revolver.

[*Takes his guitar and exit, playing.*]

YASHA. Twenty-two misfortunes! Between you and me, he's a stupid fellow. [*Yawning.*]

DUNYASHA. Heaven help him, he'll shoot himself! [A *pause.*] I have grown so nervous, I am always in a twitter. I was quite a little girl when they took me into the household, and now I have got quite disused to common life, and my hands are as white as white, like a lady's. I have grown so refined, so delicate and genteel, I am afraid of everything. I'm always frightened. And if you deceive me, Yásha, I don't know what will happen to my nerves.

YASHA [*kissing her*]. You little cucumber! Of course every girl ought to behave herself properly; there's nothing I dislike as much as when girls aren't proper in their behaviour.

DUNYASHA. I've fallen dreadfully in love with you. You're so educated; you can talk about anything! [A *pause.*]

YASHA [*yawning*]. Yes. . . . The way I look at it is this; if a girl falls in love with anybody, then I call her immoral. [A *pause.*] How pleasant it is to smoke one's cigar in the open air. [*Listening.*] There's someone coming. It's the missis and the rest of 'em. . . . [DUNYASHA *embraces him hastily.*] Go towards the house as if you'd just been for a bathe. Go by this path or else they'll meet you and think that I've been walking out with you. I can't stand that sort of thing.

DUNYASHA [*coughing softly*]. Your cigar has given me a headache.

[*Exit* DUNYASHA.]

[YASHA *remains sitting by the shrine. Enter* MADAME RANEVSKY, GAYEF *and* LOPAKHIN.]

LOPAKHIN. You must make up your minds once and for all. Time waits for no man. The question is perfectly simple. Are you going to let off the land for villas or not? Answer in one word; yes or no. Only one word!

MADAME RANEVSKY. Who's smoking horrible cigars here? [*She sits down.*]

GAYEF. How handy it is now they've built that railway. [*Sitting.*] We've been into town for lunch and back again. . . . Red in the middle! I must just go up to the house and have a game.

MADAME RANEVSKY. There's no hurry.

LOPAKHIN. Only one word—yes or no! [*Entreatingly.*] Come, answer the question!

GAYEF [*yawning*]. Who's that?

MADAME RANEVSKY [*looking into her purse*]. I had a lot of money yesterday but there's hardly any left now. Poor Barbara tries to save money by feeding us all on milk soup; the old people in the kitchen get nothing but peas, and yet I go squandering aimlessly. . . . [*Dropping her purse and scattering gold coins; vexed.*] There, I've dropped it all!

YASHA. Allow me, I'll pick it up. [*Collecting the coins.*]

MADAME RANEVSKY. Yes, please do, Yásha! Whatever made me go into town for lunch? I hate your horrid restaurant with the organ and the tablecloths all smelling of soap. Why do you drink so much, Leoníd? Why do you eat so much? Why do you talk so much? You talked too much at the restaurant again, and most unsuitably, about the seventies, and the decadents. And to whom? Fancy talking about decadents to the waiters!

LOPAKHIN. Quite true.

GAYEF [*with a gesture*]. I'm incorrigible, that's plain. [*Irritably to* YASHA.] What do you keep dodging about in front of me for?

YASHA [*laughing*]. I can't hear your voice without laughing.

GAYEF [*to* MADAME RANEVSKY]. Either he or I . . .

MADAME RANEVSKY. Go away, Yásha; run along.

YASHA [*handing* MADAME RANEVSKY *her purse*]. I'll go at once. [*Restraining his laughter with difficulty.*] This very minute.

[*Exit* YASHA.]

LOPAKHIN. Derigánof, the millionaire, wants to buy your property. They say he'll come to the auction himself.

MADAME RANEVSKY. How did you hear?

LOPAKHIN. I was told so in town.

GAYEF. Our aunt at Yaroslav has promised to send something; but I don't know when, or how much.

LOPAKHIN. How much will she send? Ten thousand pounds? Twenty thousand pounds?

MADAME RANEVSKY. Oh, come . . . A thousand or fifteen hundred at the most.

LOPAKHIN. Excuse me, but in all my life I never met anybody so frivolous as you two, so crazy and unbusinesslike! I tell you in plain Russian your property is going to be sold, and you don't seem to understand what I say.

MADAME RANEVSKY. Well, what are we to do? Tell us what you want us to do.

LOPAKHIN. Don't I tell you every day? Every day I say the same thing over and over again. You must lease off the cherry orchard and the rest of the estate for villas; you must do it at once, this very moment; the auction will be on you in two twos! Try and understand. Once you make up your mind there are to be villas, you can get all the money you want, and you're saved.

MADAME RANEVSKY. Villas and villa residents, oh, please, . . . it's so vulgar!

GAYEF. I quite agree with you.

LOPAKHIN. I shall either cry, or scream, or faint. I can't stand it! You'll be the death of me. [*To* GAYEF.] You're an old woman!

GAYEF. Who's that?

LOPAKHIN. You're an old woman! [*Going.*]

MADAME RANEVSKY [*frightened*]. No, don't go. Stay here, there's a dear! Perhaps we shall think of some way.

LOPAKHIN. What's the good of thinking!

MADAME RANEVSKY. Please don't go; I want you. At any rate it's gayer when you're here. [*A pause.*] I keep expecting something to happen, as if the house were going to tumble down about our ears.

GAYEF [*in deep abstraction*]. Off the cushion on the corner; double into the middle pocket. . . .

MADAME RANEVSKY. We have been very, very sinful!

LOPAKHIN. You! What sins have you committed?

GAYEF [*eating candy*]. They say I've devoured all my substance in sugar candy. [*Laughing.*]

MADAME RANEVSKY. Oh, the sins that I have committed . . . I've always squandered money at random like a madwoman; I married a man who made nothing but debts. My husband drank himself to death on champagne; he was a fearful drinker. Then for my sins I fell in love and went off with another man; and immediately—that was my first punishment—a blow full on the head . . . here, in this very river . . . my little boy was drowned; and I went abroad, right, right away, never to come back any more, never to see this river again. . . . I shut my eyes and ran, like a mad thing, and *he* came after me, pitiless and cruel. I bought a villa at Mentone, because he fell ill there, and for three years I knew no rest day or night; the sick man tormented and wore down my soul. Then, last year, when my villa was sold to pay my debts, I went off to Paris, and he came and robbed me of everything, left me and took up with another woman, and I tried to poison myself. . . . It was all so stupid, so humiliating. . . . Then suddenly I longed to be back in Russia, in my own country, with my little girl. . . . [*Wiping away her tears.*] Lord, Lord, be merciful to me; forgive my sins! Do not punish me any more! [*Taking a telegram from her pocket.*] I got this to-day from Paris. . . . He asks to be forgiven, begs me to go back. . . . [*Tearing up the telegram.*] Isn't that music that I hear? [*Listening.*]

GAYEF. That's our famous Jewish band. You remember? Four fiddles, a flute and a double bass.

MADAME RANEVSKY. Does it still exist? We must make them come up some time; we'll have a dance.

LOPAKHIN [*listening*]. I don't hear anything. [*Singing softly.*]

'The Germans for a fee will turn
A Russ into a Frenchman.'

[*Laughing.*] I saw a very funny piece at the theatre last night; awfully funny!

MADAME RANEVSKY. It probably wasn't a bit funny. You people ought to go and see plays; you ought to try to see yourselves; to see what a dull life you lead, and how much too much you talk.

LOPAKHIN. Quite right. To tell the honest truth, our life's an imbecile affair. [A *pause.*] My papa was a peasant, an idiot; he understood nothing; he taught me nothing; all he did was to beat me when he was drunk, with a walking-stick. As a matter of fact I'm just as big a blockhead and idiot as he was. I never did any lessons; my handwriting's abominable; I write so badly I'm ashamed before people; like a pig.

MADAME RANEVSKY. You ought to get married.

LOPAKHIN. Yes, that's true.

MADAME RANEVSKY. Why not marry Barbara? She's a nice girl.

LOPAKHIN. Yes.

MADAME RANEVSKY. She's a nice straightforward creature; works all day; and what's most important, she loves you. You've been fond of her for a long time.

LOPAKHIN. Well, why not? I'm quite willing. She's a very nice girl. [A *pause.*]

GAYEF. I've been offered a place in a bank. Six hundred pounds a year. Do you hear?

MADAME RANEVSKY. You in a bank! Stay where you are.

[*Enter* FIRS *carrying an overcoat.*]

FIRS [*to* GAYEF]. Put this on, please, master; it's getting damp.

GAYEF [*putting on the coat*]. What a plague you are, Firs!

FIRS. What's the use. . . . You went off and never told me. [*Examining his clothes.*]

MADAME RANEVSKY. How old you've got, Firs!

FIRS. I beg your pardon?

LOPAKHIN. She says how old you've got!

FIRS. I've been alive a long time. When they found me a wife, your father wasn't even born yet. [*Laughing.*] And when the Liberation came I was already chief valet. But I wouldn't have any Liberation then; I stayed with the master. [A *pause.*] I remember how happy everybody was, but why they were happy they didn't know themselves.

LOPAKHIN. It was fine before then. Anyway they used to flog 'em.

FIRS [*mishearing him*]. I should think so! The peasants minded the masters, and the masters minded the peasants, but now it's all higgledy-piggledy; you can't make head or tail of it.

GAYEF. Shut up, Firs. I must go into town again to-morrow. I've been promised an introduction to a general who'll lend money on a bill.

LOPAKHIN. You'll do no good. You won't even pay the interest; set your mind at ease about that.

MADAME RANEVSKY [*to* LOPAKHIN]. He's only talking nonsense. There's no such general at all.

[*Enter* TROPHIMOF, ANYA *and* BARBARA.]

GAYEF. Here come the others.

ANYA. Here's the mamma.

MADAME RANEVSKY [*tenderly*]. Come along, come along, . . . my little ones. . . . [*Embracing* ANYA *and* BARBARA.] If only you knew how much I love you both! Sit beside me . . . there, like that. [*Everyone sits.*]

LOPAKHIN. The Perpetual Student's always among the girls.

TROPHIMOF. It's no affair of yours.

LOPAKHIN. He's nearly fifty and still a student.

TROPHIMOF. Stop your idiotic jokes!

LOPAKHIN. What are you losing your temper for, silly?

TROPHIMOF. Why can't you leave me alone?

LOPAKHIN [*laughing*]. I should like to know what your opinion is of me?

TROPHIMOF. My opinion of you, Yermolái Alexéyitch, is this. You're a rich man; you'll soon be a millionaire. Just as a beast of prey which devours everything that comes in its way is necessary for the conversion of matter, so you are necessary too.

[*All laugh.*]

BARBARA. Tell us something about the planets, Peter, instead.

MADAME RANEVSKY. No. Let's go on with the conversation we were having yesterday.

TROPHIMOF. What about?

GAYEF. About the proud man.

TROPHIMOF. We had a long talk yesterday, but we didn't come to any conclusion. There is something mystical in the proud man in the sense in which you use the words. You may be right from your point of view, but, if we look at it simple-mindedly, what room is there for pride? Is there any sense in it, when man is so poorly constructed from the physiological point of view, when the vast majority of us are so gross and stupid and profoundly unhappy? We must give up admiring ourselves. The only thing to do is to work.

GAYEF. We shall die all the same.

TROPHIMOF. Who knows? And what does it mean, to die? Perhaps man has a hundred senses, and when he dies only the five senses that we know perish with him, and the other ninety-five remain alive.

MADAME RANEVSKY. How clever you are, Peter.

LOPAKHIN [*ironically*]. Oh, extraordinary!

TROPHIMOF. Mankind marches forward, perfecting its strength. Everything that is unattainable for us now will one day be near and clear; but we must work; we must help with all our force those who seek for truth. At present only a few men work in Russia. The vast majority of the educated people that I know seek after nothing, do nothing, and are as yet incapable of work. They call themselves the 'Intelligentsia,' they say 'thou' and 'thee' to the servants, they treat the peasants like animals, learn nothing, read nothing serious, do absolutely nothing, only talk about science, and understand little or nothing about art. They are all serious; they all have solemn faces; they only discuss important subjects; they philosophise; but meanwhile the vast majority of us, ninety-nine per cent., live like savages; at the least thing they curse and punch people's heads; they eat like beasts and sleep in dirt and bad air; there are bugs everywhere, evil smells, damp and moral degradation. . . . It's plain that all our clever conversations are only meant to distract our own attention and other people's. Show me where those crèches are, that they're always talking so much about; or those reading-rooms. They are only things people write about in novels; they don't really exist at all. Nothing exists but dirt, vulgarity and Asiatic ways. I am afraid of solemn faces; I dislike them; I am afraid of solemn conversations. Let us rather hold our tongues.

LOPAKHIN. Do you know, I get up at five every morning. I work from morning till night; I am always handling my own money or other people's, and I see the sort of men there are about me. One only has to begin to do anything to see how few honest and decent people there are. Sometimes, as I lie awake in bed, I think: 'O Lord, you have given us mighty forests, boundless fields and immeasurable horizons, and we, living in their midst, ought really to be giants.'

MADAME RANEVSKY. Oh dear, you want giants! They are all very well in fairy stories; but in real life they are rather alarming. [EPHIKHODOF *passes at the back of the scene, playing on his guitar.*] [*Pensively.*] There goes Ephikhódof.

ANYA [*pensively*]. There goes Ephikhódof.

GAYEF. The sun has set.

TROPHIMOF. Yes.

GAYEF [*as if declaiming, but not loud*]. O Nature, wonderful Nature, you glow with eternal light; beautiful and indifferent, you whom we call our mother, uniting in yourself both life and death, you animate and you destroy. . . .

BARBARA [*entreatingly*]. Uncle!

ANYA. You're at it again, uncle!

TROPHIMOF. You'd far better double the red into the middle pocket.

GAYEF. I'll hold my tongue! I'll hold my tongue!

[*They all sit pensively. Silence reigns, broken only by the mumbling of old* FIRS. *Suddenly a distant sound is heard as if from the sky, the sound of a string breaking, dying away, melancholy.*]

MADAME RANEVSKY. What's that?

LOPAKHIN. I don't know. It's a lifting-tub given way somewhere away in the mines. It must be a long way off.

GAYEF. Perhaps it's some sort of bird . . . a heron, or something.

TROPHIMOF. Or an owl. . . .

MADAME RANEVSKY [*shuddering*]. There's something uncanny about it!

FIRS. The same thing happened before the great misfortune: the owl screeched and the samovar kept humming.

GAYEF. What great misfortune?

FIRS. The Liberation. [A *pause.*]

MADAME RANEVSKY. Come, everyone, let's go in; it's getting late. [*To* ANYA.] You've tears in your eyes. What is it, little one? [*Embracing her.*]

ANYA. Nothing, mamma. I'm all right.

TROPHIMOF. There's someone coming.

[A *Tramp appears in a torn white-peaked cap and overcoat. He is slightly drunk.*]

TRAMP. Excuse me, but can I go through this way straight to the station?

GAYEF. Certainly. Follow this path.

TRAMP. I am uncommonly obliged to you, sir. [*Coughing.*] We're having lovely weather. [*Declaiming.*] 'Brother, my suffering brother' . . . 'Come forth to the Volga. Who moans?' . . . [*To* BARBARA.] Mademoiselle, please spare a sixpence for a hungry fellow-countryman.

[BARBARA, *frightened, screams.*]

LOPAKHIN [*angrily*]. There's a decency for even indecency to observe.

MADAME RANEVSKY. Take this; here you are. [*Fumbling in her purse.*] I haven't any silver. . . . Never mind, take this sovereign.

TRAMP. I am uncommonly obliged to you, madam.

[*Exit* TRAMP. *Laughter.*]

BARBARA [*frightened*]. I'm going! I'm going! Oh, mamma, there's nothing for the servants to eat at home, and you've gone and given this man a sovereign.

MADAME RANEVSKY. What's to be done with your stupid old mother? I'll give you up everything I have when I get back. Yermolái Alexéyitch, lend me some more money.

LOPAKHIN. Very good.

MADAME RANEVSKY. Come along, everyone; it's time to go in. We've settled all about your marriage between us, Barbara. I wish you joy.

BARBARA [*through her tears*]. You mustn't joke about such things, mamma.

LOPAKHIN. Amelia, get thee to a nunnery, go!

GAYEF. My hands are all trembling; it's ages since I had a game of billiards.

LOPAKHIN. Amelia, nymphlet, in thine orisons remember me.

MADAME RANEVSKY. Come along. It's nearly supper-time.

BARBARA. How he frightened me! My heart is simply throbbing.

LOPAKHIN. Allow me to remind you, the cherry orchard is to be sold on the twenty-second of August. Bear that in mind; bear that in mind!

[*Exeunt omnes except* TROPHIMOF *and* ANYA.]

ANYA [*laughing*]. Many thanks to the Tramp for frightening Barbara; at last we are alone.

TROPHIMOF. Barbara's afraid we shall go and fall in love with each other. Day after day she never leaves us alone. With her narrow mind she cannot understand that we are above love. To avoid everything petty, everything illusory, everything that prevents one from being free and happy, that is the whole meaning and purpose of our life. Forward! We march on irresistibly towards that bright star which burns far, far before us! Forward! Don't tarry, comrades!

ANYA [*clasping her hands*]. What beautiful things you say! [*A pause.*] Isn't it enchanting here to-day!

TROPHIMOF. Yes, it's wonderful weather.

ANYA. What have you done to me, Peter? Why is it that I no longer love the cherry orchard as I did? I used to love it so tenderly; I thought there was no better place on earth than our garden.

TROPHIMOF. All Russia is our garden. The earth is great and beautiful; it is full of wonderful places. [*A pause.*] Think, Anya, your grandfather, your great-grandfather and all your ancestors were serf-owners, owners of living souls. Do not human spirits look out at you from every tree in the orchard, from every leaf and every stem? Do you not hear human voices? . . . Oh! it is terrible. Your orchard frightens me. When I walk through it in the evening or at night, the rugged bark on the trees glows with a dim light, and the cherry trees seem to see all that happened a hundred and two hundred years ago in painful and oppressive dreams. Well, well, we have fallen at least two hundred years behind the times. We have achieved nothing at all as yet; we have not made up our minds how we stand with the past; we only philosophise, complain of boredom, or drink vodka. It is so plain that, before we can live in the present, we must first redeem the past, and have done with it; and it is only by suffering that we can redeem it, only by strenuous, unremitting toil. Understand that, Anya.

ANYA. The house we live in has long since ceased to be our house; and I shall go away, I give you my word.

TROPHIMOF. If you have the household keys, throw them in the well and go away. Be free, be free as the wind.

ANYA [*enthusiastically*]. How beautifully you put it!

TROPHIMOF. Believe what I say, Anya; believe what I say. I'm not thirty yet; I am still young, still a student; but what I have been through! I am hungry as the winter; I am sick, anxious, poor as a beggar. Fate has tossed me hither and thither; I have been everywhere, everywhere. But wherever I have been, every minute, day and night, my soul has been full of mysterious anticipations. I feel the approach of happiness; Anya; I see it coming. . . .

ANYA [*pensively*]. The moon is rising.

[EPHIKHODOF *is heard still playing the same sad tune on his guitar. The moon rises. Somewhere beyond the poplar trees,* BARBARA *is heard calling for* ANYA: *'Anya, where are you?'*]

TROPHIMOF. Yes, the moon is rising. [*A pause.*] There it is, there is happiness; it is coming towards us, nearer and nearer; I can hear the sound of its footsteps. . . . And if we do not see it, if we do not know it, what does it matter? Others will see it.

BARBARA [*without*]. Anya? Where are you?

TROPHIMOF. There's Barbara again! [*Angrily.*] It really is too bad!

ANYA. Never mind. Let us go down to the river. It's lovely there.

TROPHIMOF. Come on!

[*Exeunt* ANYA *and* TROPHIMOF.]

BARBARA [*without*]. Anya! Anya!

CURTAIN

Act III

A sitting-room separated by an arch from a big drawing-room behind. Chandelier lighted. The Jewish band mentioned in Act II is heard playing on the landing. Evening. In the drawing-room they are dancing the grand rond. SIMEONOF-PISHTCHIK *is heard crying: 'Promenade à une paire!'*

The dancers come down into the sitting-room. The first pair consists of PISHTCHIK *and* CHARLOTTE; *the second of* TROPHIMOF *and* MADAME RANEVSKY; *the third of* ANYA *and the* POST OFFICE OFFICIAL; *the fourth of* BARBARA *and the* STATION-MASTER, *etc., etc.* BARBARA *is crying softly and wipes away the tears as she dances. In the last pair comes* DUNYASHA. *They cross the sitting-room.*

PISHTCHIK. Grand rond, balancez. . . . Les cavaliers à genou et remerciez vos dames.

[FIRS *in evening dress carries seltzer water across on a tray.* PISHTCHIK *and* TROPHIMOF *come down into the sitting-room.*]

PISHTCHIK. I am a full-blooded man; I've had two strokes already; it's hard work dancing, but, as the saying goes: 'If you run with the pack, bark or no, but anyway wag your tail.' I'm as strong as a horse. My old father, who was fond of his joke, rest his soul, used to say, talking of our pedigree, that the ancient stock of the Simeónof-Píshtchiks was descended from that very horse that Caligula made a senator. . . . [*Sitting.*] But the worst of it is, I've got no money. A hungry dog believes in nothing but meat. [*Snoring and waking up again at once.*] I'm just the same. . . . It's nothing but money, money, with me.

TROPHIMOF. Yes, it's quite true, there is something horselike about your build.

PISHTCHIK. Well, well . . . a horse is a jolly creature . . . you can sell a horse.

[*A sound of billiards being played in the next room.* BARBARA *appears in the drawing-room beyond the arch.*]

TROPHIMOF [*teasing her*]. Madame Lopákhin! Madame Lopákhin!
BARBARA [*angrily*]. Mouldy gentleman!
TROPHIMOF. Yes, I'm a mouldy gentleman, and I'm proud of it.
BARBARA [*bitterly*]. We've hired the band, but where's the money to pay for it?

[*Exit* BARBARA.]

TROPHIMOF [*to* PISHTCHIK]. If the energy which you have spent in the course of your whole life in looking for money to pay the interest on your loans had been diverted to some other purpose, you would have had enough of it, I dare say, to turn the world upside down.
PISHTCHIK. Nietzsche, the philosopher, a very remarkable man, very famous, a man of gigantic intellect, says in his works that it's quite right to forge banknotes.
TROPHIMOF. What, have you read Nietzsche?
PISHTCHIK. Well . . . Dáshenka told me. . . . But I'm in such a hole, I'd forge 'em for two-pence. I've got to pay thirty-one pounds the day after to-morrow. . . . I've got thirteen pounds already. [*Feeling his pockets; alarmed.*] My money's gone! I've lost my money! [*Crying.*] Where's my money got to? [*Joyfully.*] Here it is, inside the lining. . . . It's thrown me all in a perspiration.

[*Enter* MADAME RANEVSKY *and* CHARLOTTE.]

MADAME RANEVSKY [*humming a lezginka*]. Why is Leoníd so long? What can he be doing in the town? [*To* DUNYASHA.] Dunyásha, ask the musicians if they'll have some tea.
TROPHIMOF. The sale did not come off, in all probability.
MADAME RANEVSKY. It was a stupid day for the musicians to come; it was a stupid day to have this dance. . . . Well, well, it doesn't matter. . . . [*She sits down and sings softly to herself.*]
CHARLOTTE [*giving* PISHTCHIK *a pack of cards*]. Here is a pack of cards. Think of any card you like.
PISHTCHIK. I've thought of one.
CHARLOTTE. Now shuffle the pack. That's all right. Give them here, O most worthy Mr. Píshtchik. Ein, zwei, drei! Now look and you'll find it in your side pocket.
PISHTCHIK [*taking a card from his side pocket*]. The Eight of Spades. You're perfectly right. [*Astonished.*] Well, I never!
CHARLOTTE [*holding the pack on the palm of her hand, to* TROPHIMOF]. Say quickly, what's the top card?

TROPHIMOF. Well, say the Queen of Spades.
CHARLOTTE. Right! [*To* PISHTCHIK.] Now then, what's the top card?
PISHTCHIK. Ace of Hearts.
CHARLOTTE. Right! [*She claps her hands; the pack of cards disappears.*] What a beautiful day we've been having.

[*A mysterious female* VOICE *answers her as if from under the floor: 'Yes, indeed, a charming day, mademoiselle.'*]

CHARLOTTE. You are my beautiful ideal.
THE VOICE. *'I think you also ferry peautiful, mademoiselle.'*
STATION-MASTER [*applauding*]. Bravo, Miss Ventriloquist!
PISHTCHIK [*astonished*]. Well, I never! Bewitching Charlotte Ivánovna, I'm head over ears in love with you.
CHARLOTTE. In love! [*Shrugging her shoulders.*] Are you capable of love? Guter Mensch, aber schlechter Musikant!
TROPHIMOF [*slapping* PISHTCHIK *on the shoulder*]. You old horse!
CHARLOTTE. Now attention, please; one more trick. [*Taking a shawl from a chair.*] Now here's a shawl, and a very pretty shawl; I'm going to sell this very pretty shawl. [*Shaking it.*] Who'll buy? who'll buy?
PISHTCHIK [*astonished*]. Well, I never!
CHARLOTTE. Ein, zwei, drei! [*She lifts the shawl quickly; behind it stands* ANYA, *who drops a curtsy, runs to her mother, kisses her, then runs up into the drawing-room amid general applause.*]
MADAME RANEVSKY [*applauding*]. Bravo! bravo!
CHARLOTTE. Once more. Ein, zwei, drei! [*She lifts up the shawl; behind it stands* BARBARA, *bowing.*]
PISHTCHIK [*astonished*]. Well, I never!
CHARLOTTE. That's all. [*She throws the shawl over* PISHTCHIK, *makes a curtsy and runs up into the drawing-room.*]
PISHTCHIK [*hurrying after her*]. You little rascal . . . there's a girl for you, there's a girl. . . .

[*Exit.*]

MADAME RANEVSKY. And still no sign of Leoníd. What he's doing in the town so long, I can't understand. It must be all over by now; the property's sold; or the auction never came off; why does he keep me in suspense so long?
BARBARA [*trying to soothe her*]. Uncle has bought it, I am sure of that.
TROPHIMOF [*mockingly*]. Of course he has!
BARBARA. Grannie sent him a power of attorney to buy it in her name and transfer the mortgage. She's done it for Anya's sake. I'm perfectly sure that Heaven will help us and uncle will buy it.

MADAME RANEVSKY. Your Yaroslav grannie sent fifteen hundred pounds to buy the property in her name—she doesn't trust us—but it wouldn't be enough even to pay the interest. [*Covering her face with her hands.*] My fate is being decided to-day, my fate. . . .

TROPHIMOF [*teasing* BARBARA]. Madame Lopákhin!

BARBARA [*angrily*]. Perpetual Student! He's been sent down twice from the University.

MADAME RANEVSKY. Why do you get angry, Barbara? He calls you Madame Lopákhin for fun. Why not? You can marry Lopákhin if you like; he's a nice, interesting man; you needn't if you don't; nobody wants to force you, my pet.

BARBARA. I take it very seriously, mamma, I must confess. He's a nice man and I like him.

MADAME RANEVSKY. Then marry him. There's no good putting it off that I can see.

BARBARA. But, mamma, I can't propose to him myself. For two whole years everybody's been talking about him to me, everyone; but he either says nothing or makes a joke of it. I quite understand. He's making money; he's always busy; he can't be bothered with me. If I only had some money, even a little, even ten pounds, I would give everything up and go right away. I would go into a nunnery.

TROPHIMOF [*mockingly*]. What bliss!

BARBARA [*to* TROPHIMOF]. A student ought to be intelligent. [*In a gentler voice, crying.*] How ugly you've grown, Peter; how old you've grown! [*She stops crying; to* MADAME RANEVSKY.] But I can't live without work, mamma. I must have something to do every minute of the day.

[*Enter* YASHA.]

YASHA [*trying not to laugh*]. Ephikhódof has broken a billiard cue.

[*Exit* YASHA.]

BARBARA. What's Ephikhódof doing here? Who gave him leave to play billiards? I don't understand these people.

[*Exit* BARBARA.]

MADAME RANEVSKY. Don't tease her, Peter. Don't you see that she's unhappy enough already?

TROPHIMOF. I wish she wouldn't be so fussy, always meddling in other people's affairs. The whole summer she's given me and Anya no peace; she is afraid we'll work up a romance between us. What business is it of hers? I'm sure I never gave her any grounds; I'm not likely to be so commonplace. We are above love!

MADAME RANEVSKY. Then I suppose I must be beneath love. [*Deeply agitated.*] Why doesn't Leoníd come? Oh, if only I knew whether the property's sold or not! It seems such an impossible disaster, that I don't know what to think. . . . I'm bewildered. . . . I shall burst out screaming, I shall do something idiotic. Save me, Peter; say something to me, say something. . . .

TROPHIMOF. Whether the property is sold to-day or whether it's not sold, surely it's all one? It's all over with it long ago; there's no turning back, the path is overgrown. Be calm, dear Lyubóf Andréyevna. You mustn't deceive yourself any longer; for once you must look the truth straight in the face.

MADAME RANEVSKY. What truth? You can see what's truth, and what's untruth, but I seem to have lost the power of vision; I see nothing. You settle every important question so boldly; but tell me, Peter, isn't that because you're young, because you have never solved any question of your own as yet by suffering? You look boldly ahead; isn't it only that you don't see or divine anything terrible in the future; because life is still hidden from your young eyes? You are bolder, honester, deeper than we are, but reflect, show me just a finger's breadth of consideration, take pity on me. Don't you see? I was born here, my father and mother lived here, and my grandfather; I love this house; without the cherry orchard my life has no meaning for me, and if it *must* be sold, then for heaven's sake sell me too! [*Embracing* TROPHIMOF *and kissing him on the forehead.*] My little boy was drowned here. [*Crying.*] Be gentle with me, dear, kind Peter.

TROPHIMOF. You know I sympathise with all my heart.

MADAME RANEVSKY. Yes, yes, but you ought to say it somehow differently. [*Taking out her handkerchief and dropping a telegram.*] I am so wretched to-day, you can't imagine! All this noise jars on me, my heart jumps at every sound. I tremble all over; but I can't shut myself up; I am afraid of the silence when I'm alone. Don't be hard on me, Peter; I love you like a son. I would gladly let Anya marry you, I swear it; but you must work, Peter; you must get your degree. You do nothing; Fate tosses you about from place to place; and that's not right. It's true what I say, isn't it? And you must do something to your beard to make it grow better. [*Laughing.*] I can't help laughing at you.

TROPHIMOF [*picking up the telegram*]. I don't wish to be an Adonis.

MADAME RANEVSKY. It's a telegram from Paris. I get them every day. One came yesterday, another to-day. That savage is ill again; he's in a bad way. . . . He asks me to forgive him, he begs me to come; and I really ought to go to Paris and be with him. You look at me sternly; but what am I to do, Peter? What am I to do? He's ill, he's lonely, he's unhappy. Who is to look after him? Who is to keep him from doing stupid things? Who is to give him his medicine when it's time? After all, why should I be ashamed to say it? I love him, that's plain. I love him, I love him. . . . My love is like a stone tied round my neck; it's dragging me down to the bottom; but I love my stone. I can't live without it. [*Squeezing* TROPHIMOF'S *hand.*] Don't think ill of me, Peter; don't say anything! Don't say anything!

TROPHIMOF [*crying*]. Forgive my bluntness, for heaven's sake; but the man has simply robbed you.

MADAME RANEVSKY. No, no, no! [*Stopping her ears.*] You mustn't say that!

TROPHIMOF. He's a rascal; everybody sees it but yourself; he's a petty rascal, a ne'er-do-well. . . .

MADAME RANEVSKY [*angry but restrained*]. You're twenty-six or twenty-seven, and you're still a Lower School boy!

TROPHIMOF. Who cares?

MADAME RANEVSKY. You ought to be a man by now; at your age you ought to understand people who love. You ought to love someone yourself, you ought to be in love! [*Angrily.*] Yes, yes! It's not purity with you; it's simply you're a smug, a figure of fun, a freak. . . .

TROPHIMOF [*horrified*]. What does she say?

MADAME RANEVSKY. 'I am above love!' You're not above love; you're simply what Firs calls a 'job-lot.' At your age you ought to be ashamed not to have a mistress!

TROPHIMOF [*aghast*]. This is awful! What does she say? [*Going quickly up into the drawing-room, clasping his head with his hands.*] This is something awful! I can't stand it; I'm off . . . [*Exit, but returns at once.*] All is over between us!

[*Exit to landing.*]

MADAME RANEVSKY [*calling after him*]. Stop, Peter! Don't be ridiculous; I was only joking! Peter!

[TROPHIMOF *is heard on the landing going quickly down the stairs, and suddenly falling down them with a crash.* ANYA *and* BARBARA *scream. A moment later the sound of laughter.*]

MADAME RANEVSKY. What has happened?

[ANYA *runs in.*]

ANYA [*laughing*]. Peter's tumbled downstairs. [*She runs out again.*]

MADAME RANEVSKY. What a ridiculous fellow he is!

[*The* STATION-MASTER *stands in the middle of the drawing-room behind the arch and recites Alexey Tolstoy's poem, 'The Sinner.' Everybody stops to listen, but after a few lines the sound of a waltz is heard from the landing and he breaks off. All dance.* TROPHIMOF, ANYA, BARBARA *and* MADAME RANEVSKY *enter from the landing.*]

MADAME RANEVSKY. Come, Peter, come, you pure spirit. . . . I beg your pardon. Let's have a dance. [*She dances with* TROPHIMOF. ANYA *and* BARBARA *dance.*]

[*Enter* FIRS, *and stands his walking-stick by the side door. Enter* YASHA *by the drawing-room; he stands looking at the dancers.*]

YASHA. Well, grandfather?

FIRS. I'm not feeling well. In the old days it was generals and barons and admirals that danced at our dances, but now we send for the Postmaster and the Station-Master, and even they make a favour of coming. I'm sort of weak all over. The old master, their grandfather, used to give us all sealing wax, when we had anything the matter. I've taken sealing wax every day for twenty years and more. Perhaps that's why I'm still alive.

YASHA. I'm sick of you, grandfather. [*Yawning.*] I wish you'd die and have done with it.

FIRS. Ah! you . . . job-lot! [*He mumbles to himself.*]

[TROPHIMOF *and* MADAME RANEVSKY *dance beyond the arch and down into the sitting-room.*]

MADAME RANEVSKY. Merci. I'll sit down. [*Sitting.*] I'm tired.

[*Enter* ANYA.]

ANYA [*agitated*]. There was somebody in the kitchen just now saying that the cherry orchard was sold to-day.

MADAME RANEVSKY. Sold? Who to?

ANYA. He didn't say who to. He's gone. [*She dances with* TROPHIMOF. *Both dance up into the drawing-room.*]

YASHA. It was some old fellow chattering; a stranger.

FIRS. And still Leoníd Andréyitch doesn't come. He's wearing his light overcoat *demi-saison;* he'll catch cold as like as not. Ah, young wood, green wood!

MADAME RANEVSKY. This is killing me. Yásha, go and find out who it was sold to.

YASHA. Why, he's gone long ago, the old man. [*Laughs.*]

MADAME RANEVSKY [*vexed*]. What are you laughing at? What are you glad about?

YASHA. He's a ridiculous fellow, is Ephikhódof. Nothing in him. Twenty-two misfortunes!

MADAME RANEVSKY. Firs, if the property is sold, where will you go to?

FIRS. Wherever you tell me, there I'll go.

MADAME RANEVSKY. Why do you look like that? Are you ill? You ought to be in bed.

FIRS [*ironically*]. Oh yes, I'll go to bed, and who'll hand the things around, who'll give orders? I've the whole house on my hands.

YASHA. Lyubóf Andréyevna! Let me ask a favour of you; be so kind; if you go to Paris again, take me with you, I beseech you. It's absolutely impossible for me to stay here. [*Looking about; sotto voce.*] What's the use of talking? You can see for yourself this is a barbarous country; the people have no morals; and the boredom! The food in the kitchen is something shocking, and on the top of it old Firs goes about mumbling irrelevant nonsense. Take me back with you; be so kind!

[*Enter* PISHTCHIK.]

PISHTCHIK. May I have the pleasure . . . a bit of a waltz, charming lady? [MADAME RANEVSKY *takes his arm.*] All the same, enchanting lady, you must let me have eighteen pounds. [*Dancing.*] Let me have . . . eighteen pounds.

[*Exeunt dancing through the arch.*]

YASHA [*singing to himself*].

'Oh, wilt thou understand
The turmoil of my soul?'

[*Beyond the arch appears a figure in grey tall hat and check trousers, jumping and waving its arms. Cries of 'Bravo, Charlotte Ivánovna.'*]

DUNYASHA [*stopping to powder her face*]. Mamselle Anya tells me I'm to dance; there are so many gentlemen and so few ladies. But dancing makes me giddy and makes my heart beat, Firs Nikoláyevitch; and just now the gentleman from the post office said something so nice to me, oh, so nice! It quite took my breath away. [*The music stops.*]

FIRS. What did he say to you?

DUNYASHA. He said, 'You are like a flower.'

YASHA [*yawning*]. Cad!

[*Exit* YASHA.]

DUNYASHA. Like a flower! I am so ladylike and refined, I dote on compliments.

FIRS. You'll come to a bad end.

[*Enter* EPHIKHODOF.]

EPHIKHODOF. You are not pleased to see me, Avdótya Fyódorovna, no more than if I were some sort of insect. [*Sighing.*] Ah! Life! Life!

DUNYASHA. What do you want?

EPHIKHODOF. Undoubtedly perhaps you are right. [*Sighing.*] But of course, if one regards it, so to speak, from the point of view, if I may allow myself the expression, and with apologies for my frankness, you have finally reduced me to a state of mind. I quite appreciate my destiny; every day some misfortune happens to me, and I have long since grown accustomed to it, and face my fortune with a smile. You have passed your word to me, and although I . . .

DUNYASHA. Let us talk of this another time, if you please; but now leave me in peace. I am busy meditating. [*Playing with her fan.*]

EPHIKHODOF. Every day some misfortune befalls me, and yet, if I may venture to say so, I meet them with smiles and even laughter.

[*Enter* BARBARA *from the drawing-room.*]

BARBARA [*to* EPHIKHODOF]. Haven't you gone yet, Simeon? You seem to pay no attention to what you're told. [*To* DUNYASHA.] You get out of here, Dunyásha. [*To* EPHIKHODOF.] First you play billiards and break a cue, and then you march about the drawing-room as if you were a guest!

EPHIKHODOF. Allow me to inform you that it's not your place to call me to account.

BARBARA. I'm not calling you to account; I'm merely talking to you. All you can do is to walk about from one place to another, without ever doing a stroke of work; and why on earth we keep a clerk at all heaven only knows.

EPHIKHODOF [*offended*]. Whether I work, or whether I walk, or whether I eat, or whether I play billiards is a question to be decided only by my elders and people who understand.

BARBARA [*furious*]. How dare you talk to me like that! How dare you! I don't understand things, don't I? You clear out of here this minute! Do you hear me? This minute!

EPHIKHODOF [*flinching*]. I must beg you to express yourself in genteeler language.

BARBARA [*beside herself*]. You clear out this instant second! Out you go! [*Following him as he retreats towards the door.*] Twenty-two misfortunes! Make yourself scarce! Get out of my sight!

[*Exit* EPHIKHODOF.]

EPHIKHODOF [*without*]. I shall lodge a complaint against you.

BARBARA. What! You're coming back, are you? [*Seizing the walking-stick left at the door by* FIRS.] Come on! Come on! Come on! I'll teach you! Are you coming? Are you coming? Then take that. [*She slashes with the stick.*]

[*Enter* LOPAKHIN.]

LOPAKHIN. Many thanks; much obliged.
BARBARA [*still angry, but ironical*]. Sorry!
LOPAKHIN. Don't mention it. I'm very grateful for your warm reception.
BARBARA. It's not worth thanking me for. [*She walks away, then looks round and asks in a gentle voice.*] I didn't hurt you?
LOPAKHIN. Oh, no, nothing to matter. I shall have a bump like a goose's egg, that's all.

[*Voices from the drawing-room: 'Lopákhin has arrived! Yermolái Alexéyitch!'*]

PISHTCHIK. Let my eyes see him, let my ears hear him! [*He and* LOPAKHIN *kiss.*] You smell of brandy, old man. We're having a high time, too.

[*Enter* MADAME RANEVSKY.]

MADAME RANEVSKY. Is it you, Yermolái Alexéyitch? Why have you been so long? Where is Leoníd?
LOPAKHIN. Leoníd Andréyitch came back with me. He's just coming.
MADAME RANEVSKY [*agitated*]. What happened? Did the sale come off? Tell me, tell me!
LOPAKHIN [*embarrassed, afraid of showing his pleasure.*] The sale was all over by four o'clock. We missed the train and had to wait till half-past eight. [*Sighing heavily.*] Ouf! I'm rather giddy. . . .

[*Enter* GAYEF. *In one hand he carries parcels; with the other he wipes away his tears.*]

MADAME RANEVSKY. What happened, Lénya? Come, Lénya! [*Impatiently, crying.*] Be quick, be quick, for heaven's sake!
GAYEF [*answering her only with an up and down gesture of the hand; to* FIRS, *crying*]. Here, take these. . . . Here are some anchovies and Black Sea herrings. I've had nothing to eat all day. Lord, what I've been through! [*Through the open door of the billiard-room comes the click of the billiard balls and* YASHA'S *voice: 'Seven, eighteen!'* GAYEF'S *expression changes; he stops crying.*] I'm frightfully tired. Come and help me change, Firs. [*He goes up through the drawing-room,* FIRS *following.*]
PISHTCHIK. What about the sale? Come on, tell us all about it.
MADAME RANEVSKY. Was the cherry orchard sold?

LOPAKHIN. Yes.

MADAME RANEVSKY. Who bought it?

LOPAKHIN. I did. [*A pause.* MADAME RANEVSKY *is overwhelmed at the news. She would fall to the ground but for the chair and table by her.* BARBARA *takes the keys from her belt, throws them on the floor in the middle of the sitting-room, and exit.*] I bought it. Wait a bit; don't hurry me; my head's in a whirl; I can't speak. . . . [*Laughing.*] When we got to the sale, Derigánof was there already. Leoníd Andréyitch had only fifteen hundred pounds, and Derigánof bid three thousand more than the mortgage right away. When I saw how things stood, I went for him and bid four thousand. He said four thousand five hundred. I said five thousand five hundred. He went up by five hundreds, you see, and I went up by thousands. . . . Well, it was soon over. I bid nine thousand more than the mortgage, and got it; and now the cherry orchard is mine! Mine! [*Laughing.*] Heaven's alive! Just think of it! The cherry orchard is mine! Tell me that I'm drunk; tell me that I'm off my head; tell me that it's all a dream! . . . [*Stamping his feet.*] Don't laugh at me! If only my father and my grandfather could rise from their graves and see the whole affair, how their Yermolái, their flogged and ignorant Yermolái, who used to run about barefooted in the winter, how this same Yermolái had bought a property that hasn't its equal for beauty anywhere in the whole world! I have bought the property where my father and grandfather were slaves, where they weren't even allowed into the kitchen. I'm asleep, it's only a vision, it isn't real. . . . 'Tis the fruit of imagination, wrapped in the mists of ignorance. [*Picking up the keys and smiling affectionately.*] She's thrown down her keys; she wants to show that she's no longer mistress here. . . . [*Jingling them together.*] Well, well, what's the odds? [*The musicians are heard tuning up.*] Hey, musicians, play! I want to hear you. Come everyone and see Yermolái Lopákhin lay his axe to the cherry orchard, come and see the trees fall down! We'll fill the place with villas; our grandsons and great-grandsons shall see a new life here. . . . Strike up, music! [*The band plays.* MADAME RANEVSKY *sinks into a chair and weeps bitterly.*] [*Reproachfully.*] Oh, why, why didn't you listen to me? You can't put the clock back now, poor dear. [*Crying.*] Oh, that all this were past and over! Oh, that our unhappy topsy-turvy life were changed!

PISHTCHIK [*taking him by the arm, sotto voce*]. She's crying. Let's go into the drawing-room and leave her alone to . . . Come on. [*Taking him by the arm, and going up towards the drawing-room.*]

LOPAKHIN. What's up? Play your best, musicians! Let everything be as I want. [*Ironically.*] Here comes the new squire, the owner of the cherry orchard! [*Knocking up by accident against a table and nearly throwing down the candelabra.*] Never mind, I can pay for everything!

[*Exit with* PISHTCHIK. *Nobody remains in the drawing-room or sitting-room except* MADAME RANEVSKY, *who sits huddled together, weeping bitterly. The band plays softly. Enter* ANYA *and* TROPHIMOF *quickly.* ANYA *goes to her mother and kneels before her.* TROPHIMOF *stands in the entry to the drawing-room.*]

ANYA. Mamma! Are you crying, mamma? My dear, good, sweet mamma! Darling, I love you! I bless you! The cherry orchard is sold; it's gone; it's quite true, it's quite true. But don't cry, mamma, you've still got life before you, you've still got your pure and lovely soul. Come with me, darling; come away from here. We'll plant a new garden, still lovelier than this. You will see it and understand, and happiness, deep, tranquil happiness will sink down on your soul, like the sun at eventide, and you'll smile, mamma. Come, darling, come with me!

CURTAIN

Act IV

Same scene as Act I. There are no window-curtains, no pictures. The little furniture left is stacked in a corner, as if for sale. A feeling of emptiness. By the door to the hall and at the back of the scene are piled portmanteaux, bundles, etc. The door is open and the voices of BARBARA *and* ANYA *are audible.*

[LOPAKHIN *stands waiting.* YASHA *holds a tray with small tumblers full of champagne.* EPHIKHODOF *is tying up a box in the hall. A distant murmur of voices behind the scene; the* PEASANTS *have come to say good-bye.*]

GAYEF [*without*]. Thank you, my lads, thank you.

YASHA. The common people have come to say good-bye. I'll tell you what I think, Yermolái Alexéyitch; they're good fellows but rather stupid.

[*The murmur of voices dies away. Enter* MADAME RANEVSKY *and* GAYEF *from the hall. She is not crying, but she is pale, her face twitches, she cannot speak.*]

GAYEF. You gave them your purse, Lyuba. That was wrong, very wrong!

MADAME RANEVSKY. I couldn't help it, I couldn't help it!

[*Exeunt both.*]

LOPAKHIN [*calling after them through the doorway*]. Please come here! Won't you come here? Just a glass to say good-bye. I forgot to bring any from town, and could only raise one bottle at the station. Come along. [*A pause.*] What, won't you have any? [*Returning from the door.*] If I'd known, I wouldn't have bought it. I shan't have any either. [YASHA *sets the tray down carefully on a chair.*] Drink it yourself, Yásha.

YASHA. Here's to our departure! Good luck to them that stay! [*Drinking.*] This isn't real champagne, you take my word for it.

LOPAKHIN. Sixteen shillings a bottle. [*A pause.*] It's devilish cold in here.

YASHA. The fires weren't lighted to-day; we're all going away. [*He laughs.*]

LOPAKHIN. What are you laughing for?

YASHA. Just pleasure.

LOPAKHIN. Here we are in October, but it's as calm and sunny as summer. Good building weather. [*Looking at his watch and speaking off.*] Don't forget that there's only forty-seven minutes before the train goes. You must start for the station in twenty minutes. Make haste.

[*Enter* TROPHIMOF *in an overcoat, from out of doors.*]

TROPHIMOF. I think it's time we were off. The carriages are round. What the deuce has become of my goloshes? I've lost 'em. [*Calling off.*] Anya, my goloshes have disappeared. I can't find them anywhere!

LOPAKHIN. I've got to go to Kharkof. I'll start in the same train with you. I'm going to spend the winter in Kharkof. I've been loafing about all this time with you people, eating my head off for want of work. I can't live without work, I don't know what to do with my hands; they dangle about as if they didn't belong to me.

TROPHIMOF. Well, we're going now, and you'll be able to get back to your beneficent labours.

LOPAKHIN. Have a glass.

TROPHIMOF. Not for me.

LOPAKHIN. Well, so you're off to Moscow?

TROPHIMOF. Yes, I'll see them into the town, and go on to Moscow to-morrow.

LOPAKHIN. Well, well. . . . I suppose the professors haven't started their lectures yet; they're waiting till you arrive.

TROPHIMOF. It is no affair of yours.

LOPAKHIN. How many years have you been up at the University?

TROPHIMOF. Try and think of some new joke; this one's getting a bit flat. [*Looking for his goloshes.*] Look here, I dare say we shan't meet again, so let me give you a bit of advice as a keepsake: Don't flap your hands about! Get out of the habit of flapping. Building villas, prophesying that villa residents will turn into small freeholders, all that sort of thing is flapping too. Well, when all's said and done, I like you. You have thin, delicate, artist fingers; you have a delicate, artist soul.

LOPAKHIN [*embracing him*]. Good-bye, old chap. Thank you for everything. Take some money off me for the journey if you want it.

TROPHIMOF. What for? I don't want it.

LOPAKHIN. But you haven't got any.

TROPHIMOF. Yes, I have. Many thanks. I got some for a translation. Here it is, in my pocket. [*Anxiously.*] I can't find my goloshes anywhere!

BARBARA [*from the next room*]. Here, take your garbage away! [*She throws a pair of goloshes on the stage.*]

TROPHIMOF. What are you so cross about, Barbara? Humph! . . . But those aren't *my* goloshes!

LOPAKHIN. In the spring I sowed three thousand acres of poppy and I have cleared four thousand pounds net profit. When my poppies were in flower, what a picture they made! So you see, I cleared four thousand pounds; and I wanted to lend you a bit because I've got it to spare. What's the good of being stuck up? I'm a peasant. . . . As man to man. . . .

TROPHIMOF. Your father was a peasant; mine was a chemist; it doesn't prove anything. [LOPAKHIN *takes out his pocket-book with paper money.*] Shut up, shut up. . . . If you offered me twenty thousand pounds I would not take it. I am a free man; nothing that you value so highly, all of you, rich and poor, has the smallest power over me; it's like thistledown floating on the wind. I can do without you; I can go past you; I'm strong and proud. Mankind marches forward to the highest truth, to the highest happiness possible on earth, and I march in the foremost ranks.

LOPAKHIN. Will you get there?

TROPHIMOF. Yes. [*A pause.*] I will get there myself or I will show others the way.

[*The sound of axes hewing is heard in the distance.*]

LOPAKHIN. Well, good-bye, old chap; it is time to start. Here we stand swaggering to each other, and life goes by all the time without heeding us. When I work for hours without getting tired, I get easy in my mind and I seem to know why I exist. But God alone knows what most of the people in Russia were born for. . . . Well, who cares? It doesn't affect the circulation of work. They say Leoníd Andréyitch has got a place; he's going to be in a bank and get six hundred pounds a year. . . . He won't sit it out, he's too lazy.

ANYA [*in the doorway*]. Mamma says, will you stop cutting down the orchard till she has gone.

TROPHIMOF. Really, haven't you got tact enough for that?

[*Exit* TROPHIMOF *by the hall.*]

LOPAKHIN. Of course, I'll stop them at once. What fools they are!

[*Exit after* TROPHIMOF.]

ANYA. Has Firs been sent to the hospital?

YASHA. I told 'em this morning. They're sure to have sent him.

ANYA [*to* EPHIKHODOF, *who crosses*]. Simeon Panteléyitch, please find out if Firs has been sent to the hospital.
YASHA [*offended*]. I told George this morning. What's the good of asking a dozen times?
EPHIKHODOF. Our centenarian friend, in my conclusive opinion, is hardly worth tinkering; it's time he was dispatched to his forefathers. I can only say I envy him. [*Putting down a portmanteau on a bandbox and crushing it flat.*] There you are! I knew how it would be!

[*Exit.*]

YASHA [*jeering*]. Twenty-two misfortunes.
BARBARA [*without*]. Has Firs been sent to the hospital?
ANYA. Yes.
BARBARA. Why didn't they take the note to the doctor?
ANYA. We must send it after them.

[*Exit* ANYA.]

BARBARA [*from the next room*]. Where's Yásha? Tell him his mother is here. She wants to say good-bye to him.
YASHA [*with a gesture of impatience*]. It's enough to try the patience of a saint!

[DUNYASHA *has been busying herself with the luggage. Seeing* YASHA *alone, she approaches him.*]

DUNYASHA. You might just look once at me, Yásha. You are going away, you are leaving me. [*Crying and throwing her arms round his neck.*]
YASHA. What's the good of crying? [*Drinking champagne.*] In six days I shall be back in Paris. To-morrow we take the express, off we go, and that's the last of us! I can hardly believe it's true. Vive la France! This place don't suit me. I can't bear it . . . it can't be helped. I have had enough barbarism; I'm fed up. [*Drinking champagne.*] What's the good of crying? You be a good girl, and you'll have no call to cry.
DUNYASHA [*powdering her face and looking into a glass*]. Write me a letter from Paris. I've been so fond of you, Yásha, ever so fond! I am a delicate creature, Yásha.
YASHA. Here's somebody coming. [*He busies himself with the luggage, singing under his breath.*]

[*Enter* MADAME RANEVSKY, GAYEF, ANYA *and* CHARLOTTE.]

GAYEF. We'll have to be off; it's nearly time. [*Looking at* YASHA.] Who is it smells of red herring?
MADAME RANEVSKY. We must take our seats in ten minutes. [*Looking*

round the room.] Good-bye, dear old house, good-bye, grandpapa! When winter is past and spring comes again, you will be here no more; they will have pulled you down. Oh, think of all these walls have seen! [*Kissing* ANYA *passionately.*] My treasure, you look radiant, your eyes flash like two diamonds. Are you happy? very happy?

ANYA. Very, very happy. We're beginning a new life, mamma.

GAYEF [*gaily*]. She's quite right, everything's all right now. Till the cherry orchard was sold we were all agitated and miserable; but once the thing was settled finally and irrevocably, we all calmed down and got jolly again. I'm a bank clerk now; I'm a financier . . . red in the middle! And you, Lyuba, whatever you may say, you're looking ever so much better, not a doubt about it.

MADAME RANEVSKY. Yes, my nerves are better; it's quite true. [*She is helped on with her hat and coat.*] I sleep well now. Take my things out, Yásha. We must be off. [*To* ANYA.] We shall soon meet again, darling. . . . I'm off to Paris; I shall live on the money your grandmother sent from Yaroslav to buy the property. God bless your grandmother! I'm afraid it won't last long.

ANYA. You'll come back very, very soon, won't you, mamma? I'm going to work and pass the examination at the Gymnase and get a place and help you. We'll read all sorts of books together, won't we, mamma? [*Kissing her mother's hands.*] We'll read in the long autumn evenings, we'll read heaps of books, and a new, wonderful world will open up before us. [*Meditating.*] . . . Come back, mamma!

MADAME RANEVSKY. I'll come back, my angel. [*Embracing her.*]

[*Enter* LOPAKHIN. CHARLOTTE *sings softly.*]

GAYEF. Happy Charlotte, she's singing.

CHARLOTTE [*taking a bundle of rugs, like a swaddled baby*]. Hush-a-bye, baby, on the tree top . . . [*The baby answers, 'Wah, wah.'*] Hush, my little one, hush, my pretty one! [*'Wah, wah.'*] You'll break your mother's heart. [*She throws the bundle down on the floor again.*] Don't forget to find me a new place, please. I can't do without it.

LOPAKHIN. We'll find you a place, Charlotte Ivánovna, don't be afraid.

GAYEF. Everybody's deserting us. Barbara's going. Nobody seems to want us.

CHARLOTTE. There's nowhere for me to live in the town. I'm obliged to go. [*Hums a tune.*] What's the odds?

[*Enter* PISHTCHIK.]

LOPAKHIN. Nature's masterpiece!

PISHTCHIK [*panting*]. Oy, oy, let me get my breath again! . . . I'm done up! . . . My noble friends! . . . Give me some water.

GAYEF. Wants some money, I suppose. No, thank you; I'll keep out of harm's way.

[*Exit.*]

PISHTCHIK. It's ages since I have been here, fairest lady. [*To* LOPAKHIN.] You here? Glad to see you, you man of gigantic intellect. Take this; it's for you. [*Giving* LOPAKHIN *money.*] Forty pounds! I still owe you eighty-four.

LOPAKHIN [*amazed, shrugging his shoulders*]. It's like a thing in a dream! Where did you get it from?

PISHTCHIK. Wait a bit. . . . I'm hot. . . . A most remarkable thing! Some Englishmen came and found some sort of white clay on my land. [*To* MADAME RANEVSKY.] And here's forty pounds for you, lovely, wonderful lady. [*Giving her money.*] The rest another time. [*Drinking water.*] Only just now a young man in the train was saying that some . . . some great philosopher advises us all to jump off roofs. . . . Jump, he says, and there's an end of it. [*With an astonished air.*] Just think of that! More water!

LOPAKHIN. Who were the Englishmen?

PISHTCHIK. I leased them the plot with the clay on it for twenty-four years. But I haven't any time now . . . I must be getting on. I must go to Znoikof's, to Kardamónof's. . . . I owe everybody money. [*Drinking.*] Good-bye to everyone; I'll look in on Thursday.

MADAME RANEVSKY. We're just moving into town, and to-morrow I go abroad.

PISHTCHIK. What! [*Alarmed.*] What are you going into town for? Why, what's happened to the furniture? . . . Trunks? . . . Oh, it's all right. [*Crying.*] It's all right. People of powerful intellect . . . those Englishmen. It's all right. Be happy . . . God be with you . . . it's all right. Everything in this world has come to an end. [*Kissing* MADAME RANEVSKY'S *hand.*] If ever the news reaches you that I have come to an end, give a thought to the old . . . horse, and say, 'Once there lived a certain Simeónof-Píshtchik, Heaven rest his soul.'. . . Remarkable weather we're having. . . . Yes. . . . [*Goes out deeply moved. Returns at once and says from the doorway.*] Dáshenka sent her compliments.

[*Exit.*]

MADAME RANEVSKY. Now we can go. I have only two things on my mind. One is poor old Firs. [*Looking at her watch.*] We can still stay five minutes.

ANYA. Firs has been sent to the hospital already, mamma. Yásha sent him off this morning.

MADAME RANEVSKY. My second anxiety is Barbara. She's used to getting up early and working, and now that she has no work to do she's like a fish out of water. She has grown thin and pale and taken to crying, poor dear. . . . [A *pause.*] You know very well, Yermolái Alexéyitch, I always hoped . . . to see her married to you, and as far as I can see, you're looking out for a wife. [*She whispers to* ANYA, *who nods to* CHARLOTTE, *and both exeunt.*] She loves you; you like her; and I can't make out why you seem to fight shy of each other. I don't understand it.

LOPAKHIN. I don't understand it either, to tell you the truth. It all seems so odd. If there's still time, I'll do it this moment. Let's get it over and have done with it; without you there, I feel as if I should never propose to her.

MADAME RANEVSKY. A capital idea! After all, it doesn't take more than a minute. I'll call her at once.

LOPAKHIN. And here's the champagne all ready. [*Looking at the glasses.*] Empty; someone's drunk it. [YASHA *coughs.*] That's what they call lapping it up and no mistake!

MADAME RANEVSKY [*animated*]. Capital! We'll all go away. . . . *Allez,* Yásha. I'll call her. [*At the door.*] Barbara, leave all that and come here. Come along!

[*Exeunt* MADAME RANEVSKY *and* YASHA.]

LOPAKHIN [*looking at his watch*]. Yes.

[*A pause. A stifled laugh behind the door; whispering; at last enter* BARBARA.]

BARBARA [*examining the luggage*]. Very odd; I can't find it anywhere . . .

LOPAKHIN. What are you looking for?

BARBARA. I packed it myself, and can't remember. [A *pause.*]

LOPAKHIN. Where are you going to-day, Varvára Mikháilovna?

BARBARA. Me? I'm going to the Ragulins'. I'm engaged to go and keep house for them, to be housekeeper or whatever it is.

LOPAKHIN. Oh, at Yáshnevo? That's about fifty miles from here. [A *pause.*] Well, so life in this house is over now.

BARBARA [*looking at the luggage*]. Wherever can it be? Perhaps I put it in the trunk. . . . Yes, life here is over now; there won't be any more . . .

LOPAKHIN. And I'm off to Kharkof at once . . . by the same train. A lot of business to do. I'm leaving Ephikhódof to look after this place. I've taken him on.

BARBARA. Have you?

LOPAKHIN. At this time last year snow was falling already, if you remember; but now it's fine and sunny. Still, it's cold for all that. Three degrees of frost.

BARBARA. Were there? I didn't look. [*A pause.*] Besides, the thermometer's broken. [*A pause.*]

A VOICE [*at the outer door*]. Yermolái Alexéyitch!

LOPAKHIN [*as if he had only been waiting to be called*]. I'm just coming! [*Exit* LOPAKHIN *quickly.*]

[BARBARA *sits on the floor, puts her head on a bundle and sobs softly. The door opens and* MADAME RANEVSKY *comes in cautiously.*]

MADAME RANEVSKY. Well? [*A pause.*] We must be off.

BARBARA [*no longer crying, wiping her eyes*]. Yes, it's time, mamma. I shall get to the Ragulins' all right to-day, so long as I don't miss the train.

MADAME RANEVSKY [*calling off*]. Put on your things, Anya.

[*Enter* ANYA, *then* GAYEF *and* CHARLOTTE. GAYEF *wears a warm overcoat with a hood. The servants and drivers come in.* EPHIKHODOF *busies himself about the luggage.*]

MADAME RANEVSKY. Now we can start on our journey.

ANYA [*delighted*]. We can start on our journey!

GAYEF. My friends, my dear, beloved friends! Now that I am leaving this house for ever, can I keep silence? Can I refrain from expressing those emotions which fill my whole being at such a moment?

ANYA [*pleadingly*]. Uncle!

BARBARA. Uncle, what's the good?

GAYEF [*sadly*]. Double the red in the middle pocket. I'll hold my tongue.

[*Enter* TROPHIMOF, *then* LOPAKHIN.]

TROPHIMOF. Come along, it's time to start.

LOPAKHIN. Ephikhódof, my coat.

MADAME RANEVSKY. I must sit here another minute. It's just as if I had never noticed before what the walls and ceilings of the house were like. I look at them hungrily, with such tender love. . . .

GAYEF. I remember, when I was six years old, how I sat in this window on Trinity Sunday, and watched father starting out for church.

MADAME RANEVSKY. Has everything been cleared out?

LOPAKHIN. Apparently everything. [*To* EPHIKHODOF, *putting on his overcoat.*] See that everything's in order, Ephikhódof.

EPHIKHODOF [*in a hoarse voice*]. You trust me, Yermolái Alexéyitch.

LOPAKHIN. What's up with your voice?

EPHIKHODOF. I was just having a drink of water. I swallowed something.

YASHA [*contemptuously*]. Cad!

MADAME RANEVSKY. We're going, and not a soul will be left here.

LOPAKHIN. Until the spring.

[BARBARA *pulls an umbrella out of a bundle of rugs, as if she were brandishing it to strike.* LOPAKHIN *pretends to be frightened.*]

BARBARA. Don't be so silly! I never thought of such a thing.
TROPHIMOF. Come, we'd better go and get in. It's time to start. The train will be in immediately.
BARBARA. There are your goloshes, Peter, by that portmanteau. [*Crying.*] What dirty old things they are!
TROPHIMOF [*putting on his goloshes*]. Come along.
GAYEF [*much moved, afraid of crying*]. The train . . . the station . . . double the red in the middle; doublette to pot the white in the corner. . . .
MADAME RANEVSKY. Come on!
LOPAKHIN. Is everyone here? No one left in there? [*Locking the door.*] There are things stacked in there; I must lock them up. Come on!
ANYA. Good-bye, house! good-bye, old life!
TROPHIMOF. Welcome, new life!

[*Exit with* ANYA. BARBARA *looks round the room, and exit slowly. Exeunt* YASHA, *and* CHARLOTTE *with her dog.*]

LOPAKHIN. Till the spring, then. Go on, everybody. So-long!

[*Exit.* MADAME RANEVSKY *and* GAYEF *remain alone. They seem to have been waiting for this, throw their arms round each other's necks and sob restrainedly and gently, afraid of being overheard.*]

GAYEF [*in despair*]. My sister! my sister!
MADAME RANEVSKY. Oh, my dear, sweet lovely orchard! My life, my youth, my happiness, farewell! Farewell!
ANYA [*calling gaily, without*]. Mamma!
TROPHIMOF [*gay and excited*]. Aoo!
MADAME RANEVSKY. One last look at the walls and the windows. . . . Our dear mother used to walk up and down this room.
GAYEF. My sister! my sister!
ANYA [*without*]. Aoo!
MADAME RANEVSKY. We're coming. [*Exeunt.*]

[*The stage is empty. One hears all the doors being locked, and the carriages driving away. All is quiet. Amid the silence the thud of the axes on the trees echoes sad and lonely. The sound of footsteps.* FIRS *appears in the doorway* R. *He is dressed, as always, in his long coat and white waistcoat; he wears slippers. He is ill.*]

FIRS [*going to the door* L. *and trying the handle*]. Locked. They've gone. [*Sitting on the sofa.*] They've forgotten me. Never mind! I'll sit here. Leoníd Andréyitch is sure to have put on his cloth coat instead of his fur. [*He sighs anxiously.*] He hadn't me to see. Young wood, green wood! [*He mumbles something incomprehensible.*] Life has gone by as if I'd never lived. [*Lying down.*] I'll lie down. There's no strength left in you; there's nothing, nothing. Ah, you . . . job-lot!

[*He lies motionless. A distant sound is heard, as if from the sky, the sound of a string breaking, dying away, melancholy. Silence ensues, broken only by the stroke of the axe on the trees far away in the cherry orchard.*]

CURTAIN

The Inspector General

CHARACTERS *

ANTÓN ANTÓNOVICH SKVÓZNIK-DMUKHANÓVSKY, *chief of police*
ANNA ANDRÉYEVNA, *his wife*
MÁRYA ANTÓNOVNA, *his daughter*
LUKÁ LÚKICH HLÓPOV, *superintendent of schools*
HIS WIFE
AMMÓS FÉDOROVICH LYÁPKIN-TYÁPKIN, *judge*
ARTÉMY FILÍPPOVICH ZEMLYANÍKA, *supervisor of charitable institutions*
IVÁN KÚZMICH SHPÉKIN, *postmaster*
PETR IVÁNOVICH DÓBCHINSKY } *landed proprietors living in the town*
PETR IVÁNOVICH BÓBCHINSKY }
IVÁN ALEXÁNDROVICH HLESTAKÓV, *an official from St. Petersburg*
OSIP, *his servant*
CHRISTIÁN IVÁNOVICH GÍBNER, *district physician*
FÉDOR ANDRÉYEVICH LYULYUKÓV } *retired officials, respected personages in the town*
IVÁN LAZARÉVICH RASTAKÓVSKY }
STEPÁN IVÁNOVICH KORÓBKIN }
STEPÁN ILYÍCH UKHOVÉRTOV, *police captain*
SVISTUNÓV } *policemen*
PÚGOVITSYN }
DERZHÍMORDA }
ABDÚLIN, *a merchant*
FEVRÓNYA PETRÓVA POSHLÉPKIN, *wife of a locksmith*
WIDOW *of a* SERGEANT
MÍSHKA, *servant of the chief of police*
INN SERVANT
Men and women guests, merchants, townsfolk, petitioners.

* Several of these names have grotesque associations; the following translations may serve: Skvoznik-Dmukhanovsky, Rascal-Puftup; Hlopov, Bedbug; Lyapkin-Tyapkin, Bungle-Steal; Zemlyanika, Strawberry; Hlestakov, Whippersnapper; Lyulyukov, Halloo; Rastakovsky, Sayyes; Korobkin, Woodenhead; Ukhovertov, Earwig; Svistunov, Whistle; Pugovitsyn, Buttons; Derzhimorda, Holdyourmug; Abdulin, Tatar; Poshlepkin (pronounced Po-shlyop'kin), Draggletail. Fedor is pronounced Fyŏ'dor; Fedorovich, Fyŏ'do-ro-vich; Shpekin, Shpyŏ'kin; Ukhovterov, U-kho-vyŏr'toff; Petr, Pyŏtr (one syllable).

CHARACTERS AND COSTUMES

NOTES FOR THE ACTORS

The CHIEF OF POLICE * has grown old in the service and is, in his own way, anything but a stupid man. Although a bribe-taker, he behaves with marked dignity; he is rather serious, and is even somewhat inclined to moralize; he speaks neither loudly nor softly, much nor little. His every word is significant. His features are harsh and coarse, such as are common in people who have advanced with difficulty from the lowest ranks. The change from fear to joy, from servility to arrogance, is very sudden, as in the case of a man with crudely developed personal traits. He is dressed in the usual manner, in his uniform with frogs, wearing high boots with spurs. His hair is cut short and shows gray streaks.

ANNA ANDREYEVNA, his wife, is a provincial coquette, still in middle life, brought up half on novels and albums, half on bustling about her housekeeping supplies and supervising her maids. She is very inquisitive, and on occasion displays vanity. Sometimes she gets the upper hand of her husband simply because he is unable to answer her, but this power extends only to trifles and consists of curtain lectures and nagging. During the course of the play she changes her costume four times.

HLESTAKOV is a young man twenty-three years old, very thin and lean; he is rather stupid, and, as they say, rattle-headed, one of those people who in their offices are called hopelessly "dumb." He speaks and acts without any reflection. He is incapable of focusing his attention on any thought whatsoever. His speech is abrupt, and the words fly out of his mouth quite unexpectedly. The more sincerity and simplicity the actor puts into this rôle, the better he will play it. He is dressed fashionably.

OSIP is the usual sort of elderly manservant. He talks seriously, and has a rather condescending air; he is inclined to moralize, and likes to sermonize his master behind his back. His voice is almost unchang-

* The office of *gorodnichy*, or chief of city police, existed from 1775 to 1862. The *gorodnichy* was appointed by the imperial authorities in St. Petersburg and was responsible to them. His duties were far more extensive than those of the chief of police of an American or an English city. The title *city manager* might suggest them more accurately.

ing: in conversation with his master he assumes a severe, abrupt, and even rather rude expression. He is cleverer than his master, and therefore grasps a situation more quickly; but he does not like to talk much, and is a silent rascal. He wears a gray or blue frock coat, much worn.

BOBCHINSKY and DOBCHINSKY are both short and stubby and very inquisitive, extraordinarily like each other: both are slightly corpulent; both speak very fast with an extraordinary amount of gesticulation. Dobchinsky is a little taller and more serious than Bobchinsky, but Bobchinsky is more expansive and lively than Dobchinsky.

LYAPKIN-TYAPKIN, the Judge, is a man who has read five or six books, and is consequently something of a freethinker. He is very fond of conjectures, and therefore gives much weight to his every word. The actor who plays the rôle must always preserve a knowing expression of countenance. He speaks in a bass voice with a prolonged drawl, with a sound of wheezing and strangling, like an old clock, which first squeaks and then strikes.

ZEMLYANIKA, the Supervisor of Charitable Institutions, is a very stout, awkward, and clumsy man, but for all that a schemer and a rogue. He is very officious and bustling.

THE POSTMASTER is simple-hearted to the point of naïveté.

The remaining rôles require no special explanations: their prototypes may be found in almost any community.

The actors should pay particular attention to the last scene. The last speech should produce upon all a sudden electric shock. The whole group should strike its pose in a twinkling. A cry of astonishment should be uttered by all the women at once, as if proceeding from a single bosom. From a disregard of these remarks may result a total loss of effect.

Don't blame the looking-glass if your mug is crooked.

POPULAR PROVERB

ACT I

A room in the house of the CHIEF OF POLICE

SCENE I

CHIEF OF POLICE, SUPERVISOR OF CHARITABLE INSTITUTIONS, SUPERINTENDENT OF SCHOOLS, JUDGE, POLICE CAPTAIN, DISTRICT PHYSICIAN, *and two* SERGEANTS OF POLICE

CHIEF OF POLICE: I have invited you here, gentlemen, in order to communicate to you a most unpleasant piece of news: a government inspector is coming to visit us.

AMMOS FEDOROVICH: What, an inspector?

ARTEMY FILIPPOVICH: What, an inspector?

CHIEF OF POLICE: An inspector from Petersburg, incognito. And furthermore, with secret instructions.

AMMOS FEDOROVICH: Well, I declare!

ARTEMY FILIPPOVICH: As if we didn't have troubles enough already!

LUKA LUKICH: Oh, my God, and with secret instructions too!

CHIEF OF POLICE: I had a sort of presentiment. All last night I kept dreaming about two most extraordinary rats. Honest, I've never seen any like them: black, and awfully big. They came, sniffled about, and went away again. And now I'm going to read you a letter that I've received from Andrey Ivanovich Chmykhov, whom you know, Artemy Filippovich. Here's what he writes: "My dear friend, godfather, and benefactor," (*He mutters in an undertone, rapidly glancing over the letter.*) . . . "and to inform you." Ah, here it is! "I hasten to inform you, by the way, that an official has arrived with instructions to inspect the whole province and especially our district. (*Raising his fingers significantly.*) I have found this out from most reliable people, although he is representing himself as a private individual. Knowing as I do that you, like everybody else, are liable to your little failings, because you're a smart chap and don't like to miss anything that fairly swims into your hands . . ." (*After a pause.*) Well, this is a friendly party. . . . "I advise you to take precautions, because he may arrive at any moment, if he hasn't already, and isn't living somewhere around now, incognito. . . . Yesterday I . . ." Well, next there's some family matters: "Cousin Anna Kirilovna has come to see us with her husband; Ivan Kirilovich has grown very stout, and he plays on the fiddle all the time . . ." and so forth, and so on. Now there's a fix for you!

AMMOS FEDOROVICH: Yes, and such an unusual fix; absolutely extraordinary! There's something up.

LUKA LUKICH: But why on earth, Anton Antonovich; what's this for? Why send an inspector here?

CHIEF OF POLICE: What for? Evidently it's fate. (*Sighing.*) Up to this time, thanks be to God, they've poked into other people's business; but now it's our turn.

AMMOS FEDOROVICH: I think, Anton Antonovich, that in this case it's for a subtle and more political reason. Here's what it means: Russia . . . yes . . . Russia's going to war; and the ministry, you see, has sent the official to find out if there's any treason brewing.

CHIEF OF POLICE: Where do you get that stuff? Aren't you the smart man! Treason in a provincial town! Is this a frontier town? Why, you can gallop away from here for three years without reaching a foreign country.

AMMOS FEDOROVICH: No, I tell you, you don't understand . . . you don't . . . The authorities have subtle ideas: even if it is a long distance, they aren't taking any chances.

CHIEF OF POLICE: Whether they are or not, gentlemen, I've warned you. See here: I've made, for my part, some kind of arrangements, and I advise you to do the same. Especially you, Artemy Filippovich! No doubt the passing official will want first of all to inspect the charitable institutions belonging to your department, and therefore you'd better see that everything's in decent shape: the nightcaps had better be clean, and the patients had better not look like blacksmiths, as they usually do, in their little home circle.

ARTEMY FILIPPOVICH: Come, that's all right. They can put on clean nightcaps if you want.

CHIEF OF POLICE: Yes. And also above each bed write up in Latin or some such language—here, that's your job, Christian Ivanovich—the name of each disease, when the person was taken ill, and the day of the week and month. . . . And it's a bad thing that your patients smoke such strong tobacco that a fellow always begins to sneeze as soon as he goes in. Yes, and it would be better if there were fewer of 'em: people will attribute it right off to bad supervision or to the doctor's lack of skill.

ARTEMY FILIPPOVICH: Oh, so far as the doctoring goes, Christian Ivanovich and I have taken our measures: the closer you get to nature, the better; we don't use expensive medicines. Man's a simple creature: if he's going to die, he dies; if he's going to get well, he gets well. And besides it would be hard for Christian Ivanovich to consult with them: he doesn't know a word of Russian.

(CHRISTIAN IVANOVICH *utters a sound somewhat like the letter "e" and a little like "a."*)

CHIEF OF POLICE: I'd also advise you, Ammos Fedorovich, to pay some attention to the courthouse. There in the hall where the petitioners usually appear, the janitors have started raising domestic geese and goslings, and they all duck under your feet as you walk. Of course it's praiseworthy for every man to look after his domestic enterprises, and why shouldn't a janitor? Only in such a place, you know, it's hardly suitable. . . . I meant to bring that to your attention before, but somehow I forgot it.

AMMOS FEDOROVICH: Well, I'll order them all taken away to my kitchen this very day. Come to dinner if you want to.

CHIEF OF POLICE: Besides that it's a bad thing that you have all kinds of rubbish drying up right in the court room, and a hunter's whip right over the cupboard where the documents are kept. I know that you like hunting, but all the same you'd better remove it for a while; and then, when the government inspector has gone away, you can hang it up there again. And your assessor likewise . . . of course, he's a well-informed man, but he smells exactly as if he'd just come out of a distillery—and that's no good either. I've been going to speak to you about that for some time back; but I was distracted, I don't remember how. There's a remedy against that smell, if, as he says, it's actually natural to him: he can be advised to eat onions or garlic or something else. In that case Christian Ivanovich might help out with some drugs.

(CHRISTIAN IVANOVICH *utters the same sound.*)

AMMOS FEDOROVICH: No, it's impossible to drive it out. He says that in his childhood his nurse bumped him and that since that time he smells a little of vodka.

CHIEF OF POLICE: Well, I only brought it to your notice. So far as internal arrangements go and what Andrey Ivanovich calls in his letter little failings, I can't say anything, and it would be queer to talk about them, for there's no man who hasn't some weaknesses or other. Why, God himself has fixed it like that, and the Voltairians make a great mistake to say anything to the contrary.

AMMOS FEDOROVICH: And what do you presume to call failings, Anton Antonovich? There are sins and sins. I tell everybody openly that I take bribes—but what kind of bribes? Wolfhound puppies. That's absolutely another matter.

CHIEF OF POLICE: Well, puppies or anything else—it's bribes, all the same.

AMMOS FEDOROVICH: Indeed not, Anton Antonovich. Here, for instance, if a man accepts a fur coat worth five hundred rubles, or a shawl for his wife . . .

CHIEF OF POLICE: Well, and what if you do accept only wolfhound puppies as bribes? To make up for it, you don't believe in God; you never go to church; but I am at least firm in the faith, and I go to church every Sunday. But you . . . Oh, I know you: if you begin to talk about the creation of the world, my hair simply stands on end.

AMMOS FEDOROVICH: But you see I reasoned it out for myself, with my own intellect.

CHIEF OF POLICE: Well, in some cases it's worse to have too much intellect than to have none at all. However, I merely wanted to mention the district court; but to tell the truth, I doubt that any one will ever take a peep at it; it's such an enviable place, God Himself must protect it. Now, as for you, Luka Lukich, as supervisor of educational institutions, you'd better take special care of the teachers. Of course they're learned people, educated in various colleges; but they have very strange ways, naturally inseparable from their learned calling. One of them, for instance, the one with the fat face . . . I don't remember his name . . . when he gets on the platform can't do without making faces, like this (*making a grimace*) and then begins to iron out his beard with his hand, from under his cravat. Of course, when he pulls a snout like that at one of the pupils, it doesn't matter much, and it may even be necessary for all I can say; but judge for yourself if he should do it to a visitor—that would be awful: the government inspector or whoever it was might consider it personal, and the devil knows what might come of it.

LUKA LUKICH: Surely, but what can I do with him? I've spoken to him about it several times already. Here, just a few days ago, when our marshal of nobility happened to drop in on the class, he cut such a mug as I've never seen before. Of course he did it with the best heart in the world, but I got called down: "Why," says they, "are our young people being exposed to the contagion of freethinking?"

CHIEF OF POLICE: I ought also to mention your history teacher. His head's full of learning, that's evident, and he's picked up information by the ton; only he gets so hot in his explanations that there's no understanding him. I once listened to him: well, while he was talking about the Assyrians and the Babylonians, it was all right; but when he got as far as Alexander of Macedon I can't tell you what came over him. Damme if I didn't think there was a fire! He ran down from the platform, and banged a chair against the door with all his might.

Of course, Alexander of Macedon was a hero; but why smash the chairs over him? It causes a loss to the treasury.

LUKA LUKICH: Yes, he's hot-headed. I've remarked the fact to him several times already. . . . He says, "Just as you please: for science I won't spare life itself."

CHIEF OF POLICE: Yes, such is the inexplicable law of the Fates: a wise man is either a drunkard or he makes such faces that you've got to carry out the holy ikons.*

LUKA LUKICH: God save us from serving in the educational line! A fellow's afraid of everybody: all sorts of people interfere, and they all want to show that they're educated, too.

CHIEF OF POLICE: But all this wouldn't amount to anything—it's that damned incognito! He'll look in all of a sudden with an "Oh, here you are, sweethearts! And who's the judge here?" he'll say.—"Lyapkin-Tyapkin."—"All right, hand over Lyapkin-Tyapkin! And who's the supervisor of charitable institutions?"—"Zemlyanika."—"Well, hand over Zemlyanika!"—That's what's bad!

SCENE II

The same and the POSTMASTER

POSTMASTER: Will you explain, gentlemen, what sort of official is coming, and why?

CHIEF OF POLICE: But haven't you heard?

POSTMASTER: I heard something from Petr Ivanovich Bobchinsky. He just called on me at the post office.

CHIEF OF POLICE: Well, then, what do you think about it?

POSTMASTER: What do I think? I think we're going to war with the Turks.

AMMOS FEDOROVICH: Right-o! That's exactly what I thought.

CHIEF OF POLICE: Yes, but you're both talking through your hat!

POSTMASTER: Sure, it's war with the Turks. The French keep spoiling everything.

CHIEF OF POLICE: War with the Turks, your grandmother! *We're* going to be in a mess, not the Turks. We know that already; I have a letter.

POSTMASTER: If that's so, then there's not going to be war with the Turks.

CHIEF OF POLICE: Well, then, how about you, Ivan Kuzmich?

POSTMASTER: About me? How about you, Anton Antonovich?

CHIEF OF POLICE: Well, what about me? I'm not afraid: that is,

* "To avoid shocking them."—Sykes.

only a little. . . . The merchants and the townspeople make me uneasy. They say that I'm somewhat hard-boiled; but if I've ever taken anything from anybody, God knows it was without the least ill-feeling. I even think (*taking him by the arm and leading him aside*), I even think there may have been some private denunciation of me. Otherwise why in the world send the inspector to us? Now listen here, Ivan Kuzmich, hadn't you better, for our mutual benefit just unseal and read every letter that arrives at the post office, both incoming and outgoing? You know, just in case there should be some sort of denunciation, or simply, correspondence. If there isn't, of course you can seal them up again; or, so far as that goes, you can even deliver them opened.

POSTMASTER: I know, I know. . . . Don't try to teach me. I do it already, not as a precaution, but more out of curiosity; I'm deadly fond of finding out what's new in the world. I tell you, it's most interesting reading. There are piles of letters that you'll thoroughly enjoy, certain passages are so descriptive . . . and they're so instructive . . . lots better than the *Moscow News*.

CHIEF OF POLICE: Well, tell me, haven't you ever come across anything about some such official from Petersburg?

POSTMASTER: No, absolutely nothing about any one from Petersburg, but there's a lot said about those from Kostroma and Saratov. However, it's a pity that *you* don't read the letters: there are some corking places in them. Not long ago a lieutenant was writing to a friend and he described a ball in the most playful way . . . it was awfully good: "My life, my dear friend, is being passed in the empyrean," he says; "there are lots of young ladies; the band is playing; the standard gallops by. . . ." He described it all with very great feeling. I kept the letter out just on purpose. Do you want me to read it to you?

CHIEF OF POLICE: Well, this is hardly the time for it. So you'll do me the favor, Ivan Kuzmich, if you accidentally come across a complaint or a denunciation, to keep it back without any question.

POSTMASTER: With the greatest of pleasure.

AMMOS FEDOROVICH: Look out, or you'll catch it for that, sometime!

POSTMASTER: Great Scott!

CHIEF OF POLICE: Never mind, never mind. It would be another story if you were to make anything public out of it; but you see, this is a family matter.

AMMOS FEDOROVICH: Yes, a nasty mess has been brewed! I admit I was going to call on you, Anton Antonovich, to make you a present of a little bitch. She's a sister to the dog you know. You've doubtless heard that Cheptovich and Varkhovinsky have started a lawsuit, so that now I'm living in luxury: I course hares now on one man's land, now on the other's.

CHIEF OF POLICE: Holy Saints, I don't care anything about your hares now! I can't get that damned incognito out of my head. You wait until the door opens, and then suddenly—

SCENE III

The same, with DOBCHINSKY *and* BOBCHINSKY, *who both come in panting*

BOBCHINSKY: An extraordinary event!

DOBCHINSKY: What unexpected news!

ALL: Why, what is it?

DOBCHINSKY: A most unforeseen affair. We went into the inn—

BOBCHINSKY (*interrupting*): Petr Ivanovich and I went into the inn—

DOBCHINSKY (*interrupting*): Hey, if you please, Petr Ivanovich, I'll tell it!

BOBCHINSKY: Hey yourself, let me . . . let me, let me . . . you haven't got the right style. . . .

DOBCHINSKY: But you'll get all balled up and won't remember everything.

BOBCHINSKY: I'll remember, by George, I'll remember! Only don't mix in, let me tell it; don't meddle! Gentlemen, please tell Petr Ivanovich not to interfere!

CHIEF OF POLICE: Yes, for God's sake, tell us what's up! My heart's in my mouth. Be seated, gentlemen; take chairs! Petr Ivanovich, here's a chair for you. (*All seat themselves around the two* PETR IVANOVICHES.) Well now, what's up?

BOBCHINSKY: Allow me, allow me; I'll tell everything in order. No sooner had I had the pleasure of leaving you after you had got all upset over the receipt of that letter—yes, sir—than I just dropped in . . . now, please don't interrupt, Petr Ivanovich! I already know all, all, all about it, sir! So, as you'll be kind enough to see, I dropped in on Korobkin. But not finding Korobkin at home, I turned in at Rastakovsky's; and not finding Rastakovsky, I went straight to Ivan Kuzmich in order to communicate to him the news you had received; and then, going away from there, I met Petr Ivanovich—

DOBCHINSKY (*interrupting*): Near the stall where they sell meat pies.

BOBCHINSKY: Near the stall where they sell meat pies. Yes, I met up with Petr Ivanovich; and I said to him, "Have you heard the news that Anton Antonovich has received in a trustworthy letter?" But Petr Ivanovich had already heard about it from your housekeeper, Avdotya, who had been sent, I don't know what for, to Filipp Antonovich Pochechuyev's.

DOBCHINSHY (*interrupting*): For a little keg for French brandy.

BOBCHINSKY (*pushing his hands aside*): For a little keg for French brandy. So Petr Ivanovich and I went to Pochechuyev's. . . . For heaven's sake, Petr Ivanovich, don't interrupt; please don't interrupt! . . . We went to Pochechuyev's, and on the way Petr Ivanovich said to me: "Let's stop," he says, "at the inn. I haven't had anything in my stomach since morning, and it's simply flopping about. . . ." Yes, sir, Petr Ivanovich's belly was. . . . "But they've just brought some fresh salmon into the inn," he says, "and we'll take a snack." Well, no sooner were we in the hotel, when suddenly a young man—

DOBCHINSKY (*interrupting*): Not bad-looking, in civilian clothes. . . .

BOBCHINSKY: Not bad-looking, in civilian clothes, was walking up and down the room with such a thoughtful expression on his face and in his actions, and here (*putting his hand over his forehead*) much of everything, very much. I had a sort of presentiment, and I says to Petr Ivanovich: "There's more in this than meets the eye." Yes, I did. But Petr Ivanovich beckoned to me with his finger and we called the innkeeper, sir, the innkeeper Vlas. His wife was confined three weeks ago; and such a smart boy, too, he's going to take care of the inn just like his daddy. Well, having called Vlas, Petr Ivanovich asked him on the quiet: "Who's that young man?" he says. And Vlas answered, "Why that . . ." Hey, don't interrupt, Petr Ivanovich; please don't interrupt; you won't be able to tell it, God knows you won't: you lisp. I know you've got a tooth in your head that whistles. . . . "That young man," he says, "is an official." Yes, sir. "He's come from Petersburg," says Vlas, "and his name is Ivan Alexandrovich Hlestakov, sir; and he's going," says Vlas, "into the Province of Saratov; and," he says, "he's certainly acting queer: this is the second week he's been here, he never goes outside of the tavern; he orders everything on account; and he won't pay a kopek." As soon as he had told me that, I saw through it at once. "Aha!" I said to Petr Ivanovich—

DOBCHINSKY: No, Petr Ivanovich, it was I who said "Aha!"

BOBCHINSKY: You said it first, but I said it next. "Aha!" said Petr Ivanovich and I. "But why has he come here if he's headed for the Province of Saratov?"—Yes, sir. And so he must be that official.

CHIEF OF POLICE: Who? What official?

BOBCHINSKY: Why, that there official that you received the notice about, the government inspector.

CHIEF OF POLICE (*frightened*): What the deuce are you saying? That can't be he!

DOBCHINSKY: Yes, it is! He doesn't pay and he doesn't go. How could it be anybody else? And his traveling papers are made out for Saratov.

BOBCHINSKY: It's he; it's he, by God, it's he. . . . And what an observing fellow: he inspected everything. He even noticed that Petr Ivanovich and I were eating salmon, chiefly because Petr Ivanovich, on account of his stomach . . . well, yes, he even took a look in our plates. I fairly shivered with fright.

CHIEF OF POLICE: O Lord, forgive us sinners! Where's he staying?

DOBCHINSKY: In number five, under the staircase.

BOBCHINSKY: In the very same room where those traveling officers had a fight last year.

CHIEF OF POLICE: Has he been here long?

DOBCHINSKY: Just two weeks. He came on the day of St. Vasily of Egypt.

CHIEF OF POLICE: Two weeks! (*Aside.*) Holy Saints and Martyrs, get us out of this! In these two weeks the sergeant's wife has been beaten up! No provisions have been issued to the prisoners! The streets are like a dramshop, such filth! Oh, shame! Disgrace! (*He clutches at his head.*)

ARTEMY FILIPPOVICH: What do you think, Anton Antonovich: shall we go in a body to the hotel?

AMMOS FEDOROVICH: No, no! Let the Chief of Police go first, then the clergy, and the merchants—isn't that the way it is in the book, *The Deeds of John the Mason*? *

CHIEF OF POLICE: No, no, please leave it to me. Difficult situations have occurred in my life, but they have turned out all right, and I have even been thanked. Maybe God will get us off this time. (*Turning to* BOBCHINSKY.) You say he's a young man?

BOBCHINSKY: He is; not much over twenty-three or four.

CHIEF OF POLICE: All the better: you can smell out a young one quicker. It's fierce when it's an old devil; but a young one is all on the surface. Get your own business fixed up, gentlemen; but I'll go by myself, or maybe with Petr Ivanovich here, privately, just for a walk, to inquire whether the transient strangers are suffering any annoyances. Hey, Svistunov!

SVISTUNOV: What, sir?

CHIEF OF POLICE: Go call the police captain right away—but no, I need you. Tell some one outside to go for him as quickly as possible, and then come back here. (*The* SERGEANT OF POLICE *runs out at full speed.*)

* The Freemasons were prohibited in Russia as a society dangerous to the government. Apparently the freethinking judge refers to a masonic book. (Adapted from Sykes.)

ARTEMY FILIPPOVICH: Let's go, let's go, Ammos Fedorovich! There may be some trouble, for a fact.

AMMOS FEDOROVICH: Aw, what are you afraid of? Put clean nightcaps on the patients, and cover up your tracks.

ARTEMY FILIPPOVICH: To hell with your nightcaps! I ordered oatmeal porridge served to the patients, but all the same the corridors stink so of cabbage that you have to hold your nose!

AMMOS FEDOROVICH: Well, I'm easy for my part. As a matter of fact, whoever 'll look into a district court? But if he does happen to glance at any paper, he'll lose all joy in life. Here I've been sitting on the judge's bench for fifteen years, and if I merely look at a report, all I can do is wave my hand! Solomon himself couldn't make out what's truth in it and what isn't.

(*The* JUDGE, *the* SUPERVISOR OF CHARITABLE INSTITUTIONS, *the* SUPERINTENDENT OF SCHOOLS, *and the* POSTMASTER *go out, and at the door encounter the returning* SERGEANT OF POLICE.)

SCENE IV

CHIEF OF POLICE, BOBCHINSKY, DOBCHINSKY, *and* SERGEANT OF POLICE

CHIEF OF POLICE: Well, is the cab waiting?

SERGEANT OF POLICE: Yes, sir.

CHIEF OF POLICE: Go down to the street . . . or no, stop! Go bring in . . . But where are the others?. Are you just alone? I certainly ordered Prokhorov to be here. Where's Prokhorov?

SERGEANT OF POLICE: Prokhorov is in a private house, but he can hardly be put on the job now.

CHIEF OF POLICE: Why not?

SERGEANT OF POLICE: Because they carried him in this morning dead drunk. They've soused him with two tubs of water, but so far he hasn't sobered up.

CHIEF OF POLICE (*clutching his head*): Oh, my God, my God! Hurry into the street; or no, run first to my room—d'you hear?—and bring me my sword and my new hat. Well, Petr Ivanovich, let's be going!

BOBCHINSKY: Me too, me too! Let me go, too, Anton Antonovich!

CHIEF OF POLICE: No, no, Petr Ivanovich, you simply can't! It's bad form, and there's not room enough in the cab.

BOBCHINSKY: Never mind, never mind; I'll manage; I'll run along behind on my own prongs. I'd just like to peep through a chink in the door to see how he behaves. . . .

CHIEF OF POLICE (*to the* POLICEMAN, *who hands him his sword*): Run right off and get the patrolmen, and have each of them take . . . How my sword has been scratched! That damned cheat of a merchant, Abdulin: he sees that the Chief of Police has nothing but an old sword, but he won't send me a new one. Oh, what a sly gang! As it is, I think those swindlers are getting complaints ready now to yank out from under their coat-tails. Have every patrolman grab a street—deuce take it—I mean a broom—and tell 'em to sweep the whole street that leads to the inn, and sweep it clean. . . . D'you hear? And look out, you; oh, I know you! You're mighty chummy with everybody, but you'll steal spoons and stick 'em in your leggings! Look out; I've got sharp ears! . . . What did you do to the merchant Chernyayev, ha? He gave you two yards of cloth for your uniform, but you swiped the whole bolt. Look out! You take tips too big for your rank! Now, get out!

SCENE V

The same and POLICE CAPTAIN

CHIEF OF POLICE: Ah, Stepan Ilyich! Say, for God's sake, where've you been hiding out? Whoever heard the like!

POLICE CAPTAIN: Why, I was right outside the gates.

CHIEF OF POLICE: Well, listen here, Stepan Ilyich! An official has come from Petersburg. What arrangements have you made out there?

POLICE CAPTAIN: Why, just as you ordered. I sent Police Sergeant Pugovitsyn with the patrolmen to clean the sidewalk.

CHIEF OF POLICE: But where's Derzhimorda?

POLICE CAPTAIN: Derzhimorda has gone off on the fire wagon.

CHIEF OF POLICE: And Prokhorov's drunk?

POLICE CAPTAIN: He is.

CHIEF OF POLICE: How did you happen to allow that?

POLICE CAPTAIN: Why, God knows. Yesterday there was a fight in the suburbs; he went out to restore order, and came back drunk.

CHIEF OF POLICE: Well, listen, here's your job: Police Sergeant Pugovitsyn . . . he's tall, so you can post him on the bridge for the sake of law and order. Then clear away the old fence next to the shoemaker's as quick as you can, and put up a straw waymark as if surveyors were doing some leveling. The more pulling-down there is, the more it shows activity on the part of the governor of the town. Oh, my God! I had forgotten that there's about forty cartloads of every sort of rubbish heaped up against that fence! What a rotten town! You no sooner set up a monument of some kind, or simply a fence, than people bring on all manner of rubbish, the devil knows where from! (*He sighs.*) And if that traveling official asks the people in service whether they're satisfied, have 'em say, "We're satisfied with everything, your Honor." And if any one is not satisfied, I'll give him something afterwards to be dissatisfied about! . . . Ow, ow, ow, I'm a sinner, a sinner in many ways! (*He picks up the cardboard hatbox instead of his hat.*) Just grant, O Lord, that I may get all this off my hands as quickly as possible, and I'll set up such a candle as was never lighted before: I'll make every brute of a merchant contribute a hundred pounds of wax. Oh, my God, my God! Let's go, Petr Ivanovich! (*He attempts to put on the box instead of his hat.*)

POLICE CAPTAIN: Anton Antonovich, that's the box, not your hat.

CHIEF OF POLICE (*throwing away the box*): Box, is it? Oh, to hell with it! And if they ask why the church for the almshouse hasn't been built, for which an appropriation was made five years ago, don't forget to say that it was started, but it burned down. I even presented a report on the matter. Even so I suppose some idiot out of sheer stupidity will forget and say that it wasn't ever started. Yes, and tell Derzhimorda not to be too free with his fists; he's always making people see stars in the name of law and order, innocent and guilty alike. Let's go, let's go, Petr Ivanovich! (*He goes out, but returns.*) And don't let the soldiers out on the street without a stitch on; that dirty garrison will put on their uniforms just over their shirts, but with absolutely nothing below! . . . (*They all go out.*)

SCENE VI

ANNA ANDREYEVNA *and* MARYA ANTONOVNA, *who come in running*

ANNA ANDREYEVNA: Where are they? Where are they? Oh, my heavens! . . . (*Opening the door.*) Husband! Antosha, Anton! (*To her daughter, speaking quickly.*) It's your fault, it's all along of you! You would be rummaging for a pin or a neckerchief. (*She runs to the window and calls out.*) Anton, where are you going? Who's come? A government inspector? With a mustache! What sort of mustache?

Voice of the CHIEF OF POLICE: I'll tell you later, dearie.

ANNA ANDREYEVNA: Later? What d'you know about that! Later! I don't want to wait till later. . . . Tell me in a word; what is he, a colonel? Ha? (*With indifference.*) He's gone! I'll remember that against you! And this girl keeps saying, "Mamma dear, mamma, wait a minute, I'm pinning my neckerchief behind; I'll come right away." Here's your right away for you! And so we haven't found out a thing! Always your darned primping! You heard that the postmaster was here, and you had to go and prink before the mirror, twisting this way and that! She imagines that he's courting her; but he's making faces at you as soon as you turn your back.

MARYA ANTONOVNA: Well, what's to be done, mamma? It's all the same! We'll find out everything in two hours.

ANNA ANDREYEVNA: In two hours! I most humbly thank you! There's an obliging answer! I wonder you never thought of saying that we'd know better yet in a month! (*Leaning out of the window.*) Hey, Avdotya! Ha? What? Avdotya, haven't you heard that somebody has arrived? . . . You haven't? What a blockhead! He waved you off? Well, let him, you might have pumped him all the same. You couldn't find that out! Your head's full of nonsense—nothing but your beaux. Ha? They went away in a hurry? Well, you could have run after the cab. Now get along with you this minute! Listen: run and ask where they've gone; and find out everything; who the newcomer is and what he's like, d'you hear? Peek through a crack and find out everything: and what kind of eyes he has, black or not; and come back this minute, d'you hear? Hurry up, hurry up, hurry up, hurry up! (*She keeps shouting until the curtain falls, both of them still standing at the window.*)

ACT II

A small room at the inn. A bed, a table, a trunk, an empty bottle, top-boots, a clothes-brush, and other objects

SCENE I

OSIP (*lying on his master's bed*): Devil take me; I'm so hungry that there's a continual rumbling in my stomach as though the whole regiment were beginning to blow their trumpets. I s'pose we'll never get home, and that's all there is to it. What do you want me to do? You came here two months ago, all the way from Petersburg! You squandered your dough on the road, my boy, and now you sit with your tail between your legs and keep cool. There would have been plenty of money for fares; but no, you had to spread yourself in every town! (*Taking him off.*) "Hey, Osip, run along and look up the best room for me, and order the best dinner possible. I can't eat a poor dinner; I have to have the best." That would be all right if he were really something decent, but he's just a junior clerk. You get acquainted with some traveler or other—then out with the cards, and first you know you're cleaned out! Bah! I'm sick of such a life! To be sure, it's better in the country: although there's not much society, there's less anxiety; you get yourself a woman and spend your life lying on the sleeping-shelf of the stove and eating meat pies. Of course if anybody wanted to argue about it and get at the truth, living in Petersburg is the best of all. If one only had money, life would be very fine and polished: there are theatres, with dancing dogs, and everything you like. All conversation's smart 'n elegant, second only to that of the nobility. You walk into the Shchukin Bazaar, and the clerks shout "Honorable sir!" at you. Crossing on the ferry boat you sit down with an official. If you want company, walk into a shop: there a military man will tell you about the camp, and explain just what each star means, so that you can see it all as plain as your hand before your face. An old officer's wife will stroll in; and such a pretty housemaid may peep in. . . . Tra, la, la! (*He bursts out laughing and shakes his head.*) Very gallant manners, deuce take it! You never hear an impolite word; every one addresses you as an equal. If you get tired of walking, you take a cab and sit back like a gentleman; and if you don't want to pay the cabby, never mind: every house has front and rear gates, and you can slip through so fast no devil can follow you up. Only one thing is bad: you eat swell one day, but the next you may croak with hunger, like now, for instance. But he's always to blame. What's to be done with him? His dad will send him money, but instead of hanging on to it—nothing of the kind; off he goes on a spree. He rides in cabs, gets a theatre ticket every day, and then at the end of a week he sends me to the old-clothes shop to sell his new dress-coat. Sometimes he'll sell even his last shirt so that he's nothing to put on but his frock-coat and his overcoat. . . . That's the truth, by God! And such fine English cloth, too! One coat cost him one hundred and fifty rubles, but the old clo' dealer got it from him for twenty. As for the trousers, there's nothing to be said: they go for nothing. And why? Because he won't attend to business. Instead of going to his work, he strolls up and down the Nevsky Prospect and plays cards. If the old gentleman should find out—wow! He wouldn't consider the fact that you're an official, but he'd snatch up your little shirt-tail and give you such a hiding that you'd rub yourself for four days. If you're in the service, do your work. Here's the innkeeper now who says he won't give us anything more to eat until we pay for what we've had; but what if we don't pay? (*Sighing.*) Oh Lord, my God, if only I had some cabbage soup, good or bad! I think I could gobble up the world. There's a knock; that's him coming, sure. (*He hops off the bed in a hurry.*)

SCENE II

Osip *and* Hlestakov

Hlestakov: Here, take this. (*He gives* Osip *his hat and cane.*) So you've been lolling on the bed again?

Osip: Why should I? Haven't I ever seen a bed before?

Hlestakov: You're lying, you were lolling! You see, it's all mussed up.

Osip: What should I muss it for? Don't you suppose I know what a bed is? I have legs; I know how to stand up. What's your bed to me?

Hlestakov (*walking about the room*): See if there's any tobacco in the bag yonder.

Osip: How could there be any? You smoked up the last four days ago.

Hlestakov (*walks about and purses up his lips in a variety of ways, finally speaking in a loud and determined voice*): Listen! . . . Hey, Osip!

Osip: What do you want?

Hlestakov (*in a loud, but not so determined voice*): You go down there.

Osip: Where?

Hlestakov (*in a voice quite lacking in determination, softer, and almost entreating*): Downstairs, to the bar . . . and tell them to . . . to send me my dinner.

Osip: Oh no, I don't want to.

Hlestakov: How dare you, blockhead!

Osip: Why, because it'll be all the same; even if I go, we won't get anything. The boss said he wouldn't give us any more dinners.

Hlestakov: How does he dare not give us any? That's nonsense.

Osip: "I'm going to the Chief of Police," says he; "the gentleman hasn't paid anything for three weeks. You and your master are swindlers," he says, "and your master's a rascal. We've seen spongers and scoundrels like you before."

Hlestakov: And I'll bet you're happy, you brute, to be telling me all that now.

Osip: He says: "A fellow like that will come, live high, run up a bill, and afterwards there's no driving him out. I'm not going to joke," he says; "I'm going to complain straight off and have him taken to the police station and then to jail."

Hlestakov: Well, that's enough. you blockhead! Get along with you and tell him! What a vulgar animal!

OSIP: It would be better for me to call the proprietor up here to you.
HLESTAKOV: Why call the proprietor? Go yourself and tell him.
OSIP: But really, sir . . .
HLESTAKOV: Well then, deuce take you, call the proprietor!
(OSIP *goes out.*)

SCENE III

HLESTAKOV *alone*

HLESTAKOV: It's awful how hungry I am! I thought that if I'd just take a walk my appetite would go; but no, damned if it would! If I hadn't gone on a spree at Penza, I'd have had the money to get home. That infantry captain hooked me for fair: he plays wonderful faro, the cheat! We sat down for a quarter of an hour in all, and he fleeced me clean. All the same I was crazy to have another go at him, but I didn't have the opportunity. What a rotten hick town! In their lousy shops they won't sell a thing on credit. I call that simply mean. (*He begins to whistle an air from "Robert the Devil," then "The Red Sarafan," and finally no particular tune.*) Nobody'll come.

SCENE IV

HLESTAKOV, OSIP, *and an* INN SERVANT

SERVANT: The proprietor told me to ask for your orders.
HLESTAKOV: Good day, my boy! How's your health?
SERVANT: Good, thank God.
HLESTAKOV: Well, how are things with the inn: everything going all right?
SERVANT: Yes, thank God, everything's all right.
HLESTAKOV: Many travelers?
SERVANT: Yes, enough.
HLESTAKOV: Listen, my boy, they haven't brought me my dinner yet, so please hurry up and bring it as quickly as possible; you see, I have something to attend to directly after dinner.
SERVANT: But the boss said he wasn't going to send up anything more. He came near going to the Chief of Police to-day with a complaint.
HLESTAKOV: But why complain? Just consider, my boy, what's the use? You see, I've got to eat. Otherwise I might get thin. I'm awfully hungry; and I'm not joking either.
SERVANT: Exactly, sir. But he said, "I shan't give him anything to eat until he's paid for what he's had." That's what his answer was.

HLESTAKOV: Well, you reason with him; talk him over.

SERVANT: What in the world shall I say to him?

HLESTAKOV: You put it to him seriously that I need to eat. The money is another matter. . . . He thinks that if a peasant like him can go without eating for a day, other people can. What an idea!

SERVANT: All right, I'll tell him.

SCENE V

HLESTAKOV *alone*

HLESTAKOV: It's rotten, all the same, if he won't give me anything at all to eat. I never was so hungry in my life. I wonder whether I could raise something on my clothes? Could I sell my trousers? No, I'd rather go hungry than not go home in my Petersburg suit. It's a pity that Joachim * wouldn't rent me a carriage. It would have been fine, confound it all, to drive up like a swell to some neighboring landowner's front door, with lanterns, and Osip behind in livery. I can imagine how excited they'd all get! "Who's there? What does he want?" And the footman would go in (*drawing himself up straight like a footman*) and announce: "Ivan Alexandrovich Hlestakov, from Petersburg; will you receive him?" They, country bumpkins as they are, don't even know what "will you receive him?" means. When any goose of a landowner goes to see them, he wallows straight into the parlor like a bear. I'd go up to some good-looking young daughter and say, "Madam, how happy I . . ." (*He rubs his hands and scrapes with one foot.*) Fah! (*Spitting.*) I'm sick at my stomach, I'm so hungry.

SCENE VI

HLESTAKOV, OSIP, *then the* SERVANT

HLESTAKOV: Well, what now?

OSIP: They're bringing dinner.

HLESTAKOV (*clapping his hands and making a slight jump in his chair*): Hurrah, they're bringing dinner!

SERVANT (*with plates and a napkin*): This is the last dinner the proprietor will send.

HLESTAKOV: Oh, the proprietor, the proprietor! . . . I spit on your proprietor! What have you got there?

SERVANT: Soup and roast.

HLESTAKOV: What, only two courses?

* "A celebrated horse and carriage dealer of St. Petersburg."—Sykes.

SERVANT: That's all, sir.

HLESTAKOV: What trash is this? I won't accept it. You tell him that this is the limit! . . . That's not enough.

SERVANT: No, the boss says that it's a lot.

HLESTAKOV: But why isn't there any sauce?

SERVANT: There isn't any sauce.

HLESTAKOV: Why isn't there any? I saw them preparing a lot of it myself when I passed by the kitchen. And in the dining-room this morning there were two rather short fellows eating salmon and a lot of other things.

SERVANT: Well, there is some, of course, and there isn't.

HLESTAKOV: What d'you mean, isn't?

SERVANT: There just ain't.

HLESTAKOV: And salmon, and fish, and cutlets?

SERVANT: They're for better people, sir.

HLESTAKOV: Oh, you blockhead!

SERVANT: Yes, sir.

HLESTAKOV: You contemptible little swine! Why do they eat when I don't? Why, damn it all, can't I do as they do? Aren't they travelers just like me?

SERVANT: Why, everybody knows that they ain't.

HLESTAKOV: What are they, then?

SERVANT: The regular sort! Everybody knows: they pay their bills!

HLESTAKOV: I don't care to argue with you, you blockhead. (*He helps himself to soup and begins to eat.*) What kind of soup is this? You've just poured water into the tureen: it hasn't any taste; it merely stinks. I don't want this soup; bring me some other.

SERVANT: I'll remove it, sir. The proprietor said, "If he doesn't want it, he needn't have it."

HLESTAKOV (*protecting the food with his hands*): Well, well, well . . . leave it, you blockhead! You may be used to treating other people like that; but I'm not that sort, my boy. . . . I advise you not to act like that with me. . . . (*He eats.*) My God, what soup! (*He continues eating.*) I think no man on earth to date has ever eaten such soup: there's some kind of feathers swimming around in it instead of grease! (*He cuts the chicken in the soup.*) Ow, ow, ow, what a bird! Give me the roast! There, Osip, there's a little soup left; take it yourself. (*He carves the roast.*) What kind of roast is this? This is no roast.

SERVANT: Why, what is it?

HLESTAKOV: The devil knows *what* it is, but it's not roast. It's roasted ax instead of ox. (*He eats.*) Swindlers, riffraff! What stuff they hand you! Your jaws begin to ache if you swallow a single bite.

(*He picks his teeth with his finger.*) Rascals! It's just like bark—you can't pull it out anyhow; and your teeth will turn black after such dishes. Swindlers! (*Wiping his mouth with his napkin.*) Isn't there anything more?

SERVANT: No.

HLESTAKOV: Riffraff! Rascals! And not even a little sauce or a pudding. Grafters! They simply fleece travelers.

(*The* SERVANT *and* OSIP *collect the dishes and carry them away.*)

SCENE VII

HLESTAKOV, *later* OSIP

HLESTAKOV: Really, I feel as if I hadn't eaten a thing: I've just whetted my appetite. If I had any small change, I'd send to the market for a bun.

OSIP (*coming in*): The Chief of Police has come on some errand; he's making inquiries and asking about you.

HLESTAKOV (*frightened*): Well, I declare! Has that brute of an innkeeper managed to complain already? What if he really drags me to jail! What then? I suppose, if he did it in a gentlemanly manner, I might . . . But no, no, I won't! There in town officers and people are strolling about, and I purposely played the swell and exchanged winks with a tradesman's daughter. . . . No, I won't. . . . But how in the world did he dare? What does he take me for, anyhow, a merchant or an artisan? (*He adopts a bold manner and straightens up.*) I'll go right to him and say, "How dare you? How dare . . . ?"

(*The door-handle turns;* HLESTAKOV *turns pale and shrinks.*)

SCENE VIII

HLESTAKOV, CHIEF OF POLICE, *and* DOBCHINSKY

Upon entering the room, the CHIEF OF POLICE *stands still. He and* HLESTAKOV *stare at each other wide-eyed in fright for several moments.*

CHIEF OF POLICE (*recovering somewhat and standing at attention*): Please accept my greetings!

HLESTAKOV (*bowing*): And mine to you, sir.

CHIEF OF POLICE: Pardon me. . . .

HLESTAKOV: Oh, certainly. . . .

CHIEF OF POLICE: It is my duty as the chief official of the town to see that travelers and members of the nobility experience no inconvenience. . . .

HLESTAKOV (*at first stammering a little, but finally speaking loudly*): But what's to be done? . . . It's not my fault. . . . I'll pay, honest. . . . They'll send me some money from the country. (BOBCHINSKY *peeks in at the door.*) He's more to blame: he sends me beef as tough as a wooden beam; as for soup, the devil knows what he slops into it; I should have thrown it out the window. He starves me out for days at a time. . . . And such queer tea: it smells of fish, but not of tea. Why should I? . . . What an idea!

CHIEF OF POLICE (*losing courage*): Pardon me, I'm really not to blame. There's always good beef in our market. Dealers from Holmogory * supply it, sober men and well-behaved. I don't know where he could get such as you describe. But if anything is not just right . . . Permit me to propose that I remove you to other lodgings.

HLESTAKOV: No, I won't. I know what you mean by other lodgings —the jail. But what right have you? How dare you? . . . Look here, I . . . I'm in the government service in Petersburg. (*Growing bolder.*) I, I, I . . .

CHIEF OF POLICE (*aside*): Oh, Lord my God, how angry he is! He's found out everything, those damned merchants have told him!

HLESTAKOV (*more bravely*): Even if you came with a whole regiment, I wouldn't go. I'll go straight to the Minister! (*Striking the table with his fist.*) What's the matter with you, anyway?

CHIEF OF POLICE (*drawing himself up straight and trembling in every limb*): Have mercy; don't ruin me! Consider my wife, my little children! . . . Don't make a man wretched!

HLESTAKOV: No, I won't go. The idea! What's all that to me? Because you have a wife and children, I have to go to jail—that's grand! (BOBCHINSKY *peeks through the door, then hides in fright.*) No, I humbly thank you, I won't go!

CHIEF OF POLICE (*trembling*): It's my inexperience, God knows, just my inexperience. The insufficiency of my income . . . Please, sir, judge for yourself: my official salary doesn't even buy our tea and sugar. If I've taken a few bribes, they were mere trifles, something or other for the table or for a suit of clothes. And as for the sergeant's widow who keeps a shop, whom I'm supposed to have flogged, that's all slander, God knows it is. All that was thought up by my enemies; they're people who are ready to make an attempt on my life.

HLESTAKOV: What of it? I have nothing to do with them. . . . (*Meditating.*) Still, I don't know why you're talking about your enemies and some sergeant's widow or other. A sergeant's widow is quite another matter, but you won't dare to flog me; you're a long way

* A small town in the province of Archangel, noted for its cattle. (Adapted from Sykes.)

from that job! . . . The idea! What a chap you are! . . . I'll pay, I'll pay the money, but I haven't it now. I'm sticking around here because I haven't a kopek.

CHIEF OF POLICE (*aside*): Oh, a sly trick! What a hint! He makes things hazy, and you can take 'em as you please! There's no knowing how to get at him. Well, I'll make a stab at it, no matter what happens. What will be, will be. I'll take a shot at random. (*Aloud.*) If you're really needing money or something else, I'm ready to help you this very minute. It's my duty to assist travelers.

HLESTAKOV: Lend me, do lend me some! I'll settle with the dirty innkeeper at once. I owe him only about two hundred rubles, a little more or less.

CHIEF OF POLICE (*producing some notes*): Exactly two hundred rubles, but don't trouble to count them.

HLESTAKOV (*taking the money*): I thank you heartily. I'll return the amount at once from the country. . . . This was a sudden embarrassment. . . . I see that you are a gentleman. Now things are very different.

CHIEF OF POLICE (*aside*): Well, thank God, he took the money! Now I think everything will go smoothly. I slipped him four hundred instead of two.

HLESTAKOV: Hey, Osip! (OSIP *comes in.*) Call that waiter here! (*To the* CHIEF OF POLICE *and* DOBCHINSKY.) But why are you standing? Do me the favor to be seated! (*To* DOBCHINSKY.) Do please sit down.

CHIEF OF POLICE: Oh, no, we're all right standing.

HLESTAKOV: Do please be seated. Now I see perfectly your candor and cordiality; I admit that at first I thought you had come to . . . (*To* DOBCHINSKY.) Sit down! (*The* CHIEF OF POLICE *and* DOBCHINSKY *sit down.* BOBCHINSKY *peeps through the door and listens.*)

CHIEF OF POLICE (*aside*): I'll have to be more daring. He wants us to consider him as traveling incognito. Very good, we can fake, too; we'll pretend we haven't the least idea who he is. (*Aloud.*) While strolling about on my official duties with Petr Ivanovich Dobchinsky, here, a landed proprietor of the vicinity, I came into the inn on purpose to inquire whether the travelers were being well entertained; because I'm not like some police chiefs who don't care about anything. Aside from my duty, out of a Christian love of humanity, I want every mortal to be given a good reception; and here, as if to reward me, chance has afforded me this pleasant acquaintance.

HLESTAKOV: I also am very glad. I confess that except for you, I should have had to stay here a long time: and I absolutely didn't know how I could pay.

CHIEF OF POLICE (*aside*): Why, how you talk! He didn't know how he was going to pay! (*Aloud.*) And may I venture to inquire where you are going?

HLESTAKOV: I'm going to my own village in the province of Saratov.

CHIEF OF POLICE (*aside, with an ironical expression of countenance*): To Saratov, he? And he doesn't blush! Oh, one needs a sharp ear with him! (*Aloud.*) You have undertaken a good task. Concerning the road, they say that while, on the one hand, there is unpleasantness because of the delay for horses, on the other, it's a distraction for the mind. I suppose that you're traveling chiefly for your own pleasure?

HLESTAKOV: No, my father wants to see me. The old gentleman is angry because so far I've not been promoted in Petersburg. He thinks that you've only to go there and they'll stick the Vladimir ribbon in your buttonhole. No—I'd like to send *him* to bustle about in the office!

CHIEF OF POLICE (*aside*): Listen to the yarns he's spinning! He's even tangling up his old daddy! (*Aloud.*) And shall you be gone long?

HLESTAKOV: Indeed, I don't know. You see, my father is obstinate and silly, the old duffer, stubborn as a post. I shall say to him right out: "Whether you like it or not, I can't live away from Petersburg. And why, as a matter of fact, must I ruin my life among peasants? Nowadays a man's needs are quite different: my soul thirsts for enlightenment."

CHIEF OF POLICE (*aside*): How well he strings it together! He lies and lies and never trips himself. And he's such an insignificant little fellow, I think I could squash him with my finger nail. Well, just hold on! I'll make you blab yet. I'll make you talk some more. (*Aloud.*) Your remark is quite correct. What can you do in the wilderness? Now, take it here, for instance: you work all night long; you labor for your fatherland; you spare yourself in no way; but as for your reward, no one knows when you'll get it. (*He glances about the room.*) It strikes me this room is a little damp?

HLESTAKOV: A beastly room, and the bugs surpass any I've ever seen: they bite like bulldogs.

CHIEF OF POLICE: You don't say! Such a cultured guest, and he suffers, from what?—from worthless bugs that should never have been born into the world! Isn't it also a little dark in this room?

HLESTAKOV: Yes, quite dark. The proprietor has introduced the custom of not allowing candles. Sometimes when I want to do something, to read a little, or if I take a fancy to compose something, I can't: it's dark, always dark.

CHIEF OF POLICE: Might I ask you—? But no, I'm unworthy.
HLESTAKOV: Why, what is it?
CHIEF OF POLICE: No, no, I'm unworthy; I'm unworthy.
HLESTAKOV: But what in the world is it?
CHIEF OF POLICE: I might venture . . . At my house there's a room that would just suit you: light, and quiet. . . . But no, I realize that it would be too great an honor for me. . . . Don't be angry! Honest to God, I offered it only in the simplicity of my soul.
HLESTAKOV: On the contrary, I'll accept with pleasure, if you please. It would be much more agreeable for me in a private home than in this dump.
CHIEF OF POLICE: How glad I shall be! And how glad my wife will be, too! That's my disposition, hospitable from my childhood, especially if the guest is a man of culture. Don't think I'm saying this in flattery: no, I haven't that vice; I am expressing myself out of the fullness of my heart.
HLESTAKOV: I thank you heartily. I'm the same: I don't like two-faced people. I'm delighted with your candor and cordiality; and I confess I ask nothing more than to be shown devotion and respect, respect and devotion.

SCENE IX

The same and the INN SERVANT, *introduced by* OSIP

BOBCHINSKY *continues peeking through the door.*

SERVANT: Did you send for me, sir?
HLESTAKOV: Yes; bring me my bill.
SERVANT: I handed it to you long ago for the second time.
HLESTAKOV: I don't remember your stupid bills. Tell me: how much is it?
SERVANT: On the first day you ordered dinner; on the second you just ate a little kippered salmon; and then you began to order everything on credit.
HLESTAKOV: Blockhead! He's begun to reckon it all over again. What does it come to in all?
CHIEF OF POLICE: Don't trouble yourself; he can wait. (*To the* SERVANT.) Go away; the money'll be sent down.
HLESTAKOV: Yes, indeed; just so. (*He puts away the money. The* SERVANT *goes out;* BOBCHINSKY *peeks through the door.*)

SCENE X

CHIEF OF POLICE, HLESTAKOV, DOBCHINSKY

CHIEF OF POLICE: Now wouldn't you like to inspect some of the institutions in our town, the charitable ones and others?

HLESTAKOV: What is there to see?

CHIEF OF POLICE: So you can see how things go with us . . . what sort of order . . .

HLESTAKOV: With great pleasure; I'm ready.

(BOBCHINSKY *sticks his head through the door.*)

CHIEF OF POLICE: Also, if you wish it, we can go next to the district school to see how the sciences are taught there.

HLESTAKOV: Yes, let's do so.

CHIEF OF POLICE: Then, if you want to visit the prison and the city jails, you will see how we treat criminals.

HLESTAKOV: But why the city jails? We'd better inspect the charitable institutions.

CHIEF OF POLICE: Just as you please. How do you intend to go: in your own carriage, or with me in a cab?

HLESTAKOV: Well, I think I'd better go with you in a cab.

CHIEF OF POLICE (*to* DOBCHINSKY): Well, Petr Ivanovich, there'll be no place for you.

DOBCHINSKY: Never mind; I'm all right.

CHIEF OF POLICE (*softly to* DOBCHINSKY): Listen: you run lickety-split and carry two notes, one to Zemlyanika at the hospital and the other to my wife. (*To* HLESTAKOV.) May I venture to ask your permission to write in your presence a line to my wife, bidding her prepare for the reception of an honored guest?

HLESTAKOV: Certainly. . . . Here's the ink; but as for paper, I don't know . . . How about the back of this bill?

CHIEF OF POLICE: I'll write on that. (*He writes, meanwhile talking to himself.*) Now we'll see how things will go after lunch and a big-bellied bottle! We have some provincial Madeira—not much to look at, but it'll knock an elephant off its feet. If I could only find out what sort of fellow he is, and how much I need to be afraid of him. (*Having written, he hands the notes to* DOBCHINSKY, *who approaches the door; but at that moment the door falls off its hinges, and* BOBCHINSKY, *who has been listening on the other side, flies into the room with it. All utter exclamations.* BOBCHINSKY *picks himself up.*)

HLESTAKOV: I hope you didn't hurt yourself anywhere?

BOBCHINSKY: Not at all, not at all, sir, not the least derangement, sir; only a little scratch over my nose. I'll run over to Christian Ivanovich; he has some kind of little plaster, sir, and it'll soon get well.

CHIEF OF POLICE (*to* HLESTAKOV, *after making a reproachful sign to* BOBCHINSKY): That's nothing, sir. If you please, we'll go now. And I'll tell your servant to bring your trunk over. (*To* OSIP.) My good fellow, just bring everything over to my house, to the Police Chief's residence—any one will show you the way. After you, sir. (*He permits* HLESTAKOV *to go out first and follows him; then, turning around, he speaks reproachfully to* BOBCHINSKY.) That's you all over! You couldn't find any other place to fall! And there you sprawled like the devil knows what! (*He goes out,* BOBCHINSKY *after him. The curtain falls.*)

ACT III

The same room as in Act I

SCENE I

ANNA ANDREYEVNA *and* MARYA ANTONOVNA *are standing at the window in the same positions.*

ANNA ANDREYEVNA: Well now, we've been waiting a whole hour, and all the time you with your silly primping: you were all dressed, but no! you still had to rummage! . . . I shouldn't have listened to her at all. What an annoyance! As if on purpose, there's not a soul about! It's as if everything had died.

MARYA ANTONOVNA: But really, mamma, in two minutes we'll find out everything. Avdotya must be back soon. (*She looks out of the window and exclaims.*) Oh, mamma, mamma! Some one's coming, there at the end of the street!

ANNA ANDREYEVNA: Where is he? You're always having crazy notions. Well, sure enough. But who is it? Medium-sized . . . in a dress coat. . . . Who can it be? Ha? Isn't that annoying! Who in the world can it be?

MARYA ANTONOVNA: It's Dobchinsky, mamma!

ANNA ANDREYEVNA: Dobchinsky, my foot! You're always imagining things! . . . It can't be Dobchinsky. (*She waves her handkerchief.*) Hey, you, come here! Hurry up!

MARYA ANTONOVNA: Really, mamma, it is Dobchinsky.

ANNA ANDREYEVNA: There you go, always quarreling! I tell you it's *not* Dobchinsky.

MARYA ANTONOVNA: Aha, mamma, what did I tell you? You see, it *is* Dobchinsky.

ANNA ANDREYEVNA: Well, yes, it's Dobchinsky; I see now—why are you arguing about it? (*Shouting out of the window.*) Hurry up, hurry up; you're too slow! Well, where are they? Huh? Go ahead and talk from where you are. What? Very severe? Huh? And my husband? Where's my husband? (*Leaning slightly out of the window, with vexation.*) What a boob: until he gets into the very room, he won't tell a thing!

SCENE II

The same and DOBCHINSKY

ANNA ANDREYEVNA: Now, please tell me: well, aren't you ashamed? I relied on you as a decent man. They all rode off in a hurry, and you after them; and I can't get a sensible word from anybody since. Aren't you ashamed? I christened your Johnny and your Lizzie, and then you act like that with me!

DOBCHINSKY: Heavens, godmother, I ran so fast to prove my respect for you that I can't catch my breath. My respects, Marya Antonovna.

MARYA ANTONOVNA: How do you do, Petr Ivanovich.

ANNA ANDREYEVNA: Well, what's the news? Tell me what happened and how.

DOBCHINSKY: Anton Antonovich has sent you a note.

ANNA ANDREYEVNA: But what's the man like? Is he a general?

DOBCHINSKY: No, he's not a general; but he's not inferior to one in education and elegant manners.

ANNA ANDREYEVNA: Aha! Then he must be the one they wrote to my husband about.

DOBCHINSKY: The very same. I was the first to discover the fact, along with Petr Ivanovich.

ANNA ANDREYEVNA: Well, tell us what happened and how.

DOBCHINSKY: Well, thank God, everything is all right. At first he wanted to treat Anton Antonovich rather rough; yes, he did. He got angry and said that everything was bad at the inn, that he wouldn't go to his house, and wouldn't go to jail on his account; but afterwards, when he found out Anton Antonovich's innocence, and had talked a little more to the point with him, he changed his attitude all at once, and, thank God, everything came out fine. Now they've gone to have a look at the charitable institutions. . . . I admit that Anton Antonovich was thinking that there had been some secret denunciation; I was a little bit scared myself.

ANNA ANDREYEVNA: What have you to be afraid of? You're not in the service.

DOBCHINSKY: Well, you know how it is when a bigwig talks: you feel scared.

ANNA ANDREYEVNA: Oh, the idea! . . . That's all nonsense. Now tell us: what's he like? Is he old or young?

DOBCHINSKY: Young—a young man, about twenty-three years old; but he talks just like an old man. "By all means," he says, "I'll go there, and there, too" . . . (*waving his hands*) and he says it all so grandly. "I like to write and to read," he says, "but I'm annoyed by the darkness of the room."

ANNA ANDREYEVNA: But what does he look like? Is he light or dark-complexioned?

DOBCHINSKY: No, more of a chestnut. And he has such quick eyes, like some little animal's; they're positively disconcerting.

ANNA ANDREYEVNA: Well, what's he written me in this note? (*She reads.*) "I hasten to inform you, my dear, that my situation was altogether lamentable; but trusting in God's clemency, item, for two salted cucumbers and for half a portion of caviar, twenty-five kopeks—" (*Pausing.*) I don't understand a thing: what's this about pickles and caviar?

DOBCHINSKY: Oh, Anton Antonovich just wrote that on a piece of scratch paper to save time: some sort of bill had been written on it.

ANNA ANDREYEVNA: Oh, I see. (*Continuing her reading.*) "But trusting in God's clemency, it looks as if everything would come out all right. Hurry and get a room ready for an important guest, the one hung with yellow wall paper; you needn't go to any extra trouble for dinner because we're going to have a bite at the hospital, with Artemy Filippovich, but order a lot of wine; tell the dealer Abdulin to send his very best; if he doesn't, I'll overhaul his whole cellar. Kissing your little hand, sweetheart, I remain your Anton Skvoznik-Dmukhanovsky." . . . Oh, good heavens! We'll have to hurry! Hey, who's there? Mishka!

DOBCHINSKY (*running to the door and shouting*): Mishka! Mishka! Mishka!

(MISHKA *comes in.*)

ANNA ANDREYEVNA: Listen: run to the merchant Abdulin . . . wait, I'll give you a note. (*She sits down at the table and writes a note, talking meanwhile.*) Give this note to the coachman, Sidor, and have him run to the merchant Abdulin's and get some wine. You yourself go at once and get the room in fine shape for a guest. Put up a bed and a washstand, and so forth.

DOBCHINSKY: Well, Anna Andreyevna, I'll hurry off now to see how the inspection's going on.

ANNA ANDREYEVNA: Go along, go along! I'm not keeping you!

SCENE III

ANNA ANDREYEVNA *and* MARYA ANTONOVNA

ANNA ANDREYEVNA: Now, Mashenka, we'll have to see about the way we're dressed. He's a Petersburg dandy; God forbid he should laugh at anything! The most becoming thing you can put on is your blue dress with the little flounces.

MARYA ANTONOVNA: Fudge, mamma, the blue! I don't like it at all! Lyapkin-Tyapkin's daughter wears blue, and so does Zemlyanika's. No, I'd better put on my flowered dress.

ANNA ANDREYEVNA: The flowered dress! . . . Really, you're saying that to be spiteful. The other'll be much better, because I want to wear my straw-colored; I'm very fond of straw color.

MARYA ANTONOVNA: Oh, mamma, it doesn't become you at all!

ANNA ANDREYEVNA: It doesn't become me?

MARYA ANTONOVNA: No, it doesn't; I'll bet anything you please, it doesn't; you've got to have dark eyes to wear straw color.

ANNA ANDREYEVNA: Well, upon my word! And haven't I got dark eyes? As dark as can be. What nonsense she's talking! How can they be otherwise when I always tell my fortune by the queen of clubs?

MARYA ANTONOVNA: Why, mamma! You usually tell it by the queen of hearts!

ANNA ANDREYEVNA: Nonsense, absolute nonsense! I never was the queen of hearts! (*She hastily goes out with* MARYA ANTONOVNA *and continues talking in the wings.*) What's she imagining now! The queen of hearts! Heaven knows what she means! (*After they have gone out a door opens, and* MISHKA *is seen throwing out some trash. Through another door* OSIP *comes in with a trunk on his head.*)

SCENE IV

MISHKA *and* OSIP

OSIP: Which way?

MISHKA: This way, uncle, this way!

OSIP: Wait, let me get my breath first. Oh, what a dog's life! Every load seems heavy on an empty belly.

MISHKA: Well, uncle, what d'you say? Will the general be here soon?

OSIP: What general?

MISHKA: Why, your boss.

OSIP: My boss? Is he a general?

MISHKA: Well, isn't he?

OSIP: He is, only over the left.

MISHKA: Is that more or less than a real general?

OSIP: More.

MISHKA: You don't say! That's why they've kicked up such a rumpus.

OSIP: Listen, my boy; I see you're a smart fellow; just get me something to eat!

MISHKA: There's nothing ready for you yet, uncle. You aren't going to eat common chow, but when your boss sits down to the table, they'll give you the same as he gets.

OSIP: What kind of common food have you got?

MISHKA: Cabbage soup, porridge, and pies.

OSIP: Give us your cabbage soup, porridge, and pies! That's all right, I'll eat everything. Well, let's carry in the trunk. Is there another way out?

MISHKA: Yes. (*They carry the trunk into a room at one side.*)

SCENE V

The POLICEMEN *open both wings of the door.* HLESTAKOV *comes in, after him the* CHIEF OF POLICE, *the* SUPERVISOR OF CHARITABLE INSTITUTIONS, *the* SUPERINTENDENT OF SCHOOLS, DOBCHINSKY *and* BOBCHINSKY, *the latter with a plaster on his nose. The* CHIEF OF POLICE *shows the* POLICEMEN *a piece of paper on the floor; they run to pick it up, bumping each other at full speed.*

HLESTAKOV: Very good institutions. I'm delighted that you show visitors everything in the town. They didn't show me anything in the other towns.

CHIEF OF POLICE: In other towns, I venture to inform you, the city managers and the other officials are more concerned about their own profit; but here, I may say, there is no other thought but to deserve by good order and vigilance the attention of the authorities.

HLESTAKOV: The lunch was very good. I quite overate myself. Do you fare like that every day?

CHIEF OF POLICE: That was especially for our welcome guest.

HLESTAKOV: I'm fond of eating. That's what we live for: to cull the flowers of pleasure. What was that fish called?

ARTEMY FILIPPOVICH (*running up*): Aberdeen cod, sir.

HLESTAKOV: Very tasty. Where was it we had lunch—in the hospital?

ARTEMY FILIPPOVICH: Just so, sir, in the charity hospital.

HLESTAKOV: I remember, I remember, there were some beds there. Have the patients all recovered? It seems to me there weren't many.

ARTEMY FILIPPOVICH: About ten remain, no more; the rest have all got well. That's the way it's arranged: such order! From the time I undertook the management—incredible as it may seem to you—all of them have been getting well, like flies.* A patient can hardly enter the hospital before he's cured, not so much by the medicines as by the reliability of the management.

CHIEF OF POLICE: The obligations of a chief of police are, I venture to inform you, simply head-breaking! So many different things devolve on him, concerning sanitation alone, repairs, and reconstruction . . . in a word, the wisest man might find himself in a quandary; but, thanks be to God, everything is coming out splendidly. Any other police chief, of course, would look out for his own profit; but—would you believe it?—even when I lie down to sleep I think: "O Lord my God, how can I bring it to pass that the authorities may perceive my zeal and be satisfied?" . . . Whether they will reward me or not is, of course, up to them; but at least I shall be at peace in my own heart. When there is order everywhere in the city, the streets swept clean, the people under arrest well cared for, and few drunkards . . . why, what more can I do? And in truth, I want no honors. Of course, honors are alluring, but compared to virtue, they are all ashes and vanity.

ARTEMY FILIPPOVICH (*aside*): Oho, the grafter, how thick he spreads it! God gave him a gift for it!

HLESTAKOV: That is true. I admit that I myself like to philosophize once in a while: I toss things off sometimes in prose, sometimes in verse.

BOBCHINSKY (*to* DOBCHINSKY): Correct, all correct, Petr Ivanovich! Such remarks . . . one can see he's studied the sciences.

HLESTAKOV: Tell me, please, don't you ever have any amusements or social gatherings—where one might, for instance, play a game of cards?

CHIEF OF POLICE (*aside*): Aha, my boy, we know what windowpane you're pebbling now! (*Aloud.*) God forbid! There's not even a rumor about such social gatherings here! I've never had cards in my hands; I don't even know how to play cards. I never could even look at them calmly; and if I ever happen to catch sight of such a thing as a king of diamonds, such disgust comes over me that I simply have to spit. It happened once that to amuse the children I built a little house of cards, but afterwards I had the damnedest dreams all night long. Deuce take them! How can people kill such precious time with them?

LUKA LUKICH (*aside*): But you cleaned me out of a hundred rubles yesterday, you scoundrel!

* The humor lies in the reference to the usual Russian phrase, "They die like flies." (Adapted from Sykes.)

CHIEF OF POLICE: I could use that time better in the service of the state.

HLESTAKOV: However, you put it too strongly. . . . All depends upon the way in which you look at the thing. If, for instance, you pass when you ought to raise your ante . . . then, of course . . . No, I disagree: sometimes playing is very tempting.

SCENE VI

The same, ANNA ANDREYEVNA, *and* MARYA ANTONOVNA

CHIEF OF POLICE: I venture to present my family: my wife and daughter.

HLESTAKOV (*making a bow*): How fortunate I am, madam, to have, as it were, the pleasure of seeing you.

ANNA ANDREYEVNA: It is even more agreeable for us to see such a personage.

HLESTAKOV (*strutting*): Pardon me, madam, quite the contrary: my pleasure is greater.

ANNA ANDREYEVNA: How can that be, sir! You are pleased to say that out of compliment. Won't you please be seated?

HLESTAKOV: Merely to stand beside you is happiness: nevertheless, if such be unmistakably your wish, I shall be seated. How happy I am at last to be sitting beside you!

ANNA ANDREYEVNA: Really, sir, I cannot take that compliment to myself. . . . I suppose that after the capital, a tour of the country has seemed very unpleasant?

HLESTAKOV: Exceedingly unpleasant. Accustomed to live, *comprenez-vous,* in society and suddenly to find oneself on the road: dirty eating-houses, the darkness of ignorance . . . I confess, that were it not for this circumstance (*glancing at* ANNA ANDREYEVNA *and posing*) which has compensated me for everything . . .

ANNA ANDREYEVNA: Indeed, how unpleasant it must have been for you.

HLESTAKOV: However, madam, at this minute it is very pleasant for me.

ANNA ANDREYEVNA: Oh, really, sir! You do me too much honor. I do not deserve it.

HLESTAKOV: Why do you not deserve it? You do deserve it, madam.

ANNA ANDREYEVNA: I live in the country. . . .

HLESTAKOV: But the country also has its hillocks and its streamlets. . . . Of course, who'd compare it with Petersburg? Oh, Petersburg! What a life, truly! You may think that I am only a copying clerk;

but no, I'm on a friendly footing with the chief of my department. He'll clap me on the shoulder and say, "Come have dinner with me, my boy!" I drop in at the office for two minutes, only long enough to say how things are to be done. And there the copy-clerk, poor rat, goes scribbling away with his pen, tr, tr. . . . They even wanted to make me a collegiate assessor; * but I thought, what for? And the porter flies up the stairs after me with a brush: "If you please, Ivan Alexandrovich," he says, "I'll clean your boots." (*To the* CHIEF OF POLICE.) Why are you standing, gentlemen? Please be seated.

CHIEF OF POLICE, ARTEMY FILIPPOVICH, LUKA LUKICH (*speaking together*): Our rank is such that we can stand. We'll just stand. Please don't disturb yourself.

HLESTAKOV: All rank aside, I beg you to be seated. (*The* CHIEF OF POLICE *and all sit down.*) I don't like ceremony. On the contrary, I try and try to slip through unnoticed. But it's impossible to hide oneself, quite impossible! I can hardly go out anywhere but they begin saying, "There goes Ivan Alexandrovich!" Once they even took me for the commander-in-chief: the soldiers jumped out of the guard-rooms and presented arms. Afterwards an officer with whom I am well acquainted said to me: "Well, my boy, we positively took you for the commander-in-chief."

ANNA ANDREYEVNA: You don't say!

HLESTAKOV: I'm acquainted with the pretty actresses. You see, I've written a few theatrical sketches. . . . I often see literary people. I'm on friendly terms with Pushkin. I often say to him, "Well, now Pushkin, my boy, how goes it?" "Oh, so-so, old chap," he'll reply, "just so-so. . . ." He's a great character!

ANNA ANDREYEVNA: And so you even write? How delightful it must be to be an author! Do you really contribute to the magazines?

HLESTAKOV: Yes, I contribute to the magazines. Besides, my works are numerous: *The Marriage of Figaro, Robert the Devil, Norma.*† I don't even remember all their titles. And it was all by accident: I didn't want to write, but the theatre management said, "Please write something, old boy." So I thought to myself, "Well, go ahead, old fellow." And then all of a sudden, one evening, I think it was, I wrote the whole thing and astonished everybody. I have extraordinary ease in thinking. Everything that has appeared under the name of Baron Brambeus ‡—*The Frigate Hope,*§ and the *Moscow Telegraph* ¶ . . . I wrote all that.

* The eighth rank in the Russian service; Hlestakov is in the fourteenth!
† Operas by Mozart, Meyerbeer, and Bellini. (Adapted from Sykes.)
‡ Pseudonym of the popular author, Sienkowski (1800-1858).
§ A novel by Bestuzhev. ¶ A newspaper.

ANNA ANDREYEVNA: You don't say! And so you were Brambeus?

HLESTAKOV: Of course; I correct all their articles. Smirdin * pays me forty thousand for doing it.

ANNA ANDREYEVNA: I dare say *Yury Miloslavsky* † is your work also.

HLESTAKOV: Yes, that's my work.

ANNA ANDREYEVNA: I guessed it at once.

MARYA ANTONOVNA: But, mamma, it says on the binding that it was written by Mr. Zagoskin.

ANNA ANDREYEVNA: There you go: I knew that you'd argue even here.

HLESTAKOV: Oh, yes, that is true: that is Zagoskin's; but there's another *Yury Miloslavsky,* and that's mine.

ANNA ANDREYEVNA: Well, it's certain that I read yours. So well written!

HLESTAKOV: I confess that I exist by literature. Mine is the foremost house in Petersburg. It's even known as Ivan Alexandrovich's house. (*Turning to all present.*) Do me the favor, ladies and gentlemen, to come to see me when you are in Petersburg. I also give balls.

ANNA ANDREYEVNA: I suppose that balls there must be given with remarkable taste and magnificence?

HLESTAKOV: It's simply beyond description. On the table, for instance, is a watermelon—a watermelon costing seven hundred rubles. Soup ready in the tureen has come directly from Paris by steamer; raise the lid and there's a fragrant steam the like of which you can't find in nature. I go to balls every day. We've formed our own whist club: the Minister of Foreign Affairs, the French Ambassador, the English, the German Ambassadors, and I. We nearly kill ourselves playing; really, you never saw anything like it. As I run up the stairs to my fourth-story apartment, I just say to the cook: "Here, Mavrushka, my overcoat! . . ." What am I lying about! I quite forgot that I live on the second floor. My staircase alone is worth . . . But it would be curious to glance into my hall before I'm awake mornings: counts and princes jostle each other and hum there like bees, you can hear nothing but buzz, buzz. . . . Sometimes even the Minister . . . (*The* CHIEF OF POLICE *and others timidly rise from their chairs.*) My mail even comes addressed to "Your Excellency." Once I was even the director of a department. It's strange: the director went away—no one knows where. Well, naturally there was a lot of talk as to who should occupy the post. Many of the generals applied eagerly and got it, but when they started to work, it was no go—too hard. The job looks easy enough, but just examine it; why, it's the very deuce! After-

* A noted St. Petersburg publisher. † A famous historical novel.

wards they saw there was nothing to do but give it to me. And that very minute they sent messengers through the streets, messengers, messengers, and messengers . . . you can imagine for yourself: thirty-five thousand messengers! What a situation, I ask you! "Ivan Alexandrovich, go take charge of the department!" I confess that I felt somewhat uneasy. I came out in my dressing gown. I wanted to decline, but I thought, this will get to the tsar; and then, there's the service record! . . . "Very well, gentlemen, I accept the post," I said; "I accept it," I said; "So be it," I said; "I accept; only look out for me; I have sharp ears! You know me. . . ." And that's the way it was: it used to be, when I walked through the department, as if an earthquake had struck them: every one was trembling and shaking like a leaf. (*The* CHIEF OF POLICE *and the others shake with fear;* HLESTAKOV *grows more excited.*) Oh, I don't like to joke; I gave them all a bawling-out. The Council of State itself is afraid of me. And why not, indeed? Because I'm that kind of man. I don't care for anybody. . . . I tell 'em all, "I know my business; shut up!" I go everywhere, everywhere! I drive to the Palace every day. Why, to-morrow they're going to make me a field-mar— (*He slips and almost sprawls upon the floor, but the officials respectfully support him.*)

CHIEF OF POLICE (*approaching, trembling in every limb, and striving to speak out*): You—your—your . . .

HLESTAKOV (*in a rapid, abrupt tone*): What is it?

CHIEF OF POLICE: You—your—

HLESTAKOV (*in the same tone*): I can't make out anything; it's all nonsense.

CHIEF OF POLICE: You . . . your . . . your Excellency, don't you wish to rest? . . . Here's your room, and everything that you need.

HLESTAKOV: Rest—bosh! All right. I'm willing to have a rest. Your lunch, gentlemen, was good. . . . I'm satisfied, I'm satisfied. . . . (*Declaiming.*) Aberdeen! Aberdeen cod! (*He goes into a side room, followed by the* CHIEF OF POLICE.)

SCENE VII

The same without HLESTAKOV *and the* CHIEF OF POLICE

BOBCHINSKY (*to* DOBCHINSKY): There's a man for you, Petr Ivanovich! That's what I call a man! Never in my life have I been in the presence of so important a personage; I all but died of fright. What do you think his rank may be, Petr Ivanovich?

DOBCHINSKY: I think almost a general.

BOBCHINSKY: And I think a general isn't fit to pull off his boots;

but if he's a general, he's a generalissimo. Did you hear how he squashed the Council of State? Let's go quick and tell Ammos Fedorovich and Korobkin. Good-by, Anna Andreyevna!

DOBCHINSKY (*to* ANNA ANDREYEVNA): Good-by, godmother!

(*They both go out.*)

ARTEMY FILIPPOVICH (*to* LUKA LUKICH): It's simply terrifying, but just why, you can't tell, yourself. We haven't even got into our uniforms. Well, do you suppose he'll send off a report to Petersburg when he wakes up? (*They go out thoughtfully along with the* SUPERINTENDENT OF SCHOOLS, *saying as they go.*) Good-by, madam!

SCENE VIII

ANNA ANDREYEVNA *and* MARYA ANTONOVNA

ANNA ANDREYEVNA: Oh, what a charming man!

MARYA ANTONOVNA: Oh, what a darling!

ANNA ANDREYEVNA: But what refinement in everything he does! You can see at once he's a Petersburg swell. His manners, and all that. . . . Oh, how nice! I'm crazy over young men like him! I simply lose my head over them. And moreover, he took a fancy to me; I noticed that he kept glancing my way.

MARYA ANTONOVNA: Why, mamma, he was looking at me!

ANNA ANDREYEVNA: I'll thank you to be off with your nonsense. It's quite out of place here.

MARYA ANTONOVNA: No, mamma, really!

ANNA ANDREYEVNA: Well, I declare! God forbid we should quarrel about it! That will do! Why should he look at you? What reason would he have for looking at you?

MARYA ANTONOVNA: Really, mamma, he kept looking at me. First when he began to talk about literature, he gave me a look; and then when he was telling about how he played whist with the ambassadors, he looked at me again.

ANNA ANDREYEVNA: Well, maybe, once or twice, but that's all it amounted to. "Oh, I'll just take a look at her!" he said to himself.

SCENE IX

The same and the CHIEF OF POLICE

CHIEF OF POLICE (*coming in on tiptoes*): Sh, sh!

ANNA ANDREYEVNA: What is it?

CHIEF OF POLICE: I'm sorry I got him drunk. What if half he says is true? (*Reflecting.*) And why shouldn't it be true? When he's on a spree, a man brings everything to the surface: whatever is in his heart is on his tongue. Of course, he lied a little; but unless you lie a little bit, no conversation is possible. He plays cards with the Ministers and drives to the Palace. . . . And so really, the more you think about it . . . the devil knows who he is. . . . I don't know what's going on in my head; it's as if I were either standing on a sort of steeple or were just about to be hanged.

ANNA ANDREYEVNA: And I felt absolutely no timidity whatever; I simply saw in him an educated, high-toned man of the world, and his rank was nothing to me.

CHIEF OF POLICE: That's the way with you women! That word "women" sums it all up! They always fall for fiddle-faddle! They wise-crack about anything that comes into their noddles. They get off with a whipping, but the husband's as good as dead. You, sweet soul, behaved as familiarly with him as if he were another Dobchinsky.

ANNA ANDREYEVNA: I advise you not to be uneasy on that score. We know a thing or two. . . . (*Glancing at her daughter.*)

CHIEF OF POLICE (*to himself*): Well, what's the use of talking to you women! . . . Here's a fix, indeed! I haven't yet been able to get over my fright. (*He opens the door and speaks off stage.*) Mishka! Call Police Sergeants Svistunov and Derzhimorda: they're outside the gate somewhere or other. (*After a brief silence.*) Everything in the world has turned queer; you might expect a man to be something to look at; but such a lean, skinny fellow—how are you going to know who he is? If a man's military, the fact shows plainly enough; but when he puts on a dress coat, he's like a fly with his wings pulled off. He whooped it up such a long time at the inn a while ago, and faked up such a lot of fairy tales and bunk that you'd never make sense of it in a lifetime. But then he finally gave in. He even blabbed more than he needed to. Evidently he's a young man.

SCENE X

The same and OSIP

They all run to meet him, beckoning.

ANNA ANDREYEVNA: Come here, my good fellow.

CHIEF OF POLICE: Sh! . . . Well, what about it? Is he asleep?

OSIP: Not yet; he's stretching a bit.

ANNA ANDREYEVNA: Listen; what's your name?

OSIP: Osip, madam.

CHIEF OF POLICE (*to his wife and daughter*): That'll do for you! (*To* OSIP.) Well now, my boy, have they fed you well?

OSIP: They have, I thank you heartily; very well indeed.

ANNA ANDREYEVNA: Tell me: an awful lot of counts and princes call on your master, don't they?

OSIP (*aside*): What shall I say? If they've fed me well now, they'll do even better later. (*Aloud.*) Yes, even counts come.

MARYA ANTONOVNA: My dear Osip, how good-looking your master is!

ANNA ANDREYEVNA: And please tell us, Osip, how he . . .

CHIEF OF POLICE: Oh, please stop! You only mix me up with such silly talk. Now then, my friend! . . .

ANNA ANDREYEVNA: What rank has your master?

OSIP: Oh, he has the usual thing.

CHIEF OF POLICE: Oh, my God, you keep asking such silly questions! You won't let me get in a word to the point. Now, my friend, what sort of man is your master? . . . Strict? Does he like to bawl people out or doesn't he?

OSIP: Yes, he likes to have things orderly. He sees to it that everything around him is kept ship-shape.

CHIEF OF POLICE: I like your face very much. My friend, you must be a good fellow. Now, what—?

ANNA ANDREYEVNA: Listen, Osip, does your master wear his uniform at home?

CHIEF OF POLICE: Really, that'll do, chatterboxes that you are! This is a serious business: it's a question of a man's life. (*To* OSIP.) Well, now, my friend, I like you very much. When traveling there's no harm, you know, in taking an extra little glass of tea—the weather has turned cooler—so here's a couple of rubles for tea.

OSIP (*taking the money*): Thank you very much, sir! God grant you the best of health! I'm a poor man, and you've helped me.

CHIEF OF POLICE: Good, good, the pleasure is mine. Now what, my friend—?

ANNA ANDREYEVNA: Listen, Osip, what kind of eyes does your master like best?

MARYA ANTONOVNA: Osip, dear, what a darling little nose your master has!

CHIEF OF POLICE: Oh, stop! Let me! . . . (*To* OSIP.) Now please tell me, my boy: to what does your master pay the most attention, that is, what pleases him most in traveling?

OSIP: What he likes depends on circumstances. Most of all he likes to be well received; he likes good entertainment.

CHIEF OF POLICE: Good entertainment?

OSIP: Yes, sir. Now take me, for instance, I'm only a serf, but he sees that I'm well treated, too. Darned if he doesn't! Sometimes when we go to a place, he'll say: "Well, Osip, did they treat you well?" "Badly, your Honor!" "Hm," he'll say, "he's a bad host, Osip. Remind me of that when I get home." "Aha," I think to myself (*waving his hand*); "I should worry; I'm a plain man."

CHIEF OF POLICE: Very good, you're talking sense. There, I've given you something for tea; here's something more for biscuits.

OSIP: Why do you favor me, your Honor? (*He pockets the money.*) I'll drink your health.

ANNA ANDREYEVNA: Come to me, Osip, and I'll give you something, too.

MARYA ANTONOVNA: Osip, dear, take your master a kiss from me! (HLESTAKOV *is heard coughing in the next room.*)

CHIEF OF POLICE: Sh! . . . (*Rising upon tiptoe, and finishing the scene in a subdued voice.*) God forbid your making any noise! Go to your own rooms—you've said enough. . . .

ANNA ANDREYEVNA: Let's go, Mashenka! I told you that I noticed something in our guest that only we two can talk about.

CHIEF OF POLICE: Oh, they'll talk enough! I think if I went to listen to them, I'd have to stuff my ears. (*Turning to* OSIP.) Now, my friend. . . .

SCENE XI

The same, DERZHIMORDA *and* SVISTUNOV

CHIEF OF POLICE: Sh! You stamp with your boots like bow-legged bears! You make a thumping like dumping a ton of rocks out of a cart! Where the devil have you been?

DERZHIMORDA: I was acting on your orders. . . .

CHIEF OF POLICE: Sh! (*Putting his hand over the* POLICEMAN'S *mouth.*) You croak like a crow! (*Imitating him.*) "I was acting on your orders!" Roaring like an empty barrel! (*To* OSIP.) Now, my friend, run along and get everything ready for your master. Command everything there is in the house. (OSIP *goes out.*) As for you two, go stand on the doorstep and don't move! And don't let any outsider into the house, especially tradesmen! If you let in a single one, I'll . . . Only see to it that if any one comes with a complaint or even looks as if he had a complaint to present against me, throw him out on his neck! Sock it to him! Like that! (*Illustrating a kick.*) Do you get me? Sh . . . sh. . . . (*He goes out on tiptoe after the* POLICEMEN.)

ACT IV

The same room in the house of the CHIEF OF POLICE

SCENE I

Enter carefully, almost on tiptoe, AMMOS FEDOROVICH, ARTEMY FILIPPOVICH, *the* POSTMASTER, LUKA LUKICH, DOBCHINSKY, *and* BOBCHINSKY *in full dress uniforms. The whole scene proceeds in an undertone.*

AMMOS FEDOROVICH (*arranging them all in a semicircle*): For God's sake, gentlemen, make a circle as quickly as possible and put on your best manner! Confound him, he rides to the Palace and bawls out the Council of State! Draw up in military order; it must be in military order. You run over to that side, Petr Ivanovich; and you, Petr Ivanovich, stand right here.

(*Both* PETR IVANOVICHES *run on tiptoe.*)

ARTEMY FILIPPOVICH. If you're willing, Ammos Fedorovich, we ought to undertake something or other.

AMMOS FEDOROVICH: Just what exactly?

ARTEMY FILIPPOVICH: Everybody knows what.

AMMOS FEDOROVICH: Slip him something?

ARTEMY FILIPPOVICH: Well, yes, slip him something.

AMMOS FEDOROVICH: It's dangerous, deuce take it! He might raise Cain—a government man like him! But how about an offering on the part of the nobility for a memorial of some sort?

POSTMASTER: Or say this: "Here is some money left unclaimed at the post office."

ARTEMY FILIPPOVICH: Look out that he doesn't send *you* away somewhere by post! Listen: things aren't done like that in a well-regulated state. Why is there a whole squadron of us here? We should introduce ourselves one by one; and then, between man and man, everything is fixed, and nothing leaks out. That's the way it's done in a well-regulated society! Now you'll be the first to begin, Ammos Fedorovich.

AMMOS FEDOROVICH: It would be better for you: our august guest broke bread in your establishment.

ARTEMY FILIPPOVICH: It would be still better for you, Luka Lukich, as the enlightener of youth.

LUKA LUKICH: I can't, I can't, gentlemen! I confess I was so brought up that if I have to talk with a man one rank higher than mine, I get heart failure and my tongue seems to stick in the mud. No, gentlemen, you really must relieve me!

ARTEMY FILIPPOVICH: Yes, Ammos Fedorovich, there's no one but you. You have only to say a word, and Cicero fairly flies off your tongue!

AMMOS FEDOROVICH: What are you talking about! Cicero! See here, what have you thought up! What if I do get carried away sometimes, talking about my house dogs or my hunting hounds? . . .

ALL (*surrounding him*): No, not only about dogs; you can talk about the Tower of Babel, too. . . .* No, Ammos Fedorovich, don't abandon us, be a father to us! . . . No, Ammos Fedorovich!

AMMOS FEDOROVICH: Let me be, gentlemen!

(*At this moment steps and coughing are heard in* HLESTAKOV'S *room. All vie with each other in their haste to reach the door, crowding and trying to get out, which they do only with some squeezing. A few exclamations are heard in undertones.*)

Voice of BOBCHINSKY: Ow! Petr Ivanovich, you stepped on my foot, Petr Ivanovich!

Voice of ARTEMY FILIPPOVICH: Let me out, gentlemen; you've squeezed me as flat as a soul in Purgatory!

(*A few gasping exclamations of* "Ow! ow!" *are heard; finally all have been pushed out, and the room remains empty.*)

SCENE II

HLESTAKOV *alone, entering sleepy-eyed*

HLESTAKOV: I think I must have snored properly. Where did they get such mattresses and feather beds? I fairly perspired. They must have slipped me something strong at lunch yesterday; my head still goes bang. So far as I can see, a fellow can spend his time agreeably here. I like cordiality; and I admit I like it best of all when people gratify me out of sheer kind-heartedness rather than for their personal interest. The Chief of Police's daughter isn't half bad to look at, and even her mamma might perhaps . . . Well, I don't know, but I sure like this life.

SCENE III

HLESTAKOV *and the* JUDGE (AMMOS FEDOROVICH)

AMMOS FEDOROVICH (*upon entering, stops, and says to himself*): My God, my God! Make this come out right! My knees will hardly hold me up. (*Aloud, drawing himself up, and grasping his sword-hilt.*)

* "The allusion is to the Judge's skepticism."—Sykes.

I have the honor to introduce myself: Judge of the local District Court, Collegiate Assessor Lyapkin-Tyapkin.

HLESTAKOV: I beg you to sit down. So you're the Judge here?

AMMOS FEDOROVICH: In 1816 I was elected to a three-year term by the will of the nobility and I have held the post ever since.

HLESTAKOV: It's profitable to be Judge, isn't it?

AMMOS FEDOROVICH: After three terms I was presented with the order of Vladimir of the Fourth Class, with the commendation of the authorities. (*Aside.*) The money is in my fist, and my fist is on fire!

HLESTAKOV: I like the Vladimir. Now the Anna of the Third Class isn't so good.

AMMOS FEDOROVICH (*little by little thrusting forward his closed fist, aside*): O Lord God! I don't know where I'm sitting. It's as if I had live coals under me.

HLESTAKOV: What have you got in your hand?

AMMOS FEDOROVICH (*flustered, and letting some notes fall to the floor*): Nothing, sir.

HLESTAKOV: Nothing, you say? I see you've dropped some money.

AMMOS FEDOROVICH (*trembling all over*): Not at all, sir! (*Aside.*) O God, here I am in the dock, and they're bringing up the police cart to get me!

HLESTAKOV (*picking it up*): Yes, it's money.

AMMOS FEDOROVICH (*aside*): Well, it's all over! I'm lost and done for!

HLESTAKOV: I say, won't you lend it to me?

AMMOS FEDOROVICH (*hastily*): Certainly, why not, sir? . . . With the greatest pleasure. (*Aside.*) Now, bolder, bolder! Pull me through, Most Holy Mother!

HLESTAKOV: On the road, you know, I spent every kopek, on this and that. . . . Of course, I'll send it to you at once from my country home.

AMMOS FEDOROVICH: Please, sir, the idea! It's honor enough without repayment. . . . Of course, in my poor, weak way, by zeal and diligent service of the authorities . . . I shall always strive to deserve . . . (*He rises from his chair and draws himself up to an attitude of attention.*) I won't venture to disturb you longer by my presence. Have you no orders for me?

HLESTAKOV: What sort of orders?

AMMOS FEDOROVICH: I considered that you might have some orders for the local District Court.

HLESTAKOV: What for? I haven't any need of it at present; no, there's nothing. Thank you very much.

AMMOS FEDOROVICH (*bowing and going out, aside*): The town is ours!

HLESTAKOV (*when alone*): The Judge is a good fellow!

SCENE IV

HLESTAKOV *and the* POSTMASTER, *who, clad in his uniform, stands at attention, hand on sword*

POSTMASTER: I have the honor to introduce myself: Postmaster and Court Councilor Shpekin.

HLESTAKOV: Ah, do come in! I'm very fond of pleasant society. Be seated. I suppose you live here all the time?

POSTMASTER: Just so, sir.

HLESTAKOV: I like this little town. Of course, it's not very populous; but what of that? It's not the capital. It's not the capital, is it?

POSTMASTER: That's perfectly true.

HLESTAKOV: You find *bong tong* only in the capital, where there are no provincial geese. What's your opinion: isn't that right?

POSTMASTER: Quite right, sir. (*Aside.*) I see he's not a bit haughty: he asks about everything.

HLESTAKOV: You'll have to admit, I suppose, that it's possible to live happily even in a small town?

POSTMASTER: Just so, sir.

HLESTAKOV: In my opinion all one needs is to be respected and sincerely liked—isn't that right?

POSTMASTER: Absolutely right.

HLESTAKOV: I confess I'm glad that you're of my opinion. Of course they call me peculiar, but that's the kind of disposition I have. (*Looking into the* POSTMASTER's *eyes and speaking to himself.*) Why not ask this postmaster for a loan? (*Aloud.*) A strange sort of thing has happened to me: I got entirely cleaned out on the road. Couldn't you lend me three hundred rubles?

POSTMASTER: Why, certainly; I'd consider it the greatest pleasure. Here you are, sir. I'm heart and soul at your service.

HLESTAKOV: I'm much obliged. I confess I hate like hell to deny myself anything when traveling; and why should I? How does that strike you?

POSTMASTER: Just so, sir.

(*He rises and stands at attention, hand on sword.*)

I won't venture to disturb you any longer by my presence. . . . Have you perchance some remarks to make upon the management of the post office?

HLESTAKOV: No, nothing.

(*The* POSTMASTER *bows and goes out.*)

HLESTAKOV (*lighting a cigar*): The Postmaster, it seems to me, is also a nice fellow; at any rate, he's obliging. I like such people.

SCENE V

HLESTAKOV *and* LUKA LUKICH, *who is almost pushed through the door. Behind him a voice says, half aloud,* "What are you afraid of?"

LUKA LUKICH (*drawing himself up in trepidation and holding tight to his sword*): I have the honor to introduce myself: Superintendent of Schools and Titular Councilor Hlopov.

HLESTAKOV: Oh, pleased to meet you. Sit down, sit down. Have a cigar? (*Handing him a cigar.*)

LUKA LUKICH (*undecidedly, to himself*): Well, I declare! I didn't expect this. Shall I take it or not?

HLESTAKOV: Go ahead, take it; that's a good cigar. Of course it's not like those you get in Petersburg. There, my dear man, I used to smoke little cigars at twenty-five rubles the hundred—they simply make you want to kiss your hand after smoking. Here's a candle; have a light! (*He holds out a candle to him.*)

(LUKA LUKICH *tries to light his cigar and trembles all over.*)

HLESTAKOV: But that's the wrong end!

LUKA LUKICH (*dropping the cigar in his fright, spitting, and waving his hand; aside*): Devil take everything! My damned timidity has ruined me!

HLESTAKOV: Well, I see you don't care for cigars. I confess they're my weakness. Also, where the fair sex is concerned, I simply can't be indifferent. How about you? Which do you like better, brunettes or blondes?

(LUKA LUKICH *finds himself in utter bewilderment as to what to say.*)

HLESTAKOV: No, tell me frankly which: brunettes or blondes?

LUKA LUKICH: I don't venture to judge.

HLESTAKOV: No, no, now, don't offer excuses! I wish positively to find out your taste.

LUKA LUKICH: I venture to inform you . . . (*Aside.*) Well, I myself don't know what I'm saying.

HLESTAKOV: Ah, ha! You don't want to say! I believe some little brunette has got you into a slight embarrassment. Admit it now: hasn't she?

(LUKA LUKICH *remains silent.*)

HLESTAKOV: Ah, ha! You blushed! You see! You see! Why don't you talk?

LUKA LUKICH: I got scared, your Hon— . . . Excel— . . . Gra— . . . (*Aside.*) My damned tongue has betrayed me!

HLESTAKOV: Got scared? Well, there is something in my eyes that inspires timidity. At least I know there's not a woman who can hold out against them, is there?

LUKA LUKICH: Quite right, sir.

HLESTAKOV: A very strange thing has happened to me: on the road I got cleaned out. Couldn't you lend me three hundred rubles?

LUKA LUKICH (*to himself, clutching at his pocket*): What a fix if I haven't got it! I have! I have! (*He produces and tremblingly hands over the notes.*)

HLESTAKOV: Thanks ever so much.

LUKA LUKICH (*drawing himself up, hand on sword*): I won't venture to disturb you longer by my presence.

HLESTAKOV: Good-by.

LUKA LUKICH (*hurries out almost running, speaking aside*): Well, thank God! Here's hoping he won't peep in on the classes!

SCENE VI

HLESTAKOV *and* ARTEMY FILIPPOVICH, *who draws himself up, hand on sword*

ARTEMY FILIPPOVICH: I have the honor to present myself: the Supervisor of Charitable Institutions, Court Councilor Zemlyanika.

HLESTAKOV: How do you do? Pray be seated.

ARTEMY FILIPPOVICH: I had the honor of escorting you, and of receiving you personally in the charitable institutions entrusted to my care.

HLESTAKOV: Ah, yes, I remember. You treated me to a very good lunch.

ARTEMY FILIPPOVICH: I'm happy to do my best in the service of my country.

HLESTAKOV: I like good cooking; I admit it's my weakness. . . . Tell me, please, weren't you a little shorter in height yesterday? It seems so to me.

ARTEMY FILIPPOVICH: It may well be. (*A brief silence.*) I may say that I spare nothing, and zealously fulfill my duties. (*He draws his chair nearer and speaks in a lower voice.*) The Postmaster here does absolutely nothing: all the business is greatly neglected: the mail is kept back—you can find it out for yourself. The Judge also, who was here before I came, does nothing but course hares; he keeps dogs in the court rooms, and his behavior, if I may admit it in your presence —of course, for the good of my country, I must do it, although he's both a relative and a friend of mine—his behavior is most reprehensible. There's a certain landowner here named Dobchinsky, whom you have seen; and no sooner does this Dobchinsky go out of his house somewhere, than the Judge goes over to sit with his wife, and I'm ready to swear . . . And you have only to look at the children: there's not one that looks like Dobchinsky, but every one of them, even the little girl, is the spit 'n image of the Judge.

HLESTAKOV: You don't say so! I never thought of it.

ARTEMY FILIPPOVICH: Then there's the Superintendent of Schools. . . . I don't know how the authorities could entrust him with such a responsibility: he's worse than a Jacobin, and he inspires in the youth such radical principles that it's hard even to express them. Don't you want me to put all this on paper for you?

HLESTAKOV: Yes, put it on paper. I'd be much pleased. You know, when I'm bored I like to read over something amusing. . . . What is your name? I've quite forgotten.

ARTEMY FILIPPOVICH: Zemlyanika.

HLESTAKOV: Ah, yes, Zemlyanika. And tell me, please, have you any children?

ARTEMY FILIPPOVICH: I should say so, sir! Five of them, two grown up.

HLESTAKOV: You don't say! Grown up! And what are they? . . . How do you . . .?

ARTEMY FILIPPOVICH: Do you wish to ask what their names are?

HLESTAKOV: Yes, what are their names?

ARTEMY FILIPPOVICH: Nikolay, Ivan, Elizaveta, Marya, and Perepetuya.

HLESTAKOV: That's nice.

ARTEMY FILIPPOVICH: I won't venture to disturb you any longer by my presence, depriving you of time dedicated to your sacred duties. . . . (*He bows and is about to go out.*)

HLESTAKOV (*accompanying him*): No, that's all right. That was all very funny, what you were telling me. Come and see me again. I enjoy it so much. (*He returns, and opening the door, calls after him.*) Hey, you! What's your name? I keep forgetting your name.

ARTEMY FILIPPOVICH: Artemy Filippovich.

HLESTAKOV: Do me a favor, Artemy Filippovich! A queer thing has happened to me: I got quite cleaned out on the road. Haven't you some money you could lend me—say four hundred rubles?

ARTEMY FILIPPOVICH: Yes.

HLESTAKOV: Well, how opportune! I thank you heartily.

SCENE VII

HLESTAKOV, BOBCHINSKY, *and* DOBCHINSKY

BOBCHINSKY: I have the honor to introduce myself: Petr Ivanovich Bobchinsky, a resident of this town.

DOBCHINSKY: Petr Ivanovich Dobchinsky, a landowner.

HLESTAKOV: Ah, yes, I've seen you before. I think you had a fall: well, how's your nose?

BOBCHINSKY: First rate! Don't feel any anxiety, please; it's quite well and dried up.

HLESTAKOV: I'm glad it's healed. I'm very glad. . . . (*Suddenly and abruptly.*) Have you any money on you?

DOBCHINSKY: What do you mean, money?

HLESTAKOV: Lend me a thousand rubles.

BOBCHINSKY: Good Lord, I haven't such a sum. But haven't you, Petr Ivanovich?

DOBCHINSKY: I haven't it about me, because my money, if you care to know, has been deposited with the Charitable Board.*

HLESTAKOV: Well, if you haven't a thousand, a hundred will do.

BOBCHINSKY (*rummaging in his pockets*): Haven't you a hundred rubles, Petr Ivanovich? I have only forty altogether, in notes.

DOBCHINSKY (*looking in his bill-fold*): Twenty-five rubles in all.

BOBCHINSKY: Just take a better look, Petr Ivanovich. I know there's a hole in your right-hand pocket, and really, something may have fallen through.

DOBCHINSKY: No, really, there's nothing in the hole.

HLESTAKOV: Well, it's all the same. I just asked. Good: sixty-five rubles will do. . . . That's all right. (*He takes the money.*)

DOBCHINSKY: I venture to ask your help about a very delicate matter.

HLESTAKOV: What is it?

DOBCHINSKY: It's a thing of very great delicacy, sir: my eldest son, you see, was born before my marriage. . . .

HLESTAKOV: Yes?

DOBCHINSKY: Of course, that's only so to speak, sir, because he was born absolutely the same as if in wedlock; and I afterwards fixed everything up properly by the lawful bonds of matrimony, sir. And so, you see, I now want him to be my son entirely, that is, legally, sir, and to bear my name, Dobchinsky, sir.

HLESTAKOV: Very good, let him; that's all right.

DOBCHINSKY: I shouldn't have troubled you, but I'm sorry for the boy, who has such talents. He fills us with the greatest hopes: he can

* This had charge of beggars, orphans, invalids, the insane.

repeat different poems by heart; and if he happens to get hold of a pocket knife, he makes a little cab right off, as skillfully as a juggler, sir. Petr Ivanovich here knows all about it.

Bobchinsky: Yes, he has great talents.

Hlestakov: Very good, very good. I'll see about it. . . . I'll speak to . . . I have hopes . . . that can all be done; yes, yes. . . . (*Turning to* Bobchinsky.) Haven't *you* something to say to me?

Bobchinsky: Why, yes, I have a very humble petition.

Hlestakov: Well, what about?

Bobchinsky: I humbly beg you, when you return to Petersburg, to say to all those various grandees, senators, and admirals, "Your Grace," or, "Your Excellency, there lives in such-and-such a town a certain Petr Ivanovich Bobchinsky." Just tell them that there is such a person as Petr Ivanovich Bobchinsky.

Hlestakov: Very well.

Bobchinsky: And likewise, if you should meet the tsar, just say to him, "Your Imperial Majesty, in such-and-such a town there lives a certain Petr Ivanovich Bobchinsky."

Hlestakov: Very well.

Dobchinsky: Excuse me for troubling you with my presence.

Bobchinsky: Excuse me for troubling you with my presence.

Hlestakov: That's all right! That's all right! It was a pleasure. (*He shows them out.*)

SCENE VIII

Hlestakov, *alone*

Hlestakov: There are a good many functionaries here. And, by the way, it strikes me that they take me for an important government official. I really threw dust in their eyes yesterday. What foolishness! I believe I'll write all about it to Tryapichkin in Petersburg; he'll write a little satire and take them off first-rate. Hey, Osip! Bring me paper and ink. (Osip *glances in at the door, saying,* "Right away.") And if Tryapichkin ever gets his tooth into anybody, let that man look out! He won't spare his own father for the sake of a lampoon, and he likes money, too. However, these officials are good fellows; it's a great point in their favor that they lent me money. I might as well see how much I've got. Here's three hundred from the Judge; three hundred from the Postmaster, six hundred, seven hundred, eight hundred. . . . What a greasy note! Eight hundred, nine hundred! Oho! more than a thousand! . . . Now, then, captain, just let me get at you now! We'll see who's who!

SCENE IX

HLESTAKOV, *and* OSIP *with ink and paper*

HLESTAKOV: Well, you blockhead, do you see how they receive and entertain me? (*He begins to write.*)

OSIP: Yes, thank God! Only do you want me to tell you something, Ivan Alexandrovich?

HLESTAKOV: What?

OSIP: Get away from here! By Heaven, it's time!

HLESTAKOV (*writing*): What nonsense! Why?

OSIP: Because. Deuce take 'em all! We've bummed two days here, and that's enough. Why tie up with 'em any longer? Spit on 'em! Before you know it some one else may arrive. . . . Yes, Ivan Alexandrovich, by Heavens! There are some splendid horses here—they'd give us a fine ride.

HLESTAKOV (*writing*): No, I'd like to stay here a little longer. Wait till to-morrow.

OSIP: But why to-morrow? Good God, let's skip, Ivan Alexandrovich! Although it's a great honor for you, all the same you know that we'd better be off quick; they've really taken you for some one else. . . . And your dad will be peeved because you've dawdled so long. Really, we'd have a grand ride! They'd furnish you tiptop horses here.

HLESTAKOV (*writing*): Well, all right. But first take this letter and get an order for post horses. And see to it that they're good horses! Tell the drivers that I'll give them a ruble apiece if they'll bowl along as if I were a special courier and sing songs! (*He continues writing.*) I imagine Tryapichkin will die laughing. . . .

OSIP: I'll send the letter by the house servant, sir; but I'd better attend to our packing to save time.

HLESTAKOV (*writing*): All right, only bring me a candle.

OSIP (*goes out and speaks behind the scene*): Hey, listen, my boy! Take this letter to the post office and tell the Postmaster to frank it; and have them send my master their best troika of post horses; tell 'em my master won't be paying the fee, because it's at the government's expense. And tell 'em to look lively or the master'll be angry. Wait, the letter isn't ready yet.

HLSETAKOV (*continuing to write*): I'm curious to know whether he lives on Post Office Street or Gorokhovaya Street. He likes to change his lodgings frequently without paying up. I'll take a chance on addressing him at Post Office Street. (*He folds up the letter and addresses it.*)

(OSIP *brings in a candle.* HLESTAKOV *seals the letter. At the same time the voice of* DERZHIMORDA *is heard outside.*)

DERZHIMORDA: Where're you going, whiskers? I tell you I can't admit anybody.

HLESTAKOV (*handing* OSIP *the letter*): There, take it away.

Voices of MERCHANTS: Let us in, please! You can't refuse; we've come on business.

DERZHIMORDA: Go away! Go away! He's not receiving; he's asleep. (*The noise increases.*)

HLESTAKOV: What's going on there, Osip? Go see what the noise is about.

OSIP (*looking out of the window*): Some merchants want to come in, but the policemen won't let 'em. They're waving some papers; they really want to see you.

HLESTAKOV (*going to the window*): What do you want, my good men?

Voices of MERCHANTS: We appeal to your kindness. Give orders to receive our petitions, your Honor.

HLESTAKOV: Let 'em in, let 'em in! Let 'em come. Osip, tell 'em to come in. (OSIP *goes out.*)

HLESTAKOV (*accepts the petitions through the window, unrolls one of them and reads*): "To his Honorable Excellency the Minister of Finance from the merchant Abdulin." . . . What the devil! There's no such rank!

SCENE X

HLESTAKOV, *and the* MERCHANTS, *who carry a basket of wine and loaf sugar*

HLESTAKOV: What do you want, my good men?

MERCHANTS: We humbly implore your favor.

HLESTAKOV: But what do you want?

MERCHANTS: Don't ruin us, sir! We are suffering insults for no cause at all.

HLESTAKOV: From whom?

ONE OF THE MERCHANTS: All from the chief of police of this town. There never was such a Chief of Police, your Honor. He invents such insults as are beyond description. He has ruined us with billeting, until we want to hang ourselves. And his behavior is simply awful. He'll seize a man by the beard and say, "Ha, you Tatar!" By Heaven, he does! It isn't as though we hadn't shown him respect; we always do the regular thing, giving him cloth for his dear wife's clothes and his daughter's—we don't object to that. But, bless you, that's not enough for him; oh, no! He walks into the shop and takes anything he can lay his hands on. He'll see a piece of cloth and say, "Hey, my dear fellow, that's a fine piece of cloth; just send it over to me." Well, you take it over—and there's pretty close to forty yards in the piece.

HLESTAKOV: Is it possible? Why, what a swindler he is!

MERCHANTS: By Heaven, nobody can remember such a chief of police. You have to hide everything in the shop when you catch sight of him. And that's not saying that he takes only delicacies; oh, no! Dried prunes that have been lying in the barrel seven years and my own clerks wouldn't eat, he'll put away by the pocketful. His name day's St. Anthony's,* and on that day we take him seems like everything he needs; but no, we've got to keep it up; he says St. Onufry's his name day too. What can we do? We bring him stuff on St. Onufry's also.

HLESTAKOV: He's a regular highwayman!

MERCHANT: I'll say! And just try to say no to him, and he'll quarter a whole regiment on you. And if you object, he'll have the doors locked on you. "I'm not going to subject you to corporal punishment," he says, "or put you to the torture—that's forbidden by law," he says; "but you're going to eat salted herrings, my man." †

HLESTAKOV: Oh, what a swindler! Why, he ought to be sent to Siberia!

MERCHANTS: We don't care where your Honor packs him off to; any place'll do so long as it's far from us. Don't scorn our bread and salt, father: we beg to present you with this loaf sugar and this basket of wine.

HLESTAKOV: No, don't think of such a thing; I accept absolutely no bribes. But, for instance, if you should propose to lend me three hundred rubles—well, that would be another matter: I can accept loans.

MERCHANTS: Please do, your Honor! (*Taking out money.*) But why three hundred? You had better take five; only help us!

HLESTAKOV: Thanks. I have nothing to say against a loan; I'll take it.

MERCHANTS (*handing him the money on a silver tray*): And please take the tray with it.

HLESTAKOV: Well, you can throw the tray in.

MERCHANTS (*bowing*): And for once you might take the sugar.

---

* In Russia the day of the saint for whom a person is named is a family holiday.

† "To produce excessive thirst. This indirect form of torture was employed, to extort confession, by the secret police."—Sykes.

HLESTAKOV: Oh, no, I never take any bribes. . . .

OSIP: Your Honor, why not take it? Do! Everything comes in good on the road. Just hand over the sugar and the sack. Give us everything; it'll all come in useful. What's that—a rope? Give us the rope, too; a rope is useful in traveling; the wagon may break down or something, and you'll have to tie it up.

MERCHANTS: Just do us the favor, your Grace! If you don't help us out as we ask you to, we shan't know what to do: we might as well hang ourselves.

HLESTAKOV: Without fail! Without fail! I'll do my best. (*The merchants go out.*)

A WOMAN'S *Voice* (*outside*): No, don't you dare refuse to admit me! I'll complain to him himself! Stop shoving so hard!

HLESTAKOV: Who's there? (*Going to the window.*) What's the matter, my good woman?

Voices of TWO WOMEN: We beseech your favor, sir! Please hear us, your Honor!

HLESTAKOV (*out of the window*): Let her in.

SCENE XI

HLESTAKOV, *the* LOCKSMITH'S WIFE, *and the* SERGEANT'S WIDOW

LOCKSMITH'S WIFE (*bowing down to his feet*): I implore your favor. . . .

SERGEANT'S WIDOW: I implore your favor. . . .

HLESTAKOV: Who are you, my good women?

SERGEANT'S WIDOW: I'm the widow of Sergeant Ivanov.

LOCKSMITH'S WIFE: I'm the wife of a locksmith of the town, Fevronya Petrova Poshlepkin, sir.

HLESTAKOV: Wait; speak one at a time. What do you want?

LOCKSMITH'S WIFE: I implore your aid against the Chief of Police! May God send him every evil! May his children, and he, the swindler, and his uncles and his aunts, prosper in nothing they ever do!

HLESTAKOV: Why?

LOCKSMITH'S WIFE: He sent my husband away as a soldier, and it wasn't our turn, the scoundrel! And it's against the law, too, he being a married man.

HLESTAKOV: How could he do that?

LOCKSMITH'S WIFE: He did it, the scoundrel, he did it! May God smite him in this world and the next! May every misfortune visit him and his aunt, too, if he has one, and if his father's living, the rascal, may he croak or choke himself forever—such a scoundrel he is! He ought to have taken the tailor's son, who's a drunkard anyway; but his parents made him a handsome present; so he jumped on the son of Mrs. Panteleyev, the shopkeeper; but Mrs. Panteleyev sent his wife three pieces of cloth, and so he came to me. "What good's your husband to you?" says he. "He's no use to you." As if I didn't know whether he's any use or not; that's my business—the scoundrel! "He's a thief," says he; "although he hasn't stolen anything yet, it's all the same," he says; "he will; and anyway he'll be sent as a recruit next year." How can I manage without my husband—the scoundrel! I'm a weak woman, and you're a villain! May none of your relatives ever see the light of God! And if you have a mother-in-law, may she—!

HLESTAKOV: All right, all right. (*He shows the old woman out. Then to the other woman.*) And you, now?

LOCKSMITH'S WIFE (*going*): Don't forget, honored sir! Be merciful to me!

SERGEANT'S WIDOW: I've come to complain against the Chief of Police, sir.

HLESTAKOV: Well, what about? Put it in a few words.

SERGEANT'S WIDOW: He beat me up, sir!

HLESTAKOV: How?

SERGEANT'S WIDOW: By mistake, your Honor! Some of our peasant women were fighting in the market, but the police didn't get there soon enough, so they nabbed me, and reported me: I couldn't sit down for two days.

HLESTAKOV: Well, what's to be done about it, now?

SERGEANT'S WIDOW: Of course, there's nothing to be done now. But you can make him pay damages for making the mistake. I can't turn my back on my own luck, and the money would help me a lot just now.

HLESTAKOV: Well, well, run along, run along; I'll see to it. (*Several hands containing petitions are thrust through the window.*) What next? (*Approaching the window.*) I don't want them! I don't want them! There's no use! There's no use! (*Going away.*) They make me tired, deuce take 'em! Don't let 'em in, Osip!

OSIP (*shouting out the window*): Go away, go away! He hasn't time now! Come back to-morrow!

(*The door opens and there appears a strange figure in a frieze overcoat, unshaven, with a swollen lip and bandaged cheek; behind him several others appear in perspective.*)

OSIP: Get out, get out! Where'd you come from?

(*He gives the first one a push in the belly and forces his own way out into the passage with him, slamming the door behind him.*)

SCENE XII

HLESTAKOV, *and* MARYA ANTONOVNA

MARYA ANTONOVNA: Oh!

HLESTAKOV: What are you afraid of, young lady?

MARYA ANTONOVNA: No, I wasn't frightened.

HLESTAKOV (*posing*): It is most gratifying to me, young lady, that you should take me for a man who . . . May I be so bold as to ask you where you were going?

MARYA ANTONOVNA: Well, really, I wasn't going anywhere.

HLESTAKOV: And why weren't you, if I may ask?

MARYA ANTONOVNA: I thought mamma might be here. . . .

HLESTAKOV: No, I'd like to know why you weren't going anywhere.

MARYA ANTONOVNA: I've disturbed you. You were engaged with important matters.

HLESTAKOV (*posing*): Your eyes are more important than mere business. . . . You couldn't possibly disturb me, not in any manner whatsoever; on the contrary, you only bring me pleasure.

MARYA ANTONOVNA: You're talking in Petersburg style.

HLESTAKOV: To such a beautiful creature as you. Dare I be so happy as to offer you a chair? But no, you need, not a chair but a throne.

MARYA ANTONOVNA: Really, I don't know . . . I think I ought to be going. (*She sits down.*)

HLESTAKOV: What a beautiful fichu you have on!

MARYA ANTONOVNA: You men are flatterers; you just want to laugh at us provincials.

HLESTAKOV: How I should like to be your fichu, young lady, that I might embrace your lily-white neck.

MARYA ANTONOVNA: I'm sure I don't know what you're talking about: a little fichu. . . . What strange weather we're having to-day!

HLESTAKOV: But your lips, young lady, are better than any kind of weather!

MARYA ANTONOVNA: You keep talking like that! . . . I'd better ask you to write me some verses in my autograph album, as a souvenir. You surely know a lot of them.

HLESTAKOV: For your sake, young lady, I'll do anything you want. Command me, what sort of verses do you wish?

MARYA ANTONOVNA: Oh, any kind . . . such as . . . good ones . . . and new.

HLESTAKOV: But what are verses! I know a lot of them.

MARYA ANTONOVNA: Just say over the kind you're going to write for me.

HLESTAKOV: Why say them? I know them without doing that.

MARYA ANTONOVNA: I'm so fond of poetry.

HLESTAKOV: Well, I know a lot of different poems. For instance, I might write this for you:

> O man, who in thine hour of grief
> Against thy God in vain complainest. . . . *

And there are others. . . . I can't recall them now; however, that's all right. Instead I had better present you with my love, which your eyes have . . . (*Moving his chair nearer.*)

MARYA ANTONOVNA: Love! I don't understand love! . . . I have never known what love is. . . . (*She moves her chair away.*)

HLESTAKOV: Why do you move your chair away? It would be better for us to sit close together.

MARYA ANTONOVNA (*moving away*): Why close together? We're as well off at a distance.

HLESTAKOV (*moving nearer*): Why at a distance? We're as well off nearer.

MARYA ANTONOVNA (*moving away*): But why is that?

HLESTAKOV (*moving nearer*): It just seems to you that we're close; but you ought to imagine we're far apart. How happy I should be, young lady, if I could only hold you in my embrace.

MARYA ANTONOVNA (*looking out the window*): I wonder what that was that flew by. Was it a magpie or some other bird?

HLESTAKOV (*kissing her shoulder and looking out the window*): That was a magpie.

MARYA ANTONOVNA (*rising in indignation*): No, this is too much! . . . Such impudence! . . .

HLESTAKOV (*detaining her*): Forgive me, young lady, I did it from love, only from love.

MARYA ANTONOVNA: You consider me only a common provincial girl. . . . (*She tries to get away.*)

HLESTAKOV (*continues to detain her*): From love, truly, only from love. I was only joking, Marya Antonovna; don't be angry. I'm ready to beg forgiveness on my knees. (*He falls upon his knees.*) Forgive me, please forgive me! You see, I'm on my knees.

---

* The opening lines of an ode by Lomonosov (1708?-1765). Hlestakov recalls a scrap of an old-fashioned poet that he learned at school! (Adapted from Sykes.)

SCENE XIII

The same and ANNA ANDREYEVNA

ANNA ANDREYEVNA (*seeing* HLESTAKOV *on his knees*): Oh, what a scene!

HLESTAKOV (*rising*): Oh, the deuce!

ANNA ANDREYEVNA (*to her daughter*): What does this mean, young lady? What sort of behavior is this?

MARYA ANTONOVNA: Mamma, I . . .

ANNA ANDREYEVNA: Go away at once, do you hear? Go away, go away! Don't you dare show yourself before my eyes. (MARYA ANTONOVNA *goes out in tears.*) Pardon me, but I confess I was carried away by astonishment. . . .

HLESTAKOV (*aside*): She's also rather appetizing, not half bad-looking. (*Throwing himself upon his knees.*) Madam, you see, I am consumed with love.

ANNA ANDREYEVNA: What, on your knees? Oh, please get up. The floor is anything but clean.

HLESTAKOV: No, upon my knees, absolutely upon my knees, I wish to know my fate. Is it life or death?

ANNA ANDREYEVNA: I beg your pardon, but I still don't entirely understand your words. If I am not mistaken, you are declaring your sentiments regarding my daughter.

HLESTAKOV: No, I am in love with you. My life hangs by a hair. If you do not crown my constant love, then I am unworthy of earthly existence. With flames in my bosom I beseech your hand.

ANNA ANDREYEVNA: Permit me to remark that I am—well, as they say . . . married.

HLESTAKOV: That's nothing! In love that makes no difference. Even Karamzin says, "The laws condemn it." * We shall flee to the shade of the streams! . . . Your hand, I ask your hand.

SCENE XIV

The same and MARYA ANTONOVNA, *who comes in running*

MARYA ANTONOVNA: Mamma, papa says for you to . . . (*Seeing* HLESTAKOV *on his knees, and exclaiming.*) Oh, what a scene!

ANNA ANDREYEVNA: Well, what's the matter with you! What did *you* come in for? What flightiness! She runs in like a cat in a fit!

* "Quoted from some verses in the romance, *Bornholm Island,* by Karamzin (1766-1826)."—Sykes.

Well, what have you found that's so surprising? What have you thought up? Really, you act like a three-year-old child. No one in the world would ever think she was eighteen years old. I don't know when you'll have any more sense, or when you'll behave like a well-brought-up girl, or when you'll know what good principles and propriety are.

MARYA ANTONOVNA (*through her tears*): Really, mamma, I didn't know . . .

ANNA ANDREYEVNA: You always have wheels in your head; you pattern after Lyapkin-Tyapkin's daughters! Much good it does you to imitate them! You needn't copy them. There are other models for you—you have your mother, for example. That's the example you ought to follow!

HLESTAKOV (*seizing the daughter's hand*): Anna Andreyevna, do not oppose our felicity, bless our constant love!

ANNA ANDREYEVNA (*astonished*): And so you're in love with *her?*

HLESTAKOV: Decide! Is it life or death?

ANNA ANDREYEVNA: There, you see, you little fool, you see: all on your account, you rubbish, our guest was on his knees; and you had to run in like a chicken with its head off. I really ought to refuse my consent: you're unworthy such good fortune.

MARYA ANTONOVNA: I won't do it again, mamma; really, I won't do it again.

SCENE XV

The same and the CHIEF OF POLICE, *who enters out of breath*

CHIEF OF POLICE: Your Excellency, don't ruin me, don't ruin me!

HLESTAKOV: What's the matter?

CHIEF OF POLICE: The merchants have been complaining to your Excellency. I assure you on my honor that not half of what they say is true. They're the ones who cheat and overreach the people. The sergeant's widow lied to you, saying I'd flogged her; she's lying, by God, she's lying! She flogged herself.

HLESTAKOV: Damn the sergeant's widow; I've nothing to do with her!

CHIEF OF POLICE: Don't believe it, don't believe it! . . . They're all liars! Not even a baby would believe them. They're known for liars all over town. And so far as swindling goes, I venture to inform you that they are swindlers such as the earth has never produced before.

ANNA ANDREYEVNA: Do you know the honor that Ivan Alexandrovich has done us? He is asking for our daughter's hand.

CHIEF OF POLICE: What in the world! . . . You've gone crazy, my dear! Don't be angry, your Excellency; she's a little bit off, and her mother was the same.

HLESTAKOV: But I actually am asking for her hand. I'm in love.

CHIEF OF POLICE: I can't believe it, your Excellency!

ANNA ANDREYEVNA: But when you're told so!

HLESTAKOV: I'm not joking you. . . . I may go mad from love.

CHIEF OF POLICE: I don't dare believe it; I'm unworthy of such an honor.

HLESTAKOV: Yes, if you do not agree to give me Marya Antonovna's hand, then I'm ready to do the devil knows what. . . .

CHIEF OF POLICE: I can't believe it! Your Excellency is having his joke!

ANNA ANDREYEVNA: Oh, what a blockhead you are! When he's explaining it to you?

CHIEF OF POLICE: I can't believe it!

HLESTAKOV: Give her, give her to me! I'm a desperate man, ready for anything: when I shoot myself, you'll be put on trial!

CHIEF OF POLICE: Oh, my God! I'm really not to blame, in intention or in fact! Please don't be angry! Just act as your Honor wishes! My poor head, really . . . I don't know myself what's going on. I've made a bigger blockhead of myself than ever.

ANNA ANDREYEVNA: Well, give 'em your blessing!

(HLESTAKOV *approaches him with* MARYA ANTONOVNA.)

CHIEF OF POLICE: May God bless you! It's not my fault! (HLESTAKOV *kisses* MARYA ANTONOVNA. *The* CHIEF OF POLICE *watches them.*) What the devil! They really are! (*Wiping his eyes.*) They're kissing! Holy Saints, they're kissing! They're actually engaged! (*Shouting and prancing with joy.*) Hey, Anton! Hey, Anton! Aha, Police Chief! That's the way it's turned out!

SCENE XVI

The same and OSIP

OSIP: The horses are ready.

HLESTAKOV: Oh, all right. . . . In a minute.

CHIEF OF POLICE: What, sir? Are you leaving?

HLESTAKOV: Yes, I am.

CHIEF OF POLICE: But when? . . . That is . . . you hinted something about a wedding, didn't you?

HLESTAKOV: Oh, as to that . . . it's only for a minute—just a day with my uncle. He's a rich old man—and to-morrow I'll be back.

CHIEF OF POLICE: We dare not detain you and we hope for your prosperous return.

HLESTAKOV: Why, of course, of course, I'll be right back. Good-by, my love. . . . No, I simply cannot express myself! Good-by, my darling! (*He kisses her hand.*)

CHIEF OF POLICE: But don't you need anything for traveling? You were somewhat short of money, weren't you?

HLESTAKOV: Oh, no, what for? (*Upon reflection.*) However, if you wish.

CHIEF OF POLICE: How much would you like?

HLESTAKOV: Well, you gave me two hundred, that is, not two hundred, but four—I don't want to profit by your mistake—so perhaps you'd be willing to let me have as much again, to make an even eight hundred.

CHIEF OF POLICE: At once! (*He takes it from his pocketbook.*) Fortunately I have it in brand-new bills.

HLESTAKOV: Ah, yes. (*He takes the notes and looks at them.*) That's fine. They say that new notes bring good luck.

CHIEF OF POLICE: Just so, sir.

HLESTAKOV: Good-by, Anton Antonovich! I'm much obliged for your hospitality. I confess from the bottom of my heart, I've never had such a kind reception. Good-by, Anna Andreyevna! Good-by, my darling Marya Antonovna! (*They go out.*)

(*Voices behind the scenes.*)

HLESTAKOV'S *Voice:* Good-by, Marya Antonovna, my soul's angel!

Voice of the CHIEF OF POLICE: What's this? You're going by the public post?

HLESTAKOV'S *Voice:* Yes, I'm used to it. Springs give me the headache.

DRIVER'S *Voice:* Whoa!

Voice of the CHIEF OF POLICE: Then at least let me spread something on the seat: a rug, for instance. Won't you let me give you a little rug?

HLESTAKOV'S *Voice:* No, what for? That's needless; still, you might let them bring a rug.

Voice of the CHIEF OF POLICE: Hey, Avdotya! Run to the storeroom and bring out the best rug—the Persian one with the blue ground. Hurry!

DRIVER'S *Voice:* Whoa!

Voice of the CHIEF OF POLICE: When may we expect you back?

HLESTAKOV'S *Voice:* To-morrow or the day after.

OSIP'S *Voice:* Ah, is that the rug? Well, give it here; fold it like this. Now put some hay on this side.

DRIVER'S *Voice:* Whoa!

OSIP'S *Voice:* Here on this side! Here! That'll do! Good! That'll be fine. (*Slapping his hand on the rug.*) Now, sit down, your Honor!

HLESTAKOV'S *Voice:* Good-by, Anton Antonovich!

Voice of the CHIEF OF POLICE: Good-by, your Excellency!

WOMEN'S *Voices:* Good-by, Ivan Alexandrovich!

HLESTAKOV'S *Voice:* Good-by, mamma!

DRIVER'S *Voice:* Giddap, my beauties! (*The harness bells jingle; the curtain falls.*)

ACT V

The same room

SCENE I

The CHIEF OF POLICE, ANNA ANDREYEVNA, *and* MARYA ANTONOVNA

CHIEF OF POLICE: Well, Anna Andreyevna, what about it? Would you ever have expected it? What a rich prize, hang it all! Now, admit it candidly: you never even dreamed of such luck! From being a mere police chief's wife suddenly to . . . oh, the deuce! . . . to make connections with such a devil as this!

ANNA ANDREYEVNA: Not at all; I knew it all the time. It seems wonderful to you, because you're an ordinary man and have never seen decent people.

CHIEF OF POLICE: I'm a decent man myself, dear. On the other hand, really, when you think of it, Anna Andreyevna, what fine birds you and I have become! Ha, Anna Andreyevna? We'll fly high, deuce take it! Just wait, now I'll pepper those guys for presenting petitions and denunciations! Hey, who's there? (*A policeman comes in.*) Oh, it's you, Ivan Karpovich. Call the merchants in, my boy. I'll give it to them, the rascals! To complain about *me!* Nothing but a damned bunch of Jews! Just wait, sweethearts! Up to date I've merely warmed your breeches, but now I'll tan your whole hides! Write down the name of every man who came to peach on me, and, above all, the scribblers who fixed up their petitions for them. And you can announce so they'll all know it, what an honor God has bestowed on the Chief of Police, who is marrying his daughter to no ordinary man, but to one whose like can't be found on earth, a man who can do everything, everything, everything! Announce it so they'll all know it. Shout it to the whole population! Ring the bells, dammit! This is a regular holiday. (*The policeman goes out.*) That's the way, Anna

Andreyevna, huh? What'll we do now, where shall we live: here or in Petersburg?

ANNA ANDREYEVNA: In Petersburg, of course. How could we stay here!

CHIEF OF POLICE: Well, if it's to be Petersburg, so be it; but it wouldn't be so bad here. And I suppose the police business may go to hell, huh, Anna Andreyevna?

ANNA ANDREYEVNA: Of course; what's a police job!

CHIEF OF POLICE: Don't you think, Anna Andreyevna, I may now land a swell title? He's chummy with all the ministers and goes to the Palace, so he may get me promoted in time to a generalship. What do you think, Anna Andreyevna, may I get to be a general?

ANNA ANDREYEVNA: Sure, of course you may.

CHIEF OF POLICE: It's damned nice to be a general! They hang decorations across your breast! Which ribbon is better, Anna Andreyevna, the red or the blue?

ANNA ANDREYEVNA: Of course the blue is best.

CHIEF OF POLICE: Eh? So that's what you fancy. Well, the red's nice, too. Why do I want to be a general? Because if it happens that you travel anywhere, messengers and adjutants gallop ahead everywhere, shouting, "Horses!" And at the posting stations they won't give any to any one else; all have to wait: all those titular councilors, captains, police chiefs—and you don't give a snap of your fingers. You dine somewhere at a governor's, and there a police chief has to stand! He, he, he! (*He laughs himself into a perspiration.*) That's what's so attractive, damn it!

ANNA ANDREYEVNA: You always like everything vulgar. You must remember that we've got to change our whole manner of living, that your acquaintances won't be like the dog fancier Judge with whom you course hares, or like Zemlyanika; on the contrary, your acquaintances will be from the most refined society, counts and swells. . . . Though I'm really scared on your account: you'll let slip occasionally some word that simply isn't heard in polite society.

CHIEF OF POLICE: What of it? A word doesn't hurt.

ANNA ANDREYEVNA: It was all right while you were a police chief; but in Petersburg life will be quite different.

CHIEF OF POLICE: Yes; they say that there are two kinds of fish there, sea-eels and sparlings, which simply make your mouth water when you begin to eat.

ANNA ANDREYEVNA: He's always thinking about fish! I want to be sure that our house is the swellest in the capital, and I want such an odor of ambergris in my drawing-room that there'll be no going into it: you'll simply have to shut your eyes. (*She shuts her eyes and sniffs.*) Oh, how nice!

SCENE II

The same and the MERCHANTS

CHIEF OF POLICE: Ah, how are you, you flock of hawks!

MERCHANTS (*bowing*): We wish you good health, sir!

CHIEF OF POLICE: Well, darlings, how are you? How's trade, eh? What, you tea-swilling cloth-stretchers, you'll complain, will you? You arch-rascals, you dirty brutes, you swollen swindlers, you'll complain, will you? Well, did you get much? They thought they'd have me thrown in the jug! . . . Do you know, I'll swear by seven devils and one witch that . . .

ANNA ANDREYEVNA: Oh, good Heavens, Antosha, what words you use!

CHIEF OF POLICE (*greatly displeased*): Words don't matter now. Do you know that that very official to whom you complained is marrying my daughter? Do you? What d'you say now? Now I'll fix you! . . . You deceive people. . . . You make a contract with the government and swindle it out of a hundred thousand by supplying rotten cloth, and then you donate twenty yards and expect to be rewarded for it! And if they found it out, you'd catch it! . . . He struts along, belly foremost: he's a merchant; nobody must touch him! "We don't give way even to the nobility," he says. As for a nobleman . . . Bah, you pigs' mugs! . . . A nobleman studies the sciences; and if they beat him at school, it's to some purpose, so that he'll learn something useful. But what about you? You begin with rascalities, and you're beaten by the master because you don't know how to cheat. While still little brats, before you know your Lord's Prayer, you give short measure; and when you've developed a belly and lined your pockets with money, how you do put on airs! Oh, you're wonders, I'll say! Because you empty sixteen samovars a day, you put on airs, do you? I spit on you and your conceit!

MERCHANTS (*bowing*): We're at fault, Anton Antonovich!

CHIEF OF POLICE: Complain, will you? But who helped you swindle when you built the bridge and charged twenty thousand for lumber when you didn't use a hundred rubles' worth? I helped you, you old billy goat!* Have you forgotten that? If I had peached on you for that, I could have sent you to Siberia. What d'you say, ha?

ONE OF THE MERCHANTS: God knows we're guilty, Anton Antono-

*"At the date of the play, only the lower classes wore beards."—Sykes.

vich! The devil misled us. We swear never to complain again. Demand any satisfaction you please, only don't be angry!

CHIEF OF POLICE: Don't be angry! And now you're wallowing at my feet. And why? Because I've got the upper hand; but if you had even the least advantage, you scum, you'd trample me in the very mud, and roll a log over me.

MERCHANTS (*bowing to his feet*): Don't ruin us, Anton Antonovich!

CHIEF OF POLICE: "Don't ruin us!" Now it's "Don't ruin us!" But what was it before? I could . . . (*Waving his hand.*) Well, God forgive you! That'll do! I'm not vindictive; only see that you look sharp from now on! I'm not marrying my daughter to any ordinary noble: let your congratulations be . . . d'you understand? Don't try to wriggle out of it with a chunk of dried sturgeon or a loaf of sugar. . . . Now, go to the devil! (*The* MERCHANTS *go out.*)

SCENE III

The same, AMMOS FEDOROVICH, ARTEMY FILIPPOVICH, *and later* RASTAKOVSKY

AMMOS FEDOROVICH (*still in the door*): Can I believe the rumors, Anton Antonovich? Has this unusual good luck really struck you?

ARTEMY FILIPPOVICH: I have the honor to congratulate you upon your unusual good fortune. I rejoiced with all my soul when I heard about it. (*He goes to kiss* ANNA ANDREYEVNA'S *hand.*) Anna Andreyevna! (*He goes to kiss* MARYA ANTONOVNA'S *hand.*) Marya Antonovna!

RASTKOVSKY (*entering*): I congratulate Anton Antonovich! May God prolong your life and that of the new pair, and give you a numerous posterity of grandchildren and great-grandchildren! Anna Andreyevna! (*Going to kiss her hand.*) Marya Antonovna! (*Going to kiss her hand.*)

SCENE IV

The same, KOROBKIN *and his wife, and* LYULYUKOV

KOROBKIN: I have the honor to congratulate Anton Antonovich! Anna Andreyevna! (*Going to kiss her hand.*) Marya Antonovna! (*Going to kiss her hand.*)

KOROBKIN'S WIFE: I congratulate you from my soul, Anna Andreyevna, upon your new happiness!

LYULYUKOV: I have the honor to congratulate you, Anna Andreyevna. (*He goes to kiss her hand, then turning towards the spectators, he makes a clicking sound with his tongue with an air of bravado.)* Marya Antonovna, I have the honor to congratulate you! (*He goes to kiss her hand and turns to the spectators with the same bravado.*)

SCENE V

A number of guests in frock coats and swallowtails come up first to kiss the hand of ANNA ANDREYEVNA, *saying her name, then to* MARYA ANTONOVNA, *saying hers.* BOBCHINSKY *and* DOBCHINSKY *push their way forward.*

BOBCHINSKY: I have the honor to congratulate you!

DOBCHINSKY: Anton Antonovich, I have the honor to congratulate you!

BOBCHINSKY: Upon this prosperous event!

DOBCHINSKY: Anna Andreyevna!

BOBCHINSKY: Anna Andreyevna! (*Both go up to kiss her hand at the same time and knock their heads together.*)

DOBCHINSKY: Marya Antonovna! (*He goes to kiss her hand.*) I have the honor to congratulate you. You will be very, very happy; you will walk in cloth of gold and eat all sorts of delicate soups, and pass your time very entertainingly.

BOBCHINSKY (*interrupting*): Marya Antonovna, I have the honor to congratulate you! May God give you all kinds of riches and gold and a baby boy no bigger than that! (*Showing with his hand.*) So small he can sit on the palm of your hand, yes, ma'am; and all the time he'll cry wa, wa, wa!

SCENE VI

Still more guests come to kiss the ladies' hands, among them LUKA LUKICH *and his* WIFE

LUKA LUKICH: I have the honor. . . .

LUKA LUKICH'S WIFE: (*running forward*): I congratulate you, Anna Andreyevna! (*They kiss.*) I was so delighted, truly. They told me, "Anna Andreyevna is marrying off her daughter." "Oh, my goodness," I thought to myself; and I was so delighted that I said to my husband, "Listen, Luky-duky, here's a new happiness for Anna Andreyevna!" "Well," I thought, "thank God!" And I said to him, "I'm so beside myself with joy that I'm burning with impatience to declare it personally to Anna Andreyevna." . . . "Oh, good heavens!" I thought to myself, "Anna Andreyevna was just waiting for a good match for her daughter, and now see what fate has done: it has all happened exactly as she wished." And truly, I was so glad that I couldn't speak. I wept and wept; why, I fairly sobbed. Luka Lukich even said, "Nastenka, what are you sobbing about?" "Luky-duky," I said, "I don't know, myself; the tears are just flowing in a stream."

CHIEF OF POLICE: I humbly beg you to be seated, ladies and gentlemen! Hey, Mishka, bring in some more chairs here! (*The guests sit down.*)

SCENE VII

The same, the POLICE CAPTAIN, *and* SERGEANTS OF POLICE

POLICE CAPTAIN: I have the honor to congratulate you, your Honor, and to wish you prosperity and long life!

CHIEF OF POLICE: Thanks, thanks! I beg you to sit down, gentlemen! (*The guests sit down.*)

AMMOS FEDOROVICH: Now please tell us, Anton Antonovich, how all this started, the whole thing, step by step.

CHIEF OF POLICE: The course of the affair was extraordinary: he was kind enough to make the proposal in person.

ANNA ANDREYEVNA: Very respectfully, and in the most refined manner. He put everything extraordinarily well. "It's only out of respect for your virtues, Anna Andreyevna," he said. And he's such a handsome, well-bred man, of the most aristocratic manners. "Believe me, Anna Andreyevna," he said, "my life isn't worth a kopek; I'm doing this only because I respect your rare qualities."

MARYA ANTONOVNA: Why, mamma, he said that to me!

ANNA ANDREYEVNA: Stop it! You don't know anything about it. Don't mix into everything! "I'm astonished, Anna Andreyevna," he says. Then he launched forth into the most flattering words . . . and when I wanted to say, "We really don't dare hope for such an honor," he suddenly fell upon his knees and said in the most aristocratic style: "Anna Andreyevna, don't make me wretched! Please consent to reciprocate my feelings, or I shall let death end it all."

MARYA ANTONOVNA: Really, mamma, he said that about me. . . .

ANNA ANDREYEVNA: Yes, of course . . . it was about you, also. . . . I don't deny it at all.

CHIEF OF POLICE: As it was he frightened me; he said he would shoot himself. "I'll shoot myself, I'll shoot myself!" he said.

NUMEROUS GUESTS: Really, you don't say!

AMMOS FEDOROVICH: Well I declare!

LUKA LUKICH: It was surely fate that brought this to pass.

ARTEMY FILIPPOVICH: Not fate, old man, fate's too flighty a bird: his merits have done it. (*Aside.*) Luck always comes to such swine as he!

AMMOS FEDOROVICH: If you want him, I'll give you that pup you were bargaining for, Anton Antonovich.

CHIEF OF POLICE: No, I've no use for pups now.

AMMOS FEDOROVICH: Well, if you don't want him, we can agree on another dog.

KOROBKIN'S WIFE: Oh, Anna Andreyevna, how glad I am of your happiness! You simply can't imagine!

KOROBKIN: And where, if I may ask, is our eminent guest now? I heard that he had gone away for some reason.

CHIEF OF POLICE: Yes, he has left for one day, on a very important matter.

ANNA ANDREYEVNA: To see his uncle and ask his blessing.

CHIEF OF POLICE: To ask his blessing; but to-morrow . . . (*He sneezes, and is greeted by a din of good wishes.*) Thanks very much! But to-morrow he'll be back. . . . (*He sneezes again; renewed chorus of good wishes; the following people speak louder than the others.*)

POLICE CAPTAIN: We wish you good health, your Honor!

BOBCHINSKY: A hundred years and a sack of gold!

DOBCHINSKY: God prolong your days forever and ever!

ARTEMY FILIPPOVICH: May you croak!

KOROBKIN'S WIFE: The devil take you!

CHIEF OF POLICE: I humbly thank you! I wish you the same.

ANNA ANDREYEVNA: We're planning to live in Petersburg now. I confess that in this town there's an atmosphere that's too . . . well, countrified! . . . I confess it's very disagreeable. . . . And my husband—he'll be made a general there.

CHIEF OF POLICE: Yes, and I admit, ladies and gentlemen, deuce take it, that I'd like awfully to be a general.

LUKA LUKICH: God grant you may be!

RASTAKOVSKY: What is impossible for man is possible for God.

AMMOS FEDOROVICH: A big ship travels far.*

ARTEMY FILIPPOVICH: Your merits deserve the honor.

AMMOS FEDOROVICH (*aside*): That will be the limit, if they actually make him a general! A generalship will suit him like a saddle on a cow! But no, it's a far cry from this to that. There are men here more respectable than you that aren't generals yet.

ARTEMY FILIPPOVICH (*aside*): And so he's crawling into a general's boots! What the devil! But there's no telling; he may get to be a

* "Russian proverb."—Sykes.

general. The devil knows he's got conceit enough for it. (*Turning to him.*) Don't forget us then, Anton Antonovich.

AMMOS FEDOROVICH: And if anything should happen—for instance, some emergency in our affairs—don't deny us your patronage!

KOROBKIN: Next year I shall take my son to the capital to enter the government service. Please do us the favor to grant him your protection; be like a father to an orphan child.

CHIEF OF POLICE: I'm quite ready, for my part, to do what I can.

ANNA ANDREYEVNA: Antosha, you're always ready to make promises. In the first place, you'll have no time to think about that. How can you, and why should you, burden yourself with such promises?

CHIEF OF POLICE: Why not, my dear? Sometimes one can do something.

ANNA ANDREYEVNA: Of course one can; but one can't patronize all the small fry.

KOROBKIN'S WIFE: Do you hear how she's treating us?

A WOMAN GUEST: Yes, she was always like that. I know her. Let her sit at the table and she'll put her feet on it.*

SCENE VIII

The same and the POSTMASTER, *who enters out of breath, with an unsealed letter in his hand*

POSTMASTER: An astonishing thing, ladies and gentlemen! The official whom we took to be the government inspector, was not the inspector at all.

ALL: What—not the inspector?

POSTMASTER: Absolutely not; I've learned from this letter.

CHIEF OF POLICE: What's that? What's that? From what letter?

POSTMASTER: Why, from his own letter. They brought me a letter to the post office. I glanced at the address and saw, "Post Office Street." I was stupefied. "Well," I thought to myself, "he's surely found some irregularity in the post office and is notifying the authorities." So I took and opened it.

CHIEF OF POLICE: How did you dare?

POSTMASTER: I don't know; some supernatural power inspired me. I was about to call a messenger to dispatch it by express; but such curiosity as I have never felt before overcame me. I couldn't let it go; I simply couldn't! I was just drawn to open it. In one ear I seemed to hear, "Don't unseal it! You'll croak on the spot!" But in the other some demon kept whispering, "Open it, open it, open it!" And when I

* "Russian proverb."—Sykes.

pressed the wax, a fire ran through my veins; and when I unsealed it, I was frozen, by Heaven I was. My hands shook, and all went black before my eyes.

CHIEF OF POLICE: But how did you dare open the letter of such an august emissary?

POSTMASTER: But that's just the point; he ain't an emissary and he ain't august!

CHIEF OF POLICE: Well, what do you think he *is?*

POSTMASTER: A mere nobody; the devil knows what he is.

CHIEF OF POLICE (*testily*): What do you mean? How dare you call him a nobody and the devil knows who? I'll have you arrested!

POSTMASTER: Who? You?

CHIEF OF POLICE: Yes, I!

POSTMASTER: You ain't the size!

CHIEF OF POLICE: Don't you know that he is marrying my daughter, that I'm to be a dignitary myself, and that I can bundle you off to Siberia?

POSTMASTER: Oh, Anton Antonovich! What's Siberia? Siberia's far away. I'd better read you the letter. Ladies and gentlemen, shall I read the letter?

ALL: Read it, read it!

POSTMASTER (*reading*): "I hasten to inform you, my dear Tryapichkin, what wonders are happening to me. On the road I was cleaned out by an infantry captain, with the result that the innkeeper was going to have me jailed. Then all of a sudden, because of my Petersburg countenance and clothes, the whole town took me for a Governor-General. And now I'm living at the Police Chief's, enjoying myself, and flirting desperately with his wife and daughter. I haven't yet decided which one to begin with—I think the mother, because she seems to be ready to go the limit. Do you remember how hard up we used to be, and dined by being foxy; and how once a confectioner grabbed me by the collar because of some pastry we had eaten, telling him to charge it to the King of England? Now it's the other way round. Everybody lends me money, all I want. They're terrific freaks: you'd die laughing at them. I know you write articles; stick them in your contributions. In the first place, there's the Police Chief, as stupid as a gray jackass. . . ."

CHIEF OF POLICE: It can't be! It isn't there!

POSTMASTER (*showing the letter*): Read it yourself.

CHIEF OF POLICE (*reading*): "As a gray jackass." It can't be! You wrote that yourself!

POSTMASTER: How was I to write it?

ARTEMY FILIPPOVICH: Read it!

LUKA LUKICH: Read it!

POSTMASTER (*continuing his reading*): "the Police Chief—as stupid as a gray jackass. . . ."

CHIEF OF POLICE: "Oh, damn you! Do you have to repeat it? As if we didn't know it was there!

POSTMASTER (*continuing his reading*): Hm . . . hm . . . hm . . . hm . . . "a gray jackass. The Postmaster is also a nice chap. . . ." (*Stopping.*) Well, then he goes on to express himself rather indecently about me.

CHIEF OF POLICE: No, read it!

POSTMASTER: What for?

CHIEF OF POLICE: What the devil! If you're reading it, read it! Read it all!

ARTEMY FILIPPOVICH: Here, just let me read it. (*Putting on his spectacles and reading.*) "The Postmaster is the exact image of our department janitor, Mikheyev; and the rascal must be just such another old soak."

POSTMASTER (*to the spectators*): Well, he's a contemptible brat who needs a hiding; that's all!

ARTEMY FILIPPOVICH (*continuing*): "The Supervisor of Charitable Insti . . . tu . . . tu . . ." (*He begins to stammer.*)

KOROBKIN: Why are you stopping?

ARTEMY FILIPPOVICH: The writing is illegible . . . however, I can see he's a scamp.

KOROBKIN: Give it to me! I think I have better eyes. (*Taking hold of the letter.*)

ARTEMY FILIPPOVICH (*holding on to it*): No, we can skip that part; further on one can make it out.

KOROBKIN: Come on, I can do it.

ARTEMY FILIPPOVICH: If it has to be read, I'll do it myself: further on, really, it's quite legible.

POSTMASTER: No, read it all! So far everything has been read.

ALL: Give him the letter, Artemy Filippovich, give him the letter! (*To* KOROBKIN.) Read it!

ARTEMY FILIPPOVICH: All right. (*Giving the letter.*) Here, if you please . . . (*Covering part with his finger.*) Read from here on. (*All gather around him.*)

POSTMASTER: Read it, read it! Nonsense! Read it all!

KOROBKIN (*reading*): "The Supervisor of Charitable Institutions, Zemlyanika, is a regular pig in a nightcap."

ARTEMY FILIPPOVICH (*to the* SPECTATORS): It isn't even witty! A pig in a nightcap! When did a pig ever have a nightcap?

KOROBKIN (*continuing*): "The Superintendent of Schools reeks of onions from head to foot."

LUKA LUKICH (*to the* SPECTATORS): By God, I never had an onion in my mouth!

AMMOS FEDOROVICH (*aside*): Thank God, at least there's nothing about me!

KOROBKIN (*reading*): "The Judge . . ."

AMMOS FEDOROVICH: Now I'll catch it! . . . (*Aloud.*) Ladies and gentlemen, I think the letter's rather long. Devil take it, why read such trash?

LUKA LUKICH: No!

POSTMASTER: No, read it!

ARTEMY FILIPPOVICH: No, just read it!

KOROBKIN (*continuing*): "The Judge, Lyapkin-Tyapkin, is *movay tone* in the highest degree. . . ." (*Stopping.*) That must be a French word.

AMMOS FEDOROVICH: The devil knows what it means! It's all right if it's nothing but swindler, but it may mean something worse!

KOROBKIN (*continuing*): "But after all they're a hospitable and kind-hearted lot. Good-by, my dear Tryapichkin. I myself, following your example, want to become a writer. It's a bore to live like this, my boy; one needs food for one's soul. I see that exactly what I need is something lofty to occupy me. Write to me in Saratov Province, to the village of Podkatilovka." (*He turns over the letter and reads the address.*) "To Ivan Vasilyevich Tryapichkin, Esquire, Third Floor, Number Ninety-seven, turning to the right from the yard entrance, Post Office Street, St. Petersburg."

ONE OF THE LADIES: What an unexpected setback!

CHIEF OF POLICE: He's as good as cut my throat! I'm killed. I'm simply killed dead. I can see absolutely nothing in front of me but pigs' snouts instead of faces. . . . Get him back, get him back! (*He waves his arm.*)

POSTMASTER: How can we get him back? It's just my luck to have ordered the superintendent to give him the fastest horses; and the devil put me up to sending similar orders ahead.

KOROBKIN'S WIFE: This is certainly confusion worse confounded!

AMMOS FEDOROVICH: But, damn it, gentlemen, he borrowed three hundred rubles from me!

ARTEMY FILIPPOVICH: Three hundred from me, too.

POSTMASTER (*sighing*): Oh, and three hundred from me!

BOBCHINSKY: And from me and Petr Ivanovich, sixty-five, sir, in notes, yes, sir!

AMMOS FEDOROVICH (*shrugging his shoulders in perplexity*): How did this happen, gentlemen? How in the world did we make such a mistake?

CHIEF OF POLICE (*striking his brow*): How could I, how could I, old blockhead that I am! Stupid old ram! I've outlived my good sense! . . . Thirty years I've been in the service; not a merchant, not a contractor has been able to impose on me; I've fooled swindlers upon swindlers; sharpers and rascals who could fool the whole world I have hooked neatly! I've bamboozled three governors! . . . What are governors! (*Waving his hand.*) Governors aren't worth mentioning!

ANNA ANDREYEVNA: But this can't be, Antosha; he's betrothed to Mashenka.

CHIEF OF POLICE (*angrily*): Betrothed! A cat and a fiddle! Betrothed indeed! She dares to throw the engagement in my face! . . . (*In desperation.*) Here, just look—all the world, all Christianity, all of you—just see how the Police Chief has made a fool of himself! Blockhead that he is! the old blockhead, the old scoundrel! (*Threatening himself with his fist.*) Oh, you thick-nosed imbecile! To take a lounge-lizard, a rag, for a man of importance! And there he skims along the road with his bells jingling! He'll spread the story all over the earth! And I'll not only be a laughingstock, but some quill-driver, some paper-spoiler will be found to put me in a comedy! That's what hurts! He won't spare my rank or my calling; and they'll all show their teeth in a grin and clap their hands. What are you laughing at? You're laughing at yourselves! . . . Damn you! . . . (*He stamps on the floor in his rage.*) I'd like to do the same to all scribblers! Bah, you quill-drivers, you damned Liberals! You devil's brood! I'd like to tie you all in a knot and grind you to powder, and ram you into the devil's cap! . . . (*He strikes out with his fist and stamps on the floor. After a brief silence.*) I simply can't get over it. Indeed it's true that when God wants to punish a man, he takes away his reason first. Now, what was there in that weathercock like a government inspector? Absolutely nothing! Not even half a finger's length of resemblance; but suddenly everybody shouts, "The inspector, the government inspector!" Now, who was the first to let out the notion that he was the government inspector? Speak up!

ARTEMY FILIPPOVICH (*shrugging his shoulders*): I couldn't tell you how it happened if my life depended on it! It's as if a fog had descended upon us and the devil had misled us.

AMMOS FEDOROVICH: Who started it? There's who: those two smart Alecks! (*Pointing to* DOBCHINSKY *and* BOBCHINSKY.)

BOBCHINSKY: Not at all! Not me! I never even thought . . .

DOBCHINSKY: I didn't do anything, absolutely not . . .

ARTEMY FILIPPOVICH: Of course you did.

LUKA LUKICH: It stands to reason. They ran in from the tavern like two lunatics, yelling: "He's come! He's come! and he doesn't pay anything! . . ." They found a rare bird!

CHIEF OF POLICE: Naturally, it was you. You town scandal-mongers, you damned liars!

ARTEMY FILIPPOVICH: May the devil take you with your inspectors and your yarns!

CHIEF OF POLICE: You just snoop about the town and mess things up, you damned chatterboxes! You scatter scandals, you bobtailed magpies!

AMMOS FEDOROVICH: You damned bunglers!

LUKA LUKICH: Dunces!

ARTEMY FILIPPOVICH: Pot-bellied little shrimps! (*They all surround them.*)

BOBCHINSKY: By God, it wasn't I, it was Petr Ivanovich!

DOBCHINSKY: It was not, Petr Ivanovich, you said it first. . . .

BOBCHINSKY: Certainly not; you were the first yourself.

LAST SCENE

The same and a GENDARME

GENDARME: The official who has come from Petersburg by imperial order demands your instant appearance before him. He is stopping at the inn.

(*The words just pronounced strike all like a thunderbolt. A sound of astonishment escapes from the lips of all the ladies at once; the whole group, having suddenly changed its position, remains as if petrified.*)

DUMB SHOW

The CHIEF OF POLICE *stands in the midst like a post, his arms outspread and his head tilted backwards; on the right his wife and his daughter appear on the verge of rushing towards him; beyond them the* POSTMASTER, *transformed into a question mark, is turned towards the spectators; beyond him* LUKA LUKICH, *in the most innocent bewilderment; beyond him, at the very edge of the scene, three lady guests are leaning towards each other with the most sarcastic expressions of countenance, aimed directly at the* POLICE CHIEF'S FAMILY. *On the* POLICE CHIEF'S *left stands* ZEMLYANIKA, *his head inclined somewhat to one side, as if he were listening to something; beyond him the* JUDGE, *with outspread arms, almost squatting on the floor, and making movements of the lips as if about to whistle or say, "So you see what you've come to, old lady!" Beyond him is* KOROBKIN, *turned towards the spectators, with one eye cocked and a derisive gesture toward the* CHIEF

OF POLICE; *beyond him, on the extreme side,* DOBCHINSKY *and* BOBCHINSKY *make movements of their hands towards each other, their mouths open, and regarding each other with bulging eyes. The other guests simply stand like statues. For nearly a minute and a half the group remains in this position.*)

THE CURTAIN FALLS

The Lower Depths

Cast of Characters

MIKHAIL IVANOFF KOSTILYOFF, *keeper of a night lodging.*
VASSILISA KARPOVNA, *his wife.*
NATASHA, *her sister.*
MIEDVIEDIEFF, *her uncle, a policeman.*
VASKA PEPEL, *a young thief.*
ANDREI MITRITCH KLESHTCH, *a locksmith.*
ANNA, *his wife.*
NASTYA, *a street-walker.*
KVASHNYA, *a vendor of meat-pies.*
BUBNOFF, *a cap-maker.*
THE BARON.
SATINE.
THE ACTOR.
LUKA, *a pilgrim.*
ALYOSHKA, *a shoemaker.*
KRIVOY ZOB } *Porters.*
THE TARTAR }
NIGHT LODGERS, TRAMPS AND OTHERS.

The action takes place in a night lodging and in "The Waste," an area in its rear.

Act I

A cellar resembling a cave. The ceiling, which merges into stone walls, is low and grimy, and the plaster and paint are peeling off. There is a window, high up on the right wall, from which comes the light. The right corner, which constitutes Pepel's room, is partitioned off by thin boards. Close to the corner of this room is Bubnoff's wooden bunk. In the left corner stands a large Russian stove. In the stone wall, left, is a door leading to the kitchen where live Kvashnya, the Baron, and Nastya. Against the wall, between the stove and the door, is a large bed covered with dirty chintz. Bunks line the walls. In the foreground, by the left wall, is a block of wood with a vise and a small anvil fastened to it, and another smaller block of wood somewhat further towards the back. Kleshtch is seated on the smaller block, trying keys into old locks. At his feet are two large bundles of various keys, wired together, also a battered tin samovar, a hammer, and pincers. In the centre are a large table, two benches, and a stool, all of which are of dirty, unpainted wood. Behind the table Kvashnya is busying herself with the samovar. The Baron sits chewing a piece of black bread, and Nastya occupies the stool, leans her elbows on the table, and reads a tattered book. In the bed, behind curtains, Anna lies coughing. Bubnoff is seated on his bunk, attempting to shape a pair of old trousers with the help of an ancient hat shape, which he holds between his knees. Scattered about him are pieces of buckram, oilcloth, and rags. Satine, just awakened, lies in his bunk, grunting. On top of the stove, the Actor, invisible to the audience, tosses about and coughs.
It is an early spring morning.

THE BARON. And then?

KVASHNYA. No, my dear, said I, keep away from me with such proposals. I've been through it all, you see—and not for a hundred baked lobsters would I marry again!

BUBNOFF [*to* SATINE]. What are you grunting about? [SATINE *keeps on grunting*]

KVASHNYA. Why should I, said I, a free woman, my own mistress, enter my name into somebody else's passport and sell myself into slavery—no! Why—I wouldn't marry a man even if he were an American prince!

KLESHTCH. You lie!

KVASHNYA. Wha-at?

KLESHTCH. You lie! You're going to marry Abramka. . . .

THE BARON [*snatching the book out of* NASTYA'S *hand and reading the title*]. "Fatal Love" . . . [*Laughs*]

NASTYA [*stretching out her hand*]. Give it back—give it back! Stop fooling!

[THE BARON *looks at her and waves the book in the air.*]

KVASHNYA [*to* KLESHTCH]. You crimson goat, you—calling me a liar! How dare you be so rude to me?

THE BARON [*hitting* NASTYA *on the head with the book*]. Nastya, you little fool!

NASTYA [*reaching for the book*]. Give it back!

KLESHTCH. Oh—what a great lady . . . but you'll marry Abramka just the same—that's all you're waiting for . . .

KVASHNYA. Sure! Anything else? You nearly beat your wife to death!

KLESHTCH. Shut up, you old bitch! It's none of your business!

KVASHNYA. Ho-ho! can't stand the truth, can you?

THE BARON. They're off again! Nastya, where are you?

NASTYA [*without lifting her head*]. Hey—go away!

ANNA [*putting her head through the curtains*]. The day has started. For God's sake, don't row!

KLESHTCH. Whining again!

ANNA. Every blessed day . . . let me die in peace, can't you?

BUBNOFF. Noise won't keep you from dying.

KVASHNYA [*walking up to* ANNA]. Little mother, how did you ever manage to live with this wretch?

ANNA. Leave me alone—get away from me. . . .

KVASHNYA. Well, well! You poor soul . . . how's the pain in the chest—any better?

THE BARON. Kvashnya! Time to go to market. . . .

KVASHNYA. We'll go presently. [*To* ANNA] Like some hot dumplings?

ANNA. No, thanks. Why should I eat?

KVASHNYA. You must eat. Hot food—good for you! I'll leave you some in a cup. Eat them when you feel like it. Come on, sir! [*To* KLESHTCH] You evil spirit! [*Goes into kitchen*]

ANNA [*coughing*]. Lord, Lord . . .

THE BARON [*painfully pushing forward* NASTYA'S *head*]. Throw it away—little fool!

NASTYA [*muttering*]. Leave me alone—I don't bother you . . .

[THE BARON *follows* KVASHNYA, *whistling.*]

SATINE [*sitting up in his bunk*]. Who beat me up yesterday?

BUBNOFF. Does it make any difference who?

SATINE. Suppose they did—but why did they?

BUBNOFF. Were you playing cards?

SATINE. Yes!

BUBNOFF. That's why they beat you.

SATINE. Scoundrels!

THE ACTOR [*raising his head from the top of the stove*]. One of these days they'll beat you to death!

SATINE. You're a jackass!

THE ACTOR. Why?

SATINE. Because a man can die only once!

THE ACTOR [*after a silence*]. I don't understand—

KLESHTCH. Say! You crawl from that stove—and start cleaning house! Don't play the delicate primrose!

THE ACTOR. None of your business!

KLESHTCH. Wait till Vassilisa comes—she'll show you whose business it is!

THE ACTOR. To hell with Vassilisa! To-day is the Baron's turn to clean. . . . Baron!

[THE BARON *comes from the kitchen.*]

THE BARON. I've no time to clean . . . I'm going to market with Kvashnya.

THE ACTOR. That doesn't concern me. Go to the gallows if you like. It's your turn to sweep the floor just the same—I'm not going to do other people's work . . .

THE BARON. Go to blazes! Nastya will do it. Hey there—fatal love! Wake up! [*Takes the book away from* NASTYA]

NASTYA [*getting up*]. What do you want? Give it back to me! You scoundrel! And that's a nobleman for you!

THE BARON [*returning the book to her*]. Nastya! Sweep the floor for me—will you?

NASTYA [*goes to kitchen*]. Not so's you'll notice it!

KVASHNYA [*to* THE BARON *through kitchen door*]. Come on—you!

They don't need you! Actor! You were asked to do it, and now you go ahead and attend to it—it won't kill you . . .

THE ACTOR. It's always I . . . I don't understand why. . . .

[THE BARON *comes from the kitchen, across his shoulders a wooden beam from which hang earthen pots covered with rags.*]

THE BARON. Heavier than ever!

SATINE. It paid you to be born a Baron, eh?

KVASHNYA [*to* ACTOR]. See to it that you sweep up! [*Crosses to outer door, letting* THE BARON *pass ahead*]

THE ACTOR [*climbing down from the stove*]. It's bad for me to inhale dust. [*With pride*] My organism is poisoned with alcohol. [*Sits down on a bunk, meditating*]

SATINE. Organism—organon. . . .

ANNA. Andrei Mitritch. . . .

KLESHTCH. What now?

ANNA. Kvashnya left me some dumplings over there—you eat them!

KLESHTCH [*coming over to her*]. And you—don't you want any?

ANNA. No. Why should I eat? You're a workman—you need it.

KLESHTCH. Frightened, are you? Don't be! You'll get all right!

ANNA. Go and eat! It's hard on me. . . . I suppose very soon . . .

KLESHTCH [*walking away*]. Never mind—maybe you'll get well—you can never tell! [*Goes into kitchen*]

THE ACTOR [*loud, as if he had suddenly awakened*]. Yesterday the doctor in the hospital said to me: "Your organism," he said, "is entirely poisoned with alcohol . . ."

SATINE [*smiling*]. Organon . . .

THE ACTOR [*stubbornly*]. Not organon—organism!

SATINE. Sibylline. . . .

THE ACTOR [*shaking his fist at him*]. Nonsense! I'm telling you seriously . . . if the organism is poisoned . . . that means it's bad for me to sweep the floor—to inhale the dust . . .

SATINE. Macrobistic . . . hah!

BUBNOFF. What are you muttering?

SATINE. Words—and here's another one for you—transcendentalistic . . .

BUBNOFF. What does it mean?

SATINE. Don't know—I forgot . . .

BUBNOFF. Then why did you say it?

SATINE. Just so! I'm bored, brother, with human words—all our words. Bored! I've heard each one of them a thousand times surely.

THE ACTOR. In Hamlet they say: "Words, words, words!" It's a good play. I played the grave-digger in it once. . . .

[KLESHTCH *comes from the kitchen.*]

KLESHTCH. Will you start playing with the broom?

THE ACTOR. None of your business. [*Striking his chest*] Ophelia! O—remember me in thy prayers!

[*Backstage is heard a dull murmur, cries, and a police whistle.* KLESHTCH *sits down to work, filing screechily.*]

SATINE. I love unintelligible, obsolete words. When I was a youngster—and worked as a telegraph operator—I read heaps of books. . . .

BUBNOFF. Were you really a telegrapher?

SATINE. I was. There are some excellent books—and lots of curious words . . . Once I was an educated man, do you know?

BUBNOFF. I've heard it a hundred times. Well, so you were! That isn't very important! Me—well—once I was a furrier. I had my own shop—what with dyeing the fur all day long, my arms were yellow up to the elbows, brother. I thought I'd never be able ever to get clean again—that I'd go to my grave, all yellow! But look at my hands now—they're plain dirty—that's what!

SATINE. Well, and what then?

BUBNOFF. That's all!

SATINE. What are you trying to prove?

BUBNOFF. Oh, well—just matching thoughts—no matter how much dye you get on yourself, it all comes off in the end—yes, yes—

SATINE. Oh—my bones ache!

THE ACTOR [*sits, nursing his knees*]. Education is all rot. Talent is the thing. I knew an actor—who read his parts by heart, syllable by syllable—but he played heroes in a way that . . . why—the whole theatre would rock with ecstasy!

SATINE. Bubnoff, give me five kopecks.

BUBNOFF. I only have two—

THE ACTOR. I say—talent, that's what you need to play heroes. And talent is nothing but faith in yourself, in your own powers—

SATINE. Give me five kopecks and I'll have faith that you're a hero, a crocodile, or a police inspector—Kleshtch, give me five kopecks.

KLESHTCH. Go to hell! All of you!

SATINE. What are you cursing for? I know you haven't a kopeck in the world!

ANNA. Andrei Mitritch—I'm suffocating—I can't breathe—

KLESHTCH. What shall I do?

BUBNOFF. Open the door into the hall.

KLESHTCH. All right. You're sitting on the bunk, I on the floor. You change places with me, and I'll let you open the door. I have a cold as it is.

BUBNOFF [*unconcernedly*]. I don't care if you open the door—it's your wife who's asking—

KLESHTCH [*morosely*]. I don't care who's asking—

SATINE. My head buzzes—ah—why do people have to hit each other over the heads?

BUBNOFF. They don't only hit you over the head, but over the rest of the body as well. [*Rises*] I must go and buy some thread—our bosses are late to-day—seems as if they've croaked. [*Exits*]

[ANNA *coughs;* SATINE *is lying down motionless, his hands folded behind his head.*]

THE ACTOR [*looks about him morosely, then goes to* ANNA]. Feeling bad, eh?

ANNA. I'm choking—

THE ACTOR. If you wish, I'll take you into the hallway. Get up, then, come! [*He helps her to rise, wraps some sort of a rag about her shoulders, and supports her toward the hall*] It isn't easy. I'm sick myself—poisoned with alcohol . . .

[KOSTILYOFF *appears in the doorway.*]

KOSTILYOFF. Going for a stroll? What a nice couple—the gallant cavalier and the lady fair!

THE ACTOR. Step aside, you—don't you see that we're invalids?

KOSTILYOFF. Pass on, please! [*Hums a religious tune, glances about him suspiciously, and bends his head to the left as if listening to what is happening in* PEPEL'*s room.* KLESHTCH *is jangling his keys and scraping away with his file, and looks askance at the other*] Filing?

KLESHTCH. What?

KOSTILYOFF. I say, are you filing? [*Pause*] What did I want to ask? [*Quick and low*] Hasn't my wife been here?

KLESHTCH. I didn't see her.

KOSTILYOFF [*carefully moving toward* PEPEL'*s room*]. You take up a whole lot of room for your two rubles a month. The bed—and your bench—yes—you take up five rubles' worth of space, so help me God! I'll have to put another half ruble to your rent—

KLESHTCH. You'll put a noose around my neck and choke me . . . you'll croak soon enough, and still all you think of is half rubles—

KOSTILYOFF. Why should I choke you? What would be the use? God be with you—live and prosper! But I'll have to raise you half a ruble—I'll buy oil for the ikon lamp, and my offering will atone for my sins, and for yours as well. You don't think much of your sins—not much! Oh, Andrushka, you're a wicked man! Your wife is dying because of your wickedness—no one loves you, no one respects you—your work is squeaky, jarring on every one.

KLESHTCH [*shouts*]. What do you come here for—just to annoy me?

[SATINE *grunts loudly.*]

KOSTILYOFF [*with a start*]. God, what a noise!

[THE ACTOR *enters.*]

THE ACTOR. I've put her down in the hall and wrapped her up.

KOSTILYOFF. You're a kindly fellow. That's good. Some day you'll be rewarded for it.

THE ACTOR. When?

KOSTILYOFF. In the Beyond, little brother—there all our deeds will be reckoned up.

THE ACTOR. Suppose you reward me right now?

KOSTILYOFF. How can I do that?

THE ACTOR. Wipe out half my debt.

KOSTILYOFF. He-ho! You're always jesting, darling—always poking fun . . . can kindliness of heart be repaid with gold? Kindliness—it's above all other qualities. But your debt to me—remains a debt. And so you'll have to pay me back. You ought to be kind to me, an old man, without seeking for reward!

THE ACTOR. You're a swindler, old man! [*Goes into kitchen*]

[KLESHTCH *rises and goes into the hall.*]

KOSTILYOFF [*to* SATINE]. See that squeaker—? He ran away—he doesn't like me!

SATINE. Does anybody like you besides the Devil?

KOSTILYOFF [*laughing*]. Oh—you're so quarrelsome! But I like you all—I understand you all, my unfortunate down-trodden, useless brethren . . . [*Suddenly, rapidly*] Is Vaska home?

SATINE. See for yourself—

KOSTILYOFF [*goes to the door and knocks*]. Vaska!

[THE ACTOR *appears at the kitchen door, chewing something.*]

PEPEL. Who is it?

KOSTILYOFF. It's I—I, Vaska!

PEPEL. What do you want?

KOSTILYOFF [*stepping aside*]. Open!

SATINE [*without looking at* KOSTILYOFF]. He'll open—and she's there—

[THE ACTOR *makes a grimace.*]

KOSTILYOFF [*in a low, anxious tone*]. Eh? Who's there? What?

SATINE. Speaking to me?

KOSTILYOFF. What did you say?

SATINE. Oh—nothing—I was just talking to myself—

KOSTILYOFF. Take care, brother. Don't carry your joking too far! [*Knocks loudly at door*] Vassily!

PEPEL [*opening door*]. Well? What are you disturbing me for?

KOSTILYOFF [*peering into room*]. I—you see—

PEPEL. Did you bring the money?

KOSTILYOFF. I've something to tell you—

PEPEL. Did you bring the money?

KOSTILYOFF. What money? Wait—

PEPEL. Why—the seven rubles for the watch—well?

KOSTILYOFF. What watch, Vaska? Oh, you—

PEPEL. Look here. Yesterday, before witnesses, I sold you a watch for ten rubles, you gave me three—now let me have the other seven. What are you blinking for? You hang around here—you disturb people—and don't seem to know yourself what you're after.

KOSTILYOFF. Sh-sh! Don't be angry, Vaska. The watch—it is—

SATINE. Stolen!

KOSTILYOFF [*sternly*]. I do not accept stolen goods—how can you imagine—

PEPEL [*taking him by the shoulder*]. What did you disturb me for? What do you want?

KOSTILYOFF. I don't want—anything. I'll go—if you're in such a state—

PEPEL. Be off, and bring the money!

KOSTILYOFF. What ruffians! I—I—[*Exits*]

THE ACTOR. What a farce!

SATINE. That's fine—I like it.

PEPEL. What did he come here for?

SATINE [*laughing*]. Don't you understand? He's looking for his wife. Why don't you beat him up once and for all, Vaska?

PEPEL. Why should I let such trash interfere with my life?

SATINE. Show some brains! And then you can marry Vassilisa—and become our boss—

PEPEL. Heavenly bliss! And you'd smash up my household and, because I'm a soft-hearted fool, you'll drink up everything I possess. [*Sits on a bunk*] Old devil—woke me up—I was having such a pleasant dream. I dreamed I was fishing—and I caught an enormous trout—such a trout as you only see in dreams! I was playing him—and I was so afraid the line would snap. I had just got out the gaff—and I thought to myself—in a moment—

SATINE. It wasn't a trout, it was Vassilisa—

THE ACTOR. He caught Vassilisa a long time ago.

PEPEL [*angrily*]. You can all go to the devil—and Vassilisa with you—

[KLESHTCH *comes from the hall.*]

KLESHTCH. Devilishly cold!

THE ACTOR. Why didn't you bring Anna back? She'll freeze, out there—

KLESHTCH. Natasha took her into the kitchen—

THE ACTOR. The old man will kick her out—

KLESHTCH [*sitting down to his work*]. Well—Natasha will bring her in here—

SATINE. Vassily—give me five kopecks!

THE ACTOR [*to* SATINE]. Oh, you—always five kopecks—Vassya—give us twenty kopecks—

PEPEL. I'd better give it to them now before they ask for a ruble. Here you are!

SATINE. Gibraltar! There are no kindlier people in the world than thieves!

KLESHTCH [*morosely*]. They earn their money easily—they don't work—

SATINE. Many earn it easily, but not many part with it so easily. Work? Make work pleasant—and maybe I'll work too. Yes—maybe. When work's a pleasure, life's, too. When it's toil, then life is a drudge. [*To* THE ACTOR] You, Sardanapalus! Come on!

THE ACTOR. Let's go, Nebuchadnezzar! I'll get as drunk as forty thousand topers!

[*They leave.*]

PEPEL [*yawning*]. Well, how's your wife?

KLESHTCH. It seems as if soon—[*Pause*]

PEPEL. Now I look at you—seems to me all that filing and scraping of yours is useless.

KLESHTCH. Well—what else can I do?

PEPEL. Nothing.

KLESHTCH. How can I live?

PEPEL. People manage, somehow.

KLESHTCH. Them? Call them people? Muck and dregs—that's

what they are! I'm a workman—I'm ashamed even to look at them. I've slaved since I was a child. . . . D'you think I shan't be able to tear myself away from here? I'll crawl out of here, even if I have to leave my skin behind—but crawl out I will! Just wait . . . my wife'll die . . . I've lived here six months, and it seems like six years.

PEPEL. Nobody here's any worse off than you . . . say what you like . . .

KLESHTCH. No worse is right. They've neither honor nor conscience.

PEPEL [*indifferently*]. What good does it do—honor or conscience? Can you get them on their feet instead of on their uppers—through honor and conscience? Honor and conscience are needed only by those who have power and energy . . .

BUBNOFF [*coming back*]. Oh—I'm frozen . . .

PEPEL. Bubnoff! Got a conscience?

BUBNOFF. What? A conscience?

PEPEL. Exactly!

BUBNOFF. What do I need a conscience for? I'm not rich.

PEPEL. Just what I said: honor and conscience are for the rich—right! And Kleshtch is upbraiding us because we haven't any!

BUBNOFF. Why—did he want to borrow some of it?

PEPEL. No—he has plenty of his own . . .

BUBNOFF. Oh—are you selling it? You won't sell much around here. But if you had some old boxes, I'd buy them—on credit . . .

PEPEL [*didactically*]. You're a jackass, Andrushka! On the subject of conscience you ought to hear Satine—or the Baron . . .

KLESHTCH. I've nothing to talk to them about!

PEPEL. They have more brains than you—even if they're drunkards . . .

BUBNOFF. He who can be drunk and wise at the same time is doubly blessed . . .

PEPEL. Satine says every man expects his neighbor to have a conscience, but—you see—it isn't to any one's advantage to have one—that's a fact.

[NATASHA *enters, followed by* LUKA *who carries a stick in his hand, a bundle on his back, a kettle and a teapot slung from his belt.*]

LUKA. How are you, honest folks?

PEPEL [*twisting his mustache*]. Aha—Natasha!

BUBNOFF [*to* LUKA]. I was honest—up to spring before last.

NATASHA. Here's a new lodger . . .

LUKA. Oh, it's all the same to me. Crooks—I don't mind them, either. For my part there's no bad flea—they're all black—and they all jump . . . Well, dearie, show me where I can stow myself.

NATASHA [*pointing to kitchen door*]. Go in there, grand-dad.

LUKA. Thanks, girlie! One place is like another—as long as an old fellow keeps warm, he keeps happy . . .

PEPEL. What an amusing old codger you brought in, Natasha!

NATASHA. A hanged sight more interesting than you! . . . Andrei, your wife's in the kitchen with us—come and fetch her after a while . . .

KLESHTCH. All right—I will . . .

NATASHA. And be a little more kind to her—you know she won't last much longer.

KLESHTCH. I know . . .

NATASHA. Knowing won't do any good—it's terrible—dying—don't you understand?

PEPEL. Well—look at me—I'm not afraid . . .

NATASHA. Oh—you're a wonder, aren't you?

BUBNOFF [*whistling*]. Oh—this thread's rotten . . .

PEPEL. Honestly, I'm not afraid! I'm ready to die right now. Knife me to the heart—and I'll die without making a sound . . . even gladly—from such a pure hand . . .

NATASHA [*going out*]. Spin that yarn for some one else!

BUBNOFF. Oh—that thread is rotten—rotten—

NATASHA [*at hallway door*]. Don't forget your wife, Andrei!

KLESHTCH. All right.

PEPEL. She's a wonderful girl!

BUBNOFF. She's all right.

PEPEL. What makes her so curt with me? Anyway—she'll come to no good here . . .

BUBNOFF. Through you—sure!

PEPEL. Why through me? I feel sorry for her . . .

BUBNOFF. As the wolf for the lamb!

PEPEL. You lie! I feel very sorry for her . . . very . . . very sorry! She has a tough life here—I can see that . . .

KLESHTCH. Just wait till Vassilisa catches you talking to her!

BUBNOFF. Vassilisa? She won't give up so easily what belongs to her—she's a cruel woman!

PEPEL [*stretching himself on the bunk*]. You two prophets can go to hell!

KLESHTCH. Just wait—you'll see!

LUKA [*singing in the kitchen*]. "In the dark of the night the way is black . . ."

KLESHTCH. Another one who yelps!

PEPEL. It's dreary! Why do I feel so dreary? You live—and everything seems all right. But suddenly a cold chill goes through you—and then everything gets dreary . . .

BUBNOFF. Dreary? Hm-hm—

PEPEL. Yes yes—

LUKA [*sings*]. "The way is black . . ."

PEPEL. Old fellow! Hey there!

LUKA [*looking from kitchen door*]. You call me?

PEPEL. Yes. Don't sing!

LUKA [*coming in*]. You don't like it?

PEPEL. When people sing well I like it—

LUKA. In other words—I don't sing well?

PEPEL. Evidently!

LUKA. Well, well—and I thought I sang well. That's always the way: a man imagines there's one thing he can do well, and suddenly he finds out that other people don't think so . . .

PEPEL [*laughs*]. That's right . . .

BUBNOFF. First you say you feel dreary—and then you laugh!

PEPEL. None of your business, raven!

LUKA. Who do they say feels dreary?

PEPEL. I do.

[THE BARON *enters.*]

LUKA. Well, well—out there in the kitchen there's a girl reading and crying! That's so! Her eyes are wet with tears . . . I say to her: "What's the matter, darling?" And she says: "It's so sad!" "What's so sad?" say I. "The book!" says she.—And that's how people spend their time. Just because they're bored . . .

THE BARON. She's a fool!

PEPEL. Have you had tea, Baron?

THE BARON. Yes. Go on!

PEPEL. Well—want me to open a bottle?

THE BARON. Of course. Go on!

PEPEL. Drop on all fours, and bark like a dog!

THE BARON. Fool! What's the matter with you? Are you drunk?

PEPEL. Go on—bark a little! It'll amuse me. You're an aristocrat. You didn't even consider us human formerly, did you?

THE BARON. Go on!

PEPEL. Well—and now I am making you bark like a dog—and you will bark, won't you?

THE BARON. All right. I will. You jackass! What pleasure can you derive from it since I myself know that I have sunk almost lower than you? You should have made me drop on all fours in the days when I was still above you.

BUBNOFF. That's right . . .

LUKA. I say so, too!

BUBNOFF. What's over, is over. Remain only trivialities. We know no class distinctions here. We've shed all pride and self-respect. Blood and bone—man—just plain man—that's what we are!

LUKA. In other words, we're all equal . . . and you, friend, were you really a Baron?

THE BARON. Who are you? A ghost?

LUKA [*laughing*]. I've seen counts and princes in my day—this is the first time I meet a baron—and one who's decaying—at that!

PEPEL [*laughing*]. Baron, I blush for you!

THE BARON. It's time you knew better, Vassily . . .

LUKA. Hey-hey—I look at you, brothers—the life you're leading . . .

BUBNOFF. Such a life! As soon as the sun rises, our voices rise, too—in quarrels!

THE BARON. We've all seen better days—yes! I used to wake up in the morning and drink my coffee in bed—coffee—with cream! Yes—

LUKA. And yet we're all human beings. Pretend all you want to, put on all the airs you wish, but man you were born, and man you must die. And as I watch I see that the wiser people get, the busier they get—and though from bad to worse, they still strive to improve—stubbornly—

THE BARON. Who are you, old fellow? Where do you come from?

LUKA. I?

THE BARON. Are you a tramp?

LUKA. We're all of us tramps—why—I've heard said that the very earth we walk on is nothing but a tramp in the universe.

THE BARON [*severely*]. Perhaps. But have you a passport?

LUKA [*after a short pause*]. And what are you—a police inspector?

PEPEL [*delighted*]. You scored, old fellow! Well, Barosha, you got it this time!

BUBNOFF. Yes—our little aristocrat got his!

THE BARON [*embarrassed*]. What's the matter? I was only joking, old man. Why, brother, I haven't a passport, either.

BUBNOFF. You lie!

THE BARON. Oh—well—I have some sort of papers—but they have no value—

LUKA. They're papers just the same—and no papers are any good—

PEPEL. Baron—come on to the saloon with me—

THE BARON. I'm ready. Good-bye, old man—you old scamp—

LUKA. Maybe I am one, brother—

PEPEL [*near doorway*]. Come on—come on!

[*Leaves,* BARON *following him quickly.*]

LUKA. Was he really once a Baron?

BUBNOFF. Who knows? A gentleman—? Yes. That much he's even now. Occasionally it sticks out. He never got rid of the habit.

LUKA. Nobility is like small-pox. A man may get over it—but it leaves marks . . .

BUBNOFF. He's all right all the same—occasionally he kicks—as he did about your passport . . .

[ALYOSHKA *comes in, slightly drunk, with a concertina in his hand, whistling.*]

ALYOSHKA. Hey there, lodgers!

BUBNOFF. What are you yelling for?

ALYOSHKA. Excuse me—I beg your pardon! I'm a well-bred man—

BUBNOFF. On a spree again?

ALYOSHKA. Right you are! A moment ago Medyakin, the precinct captain, threw me out of the police station and said: "Look here—I don't want as much as a smell of you to stay in the streets—d'you hear?" I'm a man of principles, and the boss croaks at me—and what's a boss anyway—pah!—it's all bosh—the boss is a drunkard. I don't make any demands on life. I want nothing—that's all. Offer me one ruble, offer me twenty—it doesn't affect me. [NASTYA *comes from the kitchen*] Offer me a million—I won't take it! And to think that I, a respectable man, should be ordered about by a pal of mine—and he a drunkard! I won't have it—I won't!

[NASTYA *stands in the doorway, shaking her head at* ALYOSHKA.]

LUKA [*good-naturedly*]. Well, boy, you're a bit confused—

BUBNOFF. Aren't men fools!

ALYOSHKA [*stretches out on the floor*]. Here, eat me up alive—and I don't want anything. I'm a desperate man. Show me one better! Why am I worse than others? There! Medyakin said: "If you show yourself on the streets I smash your face!" And yet I shall go out—I'll go—and stretch out in the middle of the street—let them choke me—I don't want a thing!

NASTYA. Poor fellow—only a boy—and he's already putting on such airs—

ALYOSHKA [*kneeling before her*]. Lady! Mademoiselle! *Parlez français—? Prix courrant?* I'm on a spree—

NASTYA [*in a loud whisper*]. Vassilisa!

VASSILISA [*opens door quickly; to* ALYOSHKA]. You here again?

ALYOSHKA. How do you do—? Come in—you're welcome—

VASSILISA. I told you, young puppy, that not a shadow of you should stick around here—and you're back—eh?

ALYOSHKA. Vassilisa Karpovna . . . shall I tune up a funeral march for you?

VASSILISA [*seizing him by the shoulders*]. Get out!

ALYOSHKA [*moving towards the door*]. Wait—you can't put me out this way! I learned this funeral march a little while ago! It's refreshing music . . . wait—you can't put me out like that!

VASSILISA. I'll show whether I can or not. I'll rouse the whole street against you—you foul-mouthed creature—you're too young to bark about me—

ALYOSHKA [*running out*]. All right—I'll go—

VASSILISA. Look out—I'll get you yet!

ALYOSHKA [*opens the door and shouts*]. Vassilisa Karpovna—I'm not afraid of you—[*Hides*]

[LUKA *laughs.*]

VASSILISA. Who are you?

LUKA. A passer-by—a traveler . . .

VASSILISA. Stopping for the night or going to stay here?

LUKA. I'll see.

VASSILISA. Have you a passport?

LUKA. Yes.

VASSILISA. Give it to me.

LUKA. I'll bring it over to your house—

VASSILISA. Call yourself a traveler? If you'd say a tramp—that would be nearer the truth—

LUKA [*sighing*]. You're not very kindly, mother!

[VASSILISA *goes to door that leads to* PEPEL's *room,* ALYOSHKA *pokes his head through the kitchen door.*]

ALYOSHKA. Has she left?

VASSILISA [*turning around*]. Are you still here?

[ALYOSHKA *disappears, whistling.* NASTYA *and* LUKA *laugh.*]

BUBNOFF [*to* VASSILISA]. He isn't here—

VASSILISA. Who?

BUBNOFF. Vaska.

VASSILISA. Did I ask you about him?

BUBNOFF. I noticed you were looking around—

VASSILISA. I am looking to see if things are in order, you see? Why aren't the floors swept yet? How often did I give orders to keep the house clean?

BUBNOFF. It's the actor's turn to sweep—

VASSILISA. Never mind whose turn it is! If the health inspector comes and fines me, I'll throw out the lot of you—

BUBNOFF [*calmly*]. Then how are you going to earn your living?

VASSILISA. I don't want a speck of dirt! [*Goes to kitchen; to* NASTYA] What are you hanging round here for? Why's your face all swollen up? Why are you standing there like a dummy? Go on—sweep the floor! Did you see Natalia? Was she here?

NASTYA. I don't know—I haven't seen her . . .

VASSILISA. Bubnoff! Was my sister here?

BUBNOFF. She brought him along.

VASSILISA. That one—was he home?

BUBNOFF. Vassily? Yes—Natalia was here talking to Kleshtch—

VASSILISA. I'm not asking you whom she talked to. Dirt everywhere—filth—oh, you swine! Mop it all up—do you hear? [*Exits rapidly*]

BUBNOFF. What a savage beast she is!

LUKA. She's a lady that means business!

NASTYA. You grow to be an animal, leading such a life—any human being tied to such a husband as hers . . .

BUBNOFF. Well—that tie isn't worrying her any—

LUKA. Does she always have these fits?

BUBNOFF. Always. You see, she came to find her lover—but he isn't home—

LUKA. I guess she was hurt. Oh-ho! Everybody is trying to be boss—and is threatening everybody else with all kinds of punishment—and still there's no order in life . . . and no cleanliness—

BUBNOFF. All the world likes order—but some people's brains aren't fit for it. All the same—the room should be swept—Nastya—you ought to get busy!

NASTYA. Oh, certainly! Anything else? Think I'm your servant? [*Silence*] I'm going to get drunk to-night—dead-drunk!

BUBNOFF. Fine business!

LUKA. Why do you want to get drunk, girlie? A while ago you were crying—and now you say you'll get drunk—

NASTYA [*defiantly*]. I'll drink—then I cry again—that's all there's to it!

BUBNOFF. That's nothing!

LUKA. But for what reason—tell me! Every pimple has a cause! [NASTYA *remains silent, shaking her head*] Oh—you men—what's to become of you? All right—I'll sweep the place. Where's your broom?

BUBNOFF. Behind the door—in the hall—

[LUKA *goes into the hall.*]

Nastinka!

NASTYA. Yes?

BUBNOFF. Why did Vassilisa jump on Alyoshka?

NASTYA. He told her that Vaska was tired of her and was going to get rid of her—and that he's going to make up to Natasha—I'll go away from here—I'll find another lodging-house—

BUBNOFF. Why? Where?

NASTYA. I'm sick of this—I'm not wanted here!

BUBNOFF [*calmly*]. You're not wanted anywhere—and, anyway, all people on earth are superfluous—

[NASTYA *shakes her head. Rises and slowly, quietly, leaves the cellar.* MIEDVIEDIEFF *comes in.* LUKA, *with the broom, follows him.*]

MIEDVIEDIEFF. I don't think I know you—

LUKA. How about the others—d'you know them all?

MIEDVIEDIEFF. I must know everybody in my precinct. But I don't know you.

LUKA. That's because, uncle, the whole world can't stow itself away in your precinct—some of it was bound to remain outside . . . [*Goes into kitchen*]

MIEDVIEDIEFF [*crosses to* BUBNOFF]. It's true—my precinct is rather small—yet it's worse than any of the very largest. Just now, before getting off duty, I had to bring Alyoshka, the shoemaker, to the station house. Just imagine—there he was, stretched right in the middle of the street, playing his concertina and yelping: "I want nothing, nothing!" Horses going past all the time—and with all the traffic going on, he could easily have been run over—and so on! He's a wild youngster—so I just collared him—he likes to make mischief—

BUBNOFF. Coming to play checkers to-night?

MIEDVIEDIEFF. Yes—I'll come—how's Vaska?

BUBNOFF. Same as ever—

MIEDVIEDIEFF. Meaning—he's getting along—?

BUBNOFF. Why shouldn't he? He's able to get along all right.

MIEDVIEDIEFF [*doubtfully*]. Why shouldn't he? [LUKA *goes into hallway, carrying a pail*] M-yes—there's a lot of talk about Vaska. Haven't you heard?

BUBNOFF. I hear all sorts of gossip . . .

MIEDVIEDIEFF. There seems to have been some sort of talk concerning Vassilisa. Haven't you heard about it?

BUBNOFF. What?

MIEDVIEDIEFF. Oh—why—generally speaking. Perhaps you know—and lie. Everybody knows—[*Severely*] You mustn't lie, brother!

BUBNOFF. Why should I lie?

MIEDVIEDIEFF. That's right. Dogs! They say that Vaska and Vassilisa . . . but what's that to me? I'm not her father. I'm her uncle. Why should they ridicule me? [KVASHNYA *comes in*] What are people coming to? They laugh at everything. Aha—you here?

KVASHNYA. Well—my love-sick garrison—? Bubnoff! He came up to me again on the marketplace and started pestering me about marrying him . . .

BUBNOFF. Go to it! Why not? He has money and he's still a husky fellow.

MIEDVIEDIEFF. Me—? I should say so!

KVASHNYA. You ruffian! Don't you dare touch my sore spot! I've gone through it once already, darling. Marriage to a woman is just like jumping through a hole in the ice in winter. You do it once, and you remember it the rest of your life . . .

MIEDVIEDIEFF. Wait! There are different breeds of husbands . . .

KVASHNYA. But there's only one of me! When my beloved husband kicked the bucket, I spent the whole day all by my lonely—just bursting with joy. I sat and simply couldn't believe it was true. . . .

MIEDVIEDIEFF. If your husband beat you without cause, you should have complained to the police.

KVASHNYA. I complained to God for eight years—and he didn't help.

MIEDVIEDIEFF. Nowadays the law forbids to beat your wife . . . all is very strict these days—there's law and order everywhere. You can't beat up people without due cause. If you beat them to maintain discipline—all right . . .

LUKA [*comes in with* ANNA]. Well—we finally managed to get here after all. Oh, you! Why do you, weak as you are, walk about alone? Where's your bunk?

ANNA [*pointing*]. Thank you, grand-dad.

KVASHNYA. There—she's married—look at her!

LUKA. The little woman is in very bad shape . . . she was creeping along the hallway, clinging to the wall and moaning—why do you leave her by herself?

KVASHNYA. Oh, pure carelessness on our part, little father—forgive us! Her maid, it appears, went out for a walk . . .

LUKA. Go on—poke fun at me . . . but, all the same, how can you neglect a human being like that? No matter who or what, every human life has its worth . . .

MIEDVIEDIEFF. There should be supervision! Suppose she died

suddenly—? That would cause a lot of bother . . . we must look after her!

LUKA. True, sergeant!

MIEDVIEDIEFF. Well—yes—though I'm not a sergeant—ah—yet!

LUKA. No! But you carry yourself most martially!

[*Noise of shuffling feet is heard in the hallway. Muffled cries.*]

MIEDVIEDIEFF. What now—a row?

BUBNOFF. Sounds like it?

KVASHNYA. I'll go and see . . .

MIEDVIEDIEFF. I'll go, too. It is my duty! Why separate people when they fight? They'll stop sooner or later of their own accord. One gets tired of fighting. Why not let them fight all they want to—freely? They wouldn't fight half as often—if they'd remember former beatings . . .

BUBNOFF [*climbing down from his bunk*]. Why don't you speak to your superiors about it?

KOSTILYOFF [*throws open the door and shouts*]. Abram! Come quick—Vassilisa is killing Natasha—come quick!

[KVASHNYA, MIEDVIEDIEFF, *and* BUBNOFF *rush into hallway;* LUKA *looks after them, shaking his head.*]

ANNA. Oh God—poor little Natasha . . .

LUKA. Who's fighting out there?

ANNA. Our landladies—they're sisters . . .

LUKA [*crossing to* ANNA]. Why?

ANNA. Oh—for no reason—except that they're both fat and healthy . . .

LUKA. What's your name?

ANNA. Anna . . . I look at you . . . you're like my father—my dear father . . . you're as gentle as he was—and as soft. . . .

LUKA. Soft! Yes! They pounded me till I got soft! [*Laughs tremulously*]

CURTAIN

Act II

Same as Act I—Night.

On the bunks near the stove SATINE, THE BARON, KRIVOY ZOB, *and* THE TARTAR *play cards.* KLESHTCH *and* THE ACTOR *watch them.* BUBNOFF, *on his bunk, is playing checkers with* MIEDVIEDIEFF. LUKA *sits on a stool by* ANNA'S *bedside. The place is lit by two lamps, one on the wall near the card players, the other is on* BUBNOFF'S *bunk.*

THE TARTAR. I'll play one more game—then I'll stop . . .

BUBNOFF. Zob! Sing! [*He sings*]

"The sun rises and sets . . ."

ZOB [*joining in*].

"But my prison is dark, dark . . ."

THE TARTAR [*to* SATINE]. Shuffle the cards—and shuffle them well. We know your kind—

ZOB AND BUBNOFF [*together*].

"Day and night the wardens
Watch beneath my window . . ."

ANNA. Blows—insults—I've had nothing but that all my life long . . .

LUKA. Don't worry, little mother!

MIEDVIEDIEFF. Look where you're moving!

BUBNOFF. Oh, yes—that's right . . .

THE TARTAR [*threatening* SATINE *with his fist*]. You're trying to palm a card? I've seen you—you scoundrel . . .

ZOB. Stop it, Hassan! They'll skin us anyway . . . come in, Bubnoff!

ANNA. I can't remember a single day when I didn't go hungry . . . I've been afraid, waking, eating, and sleeping . . . all my life I've trembled—afraid I wouldn't get another bite . . . all my life I've been in rags—all through my wretched life—and why . . . ?

LUKA. Yes, yes, child—you're tired—never you mind!

THE ACTOR [*to* ZOB]. Play the Jack—the Jack, devil take you!

THE BARON. And we play the King!

KLESHTCH. They always win.

SATINE. Such is our habit.

MIEDVIEDIEFF. I have the Queen!

BUBNOFF. And so have I!

ANNA. I'm dying . . .

KLESHTCH. Look, look! Prince, throw up the game—throw it up, I tell you!

THE ACTOR. Can't he play without your assistance?

THE BARON. Look out, Andrushka, or I'll beat the life out of you!

THE TARTAR. Deal once more—the pitcher went after water—and got broke—and so did I!

[KLESHTCH *shakes his head and crosses to* BUBNOFF.]

ANNA. I keep on thinking—is it possible that I'll suffer in the other world as I did in this—is it possible? There, too?

LUKA. Nothing of the sort! Don't you disturb yourself! You'll rest there . . . be patient. We all suffer, dear, each in our own way. . . . [*Rises and goes quickly into kitchen*]

BUBNOFF [*sings*].

"Watch as long as you please . . ."

ZOB. "I shan't run away . . ."

BOTH [*together*].

"I long to be free, free—
Alas! I cannot break my chains. . . ."

THE TARTAR [*yells*]. That card was up his sleeve!

THE BARON [*embarrassed*]. Do you want me to shove it up your nose?

THE ACTOR [*emphatically*]. Prince! You're mistaken—nobody—ever . . .

THE TARTAR. I saw it! You cheat! I won't play!

SATINE [*gathering up the cards*]. Leave us alone, Hassan . . . you knew right along that we're cheats—why did you play with us?

THE BARON. He lost forty kopecks and he yelps as if he had lost a fortune! And a Prince at that!

THE TARTAR [*excitedly*]. Then play honest!

SATINE. What for?

THE TARTAR. What do you mean "what for"?

SATINE. Exactly. What for?

THE TARTAR. Don't you know?

SATINE. I don't. Do you?

[THE TARTAR *spits out, furiously; the others laugh at him.*]

ZOB [*good-naturedly*]. You're a funny fellow, Hassan! Try to understand this! If they should begin to live honestly, they'd die of starvation inside of three days.

THE TARTAR. That's none of my business. You must live honestly!

ZOB. They did you brown! Come and let's have tea. . . . [*Sings*]

"O my chains, my heavy chains . . ."

BUBNOFF [*sings*].

"You're my steely, clanking wardens . . ."

ZOB. Come on, Hassanka! [*Leaves the room, singing*]

"I cannot tear you, cannot break you . . ."

[THE TARTAR *shakes his fist threateningly at* THE BARON, *and follows the other out of the room.*]

SATINE [*to* BARON, *laughing*]. Well, Your Imperial Highness, you've again sat down magnificently in a mud puddle! You've learned a lot—but you're an ignoramus when it comes to palming a card.

THE BARON [*spreading his hands*]. The devil knows how it happened. . . .

THE ACTOR. You're not gifted—you've no faith in yourself—and without that you can never accomplish anything . . .

MIEDVIEDIEFF. I've one Queen—and you've two—oh, well . . .

BUBNOFF. One's enough if she has brains—play!

KLESHTCH. You lost, Abram Ivanovitch?

MIEDVIEDIEFF. None of your business—see? Shut up!

SATINE. I've won fifty-three kopecks.

THE ACTOR. Give me three of them . . . though, what'll I do with them?

LUKA [*coming from kitchen*]. Well—the Tartar was fleeced all right, eh? Going to have some vodka?

THE BARON. Come with us.

SATINE. I wonder what you'll be like when you're drunk.

LUKA. Same as when I'm sober.

THE ACTOR. Come on, old man—I'll recite verses for you . . .

LUKA. What?

THE ACTOR. Verses. Don't you understand?

LUKA. Verses? And what do I want with verses?

THE ACTOR. Sometimes they're funny—sometimes sad.

SATINE. Well, poet, are you coming? [*Exits with* THE BARON]

THE ACTOR. I'm coming. I'll join you. For instance, old man, here's a bit of verse—I forget how it begins—I forget . . . [*brushes his hand across his forehead*]

BUBNOFF. There! Your Queen is lost—go on, play!

MIEDVIEDIEFF. I made the wrong move.

THE ACTOR. Formerly, before my organism was poisoned with alcohol, old man, I had a good memory. But now it's all over with me, brother. I used to declaim these verses with tremendous success—thunders of applause . . . you have no idea what applause means . . . it goes to your head like vodka! I'd step out on the stage—stand this way—[*Strikes a pose*]—I'd stand there and . . . [*Pause*] I can't remember a word—I can't remember! My favorite verses—isn't it ghastly, old man?

LUKA. Yes—is there anything worse than forgetting what you loved? Your very soul is in the thing you love!

THE ACTOR. I've drunk my soul away, old man—brother, I'm lost . . . and why? Because I had no faith. . . . I'm done with . . .

LUKA. Well—then—cure yourself! Nowadays they have a cure for drunkards. They treat you free of charge, brother. There's a hospital for drunkards—where they're treated for nothing. They've owned up, you see, that even a drunkard is a human being, and they're only too glad to help him get well. Well—then—go to it!

THE ACTOR [*thoughtfully*]. Where? Where is it?

LUKA. Oh—in some town or other . . . what do they call it—? I'll tell you the name presently—only, in the meanwhile, get ready. Don't drink so much! Take yourself in hand—and bear up! And then, when you're cured, you'll begin life all over again. Sounds good, brother, doesn't it, to begin all over again? Well—make up your mind!

THE ACTOR [*smiling*]. All over again—from the very beginning—that's fine . . . yes . . . all over again . . . [*Laughs*] Well—then—I can, can't I?

LUKA. Why not? A human being can do anything—if he only makes up his mind.

THE ACTOR [*suddenly, as if coming out of a trance*]. You're a queer bird! See you anon! [*Whistles*] Old man—*au revoir!* [*Exits*]

ANNA. Grand-dad!
LUKA. Yes, little mother?
ANNA. Talk to me.
LUKA [*close to her*]. Come on—let's chat . . .

[KLESHTCH, *glancing around, silently walks over to his wife, looks at her, and makes queer gestures with his hands, as though he wanted to say something.*]

LUKA. What is it, brother?
KLESHTCH [*quietly*]. Nothing . . .

[*Crosses slowly to hallway door, stands on the threshold for a few seconds, and exits.*]

LUKA [*looking after him*]. Hard on your man, isn't it?
ANNA. He doesn't concern me much . . .
LUKA. Did he beat you?
ANNA. Worse than that—it's he who's killed me—
BUBNOFF. My wife used to have a lover—the scoundrel—how clever he was at checkers!
MIEDVIEDIEFF. Hm-hm—
ANNA. Grand-dad! Talk to me, darling—I feel so sick . . .
LUKA. Never mind—it's always like this before you die, little dove—never mind, dear! Just have faith! Once you're dead, you'll have peace—always. There's nothing to be afraid of—nothing. Quiet! Peace! Lie quietly! Death wipes out everything. Death is kindly. You die—and you rest—that's what they say. It is true, dear! Because—where can we find rest on this earth?

[PEPEL *enters. He is slightly drunk, disheveled, and sullen. Sits down on bunk near door, and remains silent and motionless.*]

ANNA. And how is it—there? More suffering?
LUKA. Nothing of the kind! No suffering! Trust me! Rest—nothing else! They'll lead you into God's presence, and they'll say: "Dear God! Behold! Here is Anna, Thy servant!"
MIEDVIEDIEFF [*sternly*]. How do you know what they'll say up there? Oh, you . . .

[PEPEL, *on hearing* MIEDVIEDIEFF'S *voice, raises his head and listens.*]

LUKA. Apparently I do know, Mr. Sergeant!
MIEDVIEDIEFF [*conciliatory*]. Yes—it's your own affair—though I'm not exactly a sergeant—yet—
BUBNOFF. I jump two!

MIEDVIEDIEFF. Damn—play!

LUKA. And the Lord will look at you gently and tenderly and He'll say: "I know this Anna!" Then He'll say: "Take Anna into Paradise. Let her have peace. I know. Her life on earth was hard. She is very weary. Let Anna rest in peace!"

ANNA [*choking*]. Grandfather—if it were only so—if there were only rest and peace . . .

LUKA. There won't be anything else! Trust me! Die in joy and not in grief. Death is to us like a mother to small children . . .

ANNA. But—perhaps—perhaps I'll get well . . . ?

LUKA [*laughing*]. Why—? Just to suffer more?

ANNA. But—just to live a little longer . . . just a little longer! Since there'll be no suffering hereafter, I could bear it a little longer down here . . .

LUKA. There'll be nothing in the hereafter . . . but only . . .

PEPEL [*rising*]. Maybe yes—maybe no!

ANNA [*frightened*]. Oh—God!

LUKA. Hey—Adonis!

MIEDVIEDIEFF. Who's that yelping?

PEPEL [*crossing over to him*]. I! What of it?

MIEDVIEDIEFF. You yelp needlessly—that's what! People ought to have some dignity!

PEPEL. Block-head! And that's an uncle for you—ho-ho!

LUKA [*to* PEPEL, *in an undertone*]. Look here—don't shout—this woman's dying—her lips are already grey—don't disturb her!

PEPEL. I've respect for you, grand-dad. You're all right, you are! You lie well, and you spin pleasant yarns. Go on lying, brother—there's little fun in this world . . .

BUBNOFF. Is the woman really dying?

LUKA. You think I'm joking?

BUBNOFF. That means she'll stop coughing. Her cough was very disturbing. I jump two!

MIEDVIEDIEFF. I'd like to murder you!

PEPEL. Abramka!

MIEDVIEDIEFF. I'm not Abramka to you!

PEPEL. Abrashka! Is Natasha ill?

MIEDVIEDIEFF. None of your business!

PEPEL. Come—tell me! Did Vassilisa beat her up very badly?

MIEDVIEDIEFF. That's none of your business, either! It's a family affair! Who are you anyway?

PEPEL. Whoever I am, you'll never see Natashka again if I choose!

MIEDVIEDIEFF [*throwing up the game*]. What's that? Who are you alluding to? My niece by any chance? You thief!

PEPEL. A thief whom you were never able to catch!

MIEDVIEDIEFF. Wait—I'll catch you yet—you'll see—sooner than you think!

PEPEL. If you catch me, God help your whole nest! Do you think I'll keep quiet before the examining magistrate? Every wolf howls! They'll ask me: "Who made you steal and showed you where?" "Mishka Kostilyoff and his wife!" "Who was your fence?" "Mishka Kostilyoff and his wife!"

MIEDVIEDIEFF. You lie! No one will believe you!

PEPEL. They'll believe me all right—because it's the truth! And I'll drag you into it, too. Ha! I'll ruin the lot of you—devils—just watch!

MIEDVIEDIEFF [*confused*]. You lie! You lie! And what harm did I do to you, you mad dog?

PEPEL. And what good did you ever do me?

LUKA. That's right!

MIEDVIEDIEFF [*to* LUKA]. Well—what are you croaking about? Is it any of your business? This is a family matter!

BUBNOFF [*to* LUKA]. Leave them alone! What do we care if they twist each other's tails?

LUKA [*peacefully*]. I meant no harm. All I said was that if a man isn't good to you, then he's acting wrong . . .

MIEDVIEDIEFF [*uncomprehending*]. Now then—we all of us here know each other—but you—who are you? [*Frowns and exits*]

LUKA. The cavalier is peeved! Oh-ho, brothers, I see your affairs are a bit tangled up!

PEPEL. He'll run to complain about us to Vassilisa . . .

BUBNOFF. You're a fool, Vassily. You're very bold these days, aren't you? Watch out! It's all right to be bold when you go gathering mushrooms, but what good is it here? They'll break your neck before you know it!

PEPEL. Well—not as fast as all that! You don't catch us Yaroslavl boys napping! If it's going to be war, we'll fight . . .

LUKA. Look here, boy, you really ought to go away from here—

PEPEL. Where? Please tell me!

LUKA. Go to Siberia!

PEPEL. If I go to Siberia, it'll be at the Tsar's expense!

LUKA. Listen! You go just the same! You can make your own way there. They need your kind out there . . .

PEPEL. My way is clear. My father spent all his life in prison, and I inherited the trait. Even when I was a small child, they called me thief—thief's son.

LUKA. But Siberia is a fine country—a land of gold. Any one who has health and strength and brains can live there like a cucumber in a hot-house.

PEPEL. Old man, why do you always tell lies?

LUKA. What?

PEPEL. Are you deaf? I ask—why do you always lie?

LUKA. What do I lie about?

PEPEL. About everything. According to you, life's wonderful everywhere—but you lie . . . why?

LUKA. Try to believe me. Go and see for yourself. And some day you'll thank me for it. What are you hanging round here for? And, besides, why is truth so important to you? Just think! Truth may spell death to you!

PEPEL. It's all one to me! If that—let it be that!

LUKA. Oh—what a madman! Why should you kill yourself?

BUBNOFF. What are you two jawing about, anyway? I don't understand. What kind of truth do you want, Vaska? And what for? You know the truth about yourself—and so does everybody else . . .

PEPEL. Just a moment! Don't crow! Let him tell me! Listen, old man! Is there a God?

[LUKA *smiles silently.*]

BUBNOFF. People just drift along—like shavings on a stream. When a house is built—the shavings are thrown away!

PEPEL. Well? Is there a God? Tell me.

LUKA [*in a low voice*]. If you have faith, there is; if you haven't, there isn't . . . whatever you believe in, exists . . .

[PEPEL *looks at* LUKA *in staring surprise.*]

BUBNOFF. I'm going to have tea—come on over to the restaurant!

LUKA [*to* PEPEL]. What are you staring at?

PEPEL. Oh—just because! Wait now—you mean to say . . .

BUBNOFF. Well—I'm off.

[*Goes to door and runs into* VASSILISA.]

PEPEL. So—you . . .

VASSILISA [*to* BUBNOFF]. Is Nastasya home?

BUBNOFF. No. [*Exits*]

PEPEL. Oh—you've come—?

VASSILISA [*crossing to* ANNA]. Is she alive yet?

LUKA. Don't disturb her!

VASSILISA. What are you loafing around here for?

LUKA. I'll go—if you want me to . . .

VASSILISA [*turning toward* PEPEL'*s room*]. Vassily! I've some business with you . . .

[LUKA *goes to hallway door, opens it, and shuts it loudly, then warily climbs into a bunk, and from there to the top of the stove.*]

VASSILISA [*calling from* PEPEL'*s room*]. Vaska—come here!
PEPEL. I won't come—I don't want to . . .
VASSILISA. Why? What are you angry about?
PEPEL. I'm sick of the whole thing . . .
VASSILISA. Sick of me, too?
PEPEL. Yes! Of you, too!

[VASSILISA *draws her shawl about her, pressing her hands over her breast. Crosses to* ANNA, *looks carefully through the bed curtains, and returns to* PEPEL.]

Well—out with it!

VASSILISA. What do you want me to say? I can't force you to be loving, and I'm not the sort to beg for kindness. Thank you for telling me the truth.

PEPEL. What truth?

VASSILISA. That you're sick of me—or isn't it the truth? [PEPEL *looks at her silently. She turns to him*] What are you staring at? Don't you recognize me?

PEPEL [*sighing*]. You're beautiful, Vassilisa! [*She puts her arm about his neck, but he shakes it off*] But I never gave my heart to you. . . . I've lived with you and all that—but I never really liked you . . .

VASSILISA [*quietly*]. That so? Well—?

PEPEL. What is there to talk about? Nothing. Go away from me!

VASSILISA. Taken a fancy to some one else?

PEPEL. None of your business! Suppose I have—I wouldn't ask you to be my match-maker!

VASSILISA [*significantly*]. That's too bad . . . perhaps I might arrange a match . . .

PEPEL [*suspiciously*]. Who with?

VASSILISA. You know—why do you pretend? Vassily—let me be frank. [*With lower voice*] I won't deny it—you've offended me . . . it was like a bolt from the blue . . . you said you loved me—and then all of a sudden . . .

PEPEL. It wasn't sudden at all. It's been a long time since I . . . woman, you've no soul! A woman must have a soul . . . we men are beasts—we must be taught—and you, what have you taught me—?

VASSILISA. Never mind the past! I know—no man owns his own

heart—you don't love me any longer . . . well and good, it can't be helped!

PEPEL. So that's over. We part peaceably, without a row—as it should be!

VASSILISA. Just a moment! All the same, when I lived with you, I hoped you'd help me out of this swamp—I thought you'd free me from my husband and my uncle—from all this life—and perhaps, Vassya, it wasn't you whom I loved—but my hope—do you understand? I waited for you to drag me out of this mire . . .

PEPEL. You aren't a nail—and I'm not a pair of pincers! I thought you had brains—you are so clever—so crafty . . .

VASSILISA [*leaning closely toward him*]. Vassa—let's help each other!

PEPEL. How?

VASSILISA [*low and forcibly*]. My sister—I know you've fallen for her . . .

PEPEL. And that's why you beat her up, like the beast you are! Look out, Vassilisa! Don't you touch her!

VASSILISA. Wait. Don't get excited. We can do everything quietly and pleasantly. You want to marry her. I'll give you money . . . three hundred rubles—even more than that . . .

PEPEL [*moving away from her*]. Stop! What do you mean?

VASSILISA. Rid me of my husband! Take that noose from around my neck . . .

PEPEL [*whistling softly*]. So that's the way the land lies! You certainly planned it cleverly . . . in other words, the grave for the husband, the gallows for the lover, and as for yourself . . .

VASSILISA. Vassya! Why the gallows? It doesn't have to be yourself—but one of your pals! And supposing it were yourself—who'd know? Natalia—just think—and you'll have money—you go away somewhere—you free me forever—and it'll be very good for my sister to be away from me—the sight of her enrages me. . . . I get furious with her on account of you, and I can't control myself. I tortured the girl—I beat her up—beat her up so that I myself cried with pity for her—but I'll beat her—and I'll go on beating her!

PEPEL. Beast! Bragging about your beastliness?

VASSILISA. I'm not bragging—I speak the truth. Think now, Vassa. You've been to prison twice because of my husband—through his greed. He clings to me like a bed-bug—he's been sucking the life out of me for the last four years—and what sort of a husband is he to me? He's forever abusing Natasha—calls her a beggar—he's just poison, plain poison, to every one . . .

PEPEL. You spin your yarn cleverly . . .

VASSILISA. Everything I say is true. Only a fool could be as blind as you . . .

[KOSTILYOFF *enters stealthily and comes forward noisily.*]

PEPEL [*to* VASSILISA]. Oh—go away!
VASSILISA. Think it over! [*Sees her husband*] What? You? Following me?

[PEPEL *leaps up and stares at* KOSTILYOFF *savagely.*]

KOSTILYOFF. It's I, I! So the two of you were here alone—you were—ah—conversing? [*Suddenly stamps his feet and screams*] Vassilisa—you bitch! You beggar! You damned hag! [*Frightened by his own screams, which are met by silence and indifference on the part of the others*] Forgive me, O Lord . . . Vassilisa—again you've led me into the path of sin. . . . I've been looking for you everywhere. It's time to go to bed. You forgot to fill the lamps—oh, you . . . beggar! Swine! [*Shakes his trembling fist at her, while* VASSILISA *slowly goes to door, glancing at* PEPEL *over her shoulder*]
PEPEL [*to* KOSTILYOFF]. Go away—clear out of here—
KOSTILYOFF [*yelling*]. What? I? The Boss? I get out? You thief!
PEPEL [*sullenly*]. Go away, Mishka!
KOSTILYOFF. Don't you dare—I—I'll show you.

[PEPEL *seizes him by the collar and shakes him. From the stove come loud noises and yawns.* PEPEL *releases* KOSTILYOFF *who runs into the hallway, screaming.*]

PEPEL [*jumping on a bunk*]. Who is it? Who's on the stove?
LUKA [*raising his head*]. Eh?
PEPEL. You?
LUKA [*undisturbed*]. I—I myself—oh, dear Jesus!
PEPEL [*shuts hallway door, looks for the wooden closing bar, but can't find it*]. The devil! Come down, old man!
LUKA. I'm climbing down—all right . . .
PEPEL [*roughly*]. What did you climb on that stove for?
LUKA. Where was I to go?
PEPEL. Why—didn't you go out into the hall?
LUKA. The hall's too cold for an old fellow like myself, brother.
PEPEL. You overheard?
LUKA. Yes—I did. How could I help it? Am I deaf? Well, my boy, happiness is coming your way. Real, good fortune I call it!
PEPEL [*suspiciously*]. What good fortune—?
LUKA. In so far as I was lying on the stove . . .
PEPEL. Why did you make all that noise?

LUKA. Because I was getting warm . . . it was your good luck . . . I thought if only the boy wouldn't make a mistake and choke the old man . . .

PEPEL. Yes—I might have done it . . . how terrible . . .

LUKA. Small wonder! It isn't difficult to make a mistake of that sort.

PEPEL [*smiling*]. What's the matter? Did you make the same sort of mistake once upon a time?

LUKA. Boy, listen to me. Send that woman out of your life! Don't let her near you! Her husband—she'll get rid of him herself—and in a shrewder way than you could—yes! Don't you listen to that devil! Look at me! I am bald-headed—know why? Because of all these women. . . . Perhaps I knew more women than I had hair on the top of my head—but this Vassilisa—she's worse than the plague . . .

PEPEL. I don't understand . . . I don't know whether to thank you—or—well . . .

LUKA. Don't say a word! You won't improve on what I said. Listen: take the one you like by the arm, and march out of here—get out of here—clean out . . .

PEPEL [*sadly*]. I can't understand people. Who is kind and who isn't? It's all a mystery to me . . .

LUKA. What's there to understand? There's all breeds of men . . . they all live as their hearts tell them . . . good to-day, bad to-morrow! But if you really care for that girl . . . take her away from here and that's all there is to it. Otherwise go away alone . . . you're young—you're in no hurry for a wife. . . .

PEPEL [*taking him by the shoulder*]. Tell me! Why do you say all this?

LUKA. Wait. Let me go. I want to look at Anna . . . she was coughing so terribly . . . [*Goes to* ANNA'*s bed, pulls the curtains, looks, touches her.* PEPEL *thoughtfully and distraught, follows him with his eyes*] Merciful Jesus Christ! Take into Thy keeping the soul of this woman Anna, new-comer amongst the blessed!

PEPEL [*softly*]. Is she dead?

[*Without approaching, he stretches himself and looks at the bed.*]

LUKA [*gently*]. Her sufferings are over! Where's her husband?

PEPEL. In the saloon, most likely . . .

LUKA. Well—he'll have to be told . . .

PEPEL [*shuddering*]. I don't like corpses!

LUKA [*going to door*]. Why should you like them? It's the living who demand our love—the living . . .

PEPEL. I'm coming with you . . .

LUKA. Are you afraid?

PEPEL. I don't like it . . .

[*They go out quickly. The stage is empty and silent for a few moments. Behind the door is heard a dull, staccato, incomprehensible noise. Then* THE ACTOR *enters.*]

THE ACTOR [*stands at the open door, supporting himself against the jamb, and shouts*]. Hey, old man—where are you—? I just remembered—listen . . . [*Takes two staggering steps forward and, striking a pose, recites*]

"Good people! If the world cannot find
A path to holy truth,
Glory be to the madman who will enfold all humanity
In a golden dream . . ."

[NATASHA *appears in the doorway behind* THE ACTOR.]

Old man! [*recites*]

"If to-morrow the sun were to forget
To light our earth,
To-morrow then some madman's thought
Would bathe the world in sunshine. . . ."

NATASHA [*laughing*]. Scarecrow! You're drunk!

THE ACTOR [*turns to her*]. Oh—it's you! Where's the old man, the dear old man? Not a soul here, seems to me . . . Natasha, farewell—right—farewell!

NATASHA [*entering*]. Don't wish me farewell, before you've wished me how-d'you-do!

THE ACTOR [*barring her way*]. I am going. Spring will come—and I'll be here no longer—

NATASHA. Wait a moment! Where do you propose going?

THE ACTOR. In search of a town—to be cured—And you, Ophelia, must go away! Take the veil! Just imagine—there's a hospital to cure—ah—organisms for drunkards—a wonderful hospital—built of marble—with marble floors . . . light—clean—food—and all gratis! And a marble floor—yes! I'll find it—I'll get cured—and then I shall start life anew. . . . I'm on my way to regeneration, as King Lear said. Natasha, my stage name is . . . Svertchkoff—Zavoloushski . . . do you realize how painful it is to lose one's name? Even dogs have their names . . .

[NATASHA *carefully passes* THE ACTOR, *stops at* ANNA'S *bed and looks.*]

To be nameless—is not to exist!

NATASHA. Look, my dear—why—she's dead. . . .

THE ACTOR [*shakes his head*]. Impossible . . .

NATASHA [*stepping back*]. So help me God—look . . .

BUBNOFF [*appearing in doorway*]. What is there to look at?

NATASHA. Anna—she's dead!

BUBNOFF. That means—she's stopped coughing! [*Goes to* ANNA's *bed, looks, and returns to his bunk*] We must tell Kleshtch—it's his business to know . . .

THE ACTOR. I'll go—I'll say to him—she lost her name—[*Exits*]

NATASHA [*in centre of room*]. I, too—some day—I'll be found in the cellar—dead. . . .

BUBNOFF [*spreading out some rags on his bunk*]. What's that? What are you muttering?

NATASHA. Nothing much . . .

BUBNOFF. Waiting for Vaska, eh? Take care—Vassilisa'll break your head!

NATASHA. Isn't it the same who breaks it? I'd much rather he'd do it!

BUBNOFF [*lying down*]. Well—that's your own affair . . .

NATASHA. It's best for her to be dead—yet it's a pity . . . oh, Lord—why do we live?

BUBNOFF. It's so with all . . . we're born, live, and die—and I'll die, too—and so'll you—what's there to be gloomy about?

[*Enter* LUKA, THE TARTAR, ZOB, *and* KLESHTCH. *The latter comes after the others, slowly, shrunk up.*]

NATASHA. Sh-sh! Anna!

ZOB. We've heard—God rest her soul . . .

THE TARTAR [*to* KLESHTCH]. We must take her out of here. Out into the hall! This is no place for corpses—but for the living . . .

KLESHTCH [*quietly*]. We'll take her out—

[*Everybody goes to the bed,* KLESHTCH *looks at his wife over the others' shoulders.*]

ZOB [*to* THE TARTAR]. You think she'll smell? I don't think she will—she dried up while she was still alive . . .

NATASHA. God! If they'd only a little pity . . . if only some one would say a kindly word—oh, you . . .

LUKA. Don't be hurt, girl—never mind! Why and how should we pity the dead? Come, dear! We don't pity the living—we can't even pity our own selves—how can we?

BUBNOFF [*yawning*]. And, besides, when you're dead, no word will help you—when you're still alive, even sick, it may. . . .

THE TARTAR [*stepping aside*]. The police must be notified . . .

ZOB. The police—must be done! Kleshtch! Did you notify the police?

KLESHTCH. No—she's got to be buried—and all I have is forty kopecks—

ZOB. Well—you'll have to borrow then—otherwise we'll take up a collection—one'll give five kopecks, others as much as they can. But the police must be notified at once—or they'll think you killed her or God knows what not . . .

[*Crosses to* THE TARTAR'*s bunk and prepares to lie down by his side.*]

NATASHA [*going to* BUBNOFF'*s bunk*]. Now—I'll dream of her . . . I always dream of the dead . . . I'm afraid to go out into the hall by myself—it's dark there . . .

LUKA [*following her*]. You better fear the living—I'm telling you . . .

NATASHA. Take me across the hall, grandfather.

LUKA. Come on—come on—I'll take you across—

[*They go away. Pause.*]

ZOB [*to* THE TARTAR]. Oh-ho! Spring will soon be here, little brother, and it'll be quite warm. In the villages the peasants are already making ready their ploughs and harrows, preparing to till . . . and we . . . Hassan? Snoring already? Damned Mohammedan!

BUBNOFF. Tartars love sleep!

KLESHTCH [*in centre of room, staring in front of him*]. What am I to do now?

ZOB. Lie down and sleep—that's all . . .

KLESHTCH [*softly*]. But—she . . . how about . . .

[*No one answers him.* SATINE *and* THE ACTOR *enter.*]

THE ACTOR [*yelling*]. Old man! Come here, my trusted Duke of Kent!

SATINE. Miklookha-Maklai is coming—ho-ho!

THE ACTOR. It has been decided upon! Old man, where's the town—where are you?

SATINE. Fata Morgana, the old man bilked you from top to bottom! There's nothing—no towns—no people—nothing at all!

THE ACTOR. You lie!

THE TARTAR [*jumping up*]. Where's the boss? I'm going to the boss. If I can't sleep, I won't pay! Corpses—drunkards . . .[*Exits quickly*]

[SATINE *looks after him and whistles.*]

BUBNOFF [*in a sleepy voice*]. Go to bed, boys—be quiet . . . night is for sleep . . .

THE ACTOR. Yes—so—there's a corpse here. . . . "Our net fished up a corpse. . . ." Verses—by Béranger. . . .

SATINE [*screams*]. The dead can't hear . . . the dead do not feel—Scream!—Roar! . . . the deaf don't hear!

[*In the doorway appears* LUKA.]

CURTAIN

Act III

"The Waste," a yard strewn with rubbish and overgrown with weeds. Back, a high brick wall which shuts out the sight of the sky. Near it are elder bushes. Right, the dark, wooden wall of some sort of house, barn or stable. Left, the grey, tumbledown wall of KOSTILYOFF'*s night asylum. It is built at an angle so that the further corner reaches almost to the centre of the yard. Between it and the wall runs a narrow passage. In the grey, plastered wall are two windows, one on a level with the ground, the other about six feet higher up and closer to the brick wall. Near the latter wall is a big sledge turned upside down and a beam about twelve feet long. Right of the wall is a heap of old planks. Evening. The sun is setting, throwing a crimson light on the brick wall. Early spring, the snow having only recently melted. The elder bushes are not yet in bud.*

NATASHA *and* NASTYA *are sitting side by side on the beam.* LUKA *and* THE BARON *are on the sledge.* KLESHTCH *is stretched on the pile of planks to the right.* BUBNOFF'*s face is at the ground floor window.*

NASTYA [*with closed eyes, nodding her head in rhythm to the tale she is telling in a sing-song voice*]. So then at night he came into the garden. I had been waiting for him quite a while. I trembled with fear and grief—he trembled, too . . . he was as white as chalk—and he had the pistol in his hand . . .

NATASHA [*chewing sun-flower seeds*]. Oh—are these students really such desperate fellows . . . ?

NASTYA. And he says to me in a dreadful voice: "My precious darling . . ."

BUBNOFF. Ho-ho! Precious—?

THE BARON. Shut up! If you don't like it, you can lump it! But don't interrupt her. . . . Go on . . .

NASTYA. "My one and only love," he says, "my parents," he says, "refuse to give their consent to our wedding—and threaten to disown me because of my love for you. Therefore," he says, "I must take my life." And his pistol was huge—and loaded with ten bullets . . . "Farewell," he says, "beloved comrade! I have made up my mind for good and all . . . I can't live without you . . ." and I replied: "My unforgettable friend—my Raoul. . . ."

BUBNOFF [*surprised*]. What? What? Krawl—did you call him—?

THE BARON. Nastka! But last time his name was Gaston. . . .

NASTYA [*jumping up*]. Shut up, you bastards! Ah—you lousy mongrels! You think for a moment that you can understand love—true love? My love was real honest-to-God love! [*To* THE BARON] You good-for-nothing! . . . educated, you call yourself—drinking coffee in bed, did you?

LUKA. Now, now! Wait, people! Don't interfere! Show a little respect to your neighbors . . . it isn't the word that matters, but what's in back of the word. That's what matters! Go on, girl! It's all right!

BUBNOFF. Go on, crow! See if you can make your feathers white!

THE BARON. Well—continue!

NATASHA. Pay no attention to them . . . what are they? They're just jealous . . . they've nothing to tell about themselves . . .

NASTYA [*sits down again*]. I'm going to say no more! If they don't believe me they'll laugh. [*Stops suddenly, is silent for a few seconds, then, shutting her eyes, continues in a loud and intense voice, swaying her hands as if to the rhythm of far music*] And then I replied to him: "Joy of my life! My bright moon! And I, too, I can't live without you—because I love you madly, so madly—and I shall keep on loving you as long as my heart beats in my bosom. But—" I say—"don't take your young life! Think how necessary it is to your dear parents whose only happiness you are. Leave me! Better that I should perish from longing for you, my life! I alone! I—ah—as such, such! Better that I should die—it doesn't matter . . . I am of no use to the world—and I have nothing, nothing at all—" [*Covers her face with her hand and weeps gently*]

NATASHA [*in a low voice*]. Don't cry—don't!

[LUKA, *smiling, strokes* NASTYA'S *head.*]

BUBNOFF [*laughs*]. Ah—you limb of Satan!

THE BARON [*also laughs*]. Hey, old man? Do you think it's true? It's all from that book "Fatal Love" . . . it's all nonsense! Let her alone!

NATASHA. And what's it to you? Shut up—or God'll punish you!

NASTYA [*bitterly*]. God damn your soul! You worthless pig! Soul—bah!—you haven't got one!

LUKA [*takes* NASTYA'*s hand*]. Come, dear! It's nothing! Don't be angry—I know—I believe you! You're right, not they! If you believe you had a real love affair, then you did—yes! And as for him—don't be angry with a fellow-lodger . . . maybe he's really jealous, and that's why he's laughing. Maybe he never had any real love—maybe not—come on—let's go!

NASTYA [*pressing her hand against her breast*]. Grandfather! So help me God—it happened! It happened! He was a student, a Frenchman—Gastotcha was his name—he had a little black beard—and patent leathers—may God strike me dead if I'm lying! And he loved me so—my God, how he loved me!

LUKA. Yes, yes, it's all right. I believe you! Patent leathers, you said? Well, well, well—and you loved him, did you? [*Disappears with her around the corner*]

THE BARON. God—isn't she a fool, though? She's good-hearted—but such a fool—it's past belief!

BUBNOFF. And why are people so fond of lying—just as if they were up before the judge—really!

NATASHA. I guess lying is more fun than speaking the truth—I, too . . .

THE BARON. What—you, too? Go on!

NATASHA. Oh—I imagine things—invent them—and I wait—

THE BARON. For what?

NATASHA [*smiling confusedly*]. Oh—I think that perhaps—well—to-morrow somebody will really appear—some one—oh—out of the ordinary—or something'll happen—also out of the ordinary. . . . I've been waiting for it—oh—always. . . . But, really, what is there to wait for? [*Pause*]

THE BARON [*with a slight smile*]. Nothing—I expect nothing! What is past, is past! Through! Over with! And then what?

NATASHA. And then—well—to-morrow I imagine suddenly that I'll die—and I get frightened . . . in summer it's all right to dream of death—then there are thunder storms—one might get struck by lightning . . .

THE BARON. You've a hard life . . . your sister's a wicked-tempered devil!

NATASHA. Tell me—does anybody live happily? It's hard for all of us—I can see that . . .

KLESHTCH [*who until this moment has sat motionless and indifferent, jumps up suddenly*]. For all? You lie! Not for all! If it were so—all right! Then it wouldn't hurt—yes!

BUBNOFF. What in hell's bit you? Just listen to him yelping!

[KLESHTCH *lies down again and grunts.*]

THE BARON. Well—I'd better go and make my peace with Nastinka—if I don't, she won't treat me to vodka . . .

BUBNOFF. Hm—people love to lie . . . with Nastka—I can see the reason why. She's used to painting that mutt of hers—and now she wants to paint her soul as well . . . put rouge on her soul, eh? But the others—why do they? Take Luka for instance—he lies a lot . . . and what does he get out of it? He's an old fellow, too—why does he do it?

THE BARON [*smiling and walking away*]. All people have drab-colored souls—and they like to brighten them up a bit . . .

LUKA [*appearing from round the corner*]. You, sir, why do you tease the girl? Leave her alone—let her cry if it amuses her . . . she weeps for her own pleasure—what harm is it to you?

THE BARON. Nonsense, old man! She's a nuisance. Raoul to-day, Gaston to-morrow—always the same old yarn, though! Still—I'll go and make up with her. [*Leaves*]

LUKA. That's right—go—and be nice to her. Being nice to people never does them any harm . . .

NATASHA. You're so good, little father—why are you so good?

LUKA. Good, did you say? Well—call it that! [*Behind the brick wall is heard soft singing and the sounds of a concertina*] Some one has to be kind, girl—some one must pity people! Christ pitied everybody—and he said to us: "Go and do likewise!" I tell you—if you pity a man when he most needs it, good comes of it. Why—I used to be a watchman on the estate of an engineer near Tomsk—all right—the house was right in the middle of a forest—lovely place—winter came—and I remained all by myself. Well—one night I heard a noise—

NATASHA. Thieves?

LUKA. Exactly! Thieves creeping in! I took my gun—I went out. I looked and saw two of them opening a window—and so busy that they didn't even see me. I yell: "Hey there—get out of here!" And they turn on me with their axes—I warn them to stand back, or I'd shoot—and as I speak, I keep on covering them with my gun, first the one, then the other—they go down on their knees, as if to implore me for mercy. And by that time I was furious—because of those axes, you see—and so I say to them: "I was chasing you, you scoundrels—and you didn't go. Now you go and break off some stout branches!"—and they did so—and I say: "Now—one of you lie down and let the other one flog him!" So they obey me and flog each other—and then they begin to implore me again. "Grandfather," they say, "for God's sake give us some bread! We're hungry!" There's thieves for you, my dear! [*Laughs*] And with an ax, too! Yes—honest peasants, both of them! And I say to them, "You should have asked for bread straight away!" And they say: "We got tired of asking—you beg and beg—and nobody gives you a crumb—it hurts!" So they stayed with me all that winter—one of them, Stepan, would take my gun and go shooting in the forest—and the other, Yakoff, was ill most of the time—he coughed a lot . . . and so the three of us together looked after the house . . . then spring came . . . "Good-bye, grandfather," they said—and they went away—back home to Russia . . .

NATASHA. Were they escaped convicts?

LUKA. That's just what they were—escaped convicts—from a Siberian prison camp . . . honest peasants! If I hadn't felt sorry for them—they might have killed me—or maybe worse—and then there would have been trial and prison and afterwards Siberia—what's the sense of it? Prison teaches no good—and Siberia doesn't either—but another human being can . . . yes, a human being can teach another one kindness—very simply! [*Pause*]

BUBNOFF. Hm—yes—I, for instance, don't know how to lie . . . why—as far as I'm concerned, I believe in coming out with the whole truth and putting it on thick . . . why fuss about it?

KLESHTCH [*again jumps up as if his clothes were on fire, and screams*]. What truth? Where is there truth? [*Tearing at his ragged clothes*] Here's truth for you! No work! No strength! That's the only truth! Shelter—there's no shelter! You die—that's the truth! Hell! What do I want with the truth? Let me breathe! Why should I be blamed? What do I want with truth? To live—Christ Almighty!—they won't let you live—and that's another truth!

BUBNOFF. He's mad!

LUKA. Dear Lord . . . listen to me, brother—

KLESHTCH [*trembling with excitement*]. They say: there's truth! You, old man, try to console every one . . . I tell you—I hate every one! And there's your truth—God curse it—understand? I tell you—God curse it!

[*Rushes away round the corner, turning as he goes.*]

LUKA. Ah—how excited he got! Where did he run off to?

NATASHA. He's off his head . . .

BUBNOFF. God—don't he say a whole lot, though? As if he was playing drama—he gets those fits often . . . he isn't used to life yet . . .

PEPEL [*comes slowly round the corner*]. Peace on all this honest gathering! Well, Luka, you wily old fellow—still telling them stories?

LUKA. You should have heard how that fellow carried on!

PEPEL. Kleshtch—wasn't it? What's wrong with him? He was running like one possessed!

LUKA. You'd do the same if your own heart were breaking!

PEPEL [*sitting down*]. I don't like him . . . he's got such a nasty, bad temper—and so proud! [*Imitating* KLESHTCH] "I'm a workman!" And he thinks everyone's beneath him. Go on working if you feel like it—nothing to be so damned haughty about! If work is the standard—a horse can give us points—pulls like hell and says nothing! Natasha—are your folks at home?

NATASHA. They went to the cemetery—then to night service . . .

PEPEL. So that's why you're free for once—quite a novelty!

LUKA [*to* BUBNOFF, *thoughtfully*]. There—you say—truth! Truth doesn't always heal a wounded soul. For instance, I knew of a man who believed in a land of righteousness . . .

BUBNOFF. In what?

LUKA. In a land of righteousness. He said: "Somewhere on this earth there must be a righteous land—and wonderful people live there—good people! They respect each other, help each other, and everything is peaceful and good!" And so that man—who was always searching for this land of righteousness—he was poor and lived miserably—and when things got to be so bad with him that it seemed there was nothing else for him to do except lie down and die—even then he never lost heart—but he'd just smile and say: "Never mind! I can stand it! A little while longer—and I'll have done with this life—and I'll go in search of the righteous land!"—it was his one happiness—the thought of that land . . .

PEPEL. Well? Did he go there?

BUBNOFF. Where? Ho-ho!

LUKA. And then to this place—in Siberia, by the way—there came a convict—a learned man with books and maps—yes, a learned man who knew all sorts of things—and the other man said to him: "Do me a favor—show me where is the land of righteousness and how I can get there." At once the learned man opened his books, spread out his maps, and looked and looked and he said—no—he couldn't find this land anywhere . . . everything was correct—all the lands on earth were marked—but not this land of righteousness . . .

PEPEL [*in a low voice*]. Well? Wasn't there a trace of it?

[BUBNOFF *roars with laughter.*]

NATASHA. Wait . . . well, little father?

LUKA. The man wouldn't believe it. . . . "It must exist," he said, "look carefully. Otherwise," he says, "your books and maps are of no use if there's no land of righteousness." The learned man was offended.

"My plans," he said, "are correct. But there exists no land of righteousness anywhere." Well, then the other man got angry. He'd lived and lived and suffered and suffered, and had believed all the time in the existence of this land—and now, according to the plans, it didn't exist at all. He felt robbed! And he said to the learned man: "Ah—you scum of the earth! You're not a learned man at all—but just a damned cheat!"—and he gave him a good wallop in the eye—then another one . . . [*After a moment's silence*] And then he went home and hanged himself!

[*All are silent.* LUKA, *smiling, looks at* PEPEL *and* NATASHA.]

PEPEL [*low-voiced*]. To hell with this story—it isn't very cheerful . . .
NATASHA. He couldn't stand the disappointment . . .
BUBNOFF [*sullen*]. Ah—it's nothing but a fairytale . . .
PEPEL. Well—there is the righteous land for you—doesn't exist, it seems . . .
NATASHA. I'm sorry for that man . . .
BUBNOFF. All a story—ho-ho!—land of righteousness—what an idea! [*Exits through window*]
LUKA [*pointing to window*]. He's laughing! [*Pause*] Well, children, God be with you! I'll leave you soon . . .
PEPEL. Where are you going to?
LUKA. To the Ukraine—I heard they discovered a new religion there—I want to see—yes! People are always seeking—they always want something better—God grant them patience!
PEPEL. You think they'll find it?
LUKA. The people? They will find it! He who seeks, will find! He who desires strongly, will find!
NATASHA. If only they could find something better—invent something better . . .
LUKA. They're trying to! But we must help them girl—we must respect them . . .
NATASHA. How can I help them? I am helpless myself!
PEPEL [*determined*]. Again—listen—I'll speak to you again, Natasha—here—before him—he knows everything . . . run away with me?
NATASHA. Where? From one prison to another?
PEPEL. I told you—I'm through with being a thief, so help me God! I'll quit! If I say so, I'll do it! I can read and write—I'll work—He's been telling me to go to Siberia on my own hook—let's go there together, what do you say? Do you think I'm not disgusted with my life? Oh—Natasha—I know . . . I see . . . I console myself with the thought that there are lots of people who are honored and respected—and who

are bigger thieves than I! But what good is that to me? It isn't that I repent . . . I've no conscience . . . but I do feel one thing: One must live differently. One must live a better life . . . one must be able to respect one's own self . . .

LUKA. That's right, friend! May God help you! It's true! A man must respect himself!

PEPEL. I've been a thief from childhood on. Everybody always called me "Vaska—the thief—the son of a thief!" Oh—very well then—I am a thief . . . just imagine—now, perhaps, I'm a thief out of spite—perhaps I'm a thief because no one ever called me anything different. . . . Well, Natasha—?

NATASHA [*sadly*]. Somehow I don't believe in words—and I'm restless to-day—my heart is heavy . . . as if I were expecting something . . . it's a pity, Vassily, that you talked to me to-day . . .

PEPEL. When should I? It isn't the first time I speak to you . . .

NATASHA. And why should I go with you? I don't love you so very much—sometimes I like you—and other times the mere sight of you makes me sick . . . it seems—no—I don't really love you . . . when one really loves, one sees no fault. . . . But I do see . . .

PEPEL. Never mind—you'll love me after a while! I'll make you care for me . . . if you'll just say yes! For over a year I've watched you . . . you're a decent girl . . . you're kind—you're reliable—I'm very much in love with you . . .

[VASSILISA, *in her best dress, appears at window and listens.*]

NATASHA. Yes—you love me—but how about my sister . . . ?

PEPEL [*confused*]. Well, what of her? There are plenty like her . . .

LUKA. You'll be all right, girl! If there's no bread, you have to eat weeds . . .

PEPEL [*gloomily*]. Please—feel a little sorry for me! My life isn't all roses—it's a hell of a life . . . little happiness in it . . . I feel as if a swamp were sucking me under . . . and whatever I try to catch and hold on to, is rotten . . . it breaks . . . Your sister—oh—I thought she was different . . . if she weren't so greedy after money . . . I'd have done anything for her sake, if she were only all mine . . . but she must have someone else . . . and she has to have money—and freedom . . . because she doesn't like the straight and narrow . . . she can't help me. But you're like a young fir-tree . . . you bend, but you don't break . . .

LUKA. Yes—go with him, girl, go! He's a good lad—he's all right! Only tell him every now and then that he's a good lad so that he won't forget it—and he'll believe you. Just you keep on telling him "Vasya, you're a good man—don't you forget it!" Just think, dear, where else could you go except with him? Your sister is a savage beast . . . and as for her husband, there's little to say of him. He's rotten beyond words . . . and all this life here, where will it get you? But this lad is strong . . .

NATASHA. Nowhere to go—I know—I thought of it. The only thing is—I've no faith in anybody—and there's no place for me to turn to . . .

PEPEL. Yes, there is! But I won't let you go that way—I'd rather cut your throat!

NATASHA [*smiling*]. There—I'm not his wife yet—and he talks already of killing me!

PEPEL [*puts his arms around her*]. Come, Natasha! Say yes!

NATASHA [*holding him close*]. But I'll tell you one thing, Vassily—I swear it before God . . . the first time you strike me or hurt me any other way, I'll have no pity on myself . . . I'll either hang myself . . . or . . .

PEPEL. May my hand wither if ever I touch you!

LUKA. Don't doubt him, dear! He needs you more than you need him!

VASSILISA [*from the window*]. So now they're engaged! Love and advice!

NATASHA. They've come back—oh, God—they saw—oh, Vassily . . .

PEPEL. Why are you frightened? Nobody'll dare touch you now!

VASSILISA. Don't be afraid, Natalia! He won't beat you . . . he don't know how to love or how to beat . . . I know!

LUKA [*in a low voice*]. Rotten old hag—like a snake in the grass . . .

VASSILISA. He dares only with the word!

KOSTILYOFF [*enters*]. Natashka! What are you doing here, you parasite? Gossiping? Kicking about your family? And the samovar not ready? And the table not cleared?

NATASHA [*going out*]. I thought you were going to church . . . ?

KOSTILYOFF. None of your business what we intended doing! Mind your own affairs—and do what you're told!

PEPEL. Shut up, you! She's no longer your servant! Don't go, Natalia—don't do a thing!

NATASHA. Stop ordering me about—you're commencing too soon! [*Leaves*]

PEPEL [*to* KOSTILYOFF]. That's enough. You've used her long enough—now she's mine!

KOSTILYOFF. Yours? When did you buy her—and for how much?

[VASSILISA *roars with laughter.*]

LUKA. Go away, Vasya!

PEPEL. Don't laugh, you fools—or first thing you know I'll make you cry!

VASSILISA. Oh, how terrible! Oh—how you frighten me!
LUKA. Vassily—go away! Don't you see—she's goading you on . . . ridiculing you, don't you understand . . . ?
PEPEL. Yes . . . You lie, lie! You won't get what you want!
VASSILISA. Nor will I get what I don't want, Vasya!
PEPEL [*shaking his fist at her*]. We'll see . . . [*Exits*]
VASSILISA [*disappearing through window*]. I'll arrange some wedding for you . . .
KOSTILYOFF [*crossing to* LUKA]. Well, old man, how's everything?
LUKA. All right!
KOSTILYOFF. You're going away, they say—?
LUKA. Soon.
KOSTILYOFF. Where to?
LUKA. I'll follow my nose . . .
KOSTILYOFF. Tramping, eh? Don't like stopping in one place all the time, do you?
LUKA. Even water won't pass beneath a stone that's sunk too firmly in the ground, they say . . .
KOSTILYOFF. That's true for a stone. But man must settle in one place. Men can't live like cockroaches, crawling about wherever they want. . . . A man must stick to one place—and not wander about aimlessly . . .
LUKA. But suppose his home is wherever he hangs his hat?
KOSTILYOFF. Why, then—he's a vagabond—useless . . . a human being must be of some sort of use—he must work . . .
LUKA. That's what you think, eh?
KOSTILYOFF. Yes—sure . . . just look! What's a vagabond? A strange fellow . . . unlike all others. If he's a real pilgrim then he's some good in the world . . . perhaps he discovered a new truth. Well—but not every truth is worth while. Let him keep it to himself and shut up about it! Or else—let him speak in a way which no one can understand . . . don't let him interfere . . . don't let him stir up people without cause! It's none of his business how other people live! Let him follow his own righteous path . . . in the woods—or in a monastery—away from everybody! He mustn't interfere—nor condemn other people—but pray—pray for all of us—for all the world's sins—for mine—for yours—for everybody's. To pray—that's why he forsakes the world's turmoil! That's so! [*Pause*] But you—what sort of a pilgrim are you—? An honest person must have a passport . . . all honest people have passports . . . yes . . . !
LUKA. In this world there are people—and also just plain men . . .
KOSTILYOFF. Don't coin wise sayings! Don't give me riddles! I'm as clever as you . . . what's the difference—people and men?

LUKA. What riddle is there? I say—there's sterile and there's fertile ground . . . whatever you sow in it, grows . . . that's all . . .

KOSTILYOFF. What do you mean?

LUKA. Take yourself for instance . . . if the Lord God himself said to you: "Mikhailo, be a man!"—it would be useless—nothing would come of it—you're doomed to remain just as you are . . .

KOSTILYOFF. Oh—but do you realize that my wife's uncle is a policeman, and that if I . . .

VASSILISA [*coming in*]. Mikhail Ivanitch—come and have your tea . . .

KOSTILYOFF [*to* LUKA]. You listen! Get out! You leave this place—hear?

VASSILISA. Yes—get out, old man! Your tongue's too long! And—who knows—you may be an escaped convict . . .

KOSTILYOFF. If I ever see sign of you again after to-day—well—I've warned you!

LUKA. You'll call your uncle, eh? Go on—call him! Tell him you've caught an escaped convict—and maybe uncle'll get a reward—perhaps all of three kopecks . . .

BUBNOFF [*in the window*]. What are you bargaining about? Three kopecks—for what?

LUKA. They're threatening to sell me . . .

VASSILISA [*to her husband*]. Come . . .

BUBNOFF. For three kopecks? Well—look out, old man—they may even do it for one!

KOSTILYOFF [*to* BUBNOFF]. You have a habit of jumping up like a jack-in-the-box!

VASSILISA. The world is full of shady people and crooks—

LUKA. Hope you'll enjoy your tea!

VASSILISA [*turning*]. Shut up! You rotten toadstool!

[*Leaves with her husband.*]

LUKA. I'm off to-night.

BUBNOFF. That's right. Don't outstay your welcome!

LUKA. True enough.

BUBNOFF. I know. Perhaps I've escaped the gallows by getting away in time . . .

LUKA. Well?

BUBNOFF. That's true. It was this way. My wife took up with my boss. He was great at his trade—could dye a dog's skin so that it looked like a raccoon's—could change cat's skin into kangaroo—muskrats, all sorts of things. Well—my wife took up with him—and they were so mad about each other that I got afraid they might poison me or something like that—so I commenced beating up my wife—and the boss beat me . . . we fought savagely! Once he tore off half my whiskers—and broke one of my ribs . . . well, then I, too, got enraged. . . . I cracked my wife over the head with an iron yard-measure—well—and altogether it was like an honest-to-God war! And then I saw that nothing really could come of it . . . they were planning to get the best of me! So I started planning—how to kill my wife—I thought of it a whole lot . . . but I thought better of it just in time . . . and got away . . .

LUKA. That was best! Let them go on changing dogs into raccoons!

BUBNOFF. Only—the shop was in my wife's name . . . and so I did myself out of it, you see? Although, to tell the truth, I would have drunk it away . . . I'm a hard drinker, you know . . .

LUKA. A hard drinker—oh . . .

BUBNOFF. The worst you ever met! Once I start drinking, I drink everything in sight, I'll spend every bit of money I have—everything except my bones and my skin . . . what's more, I'm lazy . . . it's terrible how I hate work!

[*Enter* SATINE *and* THE ACTOR, *quarreling.*]

SATINE. Nonsense! You'll go nowhere—it's all a damned lie! Old man, what did you stuff him with all those fairytales for?

THE ACTOR. You lie! Grandfather! Tell him that he lies!—I am going away. I worked to-day—I swept the streets . . . and I didn't have a drop of vodka. What do you think of that? Here they are—two fifteen kopeck pieces—and I'm sober!

SATINE. Why—that's absurd! Give it to me—I'll either drink it up—or lose it at cards . . .

THE ACTOR. Get out—this is for my journey . . .

LUKA [*to* SATINE]. And you—why are you trying to lead him astray?

SATINE. Tell me, soothsayer, beloved by the Gods, what's my future going to be? I've gone to pieces, brother—but everything isn't lost yet, grandfather . . . there are sharks in this world who got more brains than I!

LUKA. You're cheerful, Constantine—and very agreeable!

BUBNOFF. Actor, come over here! [THE ACTOR *crosses to window, sits down on the sill before* BUBNOFF, *and speaks in a low voice with him*]

SATINE. You know, brother, I used to be a clever youngster. It's nice to think of it. I was a devil of a fellow . . . danced splendidly, played on the stage, loved to amuse people . . . it was awfully gay . . .

LUKA. How did you get to be what you are?

SATINE. You're inquisitive, old man! You want to know everything? What for?

LUKA. I want to understand the ways of men—I look at you, and I don't understand. You're a bold lad, Constantine, and you're no fool . . . yet, all of a sudden . . .

SATINE. It's prison, grandfather—I spent four years and seven months in prison—afterwards—where could I go?

LUKA. Aha! What were you there for?

SATINE. On account of a scoundrel—whom I killed in a fit of rage . . . and despair . . . and in prison I learned to play cards . . .

LUKA. You killed—because of a woman?

SATINE. Because of my own sister. . . . But look here—leave me alone! I don't care for these cross-examinations—and all this happened a long time ago. It's already nine years since my sister's death. . . . Brother, she was a wonderful girl . . .

LUKA. You take life easily! And only a while ago that locksmith was here—and how he did yell!

SATINE. Kleshtch?

LUKA. Yes—"There's no work," he shouted; "there isn't anything . . ."

SATINE. He'll get used to it. What could I do?

LUKA [*softly*]. Look—here he comes!

[KLESHTCH *walks in slowly, his head bowed low.*]

SATINE. Hey, widower! Why are you so down in the mouth? What are you thinking?

KLESHTCH. I'm thinking—what'll I do? I've no food—nothing—the funeral ate up all . . .

SATINE. I'll give you a bit of advice . . . do nothing! Just be a burden to the world at large!

KLESHTCH. Go on—talk—I'd be ashamed of myself . . .

SATINE. Why—people aren't ashamed to let you live worse than a dog. Just think . . . you stop work—so do I—so do hundreds, thousands of others—everybody—understand?—Everybody'll quit working . . . nobody'll do a damned thing—and then what'll happen?

KLESHTCH. They'll all starve to death . . .

LUKA [*to* SATINE]. If those are your notions, you ought to join the order of Begunes—you know—there's some such organization . . .

SATINE. I know—grandfather—and they're no fools . . .

[NATASHA *is heard screaming behind* KOSTILYOFF's *window: "What for? Stop! What have I done?"*]

LUKA [*worried*]. Natasha! That was she crying—oh, God . . .

[*From* KOSTILYOFF's *room is heard noise, shuffling, breaking of crockery, and* KOSTILYOFF's *shrill cry: "Ah! Heretic! Bitch!"*]

VASSILISA. Wait, wait—I'll teach her—there, there!
NATASHA. They're beating me—killing me . . .
SATINE [*shouts through the window*]. Hey—you there . . .
LUKA [*trembling*]. Where's Vassily—? Call Vaska—oh, God—listen, brothers . . .
THE ACTOR [*running out*]. I'll find him at once!
BUBNOFF. They beat her a lot these days . . .
SATINE. Come on, old man—we'll be witnesses . . .
LUKA [*following* SATINE]. Oh—witnesses—what for? Vassily—he should be called at once!
NATASHA. Sister—sister dear! Va-a-a . . .
BUBNOFF. They've gagged her—I'll go and see . . .

[*The noise in* KOSTILYOFF'*s room dies down gradually as if they had gone into the hallway. The old man's cry: "Stop!" is heard. A door is slammed noisily, and the latter sound cuts off all the other noises sharply. Quiet on the stage. Twilight.*]

KLESHTCH [*seated on the sledge, indifferently, rubbing his hands; mutters at first indistinguishably, then:*] What then? One must live. [*Louder*] Must have shelter—well? There's no shelter, no roof—nothing . . . there's only man—man alone—no hope . . . no help . . .

[*Exit slowly, his head bent. A few moments of ominous silence, then somewhere in the hallway a mass of sounds, which grows in volume and comes nearer. Individual voices are heard.*]

VASSILISA. I'm her sister—let go . . .
KOSTILYOFF. What right have you . . . ?
VASSILISA. Jail-bird!
SATINE. Call Vaska—quickly! Zob—hit him!

[*A police whistle.* THE TARTAR *runs in, his right hand in a sling.*]

THE TARTAR. There's a new law for you—kill only in daytime!

[*Enter* ZOB, *followed by* MIEDVIEDIEFF.]

ZOB. I handed him a good one!
MIEDVIEDIEFF. You—how dare you fight?
THE TARTAR. What about yourself? What's your duty?
MIEDVIEDIEFF [*running after*]. Stop—give back my whistle!
KOSTILYOFF [*runs in*]. Abram! Stop him! Hold him! He's a murderer—he . . .

[*Enter* KVASHNYA *and* NASTYA *supporting* NATASHA *who is disheveled.* SATINE *backs away, pushing away* VASSILISA *who is try-*

ing to attack her sister, while, near her, ALYOSHKA *jumps up and down like a madman, whistles into her ear, shrieking, roaring. Also other ragged men and women.*]

SATINE [*to* VASSILISA]. Well—you damned bitch!

VASSILISA. Let go, you jail-bird! I'll tear you to pieces—if I have to pay for it with my own life!

KVASHNYA [*leading* NATASHA *aside*]. You—Karpovna—that's enough—stand back—aren't you ashamed? Or are you crazy?

MIEDVIEDIEFF [*seizes* SATINE]. Aha—caught at last!

SATINE. Zob—beat them up! Vaska—Vaska . . .

[*They all, in a chaotic mass, struggle near the brick wall. They lead* NATASHA *to the right, and set her on a pile of wood.* PEPEL *rushes in from the hallway and, silently, with powerful movements, pushes the crowd aside.*]

PEPEL. Natalia, where are you . . . you . . .

KOSTILYOFF [*disappearing behind a corner*]. Abram! Seize Vaska! Comrades—help us get him! The thief! The robber!

PEPEL. You—you old bastard! [*Aiming a terrific blow at* KOSTILYOFF. KOSTILYOFF *falls so that only the upper part of his body is seen.* PEPEL *rushes to* NATASHA]

VASSILISA. Beat Vaska! Brothers! Beat the thief!

MIEDVIEDIEFF [*yells to* SATINE]. Keep out of this—it's a family affair . . . they're relatives . . . and who are you . . .

PEPEL [*to* NATASHA]. What did she do to you? She used a knife?

KVASHNYA. God—what beasts! They've scalded the child's feet with boiling water!

NASTYA. They overturned the samovar . . .

THE TARTAR. Maybe an accident—you must make sure—you can't exactly tell . . .

NATASHA [*half fainting*]. Vassily—take me away—

VASSILISA. Good people! Come! Look! He's dead! Murdered!

[*All crowd into the hallway near* KOSTILYOFF. BUBNOFF *leaves the crowd and crosses to* PEPEL.]

BUBNOFF [*in a low voice, to* PEPEL]. Vaska—the old man is done for!

PEPEL [*looks at him, as though he does not understand*]. Go—for help—she must be taken to the hospital . . . I'll settle with them . . .

BUBNOFF. I say—the old man—somebody's killed him . . .

[*The noise on the stage dies out like a fire under water. Distinct, whispered exclamations: "Not really?" "Well—let's go away, brothers!" "The devil!" "Hold on now!" "Let's get away before the police comes!" The crowd disappears.* BUBNOFF, THE TARTAR, NASTYA, *and* KVASHNYA, *rush up to* KOSTILYOFF'*s body.*]

VASSILISA [*rises and cries out triumphantly*]. Killed—my husband's killed! Vaska killed him! I saw him! Brothers, I saw him! Well—Vasya—the police!

PEPEL [*moves away from* NATASHA]. Let me alone. [*Looks at* KOSTILYOFF; *to* VASSILISA] Well—are you glad? [*Touches the corpse with his foot*] The old bastard is dead! Your wish has been granted! Why not do the same to you? [*Throws himself at her*]

[SATINE *and* ZOB *quickly overpower him, and* VASSILISA *disappears in the passage.*]

SATINE. Come to your senses!

ZOB. Hold on! Not so fast!

VASSILISA [*appearing*]. Well, Vaska, dear friend? You can't escape your fate. . . . police—Abram—whistle!

MIEDVIEDIEFF. Those devils tore my whistle off!

ALYOSHKA. Here it is! [*Whistles,* MIEDVIEDIEFF *runs after him*]

SATINE [*leading* PEPEL *to* NATASHA]. Don't be afraid, Vaska! Killed in a row! That's nonsense—only manslaughter—you won't have to serve a long term . . .

VASSILISA. Hold Vaska—he killed him—I saw it!

SATINE. I, too, gave the old man a couple of blows—he was easily fixed . . . you call me as witness, Vaska!

PEPEL. I don't need to defend myself . . . I want to drag Vassilisa into this mess—and I'll do it—she was the one who wanted it . . . she was the one who urged me to kill him—she goaded me on . . .

NATASHA [*sudden and loud*]. Oh—I understand—so that's it, Vassily? Good people! They're both guilty—my sister and he—they're both guilty! They had it all planned! So, Vassily, that's why you spoke to me a while ago—so that she should overhear everything—? Good people! She's his mistress—you know it—everybody knows it—they're both guilty! She—she urged him to kill her husband—he was in their way—and so was I! And now they've maimed me . . .

PEPEL. Natalia! What's the matter with you? What are you saying?

SATINE. Oh—hell!

VASSILISA. You lie. She lies. He—Vaska killed him . . .

NATASHA. They're both guilty! God damn you both!

SATINE. What a mix-up! Hold on, Vassily—or they'll ruin you between them!

ZOB. I can't understand it—oh—what a mess!

PEPEL. Natalia! It can't be true! Surely you don't believe that I—with her—

SATINE. So help me God, Natasha! Just think . . .

VASSILISA [*in the passage*]. They've killed my husband—Your Excellency! Vaska Pepel, the thief, killed him, Captain! I saw it—everybody saw it . . .

NATASHA [*tossing about in agony; her mind wandering*]. Good people—my sister and Vaska killed him! The police—listen—this sister of mine—here—she urged, coaxed her lover—there he stands—the scoundrel! They both killed him! Put them in jail! Bring them before the judge! Take me along, too! To prison! Christ Almighty—take me to prison, too!

CURTAIN

Act IV

Same as Act I. But PEPEL'*s room is no longer there, and the partition has been removed. Furthermore, there is no anvil at the place where* KLESHTCH *used to sit and work. In the corner, where* PEPEL'*s room used to be,* THE TARTAR *lies stretched out, rather restless, and groaning from time to time.* KLESHTCH *sits at one end of the table, repairing a concertina and now and then testing the stops. At the other end of the table sits* SATINE, THE BARON, *and* NASTYA. *In front of them stand a bottle of vodka, three bottles of beer, and a large loaf of black bread.* THE ACTOR *lies on top of the stove, shifting about and coughing. It is night. The stage is lit by a lamp in the middle of the table. Outside the wind howls.*

KLESHTCH. Yes . . . he disappeared during the confusion and noise . . .

THE BARON. He vanished under the very eyes of the police—just like a puff of smoke . . .

SATINE. That's how sinners flee from the company of the righteous!

NASTYA. He was a dear old soul! But you—you aren't men—you're just—oh—like rust on iron!

THE BARON [*drinks*]. Here's to you, my lady!

SATINE. He was an inquisitive old fellow—yes! Nastenka here fell in love with him . . .

NASTYA. Yes! I did! Madly! It's true! He saw everything—understood everything . . .

SATINE [*laughing*]. Yes, generally speaking, I would say that he was—oh—like mush to those who can't chew . . .

THE BARON [*laughing*]. Right! Like plaster on a boil!

KLESHTCH. He was merciful—you people don't know what pity means . . .

SATINE. What good can I do you by pitying you?

KLESHTCH. You needn't have pity—but you needn't harm or offend your fellow-beings, either!

THE TARTAR [*sits up on his bunk, nursing his wounded hand carefully*]. He was a fine old man. The law of life was the law of his heart. . . . And he who obeys this law, is good, while he who disregards it, perishes . . .

THE BARON. What law, Prince?

THE TARTAR. There are a number—different ones—you know . . .

THE BARON. Proceed!

THE TARTAR. Do not do harm unto others—such is the law!

SATINE. Oh—you mean the Penal Code, criminal and correctional, eh?

THE BARON. And also the Code of Penalties inflicted by Justices of the Peace!

THE TARTAR. No. I mean the Koran. It is the supreme law—and your own soul ought to be the Koran—yes!

KLESHTCH [*testing his concertina*]. It wheezes like all hell! But the Prince speaks the truth—one must live abiding by the law—by the teachings of the Gospels . . .

SATINE. Well—go ahead and do it!

THE BARON. Just try it!

THE TARTAR. The Prophet Mohammed gave to us the law. He said: "Here is the law! Do as it is written therein!" Later on a time will arrive when the Koran will have outlived its purpose—and time will bring forth its own laws—every generation will create its own . . .

SATINE. To be sure! Time passed on—and gave us—the Criminal Code . . . It's a strong law, brother—it won't wear off so very soon!

NASTYA [*banging her glass on the table*]. Why—why do I stay here—with you? I'll go away somewhere—to the ends of the world!

THE BARON. Without any shoes, my lady?

NASTYA. I'll go—naked, if must be—creeping on all fours!

THE BARON. That'll be rather picturesque, my lady—on all fours!

NASTYA. Yes—and I'll crawl if I have to—anything at all—as long as I don't have to see your faces any longer—oh, I'm so sick of it all—the life—the people—everything!

SATINE. When you go, please take the actor along—he's preparing to go to the very same place—he has learned that within a half mile's distance of the end of the world there's a hospital for diseased organons . . .

THE ACTOR [*raising his head over the top of the stove*]. A hospital for organisms—you fool!

SATINE. For organons—poisoned with vodka!

THE ACTOR. Yes! He will go! He will indeed! You'll see!

THE BARON. Who is he, sir?

THE ACTOR. I!

THE BARON. Thanks, servant of the goddess—what's her name—? The goddess of drama—tragedy—whatever is her name—?

THE ACTOR. The muse, idiot! Not the goddess—the muse!

SATINE. Lachesis—Hera—Aphrodite—Atropos—oh! To hell with them all! You see—Baron—it was the old man who stuffed the actor's head full with this rot . . .

THE BARON. That old man's a fool . . .

THE ACTOR. Ignoramuses! Beasts! Melpomene—that's her name! Heartless brutes! Bastards! You'll see! He'll go! "On with the orgy, dismal spirits!"—poem—ah—by Béranger! Yes—he'll find some spot where there's no—no . . .

THE BARON. Where there's nothing, sir?

THE ACTOR. Right! Nothing! "This hole shall be my grave—I am dying—ill and exhausted . . ." Why do you exist? Why?

THE BARON. You! God or genius or orgy—or whatever you are—don't roar so loud!

THE ACTOR. You lie! I'll roar all I want to!

NASTYA [*lifting her head from the table and throwing up her hands*]. Go on! Yell! Let them listen to you!

THE BARON. Where is the sense, my lady?

SATINE. Leave them alone, Baron! To hell with the lot! Let them yell—let them knock their damned heads off if they feel like it! There's a method in their madness! Don't you go and interfere with people as that old fellow did! Yes—it's he—the damned old fool—he bewitched the whole gang of us!

KLESHTCH. He persuaded them to go away—but failed to show them the road . . .

THE BARON. That old man was a humbug!

NASTYA. Liar! You're a humbug yourself!

THE BARON. Shut up, my lady!

KLESHTCH. The old man didn't like truth very much—as a matter of fact, he strongly resented it—and wasn't he right, though? Just look—where is there any truth? And yet, without it, you can't breathe! For instance, our Tartar Prince over there, crushed his hand at his work—and now he'll have to have his arm amputated—and there's the truth for you!

SATINE [*striking the table with his clenched fist*]. Shut up! You sons of bitches! Fools! Not another word about that old fellow! [*To* THE BARON] You, Baron, are the worst of the lot! You don't understand a thing, and you lie like the devil! The old man's no humbug! What's the truth? Man! Man—that's the truth! He understood man—you don't! You're all as dumb as stones! I understand the old man—yes! He lied—but lied out of sheer pity for you . . . God damn you! Lots of people lie out of pity for their fellow-beings! I know! I've read about it! They lie—oh—beautifully, inspiringly, stirringly! Some lies bring comfort, and others bring peace—a lie alone can justify the burden which crushed a workman's hand and condemns those who are starving! I know what lying means! The weakling and the one who is a parasite through his very weakness—they both need lies—lies are their support, their shield, their armor! But the man who is strong, who is his own master, who is free and does not have to suck his neighbors' blood—he needs no lies! To lie—it's the creed of slaves and masters of slaves! Truth is the religion of the free man!

THE BARON. Bravo! Well spoken! Hear, hear! I agree! You speak like an honest man!

SATINE. And why can't a crook at times speak the truth—since honest people at times speak like crooks? Yes—I've forgotten a lot—but I still know a thing or two! The old man? Oh—he's wise! He affected me as acid affects a dirty old silver coin! Let's drink to his health! Fill the glasses . . . [NASTYA *fills a glass with beer and hands it to* SATINE, *who laughs*] The old man lives within himself . . . he looks upon all the world from his own angle. Once I asked him: "Grand-dad, why do people live?" [*Tries to imitate* LUKA'*s voice and gestures*] And he replied: "Why, my dear fellow, people live in the hope of something better! For example—let's say there are carpenters in this world, and all sorts of trash . . . people . . . and they give birth to a carpenter the like of which has never been seen upon the face of the earth . . . he's way above everybody else, and has no equal among carpenters! The brilliancy of his personality was reflected on all his trade, on all the other carpenters, so that they advanced twenty years in one day! This applies to all other trades—blacksmiths and shoemakers and other workmen—and all the peasants—and even the aristocrats live in the hopes of a higher life! Each individual thinks that he's living for his own Self, but in reality he lives in the hope of something better. A hundred years—sometimes longer—do we expect, live for the finer, higher life . . ." [NASTYA *stares intently into* SATINE'*s face.* KLESHTCH *stops working and listens.* THE BARON *bows his head very low, drumming softly on the table with his fingers.* THE ACTOR, *peering down from the stove, tries to climb noiselessly into the bunk*] "Every one, brothers, every one lives in the hope of something better. That's why we must respect each and every human being! How do we know who he is, why he was born, and what he is capable of accomplishing? Perhaps his coming into the world will prove to be our good fortune . . . Especially must we respect little children! Children—need freedom! Don't interfere with their lives! Respect children!" [*Pause*]

THE BARON [*thoughtfully*]. Hm—yes—something better?—That reminds me of my family . . . an old family dating back to the time of Catherine . . . all noblemen, soldiers, originally French . . . they served their country and gradually rose higher and higher. In the days of Nicholas the First my grandfather, Gustave DeBille, held a high post—riches—hundreds of serfs . . . horses—cooks—

NASTYA. You liar! It isn't true!

THE BARON [*jumping up*]. What? Well—go on—

NASTYA. It isn't true.

THE BARON [*screams*]. A house in Moscow! A house in Petersburg! Carriages! Carriages with coats of arms!

[KLESHTCH *takes his concertina and goes to one side, watching the scene with interest.*]

NASTYA. You lie!

THE BARON. Shut up!—I say—dozens of footmen . . .

NASTYA [*delighted*]. You lie!

THE BARON. I'll kill you!

NASTYA [*ready to run away*]. There were no carriages!

SATINE. Stop, Nastenka! Don't infuriate him!

THE BARON. Wait—you bitch! My grandfather . . .

NASTYA. There was no grandfather! There was nothing!

[SATINE *roars with laughter.*]

THE BARON [*worn out with rage, sits down on bench*]. Satine! Tell that slut—what—? You, too, are laughing? You—don't believe me either? [*Cries out in despair, pounding the table with his fists*] It's true—damn the whole lot of you!

NASTYA [*triumphantly*]. So—you're crying? Understand now what a human being feels like when nobody believes him?

KLESHTCH [*returning to the table*]. I thought there'd be a fight . . .

THE TARTAR. Oh—people are fools! It's too bad . . .

THE BARON. I shall not permit any one to ridicule me! I have proofs—documents—damn you!

SATINE. Forget it! Forget about your grandfather's carriages! You can't drive anywhere in a carriage of the past!

THE BARON. How dare she—just the same—?

NASTYA. Just imagine! How dare I—?

SATINE. You see—she does dare! How is she any worse than you are? Although, surely, in her past there wasn't even a father and mother, let alone carriages and a grandfather . . .

THE BARON [*quieting down*]. Devil take you—you do know how to argue dispassionately—and I, it seems—I've no will-power . . .

SATINE. Acquire some—it's useful . . . [*Pause*] Nastya! Are you going to the hospital?

NASTYA. What for?

SATINE. To see Natashka.

NASTYA. Oh—just woke up, did you? She's been out of the hospital for some time—and they can't find a trace of her . . .

SATINE. Oh—that woman's a goner!

KLESHTCH. It's interesting to see whether Vaska will get the best of Vassilisa, or the other way around—

NASTYA. Vassilisa will win out! She's shrewd! And Vaska will go to the gallows!

SATINE. For manslaughter? No—only to jail . . .

NASTYA. Too bad—the gallows would have been better . . . that's where all of you should be sent . . . swept off into a hole—like filth . . .

SATINE [*astonished*]. What's the matter? Are you crazy?

THE BARON. Oh—give her a wallop—that'll teach her to be less impertinent . . .

NASTYA. Just you try to touch me!

THE BARON. I shall!

SATINE. Stop! Don't insult her! I can't get the thought of the old man out of my head! [*Roars with laughter*] Don't offend your fellow-beings! Suppose I were offended once in such a way that I'd remember it for the rest of my life? What then? Should I forgive ? No, no!

THE BARON [*to* NASTYA]. You must understand that I'm not your sort . . . you—ah—you piece of dirt!

NASTYA. You bastard! Why—you live off me like a worm off an apple!

[*The men laugh amusedly.*]

KLESHTCH. Fool! An apple—?

THE BARON. You can't be angry with her—she's just an ass—

NASTYA. You laugh? Liars! Don't strike you as funny, eh?

THE ACTOR [*morosely*]. Give them a good beating!

NASTYA. If I only could! [*Takes a cup from the table and throws it on the floor*] That's what I'd like to do to you all!

THE TARTAR. Why break dishes—eh—silly girl?

THE BARON [*rising*]. That'll do! I'll teach her manners in half a second!

NASTYA [*running toward door*]. Go to hell!

SATINE [*calling after her*]. Hey! That's enough! Whom are you trying to frighten? What's all the row about, anyway?

NASTYA. Dogs! I hope you'll croak! Dogs! [*Runs out*]

THE ACTOR [*morosely*]. Amen!

THE TARTAR. Allah! Mad women, these Russians! They're bold, wilful; Tartar women aren't like that! They know the law and abide by it. . . .

KLESHTCH. She ought to be given a sound hiding!

THE BARON. The slut!

KLESHTCH [*testing the concertina*]. It's ready! But its owner isn't here yet—that young fellow is burning his life away . . .

SATINE. Care for a drink—now?

KLESHTCH. Thanks . . . it's time to go to bed . . .

SATINE. Getting used to us?

KLESHTCH [*drinks, then goes to his bunk*]. It's all right . . . there are people everywhere—at first you don't notice it . . . but after a while you don't mind. . . .

[THE TARTAR *spreads some rags over his bunk, then kneels on them and prays.*]

THE BARON [*to* SATINE, *pointing at* THE TARTAR]. Look!

SATINE. Stop! He's a good fellow! Leave him alone! [*Roars with laughter*] I feel kindly to-day—the devil alone knows the reason why . . .

THE BARON. You always feel kindly when you're drunk—you're even wiser at such times . . .

SATINE. When I'm drunk? Yes—then I like everything—right—He prays? That's fine! A man may believe or not—that's his own affair—a man is free—he pays for everything himself—belief or unbelief—love—wisdom . . . a man pays for everything—and that's just why he's free! Man is—truth! And what is man? It's neither you nor I nor they—oh, no—it's you and they and I and the old man—and Napoleon—Mohammed—all in one! [*Outlines vaguely in the air the contour of a human being*] Do you understand? It's tremendous! It contains the beginning and the end of everything—everything is in man—and everything exists for him! Man alone exists—everything else is the creation of his hands and his brain! Man! It is glorious! It sounds—oh—so big! Man must be respected—not degraded with pity—but respected, respected! Let us drink to man, Baron! [*Rises*] It is good to feel that you are a man! I'm a convict, a murderer, a crook—granted!—When I'm out on the street people stare at me as if I were a scoundrel—they draw away from me—they look after me and often they say: "You dog! You humbug! Work!" Work? And what for? To fill my belly? [*Roars with laughter*] I've always despised people who worry too much about their bellies. It isn't right, Baron! It isn't! Man is loftier than that! Man stands above hunger!

THE BARON. You—reason things out. . . . Well and good—it brings you a certain amount of consolation. . . . Personally I'm incapable of it . . . I don't know how. [*Glances around him and then, softly, guardedly*] Brother—I am afraid—at times. Do you understand? Afraid!—Because—what next?

SATINE. Rot! What's a man to be afraid of?

THE BARON [*pacing up and down*]. You know—as far back as I can remember, there's been a sort of fog in my brain. I was never able to understand anything. Somehow I feel embarrassed—it seems to me that all my life I've done nothing but change clothes—and why? I don't understand! I studied—I wore the uniform of the Institute for the Sons of the Nobility . . . but what have I learned? I don't remember! I married—I wore a frock-coat—then a dressing-gown . . . but I chose a disagreeable wife . . . and why? I don't understand. I squandered everything that I possessed—I wore some sort of a grey jacket and brick-colored trousers—but how did I happen to ruin myself? I haven't the slightest idea. . . . I had a position in the Department of State. . . . I wore a uniform and a cap with insignia of rank. . . . I embezzled government funds . . . so they dressed me in a convict's garb—and later on I got into these clothes here—and it all happened as in a dream—it's funny . . .

SATINE. Not very! It's rather—silly!

THE BARON. Yes—silly! I think so, too. Still—wasn't I born for some sort of purpose?

SATINE [*laughing*]. Probably—a man is born to conceive a better man. [*Shaking his head*]—It's all right!

THE BARON. That she-devil Nastka! Where did she run to? I'll go and see—after all, she . . . [*Exits; pause*]

THE ACTOR. Tartar! [*Pause*] Prince! [THE TARTAR *looks round*] Say a prayer for me . . .

THE TARTAR. What?

THE ACTOR [*softly*]. Pray—for me!

THE TARTAR [*after a silence*]. Pray for your own self!

THE ACTOR [*quickly crawls off the stove and goes to the table, pours out a drink with shaking hands, drinks, then almost runs to passage*]. All over!

SATINE. Hey, proud Sicambrian! Where are you going?

[SATINE *whistles.* MIEDVIEDIEFF *enters, dressed in a woman's flannel shirt-waist; followed by* BUBNOFF. *Both are slightly drunk.*

BUBNOFF *carries a bunch of pretzels in one hand, a couple of smoked fish in the other, a bottle of vodka under one arm, another bottle in his coat pocket.*]

MIEDVIEDIEFF. A camel is something like a donkey—only it has no ears. . . .

BUBNOFF. Shut up! You're a variety of donkey yourself!

MIEDVIEDIEFF. A camel has no ears at all, at all—it hears through its nostrils . . .

BUBNOFF [*to* SATINE]. Friend! I've looked for you in all the saloons and all the cabarets! Take this bottle—my hands are full . . .

SATINE. Put the pretzels on the table—then you'll have one hand free—

BUBNOFF. Right! Hey—you donkey—look! Isn't he a clever fellow?

MIEDVIEDIEFF. All crooks are clever—I know! They couldn't do a thing without brains. An honest man is all right even if he's an idiot . . . but a crook must have brains. But, speaking about camels, you're wrong . . . you can ride them—they have no horns . . . and no teeth either . . .

BUBNOFF. Where's everybody? Why is there no one here? Come on out . . . I treat! Who's in the corner?

SATINE. How soon will you drink up everything you have? Scarecrow!

BUBNOFF. Very soon! I've very little this time. Zob—where's Zob?

KLESHTCH [*crossing to table*]. He isn't here . . .

BUBNOFF. Waughrr! Bull-dog! Brr-zz-zz!—Turkey-cock! Don't bark and don't growl! Drink—make merry—and don't be sullen!—I treat everybody—Brother, I love to treat—if I were rich, I'd run a free saloon! So help me God, I would! With an orchestra and a lot of singers! Come, every one! Drink and eat—listen to the music—and rest in peace! Beggars—come, all you beggars—and enter my saloon free of charge! Satine—you can have half my capital—just like that!

SATINE. You better give me all you have straight away!

BUBNOFF. All my capital? Right now? Well—here's a ruble—here's twenty kopecks—five kopecks—sun-flower seeds—and that's all!

SATINE. That's splendid! It'll be safer with me—I'll gamble with it . . .

MIEDVIEDIEFF. I'm a witness—the money was given you for safekeeping. How much is it?

BUBNOFF. You? You're a camel—we don't need witnesses . . .

ALYOSHKA [*comes in barefoot*]. Brothers, I got my feet wet!

BUBNOFF. Go on and get your throat wet—and nothing'll happen—you're a fine fellow—you sing and you play—that's all right! But it's too bad you drink—drink, little brother, is harmful, very harmful . . .

ALYOSHKA. I judge by you! Only when you're drunk do you resemble a human being . . . Kleshtch! Is my concertina fixed? [*Sings and dances*]

"If my mug were not so attractive,
My sweetheart wouldn't love me at all . . ."

Boys, I'm frozen—it's cold . . .

MIEDVIEDIEFF. Hm—and may I ask who's this sweetheart?

BUBNOFF. Shut up! From now on, brother, you are neither a policeman nor an uncle!

ALYOSHKA. Just auntie's husband!

BUBNOFF. One of your nieces is in jail—the other one's dying . . .

MIEDVIEDIEFF [*proudly*]. You lie! She's not dying—she disappeared—without trace . . .

[SATINE *roars.*]

BUBNOFF. All the same, brothers—a man without nieces isn't an uncle!

ALYOSHKA. Your Excellency! Listen to the drummer of the retired billygoats' brigade! [*Sings*]

"My sweetheart has money,
I haven't a cent.
But I'm a cheerful,
Merry lad!"

Oh—isn't it cold!

[*Enter* ZOB. *From now until the final curtain men and women drift in, undress, and stretch out on the bunks, grumbling.*]

ZOB. Bubnoff! Why did you run off?

BUBNOFF. Come here—sit down—brother, let's sing my favorite ditty, eh?

THE TARTAR. Night was made for sleep! Sing your songs in the daytime!

SATINE. Well—never mind, Prince—come here!

THE TARTAR. What do you mean—never mind? There's going to be a noise—there always is when people sing!

BUBNOFF [*crossing to* THE TARTAR]. Count—ah—I mean Prince—how's your hand? Did they cut it off?

THE TARTAR. What for? We'll wait and see—perhaps it won't be necessary . . . a hand isn't made of iron—it won't take long to cut it off . . .

ZOB. It's your own affair, Hassanka! You'll be good for nothing without your hand. We're judged by our hands and backs—without the pride of your hand, you're no longer a human being. Tobacco-carting—that's your business! Come on—have a drink of vodka—and stop worrying!

KVASHNYA [*comes in*]. Ah, my beloved fellow-lodgers! It's horrible outside—snow and slush . . . is my policeman here?

MIEDVIEDIEFF. Right here!

KVASHNYA. Wearing my blouse again? And drunk, eh? What's the idea?

MIEDVIEDIEFF. In celebration of Bubnoff's birthday . . . besides, it's cold . . .

KVASHNYA. Better look out—stop fooling about and go to sleep!

MIEDVIEDIEFF [*goes to kitchen*]. Sleep? I can—I want to—it's time— [*Exit*]

SATINE. What's the matter? Why are you so strict with him?

KVASHNYA. You can't be otherwise, friend. You have to be strict with his sort. I took him as a partner. I thought he'd be of some benefit to me—because he's a military man—and you're a rough lot . . . and I am a woman—and now he's turned drunkard—that won't do at all!

SATINE. You picked a good one for partner!

KVASHNYA. Couldn't get a better one. You wouldn't want to live with me . . . you think you're too fine! And even if you did it wouldn't last more than a week . . . you'd gamble me and all I own away at cards!

SATINE [*roars with laughter*]. That's true, landlady—I'd gamble . . .

KVASHNYA. Yes, yes. Alyoshka!

ALYOSHKA. Here he is—I, myself!

KVASHNYA. What do you mean by gossiping about me?

ALYOSHKA. I? I speak out everything—whatever my conscience tells me. There, I say, is a wonderful woman! Splendid meat, fat, bones—over four hundred pounds! But brains—? Not an ounce!

KVASHNYA. You're a liar! I've lot of brains! What do you mean by saying I beat my policeman?

ALYOSHKA. I thought you did—when you pulled him by the hair!

KVASHNYA [*laughs*]. You fool! You aren't blind, are you? Why wash dirty linen in public? And—it hurts his feelings—that's why he took to drink . . .

ALYOSHKA. It's true, evidently, that even a chicken likes vodka . . .

[SATINE *and* KLESHTCH *roar with laughter.*]

KVASHNYA. Go on—show your teeth! What sort of a man are you anyway, Alyoshka?

ALYOSHKA. Oh—I am first-rate! Master of all trades! I follow my nose!

BUBNOFF [*near* THE TARTAR'S *bunk*]. Come on! At all events—we won't let you sleep! We'll sing all night. Zob!

ZOB. Sing—? All right . . .

ALYOSHKA. And I'll play . . .

SATINE. We'll listen!

THE TARTAR [*smiling*]. Well—Bubnoff—you devil—bring the vodka—we'll drink—we'll have a hell of a good time! The end will come soon enough—and then we'll be dead!

BUBNOFF. Fill his glass, Satine! Zob—sit down! Ah—brothers—what does a man need after all? There, for instance, I've had a drink—and I'm happy! Zob! Start my favorite song! I'll sing—and then I'll cry. . . .

ZOB [*begins to sing*]

"The sun rises and sets . . ."

BUBNOFF [*joining in*]

"But my prison is all dark. . . ."

[*Door opens quickly.*]

THE BARON [*on the threshold; yells*]. Hey—you—come—come here! Out in the waste—in the yard . . . over there . . . The actor—he's hanged himself. . . .

[*Silence. All stare at* THE BARON. *Behind him appears* NASTYA, *and slowly, her eyes wide with horror, she walks to the table.*]

SATINE [*in a matter-of-fact voice*]. Damned fool—he ruined the song . . . !

CURTAIN

A Month in the Country

Cast of Characters

ARKADY SERGEYITCH ISLAYEV, *a wealthy landowner, aged 36.*

NATALYA PETROVNA, *his wife, aged 29.*

KOLYA, *their son, aged 10.*

VERA, *their ward, aged 17.*

ANNA SEMYONOVNA ISLAYEV, *mother of Islayev, aged 58.*

LIZAVETA BOGDANOVNA, *a companion, aged 37.*

SCHAAF, *a German tutor, aged 45.*

MIHAIL ALEXANDROVITCH RAKITIN, *a friend of the family, aged 30.*

ALEXEY NIKOLAYEVITCH BELIAYEV, *a student, Kolya's tutor, aged 21.*

AFANASY IVANOVITCH BOLSHINTSOV, *a neighbour, aged 48.*

IGNATY ILYITCH SHPIGELSKY, *a doctor, aged 40.*

MATVEY, *a manservant, aged 40.*

KATYA, *a maidservant, aged 20.*

The action takes place on ISLAYEV*'s estate.*

There is an interval of one day between ACTS I *and* II,
ACTS II *and* III, *and* ACTS IV *and* V.

Act I

A drawing-room. On right a card-table and a door into the study; in centre a door into an outer room; on left two windows and a round table. Sofas in the corners. At the card-table ANNA SEMYONOVNA, LIZAVETA BOGDANOVNA *and* SCHAAF *are playing preference;* NATALYA PETROVNA *and* RAKITIN *are sitting at the round table; she is embroidering on canvas; he has a book in his hand. A clock on the wall points to three o'clock.*

SCHAAF. Hearts.

ANNA SEMYONOVNA. Again? Why, if you go on like that, my good man, you will beat us every time.

SCHAAF [*phlegmatically*]. Eight hearts.

ANNA SEMYONOVNA [*to* LIZAVETA BOGDANOVNA]. What a man! There's no playing with him. [LIZAVETA BOGDANOVNA *smiles.*]

NATALYA PETROVNA [*to* RAKITIN]. Why have you left off? Go on.

RAKITIN [*raising his head slowly*]. "Monte Cristo se redressa haletant. . . ." Does it interest you, Natalya Petrovna?

NATALYA PETROVNA. Not at all.

RAKITIN. Why are we reading it then?

NATALYA PETROVNA. Well, it's like this. The other day a woman said to me: "You haven't read Monte Cristo? Oh, you must read it—it's charming." I made her no answer at the time, but now I can say that I've been reading it and found nothing at all charming in it.

RAKITIN. Oh, well, since you have already made up your mind about it. . . .

NATALYA PETROVNA. You lazy creature!

RAKITIN. Oh, I don't mind. . . . [*Looking for the place at which he stopped.*] "Se redressa haletant et. . . ."

NATALYA PETROVNA [*interrupting him*]. Have you seen Arkady today?

RAKITIN. I met him on the dam. . . . It is being repaired. He was explaining something to the workmen and to make things clearer waded up to his knees in the sand.

NATALYA PETROVNA. He gets too hot over things, he tries to do too much. It's a failing. Don't you think so?

RAKITIN. Yes, I agree with you.

NATALYA PETROVNA. How dull that is! . . . You always agree with me. Go on reading.

RAKITIN. Oh, so you want me to quarrel with you. . . . By all means.

NATALYA PETROVNA. I want . . . I want . . . I want *you* to want. . . . Go on reading, I tell you.

RAKITIN. I obey, madam. [*Takes up the book again.*]

SCHAAF. Hearts.

ANNA SEMYONOVNA. What? Again? It's insufferable! [*To* NATALYA PETROVNA.] Natasha . . . Natasha! . . .

NATALYA PETROVNA. What is it?

ANNA SEMYONOVNA. Only fancy! Schaaf wins every point. He keeps on—if it's not seven, it's eight.

SCHAAF. And now it's seven.

ANNA SEMYONOVNA. Do you hear? Its awful.

NATALYA PETROVNA. Yes . . . it is.

ANNA SEMYONOVNA. Back me up then! [*To* NATALYA PETROVNA.] Where's Kolya?

NATALYA PETROVNA. He's gone out for a walk with the new tutor.

ANNA SEMYONOVNA. Oh! Lizaveta Bogdanovna, I call on you.

RAKITIN [*to* NATALYA PETROVNA]. What tutor?

NATALYA PETROVNA. Ah! I forgot to tell you, while you've been away, we've engaged a new teacher.

RAKITIN. Instead of Dufour?

NATALYA PETROVNA. No . . . a Russian teacher. The princess is going to send us a Frenchman from Moscow.

RAKITIN. What sort of man is he, the Russian? An old man?

NATALYA PETROVNA. No, he's young. . . . But we only have him for the summer.

RAKITIN. Oh, a holiday engagement.

NATALYA PETROVNA. Yes, that's what they call it, I believe. And I tell you what, Rakitin, you're fond of studying people, analysing them, burrowing into them. . . .

RAKITIN. Oh, come, what makes you . . .

NATALYA PETROVNA. Yes, yes. . . . You study him. I like him. Thin, well made, merry eyes, something spirited in his face. . . . You'll see. It's true he is rather awkward . . . and you think that dreadful.

RAKITIN. You are terribly hard on me to-day, Natalya Petrovna.

NATALYA PETROVNA. Joking apart, do study him. I fancy he may make a very fine man. But there, you never can tell!

RAKITIN. That sounds interesting.

NATALYA PETROVNA. Really? [*Dreamily.*] Go on reading.

RAKITIN. "Se redressa haletant et . . ."

NATALYA PETROVNA [*suddenly looking round*]. Where's Vera? I haven't seen her all day. [*With a smile, to* RAKITIN.] Put away that book. . . . I see we shan't get any reading done to-day. . . . Better tell me something.

RAKITIN. By all means. . . . What am I to tell you? . . . You know I stayed a few days at the Krinitsyns'. . . . Imagine, the happy pair are bored already.

NATALYA PETROVNA. How could you tell?

RAKITIN. Well, boredom can't be concealed. . . . Anything else may be, but not boredom. . . .

NATALYA PETROVNA [*looking at him*]. Anything else can then?

RAKITIN [*after a brief pause*]. I think so.

NATALYA PETROVNA [*dropping her eyes*]. Well, what did you do at the Krinitsyns'?

RAKITIN. Nothing. Being bored with friends is an awful thing; you are at ease, you are not constrained, you like them, there's nothing to irritate you, and yet you are bored, and there's a silly ache, like hunger, in your heart.

NATALYA PETROVNA. You must often have been bored with friends.

RAKITIN. As though you don't know what it is to be with a person whom one loves and who bores one!

NATALYA PETROVNA [*slowly*]. Whom one loves, that's saying a great deal. . . . You are too subtle to-day. . . .

RAKITIN. Subtle. . . . Why subtle?

NATALYA PETROVNA. Yes, that's a weakness of yours. Do you know, Rakitin, you are very clever, of course, but . . . [*pausing*] sometimes we talk as though we were making lace. . . . Have you seen people making lace? In stuffy rooms, never moving from their seats. . . . Lace is a fine thing, but a drink of fresh water on a hot day is much better.

RAKITIN. Natalya Petrovna, you are . . .

NATALYA PETROVNA. What?

RAKITIN. You are cross with me about something.

NATALYA PETROVNA. Oh, you clever people, how blind you are, though you are so subtle! No, I'm not cross with you.

ANNA SEMYONOVNA. Ah! at last, he has lost the trick! [*To* NATALYA PETROVNA.] Natasha, our enemy has lost the trick!

SCHAAF [*sourly*]. It's Lizaveta Bogdanovna's fault.

LIZAVETA BOGDANOVNA [*angrily*]. I beg your pardon—how could I tell Anna Semyonovna had no hearts?

SCHAAF. In future I call not on Lizaveta Bogdanovna.

ANNA SEMYONOVNA [*to* SCHAAF]. Why, how is she, Lizaveta Bogdanovna, to blame?

SCHAAF [*repeats in exactly the same tone of voice*]. In future I call not on Lizaveta Bogdanovna.

LIZAVETA BOGDANOVNA. As though I care! What next! . . .

RAKITIN. You look somehow different, I see that more and more.

NATALYA PETROVNA [*with a shade of curiosity*]. Do you mean it?

RAKITIN. Yes, really. I find a change in you.

NATALYA PETROVNA. Yes? . . . If that's so, please. . . . You know me so well—guess what the change is, what has happened to me . . . will you?

RAKITIN. Well. . . . Give me time. . . . [*Suddenly* KOLYA *runs in noisily from the outer room and straight up to* ANNA SEMYONOVNA.]

KOLYA. Granny, Granny! Do look what I've got! [*Shows her a bow and arrows.*] Look!

ANNA SEMYONOVNA. Show me, darling. . . . Oh what a splendid bow! Who made it for you?

KOLYA. He did . . . he. . . . [*Points to* BELIAYEV, *who has remained at the door.*]

ANNA SEMYONOVNA. Oh! but how well it's made. . . .

KOLYA. I shot at a tree with it, Granny, and hit it twice. . . . [*Skips about.*]

NATALYA PETROVNA. Show me, Kolya.

KOLYA [*runs to her and while* NATALYA PETROVNA *is examining the bow*]. Oh, maman, you should see how Alexey Nikolaitch climbs trees! He wants to teach me and he's going to teach me to swim too. He's going to teach me all sorts of things. [*Skips about.*]

NATALYA PETROVNA. It is very good of you to do so much for Kolya.

KOLYA [*interrupting her, warmly*]. I do like him, maman, I love him.

NATALYA PETROVNA [*stroking* KOLYA's *head*]. He has been too softly brought up. . . . Make him a sturdy, active boy.

[BELIAYEV *bows.*]

KOLYA. Alexey Nikolaitch, let's go to the stable and take Favourite some bread.

BELIAYEV. Very well.

ANNA SEMYONOVNA [*to* KOLYA]. Come here and give me a kiss first. . . .

KOLYA [*running off*]. Afterwards, Granny, afterwards! [*Runs into the outer room;* BELIAYEV *goes out after him.*]

ANNA SEMYONOVNA [*looking after* KOLYA]. What a darling boy! [*To* SCHAAF *and* LIZAVETA BOGDANOVNA.] Isn't he?

LIZAVETA BOGDANOVNA. To be sure he is.

SCHAAF [*after a brief pause*]. Pass.

NATALYA PETROVNA [*with some eagerness to* RAKITIN]. Well, how does he strike you?

RAKITIN. Who?

NATALYA PETROVNA [*pausing*]. That . . . Russian tutor.

RAKITIN. Oh, I beg your pardon—I'd forgotten him. . . . I was so absorbed by the question you asked me. . . . [NATALYA PETROVNA *looks at him with a faintly perceptible smile of irony.*] But his face . . . certainly. . . . Yes, he has a good face. I like him. Only he seems very shy.

NATALYA PETROVNA. Yes.

RAKITIN [*looking at her*]. But anyway I can't quite make out . . .

NATALYA PETROVNA. How if we were to look after him a bit, Rakitin? Will you? Let us finish his education. Here is a splendid opportunity for discreet sensible people like you and me! We are very sensible, aren't we?

RAKITIN. This young man interests you. If he knew it . . . he'd be flattered.

NATALYA PETROVNA. Oh, not a bit, believe me! You can't judge him by what . . . anyone like us would feel in his place. You see he's not at all like us, Rakitin. That's where we go wrong, my dear, we study ourselves very carefully and then imagine we understand human nature.

RAKITIN. The heart of another is a dark forest. But what are you hinting at? . . . Why do you keep on sticking pins into me?

NATALYA PETROVNA. Whom is one to stick pins into if not one's friends? . . . And you are my friend. . . . You know that. [*Presses his hand.* RAKITIN *smiles and beams.*] You are my old friend.

RAKITIN. I'm only afraid . . . you may get sick of the old friend.

NATALYA PETROVNA [*laughing*]. It's only very nice things one takes enough of for that.

RAKITIN. Perhaps. But that doesn't make it any better for them.

NATALYA PETROVNA. Nonsense. . . . [*Dropping her voice.*] As though you don't know ce que vous êtes pour moi.

RAKITIN. Natalya Petrovna, you play with me like a cat with a mouse. . . . But the mouse does not complain.

NATALYA PETROVNA. Oh! poor little mouse!

ANNA SEMYONOVNA. That's twenty from you, Adam Ivanitch. . . . Aha!

SCHAAF. In future I call not on Lizaveta Bogdanovna.

MATVEY [*enters and announces*]. Ignaty Ilyitch.

SHPIGELSKY [*following him in*]. Doctors don't need showing in. [*Exit* MATVEY.] My humblest respects to all the family. [*Kisses* ANNA

SEMYONOVNA's *hand.*] How do you do, gracious lady. Winning, I expect?

ANNA SEMYONOVNA. Winning indeed! I've hardly got my own back and I'm thankful for that. It's all this villain. [*Indicates* SCHAAF.]

SHPIGELSKY [*to* SCHAAF]. Adam Ivanitch, when you're playing with ladies, it's too bad. . . . I should never have thought it of you.

SCHAAF [*muttering through his teeth*]. Blaying wif ladies. . . .

SHPIGELSKY [*going up to the round table on the left*]. Good afternoon, Natalya Petrovna! Good afternoon, Mihail Alexandritch!

NATALYA PETROVNA. Good afternoon, Doctor. How are you?

SHPIGELSKY. I like that inquiry. . . . It shows that you are quite well. What can ail me? A respectable doctor is never ill; at the most he just goes and dies. . . . Ha! ha!

NATALYA PETROVNA. Sit down. I'm quite well, certainly. . . . But I'm in a bad humour . . . and that's a sort of illness too, you know.

SHPIGELSKY [*sitting down beside* NATALYA PETROVNA]. Let me feel your pulse. [*Feels her pulse.*] Oh, nerves, nerves. . . . You don't walk enough, Natalya Petrovna, you don't laugh enough . . . that's what it is. . . . Why don't you see to it, Mihail Alexandritch? But of course I can prescribe some drops.

NATALYA PETROVNA. I'm ready enough to laugh. . . . [*Eagerly.*] Now, Doctor, . . . you have a spiteful tongue, I like it so much in you, I respect you for it, really . . . do tell me something amusing. Mihail Alexandritch is so solemn to-day.

SHPIGELSKY [*with a sly glance at* RAKITIN]. Ah, it seems, it's not only the nerves that are upset, there's just a touch of spleen too. . . .

NATALYA PETROVNA. There you are, at it, too! Be as critical as you like, Doctor, but not aloud. We all know how sharp-sighted you are. You are both so sharp-sighted.

SHPIGELSKY. I obey, madam.

NATALYA PETROVNA. Tell us something funny.

SHPIGELSKY. I obey, madam. Tell us a story straight away, it's a bit sudden. . . . Allow me a pinch of snuff. [*Takes snuff.*]

NATALYA PETROVNA. What preparations!

SHPIGELSKY. Well, you see, my dear lady, you must graciously consider there are all sorts of funny stories. One for one person, and one for another. . . . Your neighbour, Mr. Hlopushkin, for instance, roars and laughs till he cries, if I simply hold up my finger . . . while you. . . . But, there, here goes, you know Verenitsyn?

NATALYA PETROVNA. I fancy I've met him. I've heard of him anyway.

SHPIGELSKY. He has a sister who's mad. To my thinking, they are either both mad, or both sane; for really there's nothing to choose between them, but that's neither here nor there. It's the finger of destiny, dear lady, everywhere, and in everything. Verenitsyn has a daughter, a greenish little thing, you know, with little pale eyes, and a little red nose, and little yellow teeth, a charming girl in fact; plays the piano, and talks with a lisp, so everything's as it should be. She has two hundred serfs of her own besides her aunt's hundred and fifty. The aunt's still alive to be sure, and will go on living for years; mad people always live to be old, but one need never despair. She has made a will in her niece's favour anyway, and, the day before she did it, with my own hand I poured cold water on her head—it was a complete waste of time for there's no chance of curing her. Well, so Verenitsyn's daughter is a bit of a catch, you see. He has begun bringing her out, suitors are turning up, and among others Perekuzov, an anæmic young man, timid but of excellent principles. Well, the father liked our Perekuzov; and the daughter liked him, too. . . . There seemed to be no hitch, simply bless them and haste to the wedding! And, as a matter of fact, all was going swimmingly; Mr. Verenitsyn was already beginning to poke the young man in the ribs and slap him on the back, when all of a sudden, a bolt from the blue, an officer, Ardalion Protobekasov! He saw Verenitsyn's daughter at the Marshal's ball, danced three polkas with her, said to her, I suppose, rolling his eyes like this, "Oh, how unhappy I am!" and our young lady was bowled over at once. Tears, sighs, moans. . . . Not a look, not a word for Perekuzov, hysterics at the mere mention of the wedding. . . . Oh, Lord, there was the deuce of a fuss. Oh well, thinks Verenitsyn, if Protobekasov it is to be, Protobekasov let it be! Luckily he was a man of property too. Protobekasov is invited to give them the honour of his company. He does them the honour, arrives, flirts, falls in love, and finally offers his hand and heart. Verenitsyn's daughter accepts him joyfully on the spot, you'd suppose. Not a bit of it! Mercy on us, no! Tears again, sighs, hysterics! Her father is at his wits' end. What's the meaning of it? What does she want? And what do you suppose she answers? "I don't know," she says, "which of them I love." "What!?" "I really don't know which I love, and so I'd better not marry either, but I am in love!" Verenitsyn, of course, had an attack of cholera at once; the suitors can't make head or tail of it either. But she sticks to it. So you see what queer things happen in these parts.

NATALYA PETROVNA. I don't see anything wonderful in that. . . . Surely it's possible to love two people at once?

RAKITIN. Ah! you think so. . . .

NATALYA PETROVNA [*slowly*]. I think so. . . . I don't know, though . . . perhaps it only shows one doesn't love either.

SHPIGELSKY [*taking snuff and looking now at* NATALYA PETROVNA, *now at* RAKITIN]. So that's how it is.

NATALYA PETROVNA [*eagerly to* SHPIGELSKY]. Your story is very good, but you haven't made me laugh.

SHPIGELSKY. Oh, my dear lady, who'll make you laugh just now? That's not what you want at the moment.

NATALYA PETROVNA. What is it I want then?

SHPIGELSKY [*with an affectedly meek air*]. The Lord only knows!

NATALYA PETROVNA. Oh, how tiresome you are, as bad as Rakitin.

SHPIGELSKY. You do me too much honour upon my word. . . .

[NATALYA PETROVNA *makes an impatient gesture.*]

ANNA SEMYONOVNA [*getting up*]. Well, well, at last. . . . [*Sighs.*] My legs are quite stiff from sitting so long. [LIZAVETA BOGDANOVNA *and* SCHAAF *stand up also*] O-ooh!

NATALYA PETROVNA [*stands up and goes to them*]. Why do you sit still so long? [RAKITIN *and* SHPIGELSKY *stand up.*]

ANNA SEMYONOVNA. You owe me seventy kopecks, my good sir. [SCHAAF *bows frigidly.*] You can't punish us all the time. [*To* NATALYA PETROVNA.] You look pale, Natasha? Are you quite well? Shpigelsky, is she quite well?

SHPIGELSKY [*who has been whispering something to* RAKITIN]. Oh, perfectly!

ANNA SEMYONOVNA. That's right. . . . I'll go and have a little rest before dinner. . . . I'm dreadfully tired! Liza, come along. . . . Oh, my legs, my legs. . . .

[*Goes into the outer room with* LIZAVETA BOGDANOVNA. NATALYA PETROVNA *walks with her to the door.* SHPIGELSKY, RAKITIN *and* SCHAAF *are left in the front of the stage.*]

SHPIGELSKY [*offering* SCHAAF *his snuff-box*]. Well, Adam Ivanitch, wie befinden Sie sich?

SCHAAF [*taking a pinch with dignity*]. Quite vell. And you?

SHPIGELSKY. Thank you kindly, pretty middling. [*Aside to* RAKITIN.] So you don't know what's the matter with Natalya Petrovna to-day?

RAKITIN. I don't, really.

SHPIGELSKY. Well, if *you* don't. . . . [*Turns round and goes to meet* NATALYA PETROVNA *who is coming back from the door.*] I have a little matter to talk to you about, Natalya Petrovna.

NATALYA PETROVNA [*going to the window*]. Really! What is it?

SHPIGELSKY. I must speak to you alone. . . .

NATALYA PETROVNA. Oh dear! . . . You alarm me. . . .

[RAKITIN *meanwhile has taken* SCHAAF'*s arm and walks to and fro with him, murmuring something to him in German.* SCHAAF *laughs and says in an undertone,* "Ja, ja, ja! ja wohl, ja wohl, sehr gut!"]

SHPIGELSKY [*dropping his voice*]. This business, strictly speaking, does not concern you only. . . .

NATALYA PETROVNA [*looking out into the garden*]. What do you mean?

SHPIGELSKY. Well, it's like this. A good friend of mine has asked me to find out . . . that is . . . your intentions in regard to your ward . . . Vera Alexandrovna.

NATALYA PETROVNA. My intentions?

SHPIGELSKY. That is . . . to speak plainly . . . my friend. . . .

NATALYA PETROVNA. You don't mean to say he wants to marry her?

SHPIGELSKY. Just so.

NATALYA PETROVNA. Are you joking?

SHPIGELSKY. Certainly not.

NATALYA PETROVNA [*laughing*]. Good gracious! She's a child; what a strange commission!

SHPIGELSKY. Strange, Natalya Petrovna? How so? My friend . . .

NATALYA PETROVNA. You're a great schemer, Shpigelsky. And who is your friend?

SHPIGELSKY [*smiling*]. One minute. You haven't said anything definite yet in reply. . . .

NATALYA PETROVNA. Nonsense, Doctor. Vera is a child. You know that yourself, Monsieur le diplomate. [*Turning round.*] Why, here she is. [VERA *and* KOLYA *run in from the outer room.*]

KOLYA [*runs up to* RAKITIN]. Rakitin, some glue, tell them to give us some glue. . . .

NATALYA PETROVNA [*to* VERA]. Where have you been? [*Strokes her cheek.*] How flushed you are!

VERA. In the garden. . . . [SHPIGELSKY *bows to her*]. Good afternoon, Ignaty Ilyitch.

RAKITIN [*to* KOLYA]. What do you want with glue?

KOLYA. We must have it. . . . Alexey Nikolaitch is making us a kite. . . . Ask for it. . . .

RAKITIN [*is about to ring*]. Very well. In a minute.

SCHAAF. Erlauben Sie. . . . Master Kolya has not learned his lesson to-day. . . . [*Takes* KOLYA's *hand.*] Kommen Sie.

KOLYA [*gloomily*]. Morgen, Herr Schaaf, morgen. . . .

SCHAAF [*sharply*]. Morgen, morgen, nur nicht heute, sagen alle faule Leute. . . . Kommen Sie. [KOLYA *resists.*]

NATALYA PETROVNA [*to* VERA]. Whom have you been out with all this time? I've seen nothing of you all day.

VERA. With Alexey Nikolaitch . . . with Kolya. . . .

NATALYA PETROVNA. Ah! [*Turning round.*] Kolya, what's the meaning of this?

KOLYA [*dropping his voice*]. Mr. Schaaf . . . Maman . . .

RAKITIN [*to* NATALYA PETROVNA]. They are making a kite, and you see, it's time for a lesson.

SCHAAF [*with a sense of dignity*]. Gnädige Frau. . . .

NATALYA PETROVNA [*severely, to* KOLYA]. You have been playing about enough to-day, do you hear. Go along with Mr. Schaaf.

SCHAAF [*leading* KOLYA *towards the outer room*]. Es ist unerhört!

KOLYA [*to* RAKITIN *in a whisper as he goes out*]. Ask for the glue, all the same. . . . [RAKITIN *nods.*]

SCHAAF [*pulling* KOLYA]. Kommen sie, mein Herr. . . . [*Goes out with him.* RAKITIN *follows them out.*]

NATALYA PETROVNA [*to* VERA]. Sit down . . . you must be tired. . . . [*Sits down herself.*]

VERA [*sitting down*]. Not at all, Natalya Petrovna.

NATALYA PETROVNA [*to* SHPIGELSKY, *with a smile*]. Shpigelsky, look at her, she is tired, isn't she?

SHPIGELSKY. But that's good for Vera Alexandrovna, you know.

NATALYA PETROVNA. I don't say it's not. . . . [*To* VERA.] Well, what have you been doing in the garden?

VERA. Playing, running about. First we looked at the men digging the dam, then Alexey Nikolaitch climbed up a tree after a squirrel, ever so high, and began shaking the tree-top. . . . It really frightened us. . . . The squirrel dropped at last, and Trésor nearly caught it. . . . But it got away.

NATALYA PETROVNA [*glancing with a smile at* SHPIGELSKY]. And then?

VERA. Then Alexey Nikolaitch made Kolya a bow . . . and so quickly . . . and then he stole up to our cow in the meadow and all at once leapt on her back . . . and the cow was scared and set off running and kicking . . . and he laughed [*laughs herself*] and then Alexey Nikolaitch wanted to make us a kite and so we came in.

NATALYA PETROVNA [*pats her cheek*]. Child, child, you are a perfect child. . . . What do you think, Shpigelsky?

SHPIGELSKY [*slowly, looking at* NATALYA PETROVNA]. I agree with you.

NATALYA PETROVNA. I should think so.

SHPIGELSKY. But that's no hindrance. . . . On the contrary . . .

NATALYA PETROVNA. You think so? [*To* VERA.] And you've been enjoying yourself?

VERA. Yes. . . . Alexey Nikolaitch is so amusing.

NATALYA PETROVNA. Oh, he is, is he? [*After a brief pause.*] And, Vera, how old are you? [VERA *looks at her with some surprise.*] You're a child . . . a child.

[RAKITIN *comes in from the outer room.*]

SHPIGELSKY [*fussily*]. Ah, I was forgetting . . . your coachman is ill . . . and I haven't had a look at him yet. . . .

NATALYA PETROVNA. What's the matter with him?

SHPIGELSKY. He's feverish, but it's nothing serious.

NATALYA PETROVNA [*calling after him*]. You are dining with us, Doctor?

SHPIGELSKY. With your kind permission. [*Goes out by centre door.*]

NATALYA PETROVNA. Mon enfant, vous feriez bien de mettre une autre robe pour le diner. . . . [VERA *gets up.*] Come to me. . . . [*Kisses her on the forehead.*] Child. . . . Child. [VERA *kisses her hand and goes towards door on right.*]

RAKITIN [*aside to* VERA *with a wink*]. I've sent Alexey Nikolaitch all you need.

VERA [*aside*]. Thank you, Mihail Alexandritch. [*Goes out.*]

RAKITIN [*goes up to* NATALYA PETROVNA, *she holds out her hand to him. He at once presses it*]. At last, we are alone. Natalya Petrovna, tell me, what's the matter?

NATALYA PETROVNA. Nothing, Michel, nothing. And if there were, it's all over now. Sit down. [RAKITIN *sits down beside her.*] That happens to everybody. Clouds pass over the sky. Why do you look at me like that?

RAKITIN. I'm looking at you. . . . I am happy.

NATALYA PETROVNA [*smiles in answer to him*]. Open the window, Michel. How lovely it is in the garden! [RAKITIN *gets up and opens the window.*] How I welcome the wind! [*Laughs.*] It seems to have been waiting for a chance to burst in. . . . [*Looks round.*] How completely it's taken possession of the room. . . . There's no turning it out now. . . .

RAKITIN. You are as soft and sweet yourself now as an evening after a storm.

NATALYA PETROVNA [*dreamily repeating the last words*]. After a storm?. . . But has there been a storm?

RAKITIN [*shaking his head*]. It was gathering.

NATALYA PETROVNA. Really? [*Gazing at him, after a short silence.*] Do you know, Michel, I can't imagine a kinder man than you? [RAKITIN *tries to stop her.*] No, don't prevent my speaking out. You are sympathetic, affectionate, constant. You never change. I owe you so much.

RAKITIN. Natalya Petrovna, why are you telling me this just now?

NATALYA PETROVNA. I don't know; I feel light-hearted, I'm at rest; don't stop me from chattering. . . .

RAKITIN [*pressing her hand*]. You are kind as an angel. . . .

NATALYA PETROVNA [*laughing*]. You wouldn't have said so this morning. But listen, Michel, you know me, you must make allowances for me. Our relations are so pure, so genuine, . . . and at the same time, not quite natural. . . . You and I have the right to look everybody in the face, not only Arkady. . . . Yes, but . . . [*Sinking into thought.*] That's what makes me sometimes depressed and ill at ease. I feel spiteful like a child, I'm ready to vent my spite on others, especially on you. . . . You don't resent that privilege?

RAKITIN [*earnestly*]. Quite the contrary.

NATALYA PETROVNA. Yes, at times it gives one pleasure to torture the man whom one loves . . . whom one loves. . . . Like Tatyana, I too can say, why not be frank?

RAKITIN. Natalya Petrovna, you . . .

NATALYA PETROVNA [*interrupting him*]. Yes, I love you; but do you know, Rakitin? Do you know what sometimes seems strange to me? I love you . . . and the feeling is so clear, so peaceful. . . . It does not agitate me. . . . I am warmed by it. . . . [*Earnestly.*] You have never made me cry . . . and it seems as though I ought to have. . . . [*Breaking off.*] What does that show?

RAKITIN [*rather mournfully*]. That's a question that needs no answer.

NATALYA PETROVNA [*dreamily*]. And we have known each other a long while.

RAKITIN. Four years. Yes, we are old friends.

NATALYA PETROVNA. Friends. . . . No, you are more to me than a friend.

RAKITIN. Natalya Petrovna, don't touch on that. . . . I'm afraid for my happiness, I'm afraid it may vanish at your touch.

NATALYA PETROVNA. No . . . no . . . no. The whole point is that you are too good. . . . You give way to me too much. . . . You have spoilt me. . . . You are too good, do you hear?

RAKITIN [*with a smile*]. I hear, madam.

NATALYA PETROVNA [*looking at him*]. I don't know what you feel but I desire no other happiness. Many women might envy me. [*Holds out both hands to him.*] Mightn't they?

RAKITIN. I'm in your hands. . . . Do with me what you will. . . . [*The voice of* ISLAYEV *from the outer room:* "So you've sent for him, have you?"]

NATALYA PETROVNA [*getting up quickly*]. Arkady! I can't see him just now. . . . Good-bye! [*Goes out by door on right.*]

RAKITIN [*looking after her*]. What does it mean? The beginning of the end, or the end? [A *brief pause.*] Or the beginning?

[*Enter* ISLAYEV *looking worried.*]

ISLAYEV [*taking off his hat*]. Good afternoon, Michel.
RAKITIN. We've seen each other already to-day.
ISLAYEV. Oh! I beg your pardon. . . . I've had so much to see to. . . . [*Walks up and down the room.*] It's a queer thing! The Russian peasant is very intelligent, very quick of understanding, I've a respect for the Russian peasant . . . and yet sometimes, you may talk to him, and explain away. . . . It's clear enough you'd think, but it's all no use at all. The Russian peasant hasn't that . . . that . . .
RAKITIN. You're still busy with the dam, are you?
ISLAYEV. That . . . so to speak . . . love for work . . . that's just it, he has no love for it. He won't let you tell him what you think properly. "Yes, Sir." . . . Yes, indeed, when he hasn't taken in a word. Look at a German now, it's quite a different thing! The Russian has no patience. For all that, I have a respect for him. . . . Where's Natasha? Do you know?
RAKITIN. She was here just now.
ISLAYEV. What time is it? Surely, dinner-time. I've been on my feet all day—such a lot to do. . . . And I haven't been to the building yet. . . . The time goes so fast. It's dreadful! One's simply behindhand with everything—— [RAKITIN *smiles.*] You're laughing at me, I see. . . . But I can't help it, old man. People are different. I'm a practical man, born to look after my land—and nothing else. There was a time when I dreamed of other things; but I burnt my fingers—I can tell you—came to grief, you know. Why isn't Beliayev here?
RAKITIN. Who's Beliayev?
ISLAYEV. Our new teacher. He's a shy bird, but he'll get used to us. He has a head on his shoulders. I asked him to see how the building was going on to-day. . . . [*Enter* BELIAYEV.] Oh, here he is! Well, how are they getting on? Doing nothing, I expect?
BELIAYEV. No, Sir, they are working.
ISLAYEV. Have they finished the framing of the second barn?
BELIAYEV. They have begun the third.
ISLAYEV. And did you speak to them about the beams?
BELIAYEV. Yes.
ISLAYEV. Well, what did they say?
BELIAYEV. They say that's how they always do it.
ISLAYEV. Hm. . . . Is Yermil the carpenter there?
BELIAYEV. Yes.
ISLAYEV. Ah! well, thanks! [*Enter* NATALYA.] Ah! Natasha! Good afternoon.

RAKITIN. Why twenty greetings to each of us to-day?

ISLAYEV. I tell you, I'm tired out with all I've had to see to. Oh! by the way. I haven't shown you my new winnowing machine, have I? Do come along, it's worth seeing. It's marvellous, a whirlwind, a regular whirlwind. We've time before dinner. . . . What do you say?

RAKITIN. Oh, by all means.

ISLAYEV. Won't you come with us, Natasha?

NATALYA PETROVNA. As though I know anything about your machines! You go by yourselves—and mind you're not late.

ISLAYEV [*going out with* RAKITIN]. We'll be back immediately.

[BELIAYEV *is about to follow them.*]

NATALYA PETROVNA [*to* BELIAYEV]. Where are you going, Alexey Nikolaitch?

BELIAYEV. I . . . I. . . .

NATALYA PETROVNA. Of course go, if you want a walk. . . .

BELIAYEV. Why no, I've been out of doors all the morning.

NATALYA PETROVNA. Well, then, sit down. . . . Sit here. [*Motions him to a chair.*] We have not had a proper talk, Alexey Nikolaitch. We have not made friends yet. [BELIAYEV *bows and sits down.*] I want to get to know you.

BELIAYEV. I'm . . . it's very kind of you.

NATALYA PETROVNA [*with a smile*]. You are afraid of me, I see . . . but wait a little, you won't be afraid of me, when you know me. Tell me . . . tell me now how old are you?

BELIAYEV. Twenty-one.

NATALYA PETROVNA. Are your parents living?

BELIAYEV. My mother is dead, my father is living.

NATALYA PETROVNA. Has your mother been dead long?

BELIAYEV. Yes, a long time.

NATALYA PETROVNA. But you remember her?

BELIAYEV. Oh yes . . . I remember her.

NATALYA PETROVNA. And does your father live in Moscow?

BELIAYEV. Oh no, in the country.

NATALYA PETROVNA. And have you any brothers and sisters?

BELIAYEV. One sister.

NATALYA PETROVNA. Are you fond of her?

BELIAYEV. Yes. She's much younger than I am.

NATALYA PETROVNA. And what's her name?

BELIAYEV. Natalya.

NATALYA PETROVNA [*eagerly*]. Natalya! How odd! I'm Natalya too! . . . [*Pauses.*] And you are very fond of her?

BELIAYEV. Yes.

NATALYA PETROVNA. Tell me what do you think of my Kolya?

BELIAYEV. He is a dear boy.

NATALYA PETROVNA. He is, isn't he? And so affectionate. He's devoted to you already.

BELIAYEV. I'll do my best. . . . I'm glad.

NATALYA PETROVNA. You see, Alexey Nikolaitch, of course I should like to make him a thoroughly able man—I don't know whether I shall succeed in that, but anyway I want him to look back on his childhood with pleasure. Let him grow up in freedom, that's the great thing. I was brought up very differently, Alexey Nikolaitch; my father was not an unkind man, but he was stern and irritable; everyone in the house, including my mother, was afraid of him. My brother and I used to cross ourselves in terror whenever we were summoned to his room. Sometimes my father would pet me, but even in his arms I was in a panic. My brother grew up, and you may perhaps have heard of his rupture with my father. . . . I shall never forget that awful day. . . . I remained an obedient daughter up to my father's death. . . . He used to call me his consolation, his Antigone (he was blind for some years before his death) . . . but however tender he was he could never make me forget those early impressions. . . . I was afraid of him, a blind old man, and never felt at ease in his presence. The traces of timidity, of those years of repression, haven't perhaps quite disappeared even now. . . . I know that at first sight I seem . . . how shall I say? . . . frigid, perhaps. . . . But I notice I'm talking to you about myself, instead of talking about Kolya. I only meant to say that I know from my own experience how good it is for a child to grow up in freedom. You now, I imagine, have never been repressed as a child, have you?

BELIAYEV. I don't know really. . . . Of course nobody repressed me, nobody bothered about me.

NATALYA PETROVNA [*shyly*]. Why, didn't your father. . . .

BELIAYEV. He'd no time to spare. He was always going round among the neighbours . . . on business . . . or if not business exactly. . . . He got his living through them, in a way. . . . By his services. . . .

NATALYA PETROVNA. Oh! So then nobody troubled about bringing you up?

BELIAYEV. As a matter of fact, nobody did. I dare say that's evident though, I'm only too aware of my defects.

NATALYA PETROVNA. Perhaps . . . but on the other hand. . . . [*Checks herself and adds in some embarrassment.*] Oh, by the way, Alexey Nikolaitch, was that you singing in the garden yesterday?

BELIAYEV. When?

NATALYA PETROVNA. In the evening . . . by the pond . . . was it you?

BELIAYEV. Yes. [*Hurriedly.*] I didn't think . . . the pond is such a long way off. . . . I didn't think it could be heard from here.

NATALYA PETROVNA. Are you apologizing? You have a very pleasant musical voice and you sing so well. You have studied music?

BELIAYEV. No, not at all. I only sing by ear . . . only simple songs.

NATALYA PETROVNA. You sing them capitally. . . . I'll ask you some time . . . not just now, but when we know each other better, when we are friends. . . . We are going to be friends, Alexey Nikolaitch, aren't we? I feel confidence in you; the way I've been chattering is a proof of it. . . .

[*She holds out her hand for him to shake hands.* BELIAYEV *takes it irresolutely and after some hesitation, not knowing what to do with the hand, kisses it.* NATALYA PETROVNA *flushes and draws away her hand. At that moment* SHPIGELSKY *comes in from the outer room, stops short, then takes a step forward,* NATALYA PETROVNA *gets up quickly,* BELIAYEV *does the same.*]

NATALYA PETROVNA [*embarrassed*]. Oh, it's you, Doctor . . . here Alexey Nikolaitch and I have been having . . . [*Stops.*]

SHPIGELSKY [*in a loud, free and easy voice*]. Really, Natalya Petrovna, the goings on in your house! I walk into the servants' hall and ask for the sick coachman, and my patient is sitting at the table gobbling up pancake and onion. Much good it is being a doctor and relying on illness for getting a living.

NATALYA PETROVNA [*with a constrained smile*]. Really. . . . [BELIAYEV *is about to go away.*] Alexey Nikolaitch, I forgot to tell you . . .

VERA [*running in from the outer room*]. Alexey Nikolaitch! Alexey Nikolaitch! [*She stops abruptly at the sight of* NATALYA PETROVNA.]

NATALYA PETROVNA [*with some surprise*]. What is it? What do you want?

VERA [*blushing and dropping her eyes, indicates* BELIAYEV]. He is wanted.

NATALYA PETROVNA. By whom?

VERA. Kolya . . . that is Kolya asked me . . . about the kite. . . .

NATALYA PETROVNA. Oh! [*Aside to* VERA.] On n'entre pas comme cela dans une chambre. . . . Cela ne convient pas. [*Turning to* SHPIGELSKY.] What time is it, Doctor? Your watch is always right. . . . It's time for dinner.

SHPIGELSKY. Allow me. [*Takes out his watch.*] It is just . . . I beg to inform you . . . just exactly twenty minutes past four.

NATALYA PETROVNA. There, you see, it's dinner-time. [*Goes to the looking-glass and tidies her hair. Meanwhile* VERA *whispers something to*

BELIAYEV. *Both laugh.* NATALYA PETROVNA *sees them reflected in the looking-glass.* SHPIGELSKY *gives her a sidelong look.*]

BELIAYEV [*laughing, in a low voice*]. Really?

VERA [*nodding and speaking in a low voice too*]. Yes, yes, she just went flop.

NATALYA PETROVNA [*turning with assumed indifference to* VERA]. What? Who went flop?

VERA [*in confusion*]. Oh no . . . Alexey Nikolaitch made us a swing, and so nurse took it into her head . . .

NATALYA PETROVNA [*without waiting for her to finish, turns to* SHPIGELSKY]. Oh, by the way, Shpigelsky, come here. . . . [*She draws him aside and speaks again to* VERA.] She wasn't hurt, I hope?

VERA. Oh, no!

NATALYA PETROVNA. But . . . all the same, Alexey Nikolaitch, you shouldn't have done it.

MATVEY [*enters from the outer room and announces*]. Dinner is served.

NATALYA PETROVNA. Ah! But where is Arkady Sergeyitch? They'll be late again, he and Mihail Alexandritch.

MATVEY. The gentlemen are in the dining-room.

NATALYA PETROVNA. And mother?

MATVEY. Madam is in the dining-room too.

NATALYA PETROVNA. Well, then, come along. [*Motioning to* BELIAYEV.] Vera, allez en avant avec monsieur.

[MATVEY *goes out, followed by* VERA and BELIAYEV.]

SHPIGELSKY [*to* NATALYA PETROVNA]. You had something to say to me.

NATALYA PETROVNA. Oh yes! To be sure . . . you see . . . we'll have another talk about . . . about your proposal.

SHPIGELSKY. Concerning . . . Vera Alexandrovna?

NATALYA PETROVNA. Yes . . . I will think about it. I'll think about it.

[*Both go out.*]

Act II

The garden. Seats to right and to left under trees; in the foreground raspberry bushes. KATYA *and* MATVEY *come in on right.* KATYA *has a basket in her hand.*

MATVEY. So how is it to be, Katerina Vassilyevna? Kindly explain yourself, I beg you earnestly.

KATYA. Matvey Yegoritch, I really can't.

MATVEY. You are very well aware, Katerina Vassilyevna, what my feelings, I may say, are for you. To be sure, I'm older than you in years, there's no denying that, certainly; but I can still hold my own, I'm still in my prime. I'm of mild disposition, as you are aware; I should like to know what more you want?

KATYA. Matvey Yegoritch, believe me, I feel it very much, I'm very grateful, Matvey Yegoritch. . . . But you see . . . Better wait a bit, I think.

MATVEY. But, dear me, what is there to wait for, Katerina Vassilyevna? You used not to say that, allow me to tell you. And as for consideration, I can answer for that, I believe I may say— You couldn't ask for more consideration than you will get from me, Katerina Vassilyevna. And I'm not given to drink, and I never hear a word of blame from the master and mistress either.

KATYA. Really, Matvey Yegoritch, I don't know what to say. . . .

MATVEY. Ah, Katerina Vassilyevna, something's come over you lately. . . .

KATYA [*blushing a little*]. Lately? Why lately?

MATVEY. I don't know . . . but there was a time when you didn't treat me like this.

KATYA [*glancing hurriedly behind the scene*]. Mind. . . . The German's coming.

MATVEY [*with annoyance*]. Bother him, the long-nosed crane! . . . I must talk to you again. [*He goes out to right.* KATYA *is moving towards the raspberries. Enter* SCHAAF *from the left with a fishing-rod on his shoulder.*]

SCHAAF [*calling after* KATYA]. Vere you go, vere you go, Katerin?

KATYA [*stopping*]. We've been told to pick raspberries, Adam Ivanitch.

SCHAAF. Raspberries? . . . The raspberry is a pleasant fruit. You love raspberries?

KATYA. Yes, I like them.

SCHAAF. He . . . he! And I do too! I love all that you love. [*Seeing that she is going.*] Oh, Katerin, vait a leetle.

KATYA. I've no time to spare. The housekeeper will scold me.

SCHAAF. Oh! That's nothing. You see I'm going . . . [*points to the rod*] how do you say . . . to feesh, you understand, to feesh, that is, to catch feesh. You love feesh?

KATYA. Yes.

SCHAAF. He, he, I do too, I do too. Do you know vhat I vill tell you, Katerin. There's a song in German: [*sings*] Katrinchen, Katrinchen, wie lieb ich dich so sehr! that is, in Russian, O Katrinushka, Katrinushka, you are so pretty I love you! [*Tries to put one arm round her.*]

KATYA. Give over, give over, for shame. . . . Here's the mistress coming! [*Escapes into the raspberry patch.*]

SCHAAF [*assuming a glum expression, aside*]. Das ist dumm. . . .

[*Enter on right* NATALYA PETROVNA, *arm in arm with* RAKITIN.]

NATALYA PETROVNA [*to* SCHAAF]. Ah! Adam Ivanitch! Are you going fishing?

SCHAAF. Yes, madam.

NATALYA PETROVNA. Where's Kolya?

SCHAAF. With Lizaveta Bogdanovna . . . the music lesson.

NATALYA PETROVNA. Ah! [*Looking round.*] You are alone here?

SCHAAF. Yes.

NATALYA PETROVNA. You haven't seen Alexey Nikolaitch?

SCHAAF. No, madam.

NATALYA PETROVNA [*after a pause*]. We'll go with you, Adam Ivanitch, shall we? We'll look on while you fish.

SCHAAF. I am very glad.

RAKITIN [*aside to* NATALYA PETROVNA]. What possesses you?

NATALYA PETROVNA. Come along, come along, beau ténébreux.

[*All three go out on right.*]

KATYA [*cautiously raising her head above the raspberries*]. They've gone. . . . [*Comes out, stops for a little and ponders.*] That German! . . .

[*Sighs and begins picking raspberries again, singing in a low voice.*]

"No fire is burning, no ember is glowing,
But the wild heart is glowing, is burning."

Yes, Matvey Yegoritch is right! [*Goes on singing.*]

"But the wild heart is glowing, is burning,
Not for father dear, not for mother dear. . . ."

What big raspberries! . . . [*Goes on singing.*]

"Not for father dear, not for mother dear."

How hot it is! Stifling. . . . [*Goes on singing.*]

"Not for father dear, not for mother dear,
It glows and it burns for. . . ."

[*Suddenly turns round; is quiet and half hides behind the bushes. From left* BELIAYEV *and* VERA *come in;* BELIAYEV *has a kite in his hand.*]

BELIAYEV [*as he passes the raspberries, to* KATYA]. Why have you stopped, Katya? [*Sings.*]

"It glows and it burns for a maiden so fair."

KATYA [*blushing*]. That's not how we sing it.

BELIAYEV. How then? [KATYA *laughs and does not answer.*] What are you doing? Picking raspberries? Let us taste them.

KATYA [*giving him the basket*]. Take them all.

BELIAYEV. Why all? . . . Vera Alexandrovna, won't you have some? [VERA *takes some from the basket, and he does so too.*] Well, that's enough. [*Is giving back the basket to* KATYA.]

KATYA [*putting back his hand*]. Take them, take them all.

BELIAYEV. No, thanks, Katya. [*Gives her the basket.*] Thank you. [*To* VERA.] Vera Alexandrovna, let's sit down on this seat. You see [*showing the kite*] we must fasten the tail on. You'll help me. [*They go and sit down on the seat.* BELIAYEV *puts the kite in her hands.*] That's it. Mind now, hold it straight. [*Begins to tie on the tail.*] What's the matter?

VERA. I can't see you.

BELIAYEV. Why must you see me?

VERA. I mean I want to see how you fix the tail on.

BELIAYEV. Oh—wait a minute. [*Arranges the kite so that she can see him.*] Katya, why aren't you singing? Sing.

[*After a brief interval* KATYA *begins singing in a low voice.*]

VERA. Tell me, Alexey Nikolaitch, do you sometimes fly kites in Moscow too?

BELIAYEV. I've no time for kites in Moscow! Hold the string, that's right. Do you suppose we've nothing else to do in Moscow?

VERA. What do you do in Moscow?

BELIAYEV. What do we do? We study, listen to the professors.

VERA. What do they teach you?

BELIAYEV. Everything.

VERA. I expect you're a very good student. Better than all the rest.

BELIAYEV. No, I'm not very good. Better than all the rest, indeed! I'm lazy.

VERA. Why are you lazy?

BELIAYEV. Goodness knows! I was born so, apparently.

VERA [*after a pause*]. Have you any friends in Moscow?

BELIAYEV. Of course. . . . I say, this string isn't strong enough.

VERA. And are you fond of them?

BELIAYEV. I should think so. Aren't you fond of your friends?

VERA. I haven't any.

BELIAYEV. I meant the girls you know.

VERA [*slowly*]. Yes.

BELIAYEV. I suppose you have some girl-friends?

VERA. Yes . . . only I don't know why . . . for some time past I've not thought much about them. . . . I haven't even answered Lisa Moshnin, though she begged me to in her letter.

BELIAYEV. How can you say you have no friends . . . what am I?

VERA [*with a smile*]. Oh, you . . . that's a different thing. [*After a pause.*] Alexey Nikolaitch.

BELIAYEV. Well?

VERA. Do you write poetry?

BELIAYEV. No. . . . Why?

VERA. Oh, nothing. [*After a pause.*] A girl in our school used to write poetry.

BELIAYEV [*pulling the knot with his teeth*]. Did she? Was it good?

VERA. I don't know. She used to read it to us, and we cried.

BELIAYEV. What did you cry for?

VERA. Pity. We were all so sorry for her.

BELIAYEV. Were you educated in Moscow?

VERA. Yes, at Madame Beauluce's school in Moscow. Natalya Petrovna took me away last year.

BELIAYEV. Are you fond of Natalya Petrovna?

VERA. Yes, she's so kind. I'm very fond of her.

BELIAYEV [*with a smile*]. And you're afraid of her, I bet.

VERA [*also with a smile*]. A little.

BELIAYEV [*after a pause*]. And who sent you to school?

VERA. Natalya Petrovna's mother. I grew up in her house. I'm an orphan.

BELIAYEV [*letting his hands fall*]. You're an orphan? And you don't remember your father or your mother?

VERA. No.

BELIAYEV. My mother is dead too. We are both motherless. Well we must put up with it! We mustn't be down-hearted for all that.

VERA. They say orphans quickly make friends with one another.

BELIAYEV [*looking into her eyes*]. Do they? And do you think so?

VERA [*looks into his eyes with a smile*]. I think they do.

BELIAYEV [*laughs and sets to work on the kite again*]. I should like to know how long I've been in these parts.

VERA. This is the twenty-eighth day.

BELIAYEV. What a memory you have! Well, here's the kite finished. Look what a tail! We must go and fetch Kolya.

KATYA [*coming up to him with the basket*]. Won't you have some more raspberries?

BELIAYEV. No, thanks, Katya. [KATYA *goes off without speaking.*]

VERA. Kolya's with Lizaveta Bogdanovna.

BELIAYEV. How absurd to keep a child indoors in this weather!

VERA. Lizaveta Bogdanovna would only be in our way. . . .

BELIAYEV. But I'm not talking about her. . . .

VERA [*hurriedly*]. Kolya couldn't come with us without her. . . . She was praising you ever so yesterday, though.

BELIAYEV. Really?

VERA. Don't you like her?

BELIAYEV. Oh, I don't mind her. Let her enjoy her snuff, bless the woman. Why do you sigh?

VERA [*after a pause*]. I don't know. How clear the sky is!

BELIAYEV. Does that make you sigh? [A *silence.*] Perhaps you are depressed?

VERA. Depressed? No! I never know myself why I sigh. . . . I'm not depressed at all. On the contrary . . . [A *pause.*] I don't know. . . . I think I can't be quite well. Yesterday I went upstairs to fetch a book—and all at once, fancy, on the staircase, I sat down and began to cry. Goodness knows why, and my tears kept on coming into my eyes for a long while afterwards. . . . What's the meaning of it? And yet I am quite happy.

BELIAYEV. It's because you're growing. It's growing up. It does happen so. . . . Of course, I noticed your eyes looked swollen yesterday evening.

VERA. You noticed it?

BELIAYEV. Yes.

VERA. You notice everything.

BELIAYEV. Oh no, not everything.

VERA [*dreamily*]. Alexey Nikolaitch . . .

BELIAYEV. What is it?

VERA [*after a pause*]. What was it I was going to ask you? I've forgotten what I was going to say.

BELIAYEV. You are absent-minded!

VERA. No . . . but . . . oh yes! This is what I meant to ask. I think you told me—you have a sister?

BELIAYEV. Yes.

VERA. Tell me, am I like her?

BELIAYEV. Oh no. You're much better looking.

VERA. How can that be? Your sister . . . I should like to be in her place.

BELIAYEV. What? You'd like to be in our poor little house at this moment?

VERA. I didn't mean that. . . . Is your home so small?

BELIAYEV. Tiny. Very different from this house.

VERA. Well, what's the use of so many rooms?

BELIAYEV. What's the use? You'll find out one day how useful rooms are.

VERA. One day. . . . When?

BELIAYEV. When you're the mistress of a house yourself. . . .

VERA [*dreamily*]. Do you think so?

BELIAYEV. Yes, you will see. [*A pause.*] Hadn't we better go and fetch Kolya, Vera Alexandrovna?

VERA. Why don't you call me Verotchka?

BELIAYEV. You can't call me Alexey, can you?

VERA. Why not? . . . [*Suddenly starting.*] Oh!

BELIAYEV. What's the matter?

VERA [*in a low voice*]. There's Natalya Petrovna coming this way.

BELIAYEV [*also in a low voice*]. Where?

VERA [*nodding towards the right*]. Over there . . . along the path, with Mihail Alexandritch.

BELIAYEV [*getting up*]. Let's go to Kolya. . . . He must have finished his lesson by now.

VERA. Let's go . . . or I'm afraid she'll scold me. . . .

[*They get up and walk away quickly to the left.* KATYA *hides again in the raspberry bushes.* NATALYA PETROVNA *and* RAKITIN *come in on right.*]

NATALYA PETROVNA [*standing still*]. I believe that's Mr. Beliayev with Vera.

RAKITIN. Yes, it is. . . .

NATALYA PETROVNA. It looks as though they were running away from us.

RAKITIN. Perhaps they are.

NATALYA PETROVNA [*after a pause*]. But I don't think Verotchka ought . . . to be alone like this with a young man in the garden. . . . Of course, she's only a child, still, it's not the proper thing. . . . I'll tell her.

RAKITIN. How old is she?

NATALYA PETROVNA. Seventeen! She's actually seventeen. . . . It is hot to-day. I'm tired. Let's sit down. [*They sit down on the seat on which* VERA *and* BELIAYEV *have been sitting.*] Has Shpigelsky gone home?

RAKITIN. Yes, he's gone.

NATALYA PETROVNA. It's a pity you didn't keep him. I can't imagine what induced that man to become a district doctor. . . . He's very amusing. He makes me laugh.

RAKITIN. Well, I thought you were not in a very laughing humour to-day.

NATALYA PETROVNA. What made you think that?

RAKITIN. Oh, I don't know.

NATALYA PETROVNA. Because nothing sentimental appeals to me to-day? Oh, certainly, I must warn you there's absolutely nothing that could touch me to-day. . . . But that doesn't prevent me from laughing; on the contrary. Besides, there's something I had to discuss with Shpigelsky to-day.

RAKITIN. May I ask what?

NATALYA PETROVNA. No, you mayn't. As it is, you know everything I think, everything I do. That's boring.

RAKITIN. I beg your pardon. . . . I had no idea. . . .

NATALYA PETROVNA. I want to have some secrets from you.

RAKITIN. What next! From what you say, one might suppose I know everything. . . .

NATALYA PETROVNA [*interrupting*]. And don't you?

RAKITIN. You are pleased to make fun of me.

NATALYA PETROVNA. Why don't you know everything that goes on in me? If you don't I can't congratulate you on your insight. When a man watches me from morning to night. . . .

RAKITIN. What do you mean? Is that a reproach. . . .

NATALYA PETROVNA. A reproach? [*A pause.*] No, I see; you certainly have not much insight.

RAKITIN. Perhaps not . . . but since I watch you from morning to night, allow me to tell you one thing I have noticed. . . .

NATALYA PETROVNA. About me? Please do.

RAKITIN. You won't be angry with me?

NATALYA PETROVNA. Oh no! I should like to be, but I shan't.

RAKITIN. For some time past, Natalya Petrovna, you have been in a state of permanent irritability, and that irritability is something unconscious, involuntary: you seem to be in a state of inward conflict, as though you were perplexed. I had never observed anything of the sort in you before my visit to the Krinitsyns'; it has only come on lately. [NATALYA PETROVNA *draws lines in the sand before her with her parasol.*] At times you sigh—such deep, deep sighs—like a man who's very tired, so tired that he can't find rest.

NATALYA PETROVNA. And what do you deduce from that, you observant person?

RAKITIN. I deduce? Nothing. . . . But it worries me.

NATALYA PETROVNA. Humbly grateful for your sympathy.

RAKITIN. And besides . . .

NATALYA PETROVNA [*with some impatience*]. Please, change the subject.

[*A pause.*]

RAKITIN. You have no plans for going out anywhere to-day?

NATALYA PETROVNA. No.

RAKITIN. Why not? It's so fine.

NATALYA PETROVNA. Too lazy. [*A pause.*] Tell me . . . you know Bolshintsov, of course?

RAKITIN. Our neighbour, Afanasy Ivanitch?

NATALYA PETROVNA. Yes.

RAKITIN. What a question! Only the day before yesterday we were playing preference with him in your house.

NATALYA PETROVNA. I want to know what sort of man he is.

RAKITIN. Bolshintsov?

NATALYA PETROVNA. Yes, yes, Bolshintsov.

RAKITIN. Well, I must say, that I never expected that!

NATALYA PETROVNA [*impatiently*]. What didn't you expect?

RAKITIN. That you would ever be making inquiries about Bolshintsov! A foolish, fat, tedious man—though of course there's no harm in the man.

NATALYA PETROVNA. He's by no means so foolish or tedious as you think.

RAKITIN. Perhaps not. I must own, I haven't studied the gentleman very carefully.

NATALYA PETROVNA [*ironically*]. You haven't been watching him.

RAKITIN [*with a constrained smile*]. And what has induced you? . . .

NATALYA PETROVNA. Oh, nothing!

[*Again a pause.*]

RAKITIN. Look, Natalya Petrovna, how lovely that dark green oak is against the dark blue sky. It's all bathed in the sunlight and what rich colours. . . . What inexhaustible life and strength in it especially when you compare it with that young birch tree. . . . She looks as though she might pass away in radiance, her tiny leaves gleam with a liquid brilliance, as though melting, yet she is lovely too. . . .

NATALYA PETROVNA. Do you know, Rakitin, I noticed it ages ago. You have a very delicate feeling for the so-called beauties of nature, and talk very elegantly and cleverly about them . . . so elegantly and cleverly that I imagine nature ought to be unutterably grateful for your choice and happy phrases; you dance attendance on her like a perfumed marquis on high red heels dallying with a pretty peasant girl. . . . Only I'll tell you what's wrong, it sometimes seems to me that she could never understand or appreciate your subtle observations, just as the peasant girl wouldn't understand the courtly compliments of the marquis; nature is far simpler, even coarser, than you suppose, because, thank God, she's healthy. . . . Birch trees don't melt or fall into swoons like nervous ladies.

RAKITIN. Quelle tirade! Nature is healthy . . . that is, in other words, I'm a sickly creature.

NATALYA PETROVNA. You're not the only sickly creature, we are neither of us too healthy.

RAKITIN. Oh, I know that way of telling a person the most unpleasant things in the most inoffensive way. . . . Instead of telling him to his face, for instance, you're a fool, my friend, you need only tell him with a good-natured smile, we are both fools, you know.

NATALYA PETROVNA. You're offended? What nonsense! I only meant to say that we are both . . . since you don't like the word sickly . . . we are both old, very old.

RAKITIN. In what way are we old? I don't think so of myself.

NATALYA PETROVNA. Well, listen; here we are sitting . . . on this very seat a quarter of an hour ago two really young creatures have been sitting, perhaps.

RAKITIN. Beliayev and Verotchka? Of course they are younger than we are . . . there's a few years' difference between us, that's all. . . . But that doesn't make us old yet.

NATALYA PETROVNA. The difference between us is not only in years.

RAKITIN. Ah! I understand. . . . You envy them . . . their naïveté; their freshness and innocence . . . their foolishness, in fact.

NATALYA PETROVNA. You think so? Oh, you think that they are foolish? You think everybody foolish to-day, I see. No, you don't understand me. And besides . . . foolish? What does that matter? What's the good of being clever, if you're not amusing. Nothing is more depressing than that sort of gloomy cleverness.

RAKITIN. Hm. . . . Why don't you say it straight out, without these hints? I don't amuse you . . . that's what you mean. Why find fault with cleverness in general on account of one miserable sinner like me?

NATALYA PETROVNA. No, that's not what I mean. . . . [KATYA *comes out from among the bushes.*] Have you been picking raspberries, Katya?

KATYA. Yes, madam.

NATALYA PETROVNA. Show me. [KATYA *goes up to her.*] What splendid raspberries! What a colour . . . though your cheeks are redder still. [KATYA *smiles and looks down.*] Well, run along——

[KATYA *goes out.*]

RAKITIN. There's a young creature after your taste.

NATALYA PETROVNA. Of course. [*Gets up.*]

RAKITIN. Where are you going?

NATALYA PETROVNA. First, I want to see what Verotchka's doing . . . it's time she was indoors . . . and secondly I must own I don't like our conversation. We had better drop our discussions of nature and youth for a time.

RAKITIN. Perhaps you would rather walk alone?

NATALYA PETROVNA. To tell the truth, I should. We shall see each other again soon. . . . But we are parting friends? [*Holds out her hand to him.*]

RAKITIN [*getting up*]. Yes indeed! [*Presses her hand.*]

NATALYA PETROVNA. Good-bye for the present. [*She opens her parasol and goes off at left.*]

RAKITIN [*walks up and down for some time*]. What is the matter with her? [*A pause.*] Simply caprice. But is it? I have never seen that in her before. On the contrary, I know no woman less moody. What is the reason? [*Walks to and fro again and suddenly stands still.*] Ah, how absurd a man is who has only one idea in his head, one object, one interest in life. . . . Like me, for instance. It was true what she said: one keeps watching trifling things from morning to night, and one grows trivial oneself. . . . That's so; but without her I can't live, in her presence I am more than happy; the feeling can't be called happiness, I belong to her entirely, parting from her would . . . without exaggeration . . . be exactly like parting with life. What is wrong with her? What's the meaning of her agitation, the involuntary bitterness of her words? Is she beginning to be weary of me? Hm? [*Sits down.*] I have never deceived myself, I know very well how she loves me; but

I hoped that with time that quiet feeling . . . I hoped? Have I the right to hope, dare I hope? I confess my position is pretty absurd . . . almost contemptible. . . . [A *pause.*] What's the use of talking like that? She's an honest woman, and I'm not a Lovelace. [*With a bitter smile.*] More's the pity! [*Getting up quickly.*] Well, that's enough! I must put this nonsense out of my head! [*Walking up and down.*] What a glorious day! [A *pause.*] How skilfully she stung me! . . . My choice and happy expressions. . . . She's very clever, especially when she's in a bad humour. And what's this sudden adoration of youth and innocence? . . . This tutor. . . . She often talks about him. I must say I see nothing very striking in him. He's simply a student, like all students. Can she . . . impossible! She's out of humour . . . she doesn't know what she wants and so she snaps at me, as children beat their nurse. . . . A flattering comparison! But she must go her own way. When this fit of depression and uneasiness is over, she will be the first to laugh at that lanky boy, that raw youth. . . . Your explanation is not bad, Mihail Alexandritch, but is it true? God knows! Well, we shall see. It's not the first time, my dear fellow, that after endless fretting and pondering you have had suddenly to give up all your subtle conjectures, fold you hands and wait meekly for what is to come. And meanwhile you must recognize it's pretty awkward and bitter for you. . . . But that's what I'm for, it seems. . . . [*Looking round.*] Ah, here he is, our unsophisticated young man! . . . Just when he's wanted. . . . I haven't once had a real talk with him. Let's see what he's like. [BELIAYEV *comes in on left.*] Ah! Alexey Nikolaitch! So you have come out for a turn in the fresh air too?

BELIAYEV. Yes.

RAKITIN. Though I must say the air is not so very fresh to-day: the heat's terrific, but in the shade here under these lime trees it's endurable. [A *pause.*] Did you see Natalya Petrovna?

BELIAYEV. I met her just now. . . . She's gone indoors with Vera Alexandrovna.

RAKITIN. Wasn't it you I saw here half an hour ago with Vera Alexandrovna?

BELIAYEV. Yes. . . . We were having a walk.

RAKITIN. Ah! [*Takes his arm.*] Well, how do you like living in the country?

BELIAYEV. I like the country. The only thing is, the shooting is not good here.

RAKITIN. You're fond of shooting then?

BELIAYEV. Yes. . . . Aren't you?

RAKITIN. I? No; I'm a poor shot. I'm too lazy.

BELIAYEV. I'm lazy too . . . but not in that way.

RAKITIN. Oh! Are you lazy about reading then?

BELIAYEV. No, I love reading. But I'm too lazy to work long at a time, especially too lazy to go on doing the same thing.

RAKITIN [*smiling*]. Talking to ladies, for instance?

BELIAYEV. Ah, you're laughing at me. . . . I'm frightened of ladies.

RAKITIN [*slightly embarrassed*]. What an idea! Why should I laugh at you?

BELIAYEV. Oh, that's all right. . . . I don't mind! [A *pause.*] Tell me where can I get gunpowder about here?

RAKITIN. You can get it no doubt in the town; it is sold there. But do you want good powder?

BELIAYEV. No, it's not for shooting, it's for making fireworks.

RAKITIN. Oh, can you make them?

BELIAYEV. Yes; I've picked out the right place already, the other side of the pond. I heard it's Natalya Petrovna's name-day next week, so they will come in for that.

RAKITIN. Natalya Petrovna will be pleased at such an attention from you. She likes you, Alexey Nikolaitch, I may tell you.

BELIAYEV. I'm very much flattered. . . . Ah, by the way, Mihail Alexandritch, I believe you take a magazine. Could you let me have it to read?

RAKITIN. Certainly, with pleasure. . . . There's good poetry in it.

BELIAYEV. I'm not fond of poetry.

RAKITIN. How's that?

BELIAYEV. I don't know. Comic verses strike me as far-fetched, besides there aren't many; and sentimental ones. . . . I don't know. There's something unreal in them somehow.

RAKITIN. You prefer novels?

BELIAYEV. Yes. I like good novels; but critical articles—they appeal to me——

RAKITIN. Oh, why?

BELIAYEV. It's a fine man that writes them.

RAKITIN. And you don't go in for authorship yourself?

BELIAYEV. Oh no! It's silly to write if you've no talent. It only makes people laugh at you. Besides, it's a queer thing, I wish you would explain it to me, sometimes a man seems sensible enough, but when he takes up a pen he's perfectly hopeless. No, writing's not for us, we must thank God if we understand what's written.

RAKITIN. Do you know, Alexey Nikolaitch, not many young men have as much common sense as you have.

BELIAYEV. Thank you for the compliment. [A *pause.*] I'm going to let off the fireworks the other side of the pond, because I can make Roman candles, and they will be reflected in the water. . . .

RAKITIN. That will be beautiful. . . . Excuse me, Alexey Nikolaitch, by the way, do you know French?

BELIAYEV. No, I translated a novel of Paul de Kock's, "La Laitière de Montfermeil," perhaps you've heard of it, for fifty roubles; but I didn't know a word of French. For instance: quatre-vingt-dix I translated four-twenty-ten. . . . Being hard-up drove me to it, you know. But it's a pity. I should like to know French. It's my cursed laziness. I should like to read Georges Sand in French. But the accent . . . how is one to get over the accent? An, on, en, in, isn't it awful?

RAKITIN. Well, that's a difficulty that can be got over. . . .

BELIAYEV. Please tell me, what's the time?

RAKITIN [*looking at his watch*]. Half-past one.

BELIAYEV. Lizaveta Bogdanovna is keeping Kolya a long time at the piano. . . . I bet he's dying to be running about.

RAKITIN [*cordially*]. But one has to study too, you know, Alexey Nikolaitch. . . .

BELIAYEV [*with a sigh*]. You oughtn't to have to say that, Mihail Alexandritch, and I oughtn't to have to hear it. . . . Of course, it would never do for everyone to be a loafer like me.

RAKITIN. Oh, nonsense. . . .

BELIAYEV. But I know that only too well.

RAKITIN. Well, I know too, on the contrary, that just what you regard as a defect, your impulsiveness, your freedom from constraint is what's attractive.

BELIAYEV. To whom, for instance?

RAKITIN. Well, to Natalya Petrovna, for example.

BELIAYEV. Natalya Petrovna? With her I don't feel that I am free, as you call it.

RAKITIN. Ah! Is that really so?

BELIAYEV. And after all, Mihail Alexandritch, isn't education the thing that matters most in a man? It's easy for you to talk. . . . I can't make you out, really. [*Suddenly looking round.*] What's that? I thought I heard a corncrake calling in the garden. [*Is about to go.*]

RAKITIN. Perhaps. . . . But where are you off to?

BELIAYEV. To fetch my gun. . . . [*Goes to left;* NATALYA PETROVNA *comes in, meeting him.*]

NATALYA PETROVNA [*seeing him, suddenly smiles*]. Where are you going, Alexey Nikolaitch?

BELIAYEV. I was . . .

RAKITIN. To fetch his gun. . . . He heard a corncrake in the garden. . . .

NATALYA PETROVNA. No, please don't shoot in the garden. . . . Let the poor bird live. . . . Besides, you may startle Granny.

BELIAYEV. I obey, madam.

NATALYA PETROVNA [*laughing*]. Oh, Alexey Nikolaitch, aren't you ashamed? "I obey, madam," what a way to speak! How can you . . . talk like that? But wait, you see Mihail Alexandritch and I will see to your education. . . . Yes, yes . . . we have talked together about you more than once already. . . . There's a plot against you, I warn you. . . . You will let me have a hand in your education, won't you?

BELIAYEV. Why, of course. . . . I shall be only too . . .

NATALYA PETROVNA. To begin with, don't be shy, it doesn't suit you at all. Yes, we will look after you. [*Indicating* RAKITIN.] We are old people, you know, he and I, while you are young. You are, aren't you? You will see how good it will be. You will look after Kolya and I . . . we . . . will look after you.

BELIAYEV. I shall be very grateful.

NATALYA PETROVNA. That's right. What have Mihail Alexandritch and you been talking about?

RAKITIN [*smiling*]. He has been telling me how he translated a French book without knowing a word of French.

NATALYA PETROVNA. Ah! Now there, we will teach you French. What have you done with your kite, by the way?

BELIAYEV. I've taken it indoors. I thought you didn't like it.

NATALYA PETROVNA [*with some embarrassment*]. What made you think that? Was it because of Vera . . . because I took Vera indoors? No, that . . . No, you were mistaken. [*Eagerly.*] I tell you what . . . Kolya must have finished his lesson by now. Let us take him and Vera and the kite, shall we? . . . and all of us together fly it in the meadow? Yes?

BELIAYEV. With pleasure, Natalya Petrovna.

NATALYA PETROVNA. That's right then. Come, let us go, let us go. [*Holding out her arm to him.*] But take my arm, how awkward you are! Come along . . . make haste. [*They go off quickly to left.*]

RAKITIN [*looking after them*]. What eagerness . . . what gaiety. . . . I have never seen a look like that on her face. And what a sudden transformation! [*A pause.*] Souvent femme varie. . . . But . . . I am certainly not in her good books to-day. That's clear. [*A pause.*] Well, we shall see what will come later. [*Slowly.*] Is it possible? . . . [*With a gesture of dismissal.*] It can't be! . . . But that smile, that warm, soft, bright look in her eyes. . . . O God spare me from knowing the tortures of jealousy, especially a senseless jealousy! [*Suddenly looking round.*] Hullo, what do I see? [SHPIGELSKY *and* BOLSHINTSOV *enter from left.* RAKITIN *goes to meet them.*] Good day, gentlemen. . . . I confess I didn't expect to see you to-day, Shpigelsky. . . . [*Shakes hands.*]

SHPIGELSKY. Well, I didn't expect it myself. . . . I never imagined. . . . But you see I called in on him [*indicating* BOLSHINTSOV] and he was already sitting in his carriage, coming here. So I turned round and came back with him.

RAKITIN. Well, you are very welcome.

BOLSHINTSOV. I certainly was intending . . .

SHPIGELSKY [*cutting him short*]. The servants told us you were all in the garden. . . . Anyway there was nobody in the drawing-room . . .

RAKITIN. But didn't you meet Natalya Petrovna?

SHPIGELSKY. When?

RAKITIN. Why, just now.

SHPIGELSKY. No. We didn't come here straight from the house. Afanasy Ivanovitch wanted to see whether there were any mushrooms in the copse.

BOLSHINTSOV [*surprised*]. I really . . .

SHPIGELSKY. Oh, there, we know how fond you are of mushrooms. So Natalya Petrovna has gone in? Well then, we can go back again.

BOLSHINTSOV. Of course.

RAKITIN. Yes, she has gone in to fetch them all out for a walk. . . . They are going to fly a kite, I believe.

SHPIGELSKY. Ah! That's capital. It's just the weather for a walk.

RAKITIN. You can stay here . . . I'll go in and tell her you have come.

SHPIGELSKY. Why should you trouble. . . . Really, Mihail Alexandritch . . .

RAKITIN. No trouble. . . . I'm going in anyway. . . .

SHPIGELSKY. Oh, well, in that case we won't keep you . . . No ceremony, you know. . . .

RAKITIN. Good-bye for the present. . . . [*Goes out to left.*]

SHPIGELSKY. Good-bye. [*To* BOLSHINTSOV.] Well, Afanasy Ivanovitch. . . .

BOLSHINTSOV [*interrupting him*]. What did you mean about mushrooms, Ignaty Ilyitch? . . . I'm amazed, what mushrooms?

SHPIGELSKY. Upon my soul, would you have had me say my Afanasy Ivanovitch was overcome with shyness; he wouldn't go straight in, and insisted on taking another turn?

BOLSHINTSOV. That's so . . . but all the same, mushrooms. . . . I don't know, may be I'm mistaken. . . .

SHPIGELSKY. You certainly are, my dear fellow. I'll tell you what you'd better be thinking about. You see we've come here . . . done as you wished. Look out now and don't make a mess of it.

BOLSHINTSOV. But, Ignaty Ilyitch, you know you. . . . You told me, I mean . . . I should like to know for certain what answer . . .

SHPIGELSKY. My honoured friend! It's reckoned over fifteen miles from your place here; at least three times every mile you put that very question to me. . . . Isn't that enough for you? Now listen; but this is the last time I give way to you. This is what Natalya Petrovna said to me: "I . . ."

BOLSHINTSOV [*nodding*]. Yes.

SHPIGELSKY [*with annoyance*]. Yes! Why, what do you mean by "yes"? I've told you nothing yet. . . . "I don't know," says she, "Mr. Bolshintsov very well, but he seems to me a good man; on the other hand, I don't intend to force Vera's inclinations; and so, let him visit us, and if he wins . . ."

BOLSHINTSOV. Wins? She said "wins"?

SHPIGELSKY. "If he wins her affections, Anna Semyonovna and I will not oppose . . ."

BOLSHINTSOV. Will not oppose? Is that what she said? Will not oppose?

SHPIGELSKY. Yes, yes, yes. What a queer fellow you are! "We will not oppose their happiness."

BOLSHINTSOV. Hm.

SHPIGELSKY. "Their happiness." . . . Yes, but observe, Afanasy Ivanitch, what your task is now. . . . You have now to persuade Vera Alexandrovna herself that marrying you really will be happiness for her; you have to win her affection.

BOLSHINTSOV [*blinking*]. Yes, yes, win . . . exactly so. I agree with you.

SHPIGELSKY. You insisted on my bringing you here. . . . Well, let's see how you will act.

BOLSHINTSOV. Act? Yes, yes, we must act, we must win . . . exactly so. Only you see, Ignaty Ilyitch . . . May I confess, admit to you, as to my best friend, one of my weaknesses: I did, as you truly say, wish you to bring me here to-day. . . .

SHPIGELSKY. You didn't wish it, you insisted, absolutely insisted on it. . . .

BOLSHINTSOV. Oh, well, we'll grant that. . . . I agree with you. But you see . . . at home . . . I certainly . . . at home I felt I was ready for anything; but now you know I feel overcome with fears.

SHPIGELSKY. But what are you afraid of?

BOLSHINTSOV [*glancing at him from under his brows*]. The risk, sir.

SHPIGELSKY. Wha-at?

BOLSHINTSOV. The risk. There's a great risk. I must, Ignaty Ilyitch, I must confess to you that . . .

SHPIGELSKY [*interrupting him*]. As to "your best friend." We know all about it. . . . Get on. . . .

BOLSHINTSOV. Exactly so. . . . I agree with you. I must confess to you, Ignaty Ilyitch, that I have had very little to do with ladies, with the female sex, in general, if I may say so; I will confess frankly, Ignaty Ilyitch, that I simply can't imagine what one can talk about to a person of the female sex—and alone with her too . . . and especially a young lady.

SHPIGELSKY. You surprise me. I really don't know what one can't talk about to a person of the female sex, especially a young lady, and particularly alone with her.

BOLSHINTSOV. Oh . . . you . . . Good gracious, but I'm not you. So you see it's just in this case I want to appeal to you, Ignaty Ilyitch. They say that in these affairs it's the first step that counts, so couldn't you just . . . to give me a start in the conversation . . . tell me of something to say, something agreeable in the way, for instance, of an observation . . . and then I can get along. After that I could manage somehow by myself.

SHPIGELSKY. I won't tell you anything to say, Afanasy Ivanovitch, because nothing I could tell you would be of any use to you . . . but I will give you some advice if you like.

BOLSHINTSOV. My dear sir, pray do. . . . And as to my gratitude . . . you know . . .

SHPIGELSKY. Oh, come, come, I'm not bargaining with you, am I?

BOLSHINTSOV [*dropping his voice*]. You can reckon on the three horses.

SHPIGELSKY. Oh, that will do. . . . You see, Afanasy Ivanovitch . . . You are unquestionably a capital fellow in every respect . . . [BOLSHINTSOV *makes a slight bow*] a man of excellent qualities. . . .

BOLSHINTSOV. Oh dear!

SHPIGELSKY. You are, besides, the owner, I believe, of three hundred serfs.

BOLSHINTSOV. Three hundred and twenty, sir.

SHPIGELSKY. Not mortgaged?

BOLSHINTSOV. I owe nobody a farthing.

SHPIGELSKY. There you are. I've been telling you, you're an excellent man and the most eligible of suitors. But you say yourself you've had very little to do with ladies. . . .

BOLSHINTSOV [*with a sigh*]. That's just so. I may say, Ignaty Ilyitch, I've avoided the female sex from a child.

SHPIGELSKY [*with a sigh*]. Quite so. That's not a vice in a husband; quite the contrary; but still in certain circumstances, at the first declaration of love, for instance, it is essential to be able to say *something* . . . isn't it?

BOLSHINTSOV. I quite agree with you.

SHPIGELSKY. Or else, you know, Vera Alexandrovna may simply suppose that you feel unwell—and nothing more. Besides, though your exterior figure is also perfectly presentable in all respects, it does not offer any feature very striking at first sight . . . not at first sight, you know, and that's what's wanted in this case.

BOLSHINTSOV [*with a sigh*]. That's what's wanted in this case.

SHPIGELSKY. Young ladies are attracted by it, anyway. And then, your age too . . . in fact, it's not for you and me to try to please. And so it's no good for you to think of agreeable remarks. That's a poor thing to depend on. But you have something else to count upon, far firmer and more reliable, and that's virtues, my dear Afanasy Ivanovitch, and your three hundred and twenty serfs. In your place I should simply say to Vera Alexandrovna . . .

BOLSHINTSOV. Alone with her?

SHPIGELSKY. Oh, of course, alone with her! "Vera Alexandrovna!" [*From the movement of* BOLSHINTSOV's *lips it is evident that he is repeating in a whisper every word after* SHPIGELSKY.] "I love you and ask your hand in marriage. I'm a kind-hearted, good-natured, harmless man and I'm not poor. You will be perfectly free with me; I will do my best to please you in every way. And I beg you to find out about me, to take a little more notice of me than you have done hitherto, and to give me an answer as you please and when you please. I am ready to wait and shall consider it a pleasure to do so."

BOLSHINTSOV [*uttering the last words aloud*]. To do so! Yes, yes, yes. . . . I quite agree with you. Only I tell you what, Ignaty Ilyitch; I believe you used the word "harmless." . . . You said a harmless man. . . .

SHPIGELSKY. Well, aren't you a harmless man?

BOLSHINTSOV. Ye-e-es . . . but still I fancy. . . . Will it be the right thing, Ignaty Ilyitch? Wouldn't it be better to say, for instance? . . .

SHPIGELSKY. For instance?

BOLSHINTSOV. For instance . . . for instance. . . . [*A pause.*] But maybe "harmless" will do.

SHPIGELSKY. Now, Afanasy Ivanovitch, you listen to me; the more simply you express yourself, the plainer your words, the better it will go, trust me. And above all, don't be too pressing, Afanasy Ivanovitch. Vera Alexandrovna is very young; you may scare her. . . . Give her time to think over your offer. Avoid fine words and I guarantee your success. [*Looking round.*] Why, here they are all coming too—— [BOLSHINTSOV *wants to make off.*] Where are you going? To pick mushrooms again? [BOLSHINTSOV *smiles, turns red and remains.*] The great thing is not to be scared!

BOLSHINTSOV [*hurriedly*]. Vera Alexandrovna knows nothing about it yet, does she?

SHPIGELSKY. I should think not!

BOLSHINTSOV. Well, I rely on you. . . . [*Blows his nose. Enter from left* NATALYA PETROVNA, VERA, BELIAYEV *with the kite, and* KOLYA, *followed by* RAKITIN *and* LIZAVETA BOGDANOVNA. NATALYA PETROVNA *is in a very good humour.*]

NATALYA PETROVNA [*to* BOLSHINTSOV *and* SHPIGELSKY]. How do you do; how are you, Shpigelsky; I didn't expect you to-day, but I am very glad to see you. How are you, Afanasy Ivanitch. [*He bows with some embarrassment.*]

SHPIGELSKY [*to* NATALYA PETROVNA, *indicating* BOLSHINTSOV]. This gentleman here insisted on bringing me. . . .

NATALYA PETROVNA [*laughing*]. I'm very much obliged to him. . . . But do you need forcing to come to see us?

SHPIGELSKY. Oh, good heavens! but . . . I was only here . . . this morning . . . dear me. . . .

NATALYA PETROVNA. Ah! our diplomat's caught!

SHPIGELSKY. I'm delighted, Natalya Petrovna, to see that you are in a very good humour.

NATALYA PETROVNA. You think it necessary to remark it—is it so rare then with me?

SHPIGELSKY. Oh, good gracious—no . . . but . . .

NATALYA PETROVNA. Monsieur le Diplomate, you're getting more and more in a tangle.

KOLYA [*who has been all this time impatiently fidgeting about* VERA *and* BELIAYEV]. But, Maman, when are we going to fly the kite?

NATALYA PETROVNA. When you like. . . . Alexey Nikolaitch, and you Vera, let us go to the meadow. [*Turning to the others.*] You won't care about it, I expect. Lizaveta Bogdanovna, and you, Rakitin, I leave our good friend Afanasy Ivanovitch with you.

RAKITIN. But what makes you think we shan't care about it, Natalya Petrovna?

NATALYA PETROVNA. You are sensible people . . . it must seem childish to you. . . . But as you like. We don't want to prevent your following us. [*To* BELIAYEV *and* VERA.] Come along. [NATALYA PETROVNA, VERA, BELIAYEV *and* KOLYA *go off to right.*]

SHPIGELSKY [*glancing with some surprise at* RAKITIN, *says to* BOLSHINTSOV]. Our good friend Afanasy Ivanovitch, give your arm to Lizaveta Bogdanovna.

BOLSHINTSOV [*nervously*]. With the greatest pleasure.

[*Gives* LIZAVETA BOGDANOVNA *his arm.*]

SHPIGELSKY. And we'll go along together, if you'll allow me, Mihail Alexandritch. [*Takes his arm.*] My word! How they're racing along the avenue. Let's go and see them fly the kite, though we are sensible people. . . . Afanasy Ivanovitch, will you lead the way?

BOLSHINTSOV [*as they walk, to* LIZAVETA BOGDANOVNA]. The weather is certainly very agreeable to-day, one may say.

LIZAVETA BOGDANOVNA [*mincing*]. Yes, indeed, very agreeable!

SHPIGELSKY [*to* RAKITIN]. I've something I want to talk to you about, Mihail Alexandritch. . . . [RAKITIN *suddenly laughs.*] What is it?

RAKITIN. Oh . . . nothing. . . . I was amused at our following in the rear like this.

SHPIGELSKY. The front rank easily turns into the rear guard, you know. . . . It all depends which way you are going.

[*All go out to right.*]

Act III

The scene is the same as in Act I. RAKITIN *and* SHPIGELSKY *come in from the outer room.*

SHPIGELSKY. Well, how about it, Mihail Alexandritch? For goodness sake do help me.

RAKITIN. In what way can I help you, Ignaty Ilyitch?

SHPIGELSKY. In what way? Why, put yourself in my place, Mihail Alexandritch. This is no concern of mine, really. Indeed, I've been acting chiefly from a wish to serve others. . . . My kind heart will be my ruin!

RAKITIN [*laughing*]. Well, ruin's a good way off still.

SHPIGELSKY [*laughing too*]. About that there's no knowing, but my position is certainly awkward. I brought Bolshintsov here at Natalya Petrovna's wish, and have given him her answer with her permission, and now on one side I get sulky looks as though I'd done something foolish, and on the other, Bolshintsov gives me no peace. They avoid him and won't say a word to me. . . .

RAKITIN. What possessed you to take up this business, Ignaty Ilyitch? Why, Bolshintsov, between ourselves . . . he's simply a fool.

SHPIGELSKY. Well, I declare! Between ourselves! That's a piece of news! And since when have sensible men been the only ones to marry? We must leave the fools free to get married, if nothing else. You say I've taken up this business. . . . Not at all, I'll tell you how it came about: a friend asks me to put in a word for him. Well, was I to refuse? I'm a good-natured man, I don't know how to refuse. I carry out my friend's commission: the answer I get is: "Very much obliged; pray, don't trouble yourself further." I understand and don't trouble myself further. Then they take it up themselves and encourage me, so to speak. I obey; and now they're indignant with me. And in what way am I to blame?

RAKITIN. Why, who says you are to blame? . . . The only thing that puzzles me is what induces you to take so much trouble.

SHPIGELSKY. What induces . . . what induces. . . . The man gives me no peace.

RAKITIN. Come, nonsense. . . .

SHPIGELSKY. Besides, he's an old friend.

RAKITIN [*with an incredulous smile*]. Is he? Oh, well, that's another matter.

SHPIGELSKY [*smiling too*]. I'll be open with you, though. . . . There's no deceiving you. . . . Oh well—he has promised me . . . one of my horses has gone lame, so you see he has promised me . . .

RAKITIN. A horse to replace it?

SHPIGELSKY. Well, since I must own up, three new ones.

RAKITIN. You should have said that before!

SHPIGELSKY [*eagerly*]. But please don't you imagine . . . I would never have consented to be a go-between in this affair, it would have been utterly unlike me [RAKITIN *smiles*], if I had not known Bolshintsov to be a thoroughly honest man. . . . Besides, all I want even now is a definite answer—yes or no.

RAKITIN. Surely, things haven't reached that stage yet?

SHPIGELSKY. But what are you imagining? . . . It's not a question of marriage, but of permission to come, to visit. . . .

RAKITIN. But whoever forbids it?

SHPIGELSKY. Forbids . . . what a thing to say! Of course, if it were anybody else . . . but Bolshintsov's a shy man, a blessed innocent, straight out of the Golden Age, scarcely weaned from the feeding bottle. . . . He has so little self-confidence, he needs some encouragement. While his intentions are most honourable.

RAKITIN. Yes, and his horses good.

SHPIGELSKY. And his horses are good. [*Takes a pinch of snuff and offers the box to* RAKITIN.] Won't you have some?

RAKITIN. No, thanks.

SHPIGELSKY. So that's how it is, Mihail Alexandritch. As you see, I don't want to deceive you. Indeed, why should I? The thing's perfectly clear and straightforward. A man of excellent principles, with property, quite harmless. . . . If he suits—good. If he doesn't—well, they should say so.

RAKITIN. That's all very well, no doubt, but how do I come in? I really don't see what I can do about it.

SHPIGELSKY. Oh, Mihail Alexandritch! As though we don't know that Natalya Petrovna has a very great respect for you and even sometimes follows your advice. . . . Now do, Mihail Alexandritch [*puts his arm round him*], be a friend, put in a word. . . .

RAKITIN. And you think this is a good husband for little Vera?

SHPIGELSKY [*assuming a serious air*]. I'm convinced of it. You don't believe it. . . . Well, you'll see. As you know, the great thing in marriage is solid character. And Bolshintsov is solidity itself. [*Looking round.*] And here I do believe is Natalya Petrovna herself coming in. . . . My dear good friend, my benefactor! The two chestnuts as trace-horses, and the bay in the shafts! You will do your best?

RAKITIN [*smiling*]. Oh, very well, very well. . . .

SHPIGELSKY. Mind now, I rely on you. . . . [*Escapes into the outer room.*]

RAKITIN [*looking after him*]. What a sly rogue that doctor is! Vera . . . and Bolshintsov! But there you are! There are marriages worse than that. I'll do as he asks me, and then—it's not my business! [*Turns round.* NATALYA PETROVNA, *coming out of the study and seeing him, stops.*]

NATALYA PETROVNA [*irresolutely*]. It's . . . you. . . . I thought you were in the garden.

RAKITIN. You seem sorry I'm not. . . .

NATALYA PETROVNA [*interrupting*]. Oh! nonsense. [*Advancing to front of stage.*] Are you alone here?

RAKITIN. Shpigelsky has just gone.

NATALYA PETROVNA [*with a slight frown*]. Oh, that local Talleyrand. . . . What has he been saying to you? Is he still hanging about?

RAKITIN. The local Talleyrand, as you call him, is evidently in disfavour to-day . . . but yesterday, I fancy . . .

NATALYA PETROVNA. He's funny; he's amusing, certainly, but . . . he meddles in what's not his business. . . . It's disagreeable. . . . Besides, for all his obsequiousness, he is very impudent and persistent. . . . He's a great cynic.

RAKITIN [*going up to her*]. You didn't speak of him like that yesterday. . . .

NATALYA PETROVNA. Perhaps not. [*Eagerly.*] So what was he talking about?

RAKITIN. He talked to me . . . about Bolshintsov.

NATALYA PETROVNA. Oh? About that stupid creature?

RAKITIN. Of him, too, you spoke very differently yesterday.

NATALYA PETROVNA [*with a constrained smile*]. Yesterday is not to-day.

RAKITIN. True, for others . . . but it seems not for me.

NATALYA PETROVNA [*dropping her eyes*]. How's that?

RAKITIN. For me to-day is the same as yesterday.

NATALYA PETROVNA [*holding out her hand to him*]. I understand your reproach, but you are mistaken. Yesterday I wouldn't admit that I was behaving badly to you. . . . [RAKITIN *attempts to stop her.*] Don't contradict me. . . . I know and you know what I mean . . . but to-day I admit it. I have been thinking things over to-day. . . . But believe me,

Michel, whatever silly thoughts take hold of me, whatever I say, whatever I do, there is no one I depend upon as I do on you. [*Dropping her voice.*] There is no one . . . I love as I do you. . . . [*A brief silence.*] You don't believe me?

RAKITIN. I believe you . . . but you seem depressed to-day, what's the matter?

NATALYA PETROVNA [*goes on speaking without hearing him*]. But I am convinced of one thing, Rakitin; one can never answer for oneself, one can never be sure of oneself. We often don't understand our past, how can we expect to answer for the future! There's no putting the future in fetters!

RAKITIN. That's true.

NATALYA PETROVNA [*after a long silence*]. Do you know, I want to tell you the truth. Perhaps I shall wound you a little, but I know you will be more hurt by my keeping things from you. I confess, Michel, this young student . . . this Beliayev, has made rather an impression on me. . . .

RAKITIN [*in a low voice*]. I know that.

NATALYA PETROVNA. Oh? You have noticed it? For some time?

RAKITIN. Only yesterday.

NATALYA PETROVNA. Ah!

RAKITIN. The day before yesterday, you remember, I spoke of the change in you. . . . I did not know then what to put it down to. But yesterday after our talk . . . and in the meadow . . . if you could have seen yourself! I didn't know you; you were like another woman. You laughed, you skipped and played about like a little girl; your eyes were shining, your cheeks were flushed, and with what confiding interest, with what joyful attention you gazed at him, how you smiled. [*Glancing at her.*] Why, even now your face glows at the memory of it! [*Turns away.*]

NATALYA PETROVNA. No, Rakitin, for God's sake, don't turn away from me. . . . Listen, why exaggerate? This man has infected me with his youth—that's all. I have never been young myself, Michel, from childhood up to now. . . . You know what my life has been. . . . The novelty of it has gone to my head like wine, but I know it will pass as quickly as it has come. . . . It's not worth talking about. . . . [*A pause.*] Only don't turn away from me, don't take your hand away. . . . Help me. . . .

RAKITIN [*in a low voice*]. Help you—a cruel saying! [*Aloud.*] You don't know what is happening to you, Natalya Petrovna. You are sure it's not worth talking about, and you ask for help. . . . Evidently you feel you are in need of it!

NATALYA PETROVNA. That is . . . yes. . . . I appeal to you as a friend.

RAKITIN [*bitterly*]. Quite so. . . . I hope to justify your confidence . . . but let me have a moment to try and face it.

NATALYA PETROVNA. Face it? Why, are you dreading . . . anything unpleasant? Is anything changed?

RAKITIN [*bitterly*]. Oh no! everything's the same.

NATALYA PETROVNA. What are you imagining, Michel? Surely you can't suppose. . . .

RAKITIN. I suppose nothing.

NATALYA PETROVNA. Surely you can't have such a contempt for me as . . .

RAKITIN. For God's sake, stop. We'd better talk about Bolshintsov. The doctor's expecting an answer from you about Vera, you know.

NATALYA PETROVNA [*sadly*]. You're angry with me.

RAKITIN. Me? Oh no! But I'm sorry for you.

NATALYA PETROVNA. Really, it's positively annoying, Michel, aren't you ashamed? . . . [RAKITIN *is silent. She shrugs her shoulders, and goes on in a tone of vexation.*] You say the doctor is expecting an answer? But who asked him to interfere? . . .

RAKITIN. He assured me that you yourself . . .

NATALYA PETROVNA [*interrupting*]. Perhaps, perhaps. . . . Though I believe I said nothing definite. . . . Besides, I may have changed my mind. And, good gracious, what does it matter? Shpigelsky has a hand in all sorts of affairs; he can't expect to have everything his own way.

RAKITIN. He only wants to know what answer . . .

NATALYA PETROVNA. What answer. . . . [*A pause.*] Michel, don't! Give me your hand. . . . Why this indifferent expression, this cold politeness? . . . What have I done? Think a little, is it my fault? I came to you hoping for good advice, I didn't hesitate for one instant, I never thought of concealing things from you, and you . . . I see I was wrong to be open with you. . . . It would never have entered your head. You suspected nothing, you deceived me. And now, goodness knows what you're imagining.

RAKITIN. Imagining? Not at all.

NATALYA PETROVNA. Give me your hand. . . . [*He does not move; she goes on, somewhat offended.*] You turn away from me? So much the worse for you, then. But I don't blame you. . . . [*Bitterly.*] You are jealous!

RAKITIN. I have no right to be jealous, Natalya Petrovna. . . . How could I be?

NATALYA PETROVNA [*after a pause*]. As you please. About Bolshintsov, I haven't yet spoken to Verotchka.

RAKITIN. I can send her to you at once.

NATALYA PETROVNA. Why at once? . . . But as you please.

RAKITIN [*moving towards the study-door*]. So you want me to fetch her?

NATALYA PETROVNA. Michel, for the last time. . . . You said just now that you were sorry for me. . . . Is this how you show it? Can you really . . .

RAKITIN [*coldly*]. Am I to send her?

NATALYA PETROVNA [*with annoyance*]. Yes. [RAKITIN *goes into the study.* NATALYA PETROVNA *stands for some time motionless, sits down, takes a book from the table, opens it, lets it fall on her lap.*] He too! It's awful. He . . . he too! And I relied upon him. And Arkady? Good heavens! I have never even thought of him! [*Drawing herself up.*] I see it's high time to put a stop to all this. . . . [VERA *comes in from the study.*] Yes . . . high time.

VERA [*timidly*]. You sent for me, Natalya Petrovna?

NATALYA PETROVNA [*looking round quickly*]. Ah! Verotchka! Yes, I wanted you.

VERA [*going up to her*]. Are you unwell?

NATALYA PETROVNA. Me? Oh no, why?

VERA. I fancied . . .

NATALYA PETROVNA. No, it's nothing. I'm feeling the heat a little. . . . That's all. Sit down. [VERA *sits down*] Tell me, Vera, are you doing anything particular just now?

VERA. No.

NATALYA PETROVNA. I ask you because I want to have a talk with you . . . a serious talk. You see, my dear, I've always looked on you as a child; but you are seventeen; you are a sensible girl. . . . It's time for you to think about your future. You know I love you as a daughter; my house will always be your home . . . but all the same, in other people's eyes, you are an orphan; you have no fortune. You may in time grow tired of always living with strangers; tell me would you like to be mistress in your own house, absolute mistress in it?

VERA [*slowly*]. I don't understand you, Natalya Petrovna.

NATALYA PETROVNA [*after a pause*]. I have received an offer of marriage for you. [VERA *stares at her in amazement.*] You didn't expect that; I must own it seems strange to me too. You are so young. . . . I need not tell you that I do not mean to put pressure on you. . . . In my opinion you're too young to be married; but I thought it my duty to tell you. . . . [VERA *suddenly hides her face in her hands.*] Vera . . . what is it? You're crying? [*Takes her hand.*] You're trembling all over? . . . Surely you're not afraid of me, Vera?

VERA [*in a toneless voice*]. I'm in your power, Natalya Petrovna.

NATALYA PETROVNA [*taking* VERA's *hands from her face*]. Vera, aren't you ashamed to cry? Aren't you ashamed to say that you're in my power? What do you take me for? I am speaking to you as I would to a daughter, and you . . . [VERA *kisses her hands.*] What? You are in my power? Then please laugh at once! . . . I tell you to. . . . [VERA *smiles through her tears.*] That's right. [NATALYA PETROVNA *puts one arm round her and draws her closer.*] Vera, my child, treat me as though I were your mother, or no, imagine that I'm an elder sister and let us have a little talk together about all these wonderful things. . . . Will you?

VERA. Oh, yes.

NATALYA PETROVNA. Well, listen then. . . . Come a little nearer. That's right. To begin with, as you're my sister, we suppose there's no need for me to assure you that this is your home; a girl with eyes like yours is at home everywhere. So it ought never to enter your head that you are a burden to anybody in the world or that anybody wants to get rid of you. . . . You hear? But now one fine day your sister comes to you and says: Just think, Vera, you have a suitor. . . . Well? What answer would you make? That you are too young, that you are not thinking of marriage?

VERA. Yes, Natalya Petrovna.

NATALYA PETROVNA. But you wouldn't speak like that to your sister.

VERA [*smiling*]. Oh . . . yes, then.

NATALYA PETROVNA. Your sister agrees with you, the suitor is refused and there's the end of it. But suppose the suitor is a good man, and well-to-do, and if he is willing to wait, if he only asks permission to see you occasionally in the hope of gaining your affections in time?

VERA. Who is this suitor?

NATALYA PETROVNA. Ah! you would like to know! You don't guess?

VERA. No.

NATALYA PETROVNA. You have seen him to-day. [VERA *flushes crimson.*] It is true he is not very handsome, and not very young. . . . Bolshintsov.

VERA. Afanasy Ivanitch?

NATALYA PETROVNA. Yes. . . . Afanasy Ivanitch.

VERA [*gazes for some time at* NATALYA PETROVNA, *suddenly begins laughing, then stops*]. You're not joking?

NATALYA PETROVNA [*smiling*]. No . . . but I see there's no hope for Bolshintsov. If you had cried at his name, he might have hoped, but you laugh; there's nothing for him but to go his way, bless him!

VERA. I'm sorry . . . but really I didn't expect . . . Surely people don't get married at his age?

NATALYA PETROVNA. What an idea! How old is he? He's not fifty. The very age to marry.

VERA. Perhaps . . . but he has such a queer face. . . .

NATALYA PETROVNA. Well, don't let us say any more about him.

He's dead and buried . . . bless him! But it's only natural a child of your age cannot care for a man like Bolshintsov. . . . You all want to marry for love, not from prudence, don't you?

VERA. Yes, Natalya Petrovna, and you . . . didn't you marry Arkady Sergeyitch for love too?

NATALYA PETROVNA [*after a pause*]. Of course. [*Another pause, squeezing* VERA's *hands.*] Yes, Vera. . . . I called you a child just now . . . but children are right. [VERA *drops her eyes.*] And so that business is settled. Bolshintsov is dismissed. I must own it wouldn't have been quite pleasant to me to see his puffy old countenance beside your fresh young face, though he is a very good man. Do you see now how little reason you had to be afraid of me? How quickly it's all settled! . . . [*Reproachfully.*] Really, you behaved to me as though I were your patroness! You know how I hate that word. . . .

VERA [*embracing her*]. Forgive me, Natalya Petrovna.

NATALYA PETROVNA. I should hope so. Really? You're not afraid of me?

VERA. No, I love you. I'm not afraid of you.

NATALYA PETROVNA. Thank you. So now we are great friends, and will have no secrets from each other. Well, suppose I were to ask you, Verotchka, whisper in my ear; is it only because Bolshintsov is much older than you, and not a beauty, that you don't want to marry him?

VERA. Surely that's reason enough, Natalya Petrovna?

NATALYA PETROVNA. I don't deny it . . . but is there no other reason?

VERA. I don't know him at all.

NATALYA PETROVNA. Quite so; but you don't answer my question.

VERA. There's no other reason.

NATALYA PETROVNA. Really? In that case, I should advise you to think it over. It wouldn't be easy to be in love with Bolshintsov, I know . . . but I say again, he's a good man. Of course, if you cared for anyone else . . . that would be a different matter. But your heart has told you nothing so far, has it?

VERA [*timidly*]. What do you mean?

NATALYA PETROVNA. You love no one else?

VERA. I love you . . . Kolya; I love Anna Semyonovna too.

NATALYA PETROVNA. I'm not speaking of that sort of love; you don't understand me. . . . Among the young men you may have seen here, for instance, or at parties, is there no one who attracts you?

VERA. No. . . . I like some of them, but . . .

NATALYA PETROVNA. I noticed, for instance, that at the Krinitsyns' you danced three times with that tall officer, what's his name?

VERA. An officer?

NATALYA PETROVNA. Yes, that man with a big moustache.
VERA. Oh! that man! . . . No; I don't like him.
NATALYA PETROVNA. Well, and Shalansky?
VERA. Shalansky is a nice man, but he . . . I don't think he cares about me.
NATALYA PETROVNA. Oh! why?
VERA. He . . . I fancy he thinks more of Liza Velsky.
NATALYA PETROVNA [*glancing at her*]. Ah! . . . you noticed that? [*A pause.*] Well . . . Rakitin?
VERA. I love Mihail Alexandritch very much indeed.
NATALYA PETROVNA. Yes, like a brother. And, by the way, there's Beliayev?
VERA [*flushing*]. Alexey Nikolaitch? I like Alexey Nikolaitch.
NATALYA PETROVNA [*watching her*]. Yes, he's a nice fellow. But he's so shy with everybody. . . .
VERA [*innocently*]. No. . . . He's not shy with me.
NATALYA PETROVNA. Ah!
VERA. He talks to me. Perhaps you fancy that because he . . . he's afraid of you. He has not got to know you yet.
NATALYA PETROVNA. How do you know he's afraid of me?
VERA. He told me so.
NATALYA PETROVNA. Oh! he has told you. . . . So he is more unreserved with you than with other people?
VERA. I don't know how he is with other people, but with me . . . perhaps it's because we are both orphans. Besides . . . he looks on me . . . as a child.
NATALYA PETROVNA. Do you think so? But I like him very much too. He must have a very kind heart.
VERA. Oh! the kindest! If only you knew . . . everyone in the house likes him. He's so friendly. He talks to everybody, he's ready to help anyone. The day before yesterday he carried a poor old beggar-woman in his arms from the high road to the hospital. He gathered a flower for me one day from such a high crag that I shut my eyes in terror, I kept thinking he would fall and be hurt, but he's so clever! You saw yesterday in the meadow how clever he is at that sort of thing.
NATALYA PETROVNA. Yes, that's true.
VERA. Do you remember the great ditch he jumped over when he was running after the kite? It was nothing to him.
NATALYA PETROVNA. And did he really pick a flower for you from a dangerous place? He must be fond of you.
VERA [*after a pause*]. And he's always good-humoured . . . always in good spirits. . . .

NATALYA PETROVNA. It's strange, though. Why isn't he like that with me? . . .

VERA [*interrupting her*]. But I tell you he doesn't know you. Wait a little, I'll tell him. . . . I'll tell him there's no need to be afraid of you, shall I? That you're so kind. . . .

NATALYA PETROVNA [*with a constrained laugh*]. Thanks so much.

VERA. You'll see. . . . He does what I tell him though I am younger than he is.

NATALYA PETROVNA. I didn't know you were such friends. . . . But mind, Vera, be careful. Of course, he's an excellent young man . . . but you know, at your age. . . . It's not suitable, people may imagine things. . . . I mentioned that, you remember? . . . in the garden yesterday. [VERA *looks down.*] On the other hand, I don't want to check your inclinations either. I have too much confidence in you and in him . . . but still . . . you mustn't be angry with me for my scruples, my dear . . . its the duty of us old folks to worry young people with our lectures. Though I really need not say all this, you simply like him, don't you—and nothing more?

VERA [*timidly raising her eyes*]. He. . . .

NATALYA PETROVNA. Now there you are looking at me like that again! Is that the way to look at a sister? Vera, listen, and lean down to me. . . . [*Caressing her.*] What if a sister, a real sister whispered now in your ear: "Verotchka, is it true, you don't love anyone, do you?" What would you answer? [VERA *looks uncertainly at* NATALYA PETROVNA.] Those eyes want to tell me something. . . . [VERA *suddenly presses her face to* NATALYA PETROVNA'S *bosom.* NATALYA PETROVNA *turns pale—and after a pause goes on.*] You do love him? Tell me, do you?

VERA [*not raising her head*]. Oh! I don't know what I feel. . . .

NATALYA PETROVNA. Poor child! You're in love. . . . [VERA *huddles still more closely to* NATALYA PETROVNA.] You're in love . . . and he? Vera, he?

VERA [*still not raising her head*]. Why do you ask me questions? . . . I don't know. . . . Perhaps . . . I don't know, I don't know. . . . [NATALYA PETROVNA *shudders and sits motionless.* VERA *lifts her head and at once notices the change in her face.*] Natalya Petrovna, what's the matter?

NATALYA PETROVNA [*recovering herself*]. The matter . . . nothing. Why? Nothing.

VERA. You're so pale, Natalya Petrovna. . . . What's wrong? Let me ring. . . . [*Gets up.*]

NATALYA PETROVNA. No, no . . . don't ring. It's nothing. . . . It will pass. There, it's over now.

VERA. Let me fetch somebody, anyway.

NATALYA PETROVNA. No, don't, I . . . I want to be alone. Leave me alone, do you hear? We will finish our talk later. Run along.

VERA. You are not angry with me, Natalya Petrovna?

NATALYA PETROVNA. Angry? What for? Not at all. No, I'm grateful to you for your confidence. . . . Only leave me, please, just now.

[VERA *is about to take her hand, but* NATALYA PETROVNA *turns away as though not noticing her movement.*]

VERA [*with tears in her eyes*]. Natalya Petrovna. . . .

NATALYA PETROVNA. I ask you to leave me alone. [VERA *slowly goes out of the study.*]

NATALYA PETROVNA [*alone, remains for some time motionless*]. Now it's all clear to me. . . . These children love each other. . . . [*Stops and passes her hand over her face.*] Well? So much the better. . . . God give them happiness! [*Laughing.*] And I . . . I could imagine. . . . [*Stops again.*] She was not long blurting it out. . . . I must own I did not suspect it, I must own the news has startled me. . . . But wait a bit, it's not all settled yet. My God . . . what am I saying? What's wrong with me? I don't know myself. What am I coming to? [*A pause.*] What am I about? Trying to marry the poor girl to an old man! . . . I used the doctor as a go-between . . . he suspects, he drops hints . . . Arkady, Rakitin . . . while I . . . [*Shudders and suddenly raises her head.*] But what does this mean? Me jealous of Vera! Me in love with him! [*A pause.*] And you still doubt it, do you? You're in love to your misery! How it has come about . . . I don't know. It's as though I'd been poisoned. . . . All at once everything's destroyed, scattered, swept away. . . . He's afraid of me. They're all afraid of me! What could he see in me? . . . What use is a creature like me to him? He is young and she is young. While I! [*Bitterly.*] How could he think much of me? They are both foolish, as Rakitin says. . . . Oh! I hate that clever friend! And Arkady, my good trusting Arkady! My God! my God! It's killing me! [*Gets up.*] But I believe I'm going out of my mind! Why exaggerate? Yes . . . of course . . . I'm overwhelmed. . . . It's so strange to me . . . it's the first time . . . I . . . yes, the first time! I'm in love for the first time now! [*She sits down again.*] He must go away. Yes. And Rakitin too. It's time to come to my senses. I've allowed myself to take one step . . . and see! See what I've come to! And what is it in him attracts me? [*Ponders.*] So this is it, this dreadful feeling. . . . Arkady! Yes, I will fall into his arms, I will beg him to forgive me, to protect me, to save me. . . . He . . . and no one else! All the others are strangers to me and must remain strangers. . . . But can there be . . . can there be no other way out? That girl—she's a child. She may be mistaken. That's all childishness really. . . . Why should I. . . . I will talk to him myself, I will ask him. . . . [*Reproachfully.*] What? What? You are hoping? You still want to hope? And what am I hoping for? My God! don't make me despise myself! [*Drops her head on her arms.* RAKITIN *comes in from the study, pale and agitated.*]

RAKITIN [*going up to* NATALYA PETROVNA]. Natalya Petrovna. . . . [*She does not stir.*] [*To himself.*] What can have happened with Vera? [*Aloud.*] Natalya Petrovna. . . .

NATALYA PETROVNA [*raising her head*]. Who is it? Ah! you.

RAKITIN. Vera Alexandrovna told me you were unwell. . . . I . . .

NATALYA PETROVNA [*turning away*]. I am quite well. . . . What made her? . . .

RAKITIN. No! Natalya Petrovna, you are not well, you should see yourself.

NATALYA PETROVNA. Well, perhaps not . . . but what's that to you? What do you want? What have you come for?

RAKITIN [*in a voice of deep feeling*]. I'll tell you what I have come for. I have come to ask your forgiveness. Half an hour ago I was unspeakably stupid and rude. . . . Forgive me. . . . You see, Natalya Petrovna, however modest a man's desires and . . . and hopes, it is hard, for a moment anyway, for him to keep his head, when they are suddenly snatched away from him; but I have come to my senses. I understand my position and my fault, and I want only one thing . . . your forgiveness. [*He gently sits down beside her.*] Look at me . . . don't you too turn away from me. Beside you is your old Rakitin, your friend, a man who asks nothing but to be allowed to serve you, as you said . . . to help you. Don't deprive me of your confidence, rely on me and forget that I ever. . . . Forget everything that may have wounded you. . . .

NATALYA PETROVNA [*who has been all the while staring fixedly at the floor*]. Yes, yes. . . . [*Stopping.*] Oh! I'm, sorry Rakitin, I haven't heard a word of what you've been saying.

RAKITIN [*mournfully*]. I said . . . I begged you to forgive me, Natalya Petrovna, I asked you whether you would let me be your friend still.

NATALYA PETROVNA [*slowly turning to him and laying her hands on his shoulders*]. Rakitin, tell me, what's the matter with me?

RAKITIN [*after a pause*]. You're in love.

NATALYA PETROVNA [*slowly repeating it after him*]. I'm in love. . . . But it's madness, Rakitin, it's impossible. Can such things happen all of a sudden. . . . You say I'm in love. . . . [*Breaks off.*]

RAKITIN. Yes, you're in love, poor dear woman. . . . Don't deceive yourself.

NATALYA PETROVNA [*not looking at him.*] What am I to do?

RAKITIN. I can tell you, Natalya Petrovna, if you promise . . .

NATALYA PETROVNA [*interrupting, still without looking at him*]. You know that girl, Vera, loves him. . . . They are in love with each other. . . .

RAKITIN. If so, a reason the more . . .

NATALYA PETROVNA [*interrupting again*]. I've long suspected it, but she acknowledged it herself . . . just now.

RAKITIN [*in a low voice, as though to himself*]. Poor woman!

NATALYA PETROVNA [*passing her hand over her face*]. Come. . . . I must pull myself together. I believe you were going to say something. . . . For God's sake, Rakitin, advise me what to do. . . .

RAKITIN. I'm willing to advise you, Natalya Petrovna, only on one condition.

NATALYA PETROVNA. Tell me.

RAKITIN. Promise that you won't suspect my motives. Tell me that you believe in my disinterested desire to help you; do you help me too. Let your confidence give me strength, or else let me keep silence.

NATALYA PETROVNA. Speak, speak.

RAKITIN. You have no doubt of me?

NATALYA PETROVNA. Speak!

RAKITIN. Well then, listen, he must go away. [NATALYA PETROVNA *looks at him in silence.*] Yes, he must go. I'm not going to speak to you of . . . your husband, your duty. On my lips, such words are . . . out of place. . . . But those children love each other. You told me so yourself just now, imagine yourself now between them. . . . Why, your position will be awful!

NATALYA PETROVNA. He must go. . . . [*A pause.*] And you? You remain?

RAKITIN [*confused*]. I? . . . I? . . . [*A pause.*] I must go too. For the sake of your peace, your happiness, Verotchka's happiness, both he . . . and I . . . we must both go away for ever.

NATALYA PETROVNA. Rakitin . . . I have sunk so low that I . . . was almost ready to sacrifice that poor girl, an orphan entrusted to me by my mother, to marry her to a stupid, absurd old man! I couldn't bring myself to it, Rakitin, the words died away on my lips when she burst out laughing at the suggestion . . . but I have been plotting with the doctor; I have put up with his meaning smiles, I have borne with his grins, his compliments, his hints. . . . Oh, I feel I am on the brink of a precipice; save me!

RAKITIN. Natalya Petrovna, you see that I am right. . . . [*She is silent; he goes on hurriedly.*] He ought to go . . . we ought both to go. . . . There is no other way to save you.

NATALYA PETROVNA [*dejectedly*]. But what to live for afterwards?

RAKITIN. Good God, is it as bad as that? . . . Natalya Petrovna, you will get over it, believe me. . . . This will pass. What, nothing to live for!

NATALYA PETROVNA. Yes, yes, what have I to live for when all abandon me?

RAKITIN. But . . . your family. . . . [NATALYA PETROVNA *looks down.*] If you like, after he is gone, I might stay a few days just to . . .

NATALYA PETROVNA [*gloomily*]. Ah! I understand. You are reckoning on habit, on our old friendship. . . . You hope I shall come to myself, and turn to you again, don't you? I understand you.

RAKITIN [*flushing*]. Natalya Petrovna! Why do you insult me?

NATALYA PETROVNA [*bitterly*]. I understand you . . . but you are mistaken.

RAKITIN. What? After your promise, when simply for your sake, your sake only, for your happiness, for your position in society, in fact . . .

NATALYA PETROVNA. Oh! how long have you been concerned about that? Why is it you have never spoken of it before?

RAKITIN [*getting up*]. Natalya Petrovna, I will leave this place today, at once, and you shall never see me again. . . . [*Is going.*]

NATALYA PETROVNA [*stretching out her hands to him*]. Michel, forgive me; I don't know what I'm saying. . . . You see the state I'm in. Forgive me.

RAKITIN [*turning rapidly to her and taking her by the hands*]. Natalya Petrovna . . .

NATALYA PETROVNA. Oh, Michel, I'm unutterably miserable. . . . [*Leans on his shoulder and presses her handkerchief to her eyes.*] Help me, I am lost without you. [*At that instant the door of the outer room is flung open, and* ISLAYEV *and* ANNA SEMYONOVNA *walk in.*]

ISLAYEV [*loudly*]. I was always of that opinion. [*Stops in amazement at the sight of* RAKITIN *and* NATALYA PETROVNA. NATALYA PETROVNA *looks round and goes out quickly.* RAKITIN *remains where he is, overwhelmed with confusion.*]

ISLAYEV [*to* RAKITIN]. What's the meaning of this? What's this scene?

RAKITIN. Oh . . . nothing . . . it's . . .

ISLAYEV. Is Natalya Petrovna unwell?

RAKITIN. No . . . but . . .

ISLAYEV. And why has she run away so suddenly? What were you talking about? She seemed to be crying. . . . You were consoling her. . . . What's the matter?

RAKITIN. Nothing really.

ANNA SEMYONOVNA. How can there be nothing the matter, Mihail Alexandritch? [*After a pause.*] I'll go and see. . . . [*Is about to go into the study.*]

RAKITIN [*stopping her*]. No, you had better leave her in peace, please.

ISLAYEV. But what does it all mean? Tell us.

RAKITIN. Nothing, I assure you. . . . I promise to explain it to you both to-day. I give you my word. But now, please, if you have any trust in me, don't ask me . . . and don't worry Natalya Petrovna.

ISLAYEV. Very well . . . but it is strange. This sort of thing has never happened with Natasha before. It's something quite out of the way.

ANNA SEMYONOVNA. What I want to know is what could make Natasha cry? And why has she gone away? . . . Are we strangers?

RAKITIN. Of course not. What an idea! But as a matter of fact, we had not finished our conversation. . . . I must ask you . . . both—to leave us alone for a little while.

ISLAYEV. Indeed? There's some secret between you, then?

RAKITIN. Yes . . . but you shall know it.

ISLAYEV [*after a moment's thought*]. Come along, Mamma. . . . Let us leave them. Let them finish their mysterious conversation.

ANNA SEMYONOVNA. But . . .

ISLAYEV. Come, let us go. You hear he promises to explain.

RAKITIN. You needn't worry. . . .

ISLAYEV [*coldly*]. I'm not worrying. [*To* ANNA SEMYONOVNA.] Let us go. [*They go out.*]

RAKITIN [*looks after them and goes quickly to the study door*]. Natalya Petrovna, Natalya Petrovna, please come back.

NATALYA PETROVNA [*comes out of the study. She is very pale*]. What did they say?

RAKITIN. Nothing, don't worry yourself. . . . They were rather surprised, certainly. Arkady thought you were ill. . . . He noticed how upset you were. . . . Sit down, you can hardly stand. . . . [NATALYA PETROVNA *sits down.*] I said . . . I begged him not to worry you . . . to leave us alone.

NATALYA PETROVNA. And he agreed?

RAKITIN. Yes. I had, I must say, to promise I'd explain it all tomorrow. Why did you go away?

NATALYA PETROVNA [*bitterly*]. Why indeed! What are you going to say?

RAKITIN. I'll . . . I'll think of something to say. But that's no matter just now. We must take advantage of this reprieve. You see that this can't go on. . . . These violent emotions are too much for you. . . . They are unworthy of you. . . . I myself . . . But that's not the point. Only be firm and I'll manage. You agreed with me, you know.

NATALYA PETROVNA. About what?

RAKITIN. The necessity of . . . our going. You do agree? If that's so, it's no good to delay. If you'll let me, I'll talk to Beliayev at once. . . . He's a decent fellow, he'll understand.

NATALYA PETROVNA. You want to talk to him? You? But what can you say to him?

RAKITIN [*in embarrassment*]. I'll . . .

NATALYA PETROVNA [*after a brief pause*]. Rakitin, listen, don't you think that we're both behaving like lunatics? . . . I was in a panic, I frightened you, and perhaps it's all about nothing that matters.

RAKITIN. What?

NATALYA PETROVNA. Really? What's the matter with us? It seems only a little while ago everything was so quiet and peaceful in this house . . . and all at once . . . goodness knows how! Really we've all gone out of our minds. Come, it's time to stop, we've been silly enough. . . . Let us go on as before. . . . And there'll be no need to explain anything to Arkady; I'll tell him about our antics myself and we'll laugh over them together. I need no one to intercede between my husband and me!

RAKITIN. Natalya Petrovna, you are frightening me now. You are smiling and you're as pale as death. . . . Do remember what you said to me only a quarter of an hour ago. . . .

NATALYA PETROVNA. I dare say! But I see what it is. . . . You're raising this storm . . . that you may not sink alone.

RAKITIN. Again, again suspicion, again reproaches, Natalya Petrovna. . . . God forgive you . . . but you torture me. Or do you regret having spoken so freely?

NATALYA PETROVNA. I regret nothing.

RAKITIN. Then how am I to understand you?

NATALYA PETROVNA [*eagerly*]. Rakitin, if you say a single word from me or about me to Beliayev, I will never forgive you.

RAKITIN. Oh! so that's it! . . . Don't worry, Natalya Petrovna. So far from telling Mr. Beliayev anything, I won't even say good-bye to him, when I take my departure. I don't mean to pester you with my services.

NATALYA PETROVNA [*with some embarrassment*]. You imagine perhaps that I have changed my mind about . . . his going?

RAKITIN. I imagine nothing.

NATALYA PETROVNA. That's not so. I'm so convinced of the necessity, as you say, of his leaving that I mean to dismiss him myself. [*A pause.*] Yes, I will dismiss him myself.

RAKITIN. You?

NATALYA PETROVNA. Yes. And at once. I beg you to send him to me.

RAKITIN. What? This minute?

NATALYA PETROVNA. This very minute. I ask you to do so, Rakitin. You see I am composed now. Besides, I shan't be interrupted just now. I must seize the opportunity. . . . I shall be very much obliged to you. I'll question him.

RAKITIN. But he won't tell you anything. I can assure you. He admitted to me that he felt awkward with you.

NATALYA PETROVNA [*suspiciously*]. Ah! You've been talking to him about me. [RAKITIN *shrugs his shoulders.*] Oh, forgive me, forgive me, Michel, and send him to me. You'll see, I will dismiss him and all will be over. It will all pass and be forgotten, like a bad dream. Please fetch him. I absolutely must have a final conversation with him. You will be pleased with me. Pray do.

RAKITIN [*who has not taken his eyes off her all this time, coldly and mournfully*]. Certainly. Your wishes shall be obeyed. [*Goes towards door of outer room.*]

NATALYA PETROVNA [*after him*]. Thank you, Michel.

RAKITIN [*turning*]. Oh, spare me your thanks, at least. . . . [*Goes out quickly.*]

NATALYA PETROVNA [*alone, after a pause*]. He's a good man. . . . But is it possible I ever loved him? [*Stands up.*] He is right. *He* must go. But how can I dismiss him? I only want to know whether he really cares for that girl. Perhaps it's all nonsense. . . . How could I be worked up into such a state? What was the object of all that outburst? Well, it can't be helped now. I want to know what he is going to say. But he must go. . . . He must . . . he must. . . . He may not be willing to answer. . . . He's afraid of me, of course. . . . Well? So much the better. There's no need for me to say much to him. . . . [*Lays her hand on her forehead.*] My head aches. Shall I put it off till to-morrow? Yes. I keep fancying they are all watching me to-day. . . . What am I coming to! No, better make an end of it at once. . . . Just one last effort and I am free. . . . Oh yes! I yearn for freedom and peace.

[BELIAYEV *comes in from the outer room.*]

Here he is. . . .

BELIAYEV [*going up to her*]. Natalya Petrovna, Mihail Alexandritch tells me you want to see me.

NATALYA PETROVNA [*with some effort*]. Yes, certainly . . . I have to . . . speak to you. . . .

BELIAYEV. Speak to me?

NATALYA PETROVNA [*without looking at him*]. Yes . . . speak to you. [*A pause.*] I must tell you, Alexey Nikolaitch, I'm . . . I'm displeased with you.

BELIAYEV. May I ask on what ground?

NATALYA PETROVNA. Listen. . . . I . . . I really don't know how to begin. However, I must tell you first that my dissatisfaction is not due to any remissness in your work. On the contrary, I am pleased with your methods with Kolya.

BELIAYEV. Then what can it be?

NATALYA PETROVNA [*glancing at him*]. You need not be alarmed. . . . Your fault is not so serious. You are young, you have probably never before stayed with strangers, you could not foresee . . .

BELIAYEV. But, Natalya Petrovna. . . .

NATALYA PETROVNA. You want to know what is wrong? I understand your impatience. So I must tell you that Verotchka . . . [*Glancing at him.*] Verotchka has confessed everything.

BELIAYEV [*in amazement*]. Vera Alexandrovna? What can Vera Alexandrovna have confessed? And what have I to do with it?

NATALYA PETROVNA. So you really don't know what she can have confessed? You can't guess?

BELIAYEV. I? No, I can't.

NATALYA PETROVNA. If so, I beg your pardon. If you really can't guess, I must apologize. I supposed . . . I was mistaken. But allow me to say, I don't believe you. I understand what makes you say so. . . . I respect your discretion.

BELIAYEV. I haven't the least idea what you mean, Natalya Petrovna.

NATALYA PETROVNA. Really? Do you expect to persuade me that you haven't noticed that child's feeling for you?

BELIAYEV. Vera Alexandrovna's feeling for me? I really don't know what to say to that. . . . Good gracious! I believe I have always behaved with Vera Alexandrovna as a——

NATALYA PETROVNA. As with everybody else, haven't you? [*After a brief silence.*] However that may be, whether you are really unaware of it, or are pretending to be, the fact is the girl loves you. She admitted it to me herself. Well, now I am asking you, what do you mean to do?

BELIAYEV [*with embarrassment*]. What do I mean to do?

NATALYA PETROVNA [*folding her arms*]. Yes.

BELIAYEV. All this is so unexpected, Natalya Petrovna. . . .

NATALYA PETROVNA [*after a pause*]. Alexey Nikolaitch, I see . . . I have not put the matter properly. You don't understand me. You think I'm angry with you . . . but I'm . . . only . . . a little upset. And that's very natural. Calm yourself. Let us sit down. [*They sit down.*] I will be frank with you, Alexey Nikolaitch, and you too be a little less reserved with me. You have really no need to be on your guard with me. Vera loves you. . . . Of course, that's not your fault, I am willing to assume that you are in no way responsible for it. . . . But you see, Alexey Nikolaitch, she is an orphan, she is my ward. I am responsible for her, for her future, for her happiness. She is very young, and I feel sure that the feeling you have inspired in her may soon pass off. . . . At her age, love does not last long. But you understand, it was my duty to warn you. It's always dangerous to play with fire . . . and I do not doubt that, knowing her feeling for you, you will adopt a different behaviour with her, will avoid seeing her alone, walking in the garden. . . . Won't you? I can rely on you. With another man I should be afraid to speak so plainly.

BELIAYEV. Natalya Petrovna, I assure you I appreciate. . . .

NATALYA PETROVNA. I tell you that I do not distrust. . . . Besides, all this will remain a secret between us.

BELIAYEV. I must own, Natalya Petrovna, all you have told me seems to me so strange . . . of course, I can't venture to disbelieve you, but . . .

NATALYA PETROVNA. Listen, Alexey Nikolaitch. All I said to you just now . . . I said it on the supposition that on your side there is nothing . . . [*breaks off*] because if that's not so . . . of course I don't know you well, but I do know you well enough to see no reason to make serious objections. You have no fortune . . . but you are young, you have your future before you, and when two people love each other . . . I tell you again, I thought it my duty to warn you, as a man of honour, of the consequences of your friendship with Vera, but if you . . .

BELIAYEV [*in perplexity*]. I really don't know what you mean, Natalya Petrovna.

NATALYA PETROVNA [*hurriedly*]. Oh! believe me, I'm not trying to wring out a confession, there's no need. . . . I shall see from your manner how it is. . . . [*Glancing at him.*] But I ought to tell you that Vera fancied that you were not quite indifferent to her.

BELIAYEV [*after a brief silence, stands up*]. Natalya Petrovna, I see that I can't go on living in your house.

NATALYA PETROVNA [*firing up*]. You might have waited for me to decide that. . . . [*Stands up.*]

BELIAYEV. You have been frank with me. Let me be frank with you. I don't love Vera Alexandrovna, at least, I don't love her in the way you suppose.

NATALYA PETROVNA. But I didn't . . . [*Stops short.*]

BELIAYEV. And if Vera Alexandrovna cares for me, if she fancied, as you say, that I care for her, I don't want to deceive her; I will tell her the whole truth myself. But after such plain speaking, you must see, Natalya Petrovna, that it would be difficult for me to stay here, my position would be too awkward. I can't tell you how sorry I shall be to leave . . . but there's nothing else for me to do. I shall always think of you with gratitude. . . . May I go now? . . . I shall come to say good-bye properly later on.

NATALYA PETROVNA [*with affected indifference*]. As you please . . . but I own I did not expect this. That was not my object in wishing to speak to you. . . . I only wanted to warn you . . . Vera is still a child . . .

I have perhaps taken it all too seriously. I don't see the necessity of your leaving us. However, as you please.

BELIAYEV. Natalya Petrovna . . . it's really impossible for me to go on staying here.

NATALYA PETROVNA. I see you are very ready to leave us!

BELIAYEV. No, Natalya Petrovna, I'm not.

NATALYA PETROVNA. I'm not in the habit of keeping people against their will, but I must own I don't like it at all.

BELIAYEV [*after some indecision*]. Natalya Petrovna, I shouldn't like to cause you the slightest annoyance. . . . I'll stay.

NATALYA PETROVNA [*suspiciously*]. Ah! [*After a pause.*] I didn't expect you would change your mind so quickly. . . . I am grateful, but . . . Let me think it over. Perhaps you are right, perhaps you ought to go. I'll think it over. I'll let you know. . . . May I leave you in uncertainty till this evening?

BELIAYEV. I am willing to wait as long as you like. [*Bows and is about to go.*]

NATALYA PETROVNA. You promise me. . . .

BELIAYEV [*stopping*]. What?

NATALYA PETROVNA. I believe you meant to speak to Vera. . . . I'm not sure that it's the right thing. But I'll let you know what I decide. I begin to think that you really ought to go away. Good-bye for now. [BELIAYEV *bows again and goes off into the outer room.* NATALYA PETROVNA *looks after him.*] My mind's at rest! He does not love her. . . . [*Walks up and down the room.*] And so instead of sending him away, I've myself prevented his going. . . . He'll stay. . . . But what shall I say to Rakitin? What have I done? [A *pause.*] And what right had I to publish abroad the poor girl's love? I trapped her into confessing it . . . a half-confession, and then I go . . . so ruthlessly, so brutally. . . . [*Hides her face in her hands.*] Perhaps he was beginning to care for her. . . . What right had I to trample on that flower in the bud? . . . But have I trampled on it? He may have deceived me. . . . I tried to deceive him! Oh! no! He's too good for that. . . . He's not like me! And why was I in such haste? Blurting it all out at once? [*Sighing.*] I needn't have done it! If I could have foreseen. . . . How sly I was, how I lied to him! And he! How boldly and independently he spoke! . . . I felt humbled by him. . . . He is a man! I didn't know him before. . . . He must go away. If he stays . . . I feel that I shall end by losing all self-respect. . . . He must go, or I am lost! I will write to him before he has had time to see Vera. . . . He must go! [*Goes quickly into the study.*]

Act IV

A large unfurnished outer room. The walls are bare, the stone floor is uneven; the ceiling is supported by six brick columns, three each side, covered with whitewash which is peeling off. On left two open windows and a door into the garden. On right a door into the corridor leading to the main building; in centre an iron door opening into the storeroom. Near first column on right a green garden seat; in a corner spades, watering-cans and flower-pots. Evening. The red rays of the sun fall through the windows on the floor.

KATYA [*comes in from door on right, goes briskly to the window and stands for some time looking into the garden*]. No, he's not to be seen. They told me he'd gone into the conservatory. I suppose he hasn't come out yet. Well, I'll wait till he comes by. There's no other way he can go. . . . [*Sighs and leans against the window.*] They say he's going away. [*Sighs again.*] However shall we get on without him. . . . Poor young lady! How she did beseech me. . . . And why shouldn't I oblige her? Let him have a last talk with her. How warm it is to-day. And I do believe it's beginning to spot with rain. . . . [*Again glances out of window and at once draws back.*] Surely they're not coming in here? They are. My gracious. . . . [*Tries to run off, but has not time to reach the door before* SHPIGELSKY *and* LIZAVETA BOGDANOVNA *come in from the garden.* KATYA *hides behind a column.*]

SHPIGELSKY [*shaking his hat*]. We can shelter here from the rain . . . it will soon be over.

LIZAVETA BOGDANOVNA. If you like.

SHPIGELSKY [*looking round*]. What is this building? A storehouse or what?

LIZAVETA BOGDANOVNA [*pointing to the iron door*]. No, the storeroom's there. This room, I'm told, Arkady Sergeyitch's father built when he came back from abroad.

SHPIGELSKY. Oh, I see the idea, Venice, if you please. [*Sits down on the seat.*] Let's sit down. [LIZAVETA BOGDANOVNA *sits down.*] You must confess, Lizaveta Bogdanovna, the rain has come in an unlucky moment. It has interrupted our talk at the most touching point.

LIZAVETA BOGDANOVNA [*casting down her eyes*]. Ignaty Ilyitch. . . .

SHPIGELSKY. But there's nobody to hinder our beginning again. . . . You say, by the way, that Anna Semyonovna is out of humour to-day?

LIZAVETA BOGDANOVNA. Yes, she's put out. She actually did not come down to dinner, but had it in her room.

SHPIGELSKY. You don't say so! What a calamity, upon my word!

LIZAVETA BOGDANOVNA. She came upon Natalya Petrovna in tears this morning . . . with Mihail Alexandritch. . . . Of course he's almost like one of the family, but still. . . . However, Mihail Alexandritch has promised to explain it.

SHPIGELSKY. Ah! well, she need not worry herself. Mihail Alexandritch has never, to my thinking, been a dangerous person, and now he's less so than ever.

LIZAVETA BOGDANOVNA. Why?

SHPIGELSKY. Oh, he talks a bit too cleverly. Where other people would come out in a rash, they work it all off in talk. Don't be afraid of chatterers in future, Lizaveta Bogdanovna; they're not dangerous; it's these silent men, slow in the uptake, with no end of temperament and thick necks, who are dangerous.

LIZAVETA BOGDANOVNA [*after a pause*]. Tell me, is Natalya Petrovna really ill?

SHPIGELSKY. She's no more ill than you or I.

LIZAVETA BOGDANOVNA. She ate nothing at dinner.

SHPIGELSKY. Illness isn't the only thing that spoils the appetite.

LIZAVETA BOGDANOVNA. Did you dine at Bolshintsov's?

SHPIGELSKY. Yes. . . . I went to see him. And it's only on your account I came back here, upon my soul.

LIZAVETA BOGDANOVNA. Oh, nonsense. And do you know, Ignaty Ilyitch, Natalya Petrovna is cross with you. . . . She said something not very complimentary about you at dinner.

SHPIGELSKY. Really? Ladies don't like us poor fellows to have sharp eyes, it seems. You must do what they want, you must help them, and you must pretend not to know what they're up to. A pretty set! But we shall see. And Rakitin, I dare say, looked rather in the dumps, too?

LIZAVETA BOGDANOVNA. Yes, he, too, seemed, as it were, out of sorts. . . .

SHPIGELSKY. Hm. And Vera Alexandrovna? And Beliayev?

LIZAVETA BOGDANOVNA. Everyone, absolutely everyone seemed depressed. I really can't imagine what's the matter with them all to-day.

SHPIGELSKY. If you know too much, you'll grow old before your time, Lizaveta Bogdanovna. . . . But never mind them. We had better talk about our affairs. The rain hasn't left off. . . . Shall we?

LIZAVETA BOGDANOVNA [*casting down her eyes primly*]. What are you asking me, Ignaty Ilyitch?

SHPIGELSKY. Oh, Lizaveta Bogdanovna, if you'll allow me to say so, there's no need to put on airs, and to drop your eyes like that! We're not young people, you know! These performances, these sighs and soft nothings—they don't suit us. Let us talk calmly, practically, as is proper for people of our years. And so—this is the question: we like each other . . . at least, I presume that you like me.

LIZAVETA BOGDANOVNA [*a little affectedly*]. Ignaty Ilyitch, really. . . .

SHPIGELSKY. Oh, all right, very well. After all, perhaps, airs and graces are . . . only proper in a lady. So then, we like each other. And in other respects too we are well matched. Of course, I am bound to say about myself that I am not a man of good family: well, you're not of illustrious birth either. I'm not a rich man; if I were, I shouldn't be where I am—— [*Laughs.*] But I've a decent practice, not all my patients die; you have, as you say, fifteen thousand roubles of your own, all that's not at all bad, you see. At the same time, you're tired, I imagine, of living for ever as a governess, and then fussing round an old lady, backing her up at preference, and falling in with her whims isn't much fun, I should say. On my side, it's not so much that I'm weary of bachelor-life, but I'm growing old, and then, my cooks rob me; so you see, it all fits in nicely. But here's the difficulty, Lizaveta Bogdanovna; we don't know each other at all, that is, to be exact, you don't know me . . . I know you well enough. I understand your character. I don't say you have no faults. Being a spinster, you're little old-maidish, but that's no harm. In the hands of a good husband, a wife is soft as wax. But I should like you to know me before marriage; or else you'll, maybe, blame me afterwards. . . . I don't want to deceive you.

LIZAVETA BOGDANOVNA [*with dignity*]. But, Ignaty Ilyitch, I believe I too have had opportunities of discovering your character.

SHPIGELSKY. You? Oh! nonsense. . . . That's not a woman's job. Why, I dare say you imagine I'm a man of cheerful disposition, an amusing fellow, don't you?

LIZAVETA BOGDANOVNA. I have always thought you a very amiable man. . . .

SHPIGELSKY. There you are. You see how easily one may be mistaken. Because I play the fool before outsiders, tell them anecdotes and humour them, you imagine that I'm really a light-hearted man. If I didn't need these people, I shouldn't even look at them. . . . As it is, whenever I can, without much danger, you know, I turn them into ridicule. . . . I don't deceive myself, though: I'm well aware that certain gentry, who can't take a step without me and are bored when I'm not there, consider themselves entitled to look down on me; but I pay them out, you may be sure. Natalya Petrovna, for instance. . . . Do you suppose I don't see through her? [*Mimics* NATALYA PETROVNA.] "Dear Doctor, I really like you so much . . . you have such a wicked tongue," ha, ha, coo away, my dove, coo away. Ugh! these ladies! And they smile and make eyes at you, while disdain is written on their faces. . . . They despise us, do what you will! I quite understand why she is saying harsh things of me to-day. Upon my soul, these ladies are wonderful people! Because they sprinkle themselves with eau-de-Cologne every day and speak so carelessly—as though they were just dropping their words for you to pick them up—they fancy there's no catching them by the tail. Oh, isn't there, though! They're just mortals the same as all of us poor sinners!

LIZAVETA BOGDANOVNA. Ignaty Ilyitch . . . you surprise me.

SHPIGELSKY. I knew I should surprise you. So you see I'm not a light-hearted man at all, and not too good-natured even. . . . But at the same time, I don't want to make myself out what I never have been. Though I may put it on a bit before the gentry, no one's ever seen me play the fool in a low way, no one's ever dared to take insulting liberties with me. Indeed, I think they're a bit afraid of me; in fact, they know I bite. On one occasion, three years ago, a gentleman—a regular son of the soil—by way of fun at the dinner-table, stuck a radish in my hair. What do you think I did? Why, on the spot, without any show of anger, you know, in the most courteous manner, I challenged him to a duel. The son of the soil almost had a stroke, he was so terrified; our host made him apologize—it made a great sensation. As a matter of fact, I knew beforehand that he wouldn't fight. So you see, Lizaveta Bogdanovna, my vanity's immense; but my life's not been much. My talents are not great either. . . . I got through my studies somehow. I'm not much good as a doctor, it's no use my pretending to you, and if you're ever taken ill, I shan't prescribe for you myself. If I'd had talent and a good education, I should have bolted to the capital. For the aborigines here, no better doctor is wanted, to be sure. As regards my personal character, Lizaveta Bogdanovna, I ought to warn you: at home I'm ill-humoured, silent and exacting, I'm not cross as long as everything's done for me to my satisfaction; I like to be well fed and to have my habits respected; however, I'm not jealous and I'm not mean, and in my absence, you can do just as you like. Of romantic love and all that between us, you understand it's needless to speak; and yet I imagine one might live under the same roof with me . . . so long as you try to please me, and don't shed tears in my presence, that I can't endure! But I'm not given to fault-finding. There you have my confession. Well, what do you say now?

LIZAVETA BOGDANOVNA. What am I to say to you, Ignaty Ilyitch? . . . If you have not been blackening your character on purpose to . . .

SHPIGELSKY. But how have I blackened my character? Don't forget that another man in my place would, with perfect complacency, have kept quiet about his faults, as you've not noticed them, and after the wedding, it's all up then, it's too late. But I'm too proud to do that. [LIZAVETA BOGDANOVNA *glances at him.*] Yes, yes, too proud . . . you needn't look at me like that. I don't mean to pose and lie before my future wife, not if it were for a hundred thousand instead of fifteen thousand, though to a stranger I'm ready to humble myself for a sack of flour. I'm like that. . . . I'll smirk to a stranger while inwardly I'm thinking, you're a blockhead, my friend, you'll be caught by my bait; but with you, I say what I think. That is, let me explain; I don't say everything I think, even to you; but at any rate, I'm not deceiving you. I must strike you as a very queer fish certainly, but there, wait a bit, one day I'll tell you the story of my life and you'll wonder that I've come through as well as I have. You weren't born with a silver spoon in your mouth, I expect, either, but yet, my dear, you can't conceive what real hopeless poverty is like. . . . I'll tell you all about that, though, some other time. But now you had better think over the proposition I have had the honour of laying before you. . . . Consider this little matter well, in solitude, and let me know your decision. So far as I can judge, you're a sensible woman. And by the way, how old are you?

LIZAVETA BOGDANOVNA. I . . . I . . . I'm thirty.

SHPIGELSKY [*calmly*]. And that's not true, you're quite forty.

LIZAVETA BOGDANOVNA [*firing up*]. I'm *not* forty, only thirty-six.

SHPIGELSKY. That's not thirty, anyway. Well, Lizaveta Bogdanovna, that's a habit you must get out of . . . especially as thirty-six isn't old for a married woman. And you shouldn't take snuff either. [*Getting up.*] I fancy the rain has stopped.

LIZAVETA BOGDANOVNA [*getting up also*]. Yes, it has.

SHPIGELSKY. And so you'll give me an answer in a day or two?

LIZAVETA BOGDANOVNA. I will tell you my decision to-morrow.

SHPIGELSKY. Now, I like that! That's really sensible! Bravo! Lizaveta Bogdanovna! Come, give me your arm. Let us go indoors.

LIZAVETA BOGDANOVNA [*taking his arm*]. Let us go.

SHPIGELSKY. And by the way, I haven't kissed your hand . . . and I believe it's what's done. Well, for once, here goes! [*Kisses her hand.* LIZAVETA BOGDANOVNA *blushes.*] That's right. [*Moves towards door into garden.*]

LIZAVETA BOGDANOVNA [*stopping*]. So you think, Ignaty Ilyitch, that Mihail Alexandritch is really not a dangerous man?

SHPIGELSKY. I think not.

LIZAVETA BOGDANOVNA. Do you know what, Ignaty Ilyitch? I fancy that for some time past Natalya Petrovna . . . I fancy that Mr. Beliayev. . . . She takes a good deal of notice of him . . . doesn't she! And Verotchka too, what do you think? Isn't that why to-day? . . .

SHPIGELSKY [*interrupting her*]. There's one other thing I've forgotten to tell you, Lizaveta Bogdanovna. I'm awfully inquisitive myself, but I can't endure inquisitive women. That is, I'll explain. To my thinking, a wife ought to be inquisitive and observant only with other people (indeed it's an advantage to her husband). . . . You understand me—with others only. However, if you really want to know my opinion concerning Natalya Petrovna, Vera Alexandrovna, Mr. Beliayev, and the folks here generally, listen and I'll sing you a little song. I've a horrible voice but you mustn't mind that.

LIZAVETA BOGDANOVNA [*with surprise*]. A song!

SHPIGELSKY. Listen! The first verse:

> "Granny had a little kid,
> Granny had a little kid,
> A little grey kid!
> Yes, she did, yes, she did!"

The second verse:

> "The kid would in the forest play,
> The kid would in the forest play,
> Yes, I say, yes, I say,
> He would in the forest play."

LIZAVETA BOGDANOVNA. But I don't understand. . . .

SHPIGELSKY. Listen then! The third verse:

> "The grey wolves ate that little kid [*skipping about*],
> The grey wolves ate that little kid,
> They ate him up, they ate him up,
> Yes, I say, they ate him up."

And now let us go. I must have a talk with Natalya Petrovna, by the way. Let us hope she won't bite me. If I'm not mistaken, she still has need of me. Come along.

[*They go out into the garden*]

KATYA [*cautiously coming out from behind the column*]. They've gone at last! What a spiteful man that doctor is . . . talked and talked and what didn't he say? And what a way to sing! I'm afraid Alexey

Nikolaitch may have gone back indoors meanwhile. . . . Why on earth need they have come in here! [*Goes to the window.*] So Lizaveta Bogdanovna is to be the doctor's wife. . . . [*Laughs.*] So that's it! . . . Well, I don't envy her. . . . [*Keeps looking out of window.*] The grass looks as though it had been washed. . . . What a nice smell . . . it's the wild cherry. . . . Oh! here he comes! [*After waiting a moment.*] Alexey Nikolaitch! . . . Alexey Nikolaitch!

BELIAYEV [*behind the scenes*]. Who's calling me? Oh! is it you, Katya? [*Comes up to window.*] What do you want?

KATYA. Come in here. . . . I've something to say to you.

BELIAYEV. Oh! very well. [*Moves away from window and a moment later comes in at door.*] Here I am.

KATYA. Aren't you wet?

BELIAYEV. No . . . I've been sitting in the greenhouse with Potap . . . he's your uncle, isn't he?

KATYA. Yes, he's my uncle.

BELIAYEV. How pretty you are to-day! [KATYA *smiles and looks down. He takes a peach out of his pocket.*] Would you like it?

KATYA [*refusing*]. Thank you very much . . . eat it yourself.

BELIAYEV. I didn't refuse your raspberries when you gave me some yesterday. Take it, I picked it for you . . . really.

KATYA. Oh! thank you very much. [*Takes the peach.*]

BELIAYEV. That's right. What did you want to tell me?

KATYA. My young lady . . . Vera Alexandrovna, asked me . . . she wants to see you.

BELIAYEV. Ah! well, I'll go to her at once.

KATYA. No . . . she'll come here. She wants to have a talk with you.

BELIAYEV [*with some surprise*]. She wants to come here?

KATYA. Yes. . . . Here, you see. . . . Nobody comes in here. You won't be interrupted here. . . . [*Sighs.*] She likes you very much, Alexey Nikolaitch. . . . She's so kind. I'll go and fetch her. And you'll wait, won't you?

BELIAYEV. Of course, of course.

KATYA. In a minute. . . . [*Is going and stops.*] Alexey Nikolaitch, is it true what they are saying, that you are leaving us?

BELIAYEV. I? No. . . . Who told you so?

KATYA. So you're not going away? Thank goodness! [*In confusion.*] We'll be back in a minute. [*Goes out by door leading to the house.*]

BELIAYEV [*remains for some time without moving*]. How strange it all is! Strange things are happening to me. I must say I never expected all this. . . . Vera loves me. . . . Natalya Petrovna knows it. . . . Vera has confessed it herself . . . extraordinary! Vera . . . such a sweet, dear child; but . . . what's the meaning of this note? [*Takes a scrap of paper out of his pocket.*] From Natalya Petrovna . . . in pencil. "Don't go away, don't decide on anything till I have had a talk with you." What does she want to talk about? [*A pause.*] Such idiotic ideas come into my head! I must say all this is very embarrassing. If anybody had told me a month ago that I . . . I . . . I simply can't get over that conversation with Natalya Petrovna. Why is my heart throbbing like this? And now Vera wants to see me. . . . What am I going to say to her? Anyway, I shall find out what's the matter. . . . Perhaps Natalya Petrovna's angry with me. . . . But whatever for? [*Looks at the note again.*] It's all queer, very queer.

[*The door is opened softly. He quickly hides the note.* VERA *and* KATYA *appear in the doorway. He goes up to them.* VERA *is very pale, she does not raise her eyes, nor move from the spot.*]

KATYA. Don't be afraid, miss, go up to him; I'll be on the look-out. Don't be afraid. [*To* BELIAYEV.] Oh! Alexey Nikolaitch! [*She shuts the windows, goes out into the garden and closes the door behind her.*]

BELIAYEV. Vera Alexandrovna . . . you wanted to see me. Come here, sit down here. [*Takes her by the hand and leads her to the seat.* VERA *sits down.*] That's it. [*Looking at her with surprise.*] You've been crying?

VERA [*without looking up*]. That doesn't matter. . . . I've come to beg you to forgive me, Alexey Nikolaitch.

BELIAYEV. What for?

VERA. I heard . . . you have had an unpleasant interview with Natalya Petrovna . . . you are going . . . you're being sent away.

BELIAYEV. Who told you that?

VERA. Natalya Petrovna herself. . . . I met her just after you had been with her. . . . She told me you yourself are unwilling to stay. But I believe you are being sent away.

BELIAYEV. Tell me, do they know this in the house?

VERA. No . . . only Katya knows. . . . I had to tell her. . . . I wanted to see you, to beg you to forgive me. Imagine now how wretched I must be. . . . I'm the cause of it, Alexey Nikolaitch, it's all my fault.

BELIAYEV. Your fault, Vera Alexandrovna?

VERA. I never could have thought . . . Natalya Petrovna. . . . But I don't blame her. Don't you blame me either. . . . This morning I was a silly child, but now. . . . [*Breaks off.*]

BELIAYEV. Nothing's settled yet, Vera Alexandrovna. . . . I may be staying.

VERA [*sadly*]. You say nothing's settled yet, Alexey Nikolaitch. . . . No, everything's settled, everything's over. See how you are with me now, and remember only yesterday, in the garden. . . . [*A pause.*] Ah! I see Natalya Petrovna has told you everything.

BELIAYEV [*embarrassed*]. Vera Alexandrovna . . .

VERA. She has told you, I see it. . . . She tried to catch me, and I, like a silly, fell into her trap. But she betrayed herself too. . . . I'm not such a child. [*Dropping her voice.*] Oh no!

BELIAYEV. What do you mean?

VERA [*glancing at him*]. Alexey Nikolaitch, did you really want to leave us yourself?

BELIAYEV. Yes.

VERA. Why? [BELIAYEV *is silent.*] You don't answer?

BELIAYEV. Vera Alexandrovna, you are not mistaken. . . . Natalya Petrovna told me everything.

VERA [*faintly*]. What, for instance?

BELIAYEV. Vera Alexandrovna . . . I really can't. . . . You understand.

VERA. She told you perhaps that I love you?

BELIAYEV [*hesitating*]. Yes.

VERA [*quickly*]. But it's untrue. . . .

BELIAYEV [*in confusion*]. What! . . .

VERA [*hides her face in her hands and whispers in a toneless voice through her fingers*]. Anyway, I didn't tell her that, I don't remember. . . . [*Lifting her head.*] Oh! how cruelly she has treated me! And you . . . you meant to go away because of that?

BELIAYEV. Vera Alexandrovna, only consider. . . .

VERA [*glancing at him*]. He does not love me! [*Hides her face again.*]

BELIAYEV [*sits down beside her and takes her hands*]. Vera Alexandrovna, give me your hand. . . . Listen, there must not be misunderstandings between us. I love you as a sister; I love you because no one could help loving you. Forgive me if I . . . I've never in my life been in such a position. . . . I can't bear to wound you. . . . [*She hides her face again.*] I'm not going to pretend with you, I know that you like me, that you've grown fond of me. . . . But think, what can come of it? I'm only twenty, I haven't a farthing. Please don't be angry with me. I really don't know what to say.

VERA [*taking her hands from her face and looking at him*]. And as though I expected anything, my God! But why so cruelly, so heartlessly. . . . [*She breaks off.*]

BELIAYEV. Vera Alexandrovna, I didn't mean to hurt you.

VERA. I'm not blaming you, Alexey Nikolaitch. How are you to blame? It's all my fault. . . . And how I am punished! I don't blame her either, I know she's a kind-hearted woman but she couldn't help herself. . . . She didn't know what she was doing.

BELIAYEV [*in amazement*]. Didn't know what she was doing?

VERA [*turning to him*]. Natalya Petrovna loves you, Beliayev.

BELIAYEV. What?

VERA. She's in love with you.

BELIAYEV. What are you saying?

VERA. I know what I'm saying. To-day has made me years older. . . . I'm not a child now, believe me. She was actually jealous . . . of me! [*With a bitter smile.*] What do you think of that?

BELIAYEV. But it's impossible!

VERA. Impossible. . . . Then why has she suddenly taken it into her head to marry me to that gentleman, what's his name, Bolshintsov? Why did she send the doctor to me, why did she try to persuade me to it herself? Oh! I know what I am saying! If you could have seen, Beliayev, how her whole face changed when I told her. . . . Oh! you can't imagine how cunningly, how treacherously she trapped me into admitting it. Yes, she's in love with you; it's only too evident. . . .

BELIAYEV. Vera Alexandrovna, you're mistaken, I assure you.

VERA. No, I'm not mistaken. I tell you I'm not mistaken. If she doesn't love you, why has she tortured me like this? What have I done to her? [*Bitterly.*] Jealousy is an excuse for anything. But what's the good of talking! . . . And now why is she sending you away? She imagines that you . . . that we . . . Oh! she need not worry herself! You can stay! [*Hides her face in her hands.*]

BELIAYEV. She hasn't sent me away so far, Vera Alexandrovna. . . . As I've told you already, nothing is decided yet. . . .

VERA [*suddenly lifting her head and looking at him*]. Really?

BELIAYEV. Yes . . . but why do you look at me like that?

VERA [*as though to herself*]. Ah! I see. . . . Yes, yes. . . . She is still hoping. . . . [*The door into the corridor is quickly opened and* NATALYA PETROVNA *appears in the doorway. She stops short on seeing* VERA *and* BELIAYEV.]

BELIAYEV. What did you say?

VERA. Yes, now it's all clear to me. . . . She has thought better of it. She sees I'm no danger to her, and indeed what am I? A silly girl, while she! . . .

BELIAYEV. Vera Alexandrovna, how can you imagine . . .

VERA. But who knows? Perhaps she's right . . . perhaps you love her. . . .

BELIAYEV. I?

VERA [*standing up*]. Yes, you. Why are you blushing?

BELIAYEV. Me blushing? . . .

VERA. You like her, you may come to love her? . . . You don't answer my question.

BELIAYEV. But, good Lord, what do you want me to say? Vera Alexandrovna, you're so excited. . . . Do be calm for goodness sake. . . .

VERA [*turning away from him*]. Oh! you treat me as a child. . . . You don't deign to give me a serious answer. . . . You simply want to get rid of me. You try to comfort me! [*Turns to go out but but stops short at sight of* NATALYA PETROVNA.] Natalya Petrovna! . . . [BELIAYEV *looks round instantly.*]

NATALYA PETROVNA [*taking a few steps forward*]. Yes, I'm here. [*She speaks with some effort.*] I came for you, Verotchka.

VERA [*coldly and deliberately*]. What made you come here? So you've been looking for me?

NATALYA PETROVNA. Yes, I've been looking for you. You're indiscreet, Verotchka. . . . I've spoken of it more than once. . . . And you, Alexey Nikolaitch, you've forgotten your promise . . . you've deceived me.

VERA. Oh! stop that, Natalya Petrovna, leave off, do! [NATALYA PETROVNA *looks at her in amazement.*] Give up speaking to me as though I were a child. . . . [*Dropping her voice.*] From to-day I'm a woman. . . . I'm as much a woman as you are.

NATALYA PETROVNA [*embarrassed*]. Vera. . . .

VERA [*almost in a whisper*]. He hasn't deceived you. . . . Our meeting here is not his doing. He doesn't care for me, you know that, you've no need to be jealous.

NATALYA PETROVNA [*with rising amazement*]. Vera!

VERA. It's the truth . . . don't go on pretending. These pretences are no use now. . . . I see through them now, I can assure you. To you I'm not the ward you are watching over [*ironically*] like an elder sister. . . . [*Moves closer to her.*] I'm your rival.

NATALYA PETROVNA. Vera, you forget yourself. . . .

VERA. Perhaps . . . but who has driven me to it? I don't understand what has given me courage to speak to you like this. . . . Perhaps it's because I have nothing to hope for, because it has pleased you to trample upon me. . . . And you have succeeded . . . completely. But let me tell you, I don't mean to be as underhand with you as you have been with me. . . . I'll let you know I've told him everything. [*Indicating* BELIAYEV.]

NATALYA PETROVNA. What could you tell him?

VERA. What? [*With irony.*] Why, everything I have noticed. You hoped to worm everything out of me without betraying yourself. You made a mistake, Natalya Petrovna, you overrated your self-control.

NATALYA PETROVNA. Vera, think what you're saying . . .

VERA [*in a whisper and coming still closer to her*]. Tell me that I'm wrong. . . . Tell me that you're not in love with him. . . . He has told me that he doesn't love me! [NATALYA PETROVNA, *overwhelmed with confusion, is silent.* VERA *remains for some time motionless, then suddenly presses her hand to her forehead.*] Natalya Petrovna . . . forgive me . . . I . . . don't know . . . what's come over me . . . forgive me, don't be hard on me. . . . [*Bursts into tears and goes out rapidly by door into corridor. A silence.*]

BELIAYEV [*going up to* NATALYA PETROVNA]. I can assure you, Natalya Petrovna. . . .

NATALYA PETROVNA [*looking fixedly at the floor, holds out her hand in his direction*]. Stop, Alexey Nikolaitch. The truth is . . . Vera is right. . . . It's time I . . . time I laid aside deceit. I have wronged her, and you—you have a right to despise me. [BELIAYEV *makes an involuntary gesture.*] I am degraded in my own eyes. The only way left me to regain your respect is openness, complete openness, whatever the consequences. Besides, I am seeing you for the last time, for the last time I am speaking with you. I love you. [*She does not look at him.*]

BELIAYEV. You, Natalya Petrovna! . . .

NATALYA PETROVNA. Yes, yes, I love you. Vera was not deceived and has not deceived you. I have loved you from the very day you arrived here, but I only recognized it yesterday. I don't mean to justify my conduct. It has been unworthy of me . . . but anyway you can understand now, you can make allowance for me. Yes, I was jealous of Vera; yes, I was planning to marry her to Bolshintsov, so as to get her away from you and from myself; yes, I took advantage of my position, of my being older, to find out her secret and—of course I didn't reckon on that—I betrayed myself. I love you, Beliayev; but let me say, it's only pride that forces me to confess it . . . the farce I have been playing revolts me at last. You cannot stay here. . . . Indeed, after what I have just told you, you will no doubt feel very awkward in my company, and you will want to get away as quickly as possible. I am certain of that. It is that certainty has given me courage. I confess I shouldn't like you to think badly of me. Now you know everything. . . . Perhaps I have spoilt things for you . . . perhaps, if all this had not happened, you might have cared for Verotchka. . . . I have only one plea to urge, Alexey Nikolaitch. . . . It has all been beyond my control. [*She pauses. She has said all this in a rather calm and measured voice, not looking at* BELIAYEV. *He is silent. She goes on with some agitation, still not looking at him.*] You don't answer me? But I understand that. There's nothing for you to say to me. The position of a man receiving a declaration of love when he feels no love is too painful. I thank you for your silence. Believe me, when I told you . . . I love you, I was not pretending . . . as before; I was not counting on anything; on the contrary, I wanted at last to throw off the mask, which I can assure you I'm not used to wearing. . . . And indeed, what's the use of affectation and duplicity, when everything's known; why pretend when there's no one to deceive? Everything is over between us now. I will not keep you. You can go away without saying another word to me, without taking leave of me. I shall not think it discourteous, I shall be grateful to you. There are circumstances in which delicacy is out of place . . . worse than rudeness. It seems we were not destined to know each other better. Good-bye! Yes, we were not destined to know each other . . . but at least I hope that now you no longer look on me as an oppressor, a furtive and deceitful creature. . . . Good-bye for ever. [BELIAYEV *in distress tries to say something, but cannot.*] You are not going?

BELIAYEV [*bows, is about to go, and after a struggle with himself turns back*]. No, I can't go. . . . [NATALYA PETROVNA *for the first time looks at him.*] I can't go away like this! Natalya Petrovna, you said just now . . . you didn't want me to carry away unpleasant memories of you, and I don't want you to think of me as a man who . . . Oh dear! I don't know how to say it. . . . Natalya Petrovna, I'm sorry. . . . I don't know how to talk to women like you. . . . Up to now I've only known . . . quite ordinary women. You said that we were not destined to be friends, but, good God, how could an ordinary almost uneducated fellow like me ever dream of being anything to you? Think what you are and what I am! Think, could I dare to dream? . . . With your bringing up. . . . But why talk of that. . . . Just look at me . . . this old coat and your sweet-scented clothes. . . . My God! Oh yes, I was afraid of you and I'm afraid of you still. . . . I thought of you, without any exaggeration, as a being of higher order, and now . . . you, you tell me that you love me . . . you, Natalya Petrovna! Me! . . . I feel my heart beating as it never has in my life; it's not beating merely from amazement, it's not that my vanity's flattered. . . . No, indeed . . . vanity doesn't come in now. . . . But I . . . I can't go away like this, say what you like!

NATALYA PETROVNA [*after a pause, as though to herself*]. What have I done?

BELIAYEV. Natalya Petrovna, for God's sake, I assure you . . .

NATALYA PETROVNA [*in a changed voice*]. Alexey Nikolaitch. If I did not know you are an honest man, and incapable of deceit, God knows what I should think. I might regret having spoken. But I trust you. I don't want to hide my feelings from you; I am grateful for what you have just said. Now I know why we have not been friends. . . . So it was nothing in me myself that repelled you. . . . Only my position. . . . [*Breaks off.*] It's all for the best, of course . . . but now it will be easier for me to part from you. . . . Good-bye. [*Is about to go out.*]

BELIAYEV [*after a pause*]. Natalya Petrovna, I know that it's impossible for me to stay here . . . but I can't tell you what's going on in me. You love me. . . . I'm positively terrified to utter those words . . . it's all so new to me . . . it seems as though I'm seeing you for the first time, hearing you for the first time, but I feel one thing, I must go. . . . I feel I can't answer for anything. . . .

NATALYA PETROVNA [*in a faint voice*]. Yes, Beliayev, you must go. . . . Now after what you have said, you can go. . . . And can it be really, in spite of all I have done. . . . Oh, believe me, if I had had the remotest suspicion of all you have just told me, that confession would have died in me, Beliayev. . . . I only meant to put an end to all misunderstandings, I meant to expiate, to punish myself, I meant to cut the last thread. If I could have imagined. . . . [*Hides her face.*]

BELIAYEV. I do believe you, Natalya Petrovna, I do. And I, too . . . a quarter of an hour ago . . . could I have imagined. . . . It's only to-day, during our interview before dinner that I felt for the first time something extraordinary, incredible, as though a hand had squeezed my heart, and such a burning ache. . . . It is true that before then I had, more or less, avoided you and even not liked you particularly, but when you told me to-day that Vera Alexandrovna fancied . . . [*Breaks off.*]

NATALYA PETROVNA [*with an involuntary smile of happiness on her lips*]. Hush, hush, Beliayev; we mustn't think of that. We must not forget that we are speaking to each other for the last time . . . that you are going to-morrow. . . .

BELIAYEV. Oh yes! I'll go to-morrow! Now I can go. . . . All this will pass. . . . You see I don't want to exaggerate. . . . I'm going . . . to take what God gives! I shall take with me a memory, I shall never forget that you cared for me. . . . But how was it I didn't know you till now? Here you are looking at me now. . . . Can I have ever tried to avoid your eyes? . . . Can I ever have felt shy with you?

NATALYA PETROVNA [*with a smile*]. You said just now that you're afraid of me.

BELIAYEV. Did I? [*A pause.*] Really. . . . I wonder at myself. . . . Is it I, I talking so boldly to you? I don't know myself.

NATALYA PETROVNA. And you're not deceiving yourself?

BELIAYEV. How?

NATALYA PETROVNA. In thinking that you . . . [*Shuddering.*] Oh? good God, what am I doing? . . . Beliayev. . . . Help me. . . . No woman has ever been in such a position. It's more than I can bear indeed. . . . Perhaps it's for the best, everything is ended at once; but anyway, we have come to know each other. . . . Give me your hand and good-bye for ever.

BELIAYEV [*takes her hand*]. Natalya Petrovna . . . I don't know what to say at parting . . . my heart is so full. God give you. . . . [*Breaks off and presses her hand to his lips.*] Good-bye. [*Is about to go out by door into garden.*]

NATALYA PETROVNA [*looking after him*]. Beliayev. . . .

BELIAYEV [*turning*]. Natalya Petrovna. . . .

NATALYA PETROVNA [*pausing for some time, then in a weak voice*]. Stay. . . .

BELIAYEV. What?

NATALYA PETROVNA. Stay, and may God be our judge! [*She hides her head in her hands.*]

BELIAYEV [*goes swiftly to her and holds out his hands to her*]. Natalya Petrovna. . . .

[*At that instant the garden door opens and* RAKITIN *appears in the doorway. He gazes at them for some time, then goes suddenly up to them.*]

RAKITIN [*in a loud voice*]. They are looking for you everywhere, Natalya Petrovna. . . . [NATALYA PETROVNA *and* BELIAYEV *look round.*]

NATALYA PETROVNA [*taking her hands from her face and seeming to come to herself*]. Ah, it's you. . . . Who is looking for me? [BELIAYEV *in confusion bows to* NATALYA PETROVNA *and is going out.*] Are you going, Alexey Nikolaitch? . . . Don't forget, you know what. . . . [*He bows to her a second time and goes out into the garden.*]

RAKITIN. Arkady is looking for you. . . . I must say I didn't expect to find you here . . . but as I passed by . . .

NATALYA PETROVNA [*with a smile*]. You heard our voices. . . . I met Alexey Nikolaitch here and have had a complete explanation with him. . . . To-day seems a day of explanations; but now we can go into the house. . . . [*Goes towards door into corridor.*]

RAKITIN [*with some emotion*]. May I ask . . . what decision?

NATALYA PETROVNA [*affecting surprise*]. Decision? . . . I don't understand you.

RAKITIN [*after a long pause, sadly*]. If that's so, I understand.

NATALYA PETROVNA. Well, there it is. . . . Mysterious hints again! Oh, well, I have spoken to him and now everything is set right. . . . It was all nonsense, exaggeration. . . . All you and I talked about was childish. It must be forgotten now.

RAKITIN. I am not asking you for explanations, Natalya Petrovna.

NATALYA PETROVNA [*with forced ease*]. What on earth was it I wanted to say to you. . . . I don't remember. Never mind. Let us go. It's all at an end . . . it's over.

RAKITIN [*looking at her intently*]. Yes, it's all at an end. How vexed you must be with yourself now . . . for your openness this morning. [*She turns away.*]

NATALYA PETROVNA. Rakitin. . . . [*He glances at her again; she obviously does not know what to say.*] You've not spoken to Arkady yet?

RAKITIN. No . . . I haven't thought of anything yet. . . . You see I must make up some story. . . .

NATALYA PETROVNA. How insufferable it is! What do they want of me? I'm followed about at every step I take. Rakitin, I'm really conscience-stricken you should have . . .

RAKITIN. Oh, Natalya Petrovna, pray don't distress yourself. . . . Why, it's all in the natural order of things. But how obviously this is Mr. Beliayev's first experience! Why was he so embarrassed, why did he take to flight? . . . But with time . . . [*in an undertone*] you will both learn to keep up appearances. . . . [*Aloud.*] Let us go.

[NATALYA PETROVNA *is about to go up to him but stops short. At that instant* ISLAYEV'S *voice is heard in the garden:* "He went in here, you say?" *and then* ISLAYEV *and* SHPIGELSKY *come in.*]

ISLAYEV. To be sure . . . here he is. Well, well, well! And Natalya Petrovna too! [*Going up to her.*] How's this? The continuation of this morning's talk? It's evidently an important matter.

RAKITIN. I met Natalya Petrovna here as I walked.

ISLAYEV. Met her? [*Looking round.*] A queer place for a walk!

NATALYA PETROVNA. Well, you've walked in, too . . .

ISLAYEV. I came in because . . . [*Breaks off.*]

NATALYA PETROVNA. You were looking for me?

ISLAYEV [*after a pause*]. Yes—I was looking for you. Won't you come into the house? Tea's ready. It will soon be dark.

NATALYA PETROVNA [*taking his arm*]. Come along.

ISLAYEV [*looking round*]. This place might be turned into two good rooms for the gardeners—or another servants' hall—don't you think, Shpigelsky?

SHPIGELSKY. To be sure it could.

ISLAYEV. Let us go by the garden, Natasha. [*Goes towards the garden door. Throughout the scene he has not once looked at* RAKITIN. *In the doorway he turns half round.*] Well, gentlemen. Let us go in to tea.

[*Goes out with* NATALYA PETROVNA.]

SHPIGELSKY [*to* RAKITIN]. Well, Mihail Alexandritch, come along. . . . Give me your arm. . . . It's clear we are destined to follow in the rear. . . .

RAKITIN [*wrathfully*]. Oh, Doctor, I'm sick of you.

SHPIGELSKY [*with affected good-humour*]. Ah, Mihail Alexandritch, if only you know how sick I am of myself! [RAKITIN *cannot help smiling.*] Come along, come along. [*They go out into the garden.*]

Act V

[*The scene is the same as in the 1st and 3rd Acts. Morning.* ISLAYEV *is sitting at the table looking through papers. He suddenly jumps up.*]

ISLAYEV. No! impossible. I can't work to-day. I can't get it out of my mind. [*Walks up and down.*] I confess I didn't expect this; I didn't expect I should be so upset . . . as I am now. How is one to act? . . . that's the problem. [*Ponders and suddenly shouts.*] Matvey!

MATVEY [*entering*]. Yes, Sir?

ISLAYEV. Send the bailiff to me. . . . And tell the men digging at the dam to wait for me. . . . Run along.

MATVEY. Yes, Sir. [*Goes out.*]

ISLAYEV [*going back to the table and turning over the papers*]. Yes . . . it's a problem!

ANNA SEMYONOVNA [*comes in and goes up to* ISLAYEV]. Arkasha. . . .

ISLAYEV. Ah! it's you, Mamma. How are you this morning?

ANNA SEMYONOVNA [*sitting down on the sofa*]. I'm quite well, thank God. [*Sighs.*] I'm quite well. [*Sighs still more audibly.*] Thank God. [*Seeing that* ISLAYEV *is not attending to her, she sighs very emphatically, with a faint moan.*]

ISLAYEV. You're sighing . . . what's the matter?

ANNA SEMYONOVNA [*sighs again but less emphatically*]. Oh! Arkasha, as though you don't know what makes me sigh!

ISLAYEV. What do you want to say?

ANNA SEMYONOVNA [*after a pause*]. I'm your mother, Arkasha. Of course you're a man, grown-up and sensible; but still—I'm your mother. It's a great word—mother!

ISLAYEV. Please explain.

ANNA SEMYONOVNA. You know what I am hinting at, my dear. Your wife, Natasha . . . of course, she's an excellent woman . . . and her conduct hitherto has been most exemplary . . . but she is still so young, Arkasha! And youth. . . .

ISLAYEV. I see what you want to say. . . . You fancy her relations with Rakitin. . . .

ANNA SEMYONOVNA. God forbid! I never thought of such a thing.

ISLAYEV. You didn't let me finish. . . . You fancy her relations with Rakitin are not altogether . . . clear. These mysterious conversations, these tears—all strike you as strange.

ANNA SEMYONOVNA. Well, Arkasha, has he told you at last what their talks were about? . . . He has told me nothing.

ISLAYEV. I haven't asked him, Mamma, and he is apparently in no hurry to satisfy my curiosity.

ANNA SEMYONOVNA. Then what do you intend to do now?

ISLAYEV. Do, Mamma? Why, nothing.

ANNA SEMYONOVNA. Nothing?

ISLAYEV. Why, certainly, nothing.

ANNA SEMYONOVNA [*getting up*]. I must say, I'm surprised to hear it. Of course you are master in your own house and know better than I do what is for the best. But only think of the consequences. . . .

ISLAYEV. Really, Mamma, there's no need to worry yourself.

ANNA SEMYONOVNA. My dear, I'm a mother . . . you know best. [*A pause.*] I must own I came to see whether I could do anything to help.

ISLAYEV [*earnestly*]. No, as far as that goes, I must beg you, Mamma, not to trouble yourself. . . . Pray don't!

ANNA SEMYONOVNA. As you wish, Arkasha, as you wish. I won't say another word. I have warned you, I have done my duty, and now I won't open my lips. [*A brief silence.*]

ISLAYEV. Are you going anywhere to-day?

ANNA SEMYONOVNA. Only I must warn you; you are too trustful, my dear boy; you judge everybody by yourself! Believe me, true friends are only too rare nowadays!

ISLAYEV [*with impatience*]. Mamma. . . .

ANNA SEMYONOVNA. Oh, I'll say no more, I'll say no more! And what's the use, an old woman like me! I'm in my dotage, I suppose! But I was brought up on different principles, and have tried to instil them in you . . . there, there, go on with your work, I won't interrupt you. . . . I'm going. [*Goes to door and stops.*] Well, you know best. [*Goes out.*]

ISLAYEV [*looking after her*]. Queer that people who really love you have such a passion for poking their fingers into your wounds. And of course they're convinced it's doing you good . . . that's what's so funny! I don't blame Mother, though; of course she means well, and how could she help giving advice? But that's no matter. . . . [*Sitting down.*] How am I to act? [*After a moment's thought, gets up.*] Oh! the more simply, the better! Diplomatic subtleties don't suit me. . . . I should be the first to make a muddle of them. [*Rings,* MATVEY *enters.*] Is Mihail Alexandritch at home, do you know?

MATVEY. Yes, Sir. I saw his honour in the billiard-room just now.

ISLAYEV. Ah, well, ask him to come to me.

MATVEY. Yes, Sir. [*Goes out.*]

ISLAYEV [*walking up and down*]. I'm not used to these upheavals. . . . I hope they won't happen often . . . strong as I am, I can't stand them. [*Puts his hand on his heart.*] Ough! . . . [RAKITIN, *embarrassed, comes in from the outer room.*]

RAKITIN. You sent for me?

ISLAYEV. Yes. . . . [*A pause.*] Michel, you know you owe me something?

RAKITIN. I owe you?

ISLAYEV. Why, yes. Have you forgotten your promise? About . . . Natasha's tears . . . and altogether . . . When my Mother and I came upon you, you remember—you told me you had a secret which you would explain.

RAKITIN. I said a secret?

ISLAYEV. You said so.

RAKITIN. But what secret could we have? We had had a talk.

ISLAYEV. What about? And why was she crying?

RAKITIN. You know, Arkady . . . there are moments in the life of a woman . . . even the happiest . . .

ISLAYEV. Rakitin, stop, we can't go on like this. I can't bear to see you in such a position. . . . Your confusion distresses me more than it does yourself. [*Takes his hand.*] We are old friends—you've known me from a child; I don't know how to pretend and you have always been open with me. Let me put one question to you. . . . I give you my word beforehand that I shall not doubt the sincerity of your answer. You love my wife, don't you? [RAKITIN *looks at* ISLAYEV.] You understand me, you love her as . . . Well, that is you love her with the sort of love that . . . it's difficult to admit to her husband?

RAKITIN [*after a pause, in a toneless voice*]. Yes, I love your wife . . . with that sort of love.

ISLAYEV [*also after a pause*]. Michel, thank you for your frankness. You're an honourable man. But what's to be done now? Sit down, we'll think it over together. [RAKITIN *sits down.* ISLAYEV *walks about the room.*] I know Natasha; I know how to appreciate her. But I know how much I'm worth myself too. I'm not your equal. Michel . . . don't interrupt me, please—I'm not your equal. You're cleverer, better, more attractive, in fact. I'm an ordinary person. Natasha loves me—I think, but she has eyes, well, of course, she must find you attractive. And there's another thing I must tell you: I noticed your affection for each other long ago. . . . But I was always so sure of you both—and as long as nothing came to the surface . . . Ough! I don't know how to say things! [*Breaks off.*] But after the scene yesterday, after your second interview in the evening—what are we to do? And if only I had come upon you alone, but other people are mixed up in it; Mamma, and that sly fox, Shpigelsky. . . . Come, what do you say, Michel?

RAKITIN. You are perfectly right, Arkady.

ISLAYEV. That's not the point . . . what's to be done? I must tell you, Michel, that though I am a simple person—so much I do understand, that it's not the thing to spoil other people's lives—and that there are cases when it's wicked to insist on one's rights. That I've not picked out of books, Michel . . . it's my conscience tells me so. Leave others free. . . . Well, yes, let them be free. Only it wants some thinking over. It's too important.

RAKITIN [*getting up*]. But I have thought it over already.

ISLAYEV. How so?

RAKITIN. I must go. . . . I'm going away.

ISLAYEV [*after a pause*]. You think so? . . . Right away from here altogether?

RAKITIN. Yes.

ISLAYEV [*begins walking up and down again*]. That is . . . that is a hard saying! But perhaps you are right. We shall miss you dreadfully. . . . God knows, perhaps it won't mend matters either. . . . But you can see more clearly, you know best. I expect you are right. You're a danger to me, Michel. . . . [*With a mournful smile.*] Yes . . . you are. You know what I said just now . . . about freedom. . . . And yet perhaps I couldn't survive it! For me to be without Natasha. . . . [*Waving his hand in dismissal of the idea.*] And another thing, Michel: for some time past, and especially these last few days, I've noticed a great change in her. She's all the time in a state of intense agitation and I'm alarmed about it. I'm not mistaken, am I?

RAKITIN [*bitterly*]. Oh no! you're not mistaken!

ISLAYEV. Well, you see! So you are going away?

RAKITIN. Yes.

ISLAYEV. H'm! And how suddenly this has burst on us! If only you had not been so confused when my Mother and I came upon you. . . .

MATVEY [*coming in*]. The bailiff is here.

ISLAYEV. Ask him to wait! [MATVEY *goes out.*] But, Michel, you won't be away for long? That's nonsense.

RAKITIN. I don't know . . . really . . . a good time, I expect.

ISLAYEV. But you don't take me for an Othello, do you? Upon my word, I don't believe there has been such a conversation between two friends since the world began! I can't part from you like this. . . .

RAKITIN [*pressing his hand*]. You'll let me know when I can come back. . . .

ISLAYEV. There's nobody who can fill your place here! Not Bolshintsov, anyway!

RAKITIN. There are others. . . .

ISLAYEV. Who? Krinitsyn? That conceited fool? Beliayev, of course, is a good-natured lad . . . but you can't speak of him in the same breath.

RAKITIN [*ironically*]. Do you think so? You don't know him, Arkady. . . . Look at him more attentively. . . . I advise you. . . . Do you hear? He's a very . . . very remarkable fellow!

ISLAYEV. Pooh! To be sure, Natasha and you were always meaning to finish his education! [*Glancing towards the door.*] Ah! here he is, coming here, I do believe. . . . [*Hurriedly.*] And so, dear Michel, it's settled . . . you are going away . . . for a short time . . . some days. . . . No need to hurry . . . we must prepare Natasha. . . . I'll soothe my Mother. . . . And God give you happiness! You've lifted a load off my heart. . . . Embrace me, dear boy! [*Hastily embraces him and turns to* BELIAYEV *who is coming in.*] Ah! . . . it's you! Well. . . well, how are you?

BELIAYEV. Very well, thank you, Arkady Sergeyitch.

ISLAYEV. And where's Kolya?

BELIAYEV. He's with Herr Schaaf.

ISLAYEV. Ah . . . that's right! [*Takes his hat.*] Well, I must be off, my friends. I've not been anywhere this morning, neither to the dam nor the building. . . . Here, I've not even looked through my papers. [*Gathers them up under his arm.*] Good-bye for now! Matvey! Matvey! Come with me! [*Goes out.* RAKITIN *remains in front of stage, plunged in thought.*]

BELIAYEV [*goes up to him*]. How are you feeling this morning, Mihail Alexandritch?

RAKITIN. Thank you. Just as usual. And you?

BELIAYEV. I'm quite well.

RAKITIN. That's obvious!

BELIAYEV. How so?

RAKITIN. Why . . . from your face. . . . And oh! you've put on your new coat this morning. . . . And what do I see? A flower in your buttonhole! [BELIAYEV, *blushing, snatches it out.*] Oh! why . . . why. . . . It's charming. [A *pause.*] By the way, Alexey Nikolaitch, if there's anything you want . . . I'm going to the town to-morrow.

BELIAYEV. To-morrow?

RAKITIN. Yes . . . and from there on to Moscow, perhaps.

BELIAYEV [*with surprise*]. To Moscow? Why, only yesterday you said you meant to be here another month or so. . . .

RAKITIN. Yes . . . but business . . . things have turned up. . . .

BELIAYEV. And shall you be away for long?
RAKITIN. I don't know . . . a long time, perhaps.
BELIAYEV. Do you mind telling me—does Natalya Petrovna know of your intention?
RAKITIN. No. Why do you ask me about her?
BELIAYEV. Why? [*A little embarrassed.*] Oh, nothing.
RAKITIN [*pausing and looking round*]. Alexey Nikolaitch, there's nobody in the room but ourselves; isn't it queer that we should keep up a farce before each other? Don't you think so?
BELIAYEV. I don't understand you, Mihail Alexandritch.
RAKITIN. Oh, you don't? Do you really not understand why I'm going away?
BELIAYEV. No.
RAKITIN. That's strange. . . . However, I'm willing to believe you. Perhaps you really don't know the reason . . . would you like me to tell you why I'm going?
BELIAYEV. Please do.
RAKITIN. Well, you see, Alexey Nikolaitch—but I rely on your discretion—you found me just now with Arkady Sergeyitch. . . . We have had a rather important conversation. In consequence of which I have decided to depart. And do you know why? I'm telling you all this because I think you are a really good fellow. . . . He imagined that I . . . oh! well, that I'm in love with Natalya Petrovna. What do you think of that? It's a queer notion, isn't it? But I am grateful to him for speaking to me simply, straight out instead of being underhand, keeping watch on us and all that. Come, tell me now what would you have done in my place? Of course, there are no grounds at all for his suspicions, still he's worried by them. . . . For the peace of mind of his friends, a decent man must be ready at times to sacrifice . . . his own pleasure. So that's why I'm going away. . . . I'm sure you think I'm right, don't you? You too . . . you would certainly do the same in my place, wouldn't you? You would go away too?
BELIAYEV [*after a pause*]. Perhaps.
RAKITIN. I am very glad to hear that. . . . Of course, I can't deny that my making off has its comic side. It's as though I imagine I'm dangerous; but you see, Alexey Nikolaitch, a woman's honour is such an important thing. . . . And at the same time—of course, I don't say this of Natalya Petrovna—but I have known women pure and innocent at heart, perfect children for all their cleverness, who just through that very purity and innocence, are more apt than others to give way to sudden passion. . . . And so, who knows? One can't be too discreet in such cases, especially as . . . By the way, Alexey Nikolaitch, you may perhaps still imagine that love is the greatest bliss on earth?

BELIAYEV [*coldly*]. I have had no experience, but imagine that to be loved by a woman one loves is a great happiness.

RAKITIN. God grant you long preserve such pleasant convictions! It's my belief, Alexey Nikolaitch, that love of every kind, happy as much as unhappy, is a real calamity if you give yourself up to it completely. . . . Wait a bit! You may learn yet how those soft little hands can torture you, with what sweet solicitude they can tear your heart to rags. . . . Wait a bit! You will learn what burning hatred lies hidden under the most ardent love! You will think of me when you yearn for peace, for the dullest, most commonplace peace as a sick man yearns for health, when you will envy any man who is free and light-hearted. . . . You wait! You will know what it means to be tied to a petticoat, to be enslaved and poisoned—and how shameful and agonizing that slavery is! . . . You will learn at last how little you get for all your sufferings. . . . But why am I saying all this to you, you won't believe me now. The fact is that I am very glad of your approval . . . yes, yes . . . in such cases one ought to be careful.

BELIAYEV [*who has kept his eyes fixed on* RAKITIN]. Thanks for the lesson, Mihail Alexandritch, though I didn't need it.

RAKITIN [*takes his hand*]. Please forgive me, I had no intention . . . it's not for me to give lessons to anyone whatever . . . I was just talking. . . .

BELIAYEV [*with slight irony*]. Not apropos of anything?

RAKITIN [*a little embarrassed*]. Just so, not apropos of anything in particular. . . . I only meant. . . . You haven't hitherto had occasion, Alexey Nikolaitch, to study women. Women are peculiar creatures.

BELIAYEV. But of whom are you speaking?

RAKITIN. Oh . . . no one in particular.

BELIAYEV. Of women in general?

RAKITIN [*with a constrained smile*]. Yes, perhaps. I really don't know what business I have to adopt this lecturing tone, but do let me at parting give you this one piece of advice. [*Breaking off with a gesture of dismissal.*] But there! I'm not the man to give anyone advice! Please forgive my running on like this. . . .

BELIAYEV. Oh, not at all. . . .

RAKITIN. So you don't want anything in the town?

BELIAYEV. Nothing, thank you. But I'm sorry you're going away.

RAKITIN. Thanks very much. . . . So am I, I can assure you. . . . [NATALYA PETROVNA *and* VERA *come in from the study.* VERA *is very sad and pale.*] I am very glad to have made your acquaintance. . . . [*Presses his hand again.*]

NATALYA PETROVNA [*looks at them and then goes up to them*]. Good morning.

RAKITIN [*turning quickly*]. Good morning, Natalya Petrovna. . . . Good morning Vera Alexandrovna. . . . [BELIAYEV *bows to* NATALYA PETROVNA *and* VERA *without speaking. He is confused.*]

NATALYA PETROVNA [*to* RAKITIN]. What are you doing this morning?

RAKITIN. Oh, nothing. . . .

NATALYA PETROVNA. Vera and I have been walking in the garden. . . . It's a lovely day . . . The scent of the lime trees is so delicious. We've been walking under the lime trees. . . . It's delightful to listen to the humming of the bees in the shade overhead. . . . [*Timidly to* BELIAYEV.] We expected to meet you there. [BELIAYEV *is silent.*]

RAKITIN [*to* NATALYA PETROVNA]. Ah! You too can admire the beauties of nature to-day. . . . [*A pause.*] Alexey Nikolaitch couldn't go into the garden. . . . He has got his new coat on.

BELIAYEV [*reddening*]. Of course, it's the only one I have, and I dare say it might get torn in the garden. . . . I suppose that's what you mean?

RAKITIN [*blushing*]. Oh no . . . I didn't mean that. . . . [VERA *goes in silence to sofa on right, sits down and takes up her work.* NATALYA PETROVNA *gives* BELIAYEV *a constrained smile. A brief, rather oppressive silence.* RAKITIN *goes on with malicious carelessness.*] Ah, I'd forgotten to tell you, Natalya Petrovna, I'm going away to-day. . . .

NATALYA PETROVNA [*with some agitation*]. Going? Where?

RAKITIN. To the town. . . . On business.

NATALYA PETROVNA. Not for long, I hope.

RAKITIN. That's as my business goes.

NATALYA PETROVNA. Mind you come back as soon as you can. [*To* BELIAYEV *without looking at him.*] Alexey Nikolaitch, was it your sketches Kolya was showing me? Did you draw them?

BELIAYEV. Yes . . . they're nothing much.

NATALYA PETROVNA. Not at all, they are very charming. You have talent.

RAKITIN. I see you are discovering new talents in Mr. Beliayev every day.

NATALYA PETROVNA [*coldly*]. Perhaps . . . so much the better for him. [*To* BELIAYEV.] I expect you have some other sketches, you must show them to me. [BELIAYEV *bows.*]

RAKITIN [*who stands all this time as though on thorns*]. But I remember it's time to pack. . . . Good-bye. [*Goes to door of outer room.*]

NATALYA PETROVNA. But you'll come to say good-bye to us. . . .

RAKITIN. Of course.

BELIAYEV [*after some hesitation*]. Mihail Alexandritch, wait a minute, I'm coming with you. I must have a few words with you. . . .

RAKITIN. Ah! [*They go out together.* NATALYA PETROVNA *is left in the middle of the stage; after a little while, she sits down on left.*]

NATALYA PETROVNA [*after an interval of silence*]. Vera!

VERA [*not lifting her head*]. What is it?

NATALYA PETROVNA. Vera for goodness sake, don't treat me like this . . . for goodness sake, Vera . . . Verotchka. [VERA *says nothing.* NATALYA PETROVNA *gets up, walks across the stage and slowly sinks on her knees before* VERA. VERA *tries to make her get up, turns away and hides her face.* NATALYA PETROVNA *speaks on her knees.*] Vera, forgive me; don't cry, Vera. I've behaved badly to you, I'm to blame. Can't you forgive me?

VERA [*through her tears*]. Get up, get up. . . .

NATALYA PETROVNA. I won't get up, Vera, till you forgive me. It's hard for you . . . but think, is it any easier for me . . . think, Vera. . . . You know everything. . . . The only difference between us is that you have done no wrong, while I . . .

VERA [*bitterly*]. That's all the difference! No, Natalya Petrovna, there's another difference between us. . . . You're so soft, so kind, so warm this morning. . . .

NATALYA PETROVNA [*interrupting her*]. Because I feel how wrong I've been. . . .

VERA. Really? Is it only that?

NATALYA PETROVNA [*gets up and sits beside her*]. What other reason can there be?

VERA. Natalya Petrovna, don't torture me any more, don't ask me questions. . . .

NATALYA PETROVNA [*with a sigh*]. Vera, I see you can't forgive me.

VERA. You're so kind and soft to-day because you feel you are loved.

NATALYA PETROVNA [*embarrassed*]. Vera?

VERA [*turning to her*]. Well, isn't it the truth?

NATALYA PETROVNA [*sadly*]. I assure you we are both equally unhappy.

VERA. He loves you!

NATALYA PETROVNA. Vera, why do we torture each other? It's time for both of us to think what we're doing. Remember the position I'm in, the position we are both in. Remember that our secret, though my fault, of course, is known to two men here already. . . . [*Breaks off.*] Vera, instead of tormenting each other with suspicions and reproaches, hadn't we better consider together how to get out of this dreadful position . . . how to save ourselves! Do you imagine I can stand these shocks and agitations? Have you forgotten who I am? But you're not listening.

VERA [*looking dreamily at the floor*]. He loves you. . . .

NATALYA PETROVNA. Vera, he's going away.

VERA [*turning away*]. Oh, leave me alone. . . . [NATALYA PETROVNA *looks at her irresolutely. At that instant,* ISLAYEV'S *voice calls from the study:* "Natasha, Natasha, where are you?"]

NATALYA PETROVNA [*gets up quickly and goes to study-door*]. I'm here . . . what is it?

ISLAYEV [*from the study*]. Come here, I've something to tell you. . . .

NATALYA PETROVNA. In a minute. [*She turns to* VERA *and holds out her hand.* VERA *does not stir.* NATALYA PETROVNA *sighs and goes out into the study.*]

VERA [*alone; after a silence*]. He loves her! . . . And I must stay in her house. . . . Oh! it's too much . . . [*She hides her face in her hands and sits motionless.* SHPIGELSKY *puts his head in at the door leading to the outer room. He looks round cautiously and goes on tip-toe up to* VERA, *who does not notice him.*]

SHPIGELSKY [*standing before her, his arms crossed and a malicious grin on his face*]. Vera Alexandrovna! . . . Vera Alexandrovna!

VERA [*raising her head*]. Who is it? You, Doctor. . . .

SHPIGELSKY. What is it, my young lady, not well, or what?

VERA. Oh, nothing.

SHPIGELSKY. Let me feel your pulse. [*Feels her pulse.*] H'm! Why is it so quick? Ah, young lady, young lady. . . . You won't listen to me. . . . And yet it's your welfare I wish for.

VERA [*looking at him resolutely*]. Ignaty Ilyitch . . .

SHPIGELSKY [*alertly*]. I'm all ears, Vera Alexandrovna. . . . What a look, upon my word. . . . I'm all ears.

VERA. That gentleman . . . Bolshintsov, your friend, is he really a good man?

SHPIGELSKY. My friend Bolshintsov? The most excellent, the best of men . . . a pattern and paragon of all the virtues.

VERA. He's not ill-natured?

SHPIGELSKY. Most kind-hearted, upon my soul. He's not a man, he's made of dough, really. You've only to take him and mould him. You wouldn't find another such good-natured fellow if you searched with a candle by daylight. He's a dove, not a man.

VERA. You answer for him?

SHPIGELSKY [*lays one hand on his heart and raises the other upwards*]. As I would for myself!

VERA. Then, you can tell him . . . that I am willing to marry him.

SHPIGELSKY [*with joyful amazement*]. You don't say so!

VERA. But as soon as possible—do you hear? . . . As soon as possible. . . .

SHPIGELSKY. To-morrow, if you like. . . . I should rather think so!

Bravo, Vera Alexandrovna! You're a young lady of spirit! I'll gallop over to him at once. Won't he be overjoyed. . . . Well, this is an unexpected turn of affairs! Why, he worships the ground you tread on, Vera Alexandrovna. . . .

VERA [*with impatience*]. I didn't ask you that, Ignaty Ilyitch.

SHPIGELSKY. As you please, Vera Alexandrovna, as you please. Only you'll be happy with him, you'll be grateful to me, you'll see. . . . [VERA *makes a gesture of impatience.*] There, I'll hold my tongue. . . . So then I can tell him? . . .

VERA. You can, you can.

SHPIGELSKY. Very good. So I'll set off at once. Good-bye. [*Listens.*] And here's somebody coming, by the way. [*Goes towards study and in the doorway makes a grimace expressing surprise to himself.*] Good-bye for the present. [*Goes out.*]

VERA [*looking after him*]. Anything in the world is better than staying here. [*Stands up.*] Yes, I have made up my mind. I won't stop in this house . . . not for anything. I can't endure her soft looks, her smiles, I can't bear the sight of her, basking and purring in her happiness. . . . She's happy, however she pretends to be sad and sorrowful. . . . Her caresses are unbearable. . . .

[BELIAYEV *appears in the door of the outer room. He looks round and goes up to* VERA.]

BELIAYEV [*in a low voice*]. Vera Alexandrovna, you're alone?

VERA [*looks round, starts, and after a moment, brings out*]. Yes.

BELIAYEV. I'm glad to find you alone. . . . I should not have come in here otherwise. Vera Alexandrovna, I've come to say good-bye to you.

VERA. Good-bye?

BELIAYEV. Yes, I'm going away.

VERA. You are going away? You too?

BELIAYEV. Yes . . . I too. [*With intense suppressed feeling.*] You see, Vera Alexandrovna, I can't stay here. I've done so much harm here already. Apart from my having—I don't know how—disturbed your peace of mind and Natalya Petrovna's, I've broken up old friendships. Thanks to me, Mr. Rakitin is leaving this house, you have quarrelled with your benefactress. . . . It's time to put a stop to it all. After I am gone, I hope everything will settle down and be right again. . . . Turning rich women's heads and breaking young girls' hearts is not in my line. . . . You will forget about me, and, in time perhaps, will wonder how all this could have happened. . . . I wonder even now. . . . I don't want to deceive you, Vera Alexandrovna; I'm frightened, I'm terrified of staying here. . . . I can't answer for anything. . . . And you know I'm not used to all this. I feel awkward. . . . I feel as though everybody's looking at me. . . . And in fact it would be impossible for me . . . now . . . with you both. . . .

VERA. Oh, don't trouble yourself on my account! I'm not staying here long.

BELIAYEV. What do you mean?

VERA. That's my secret. But I shan't be in your way, I assure you.

BELIAYEV. Well, but, you see, I must go. Think; I seem to have brought a plague into this house, everyone's running away. . . . Isn't it better for me to disappear before more harm's done? I have just had a great talk with Mr. Rakitin. . . . You can't imagine how bitterly he spoke. . . . And he might well jeer at my new coat. . . . He's right. Yes, I must go. Would you believe it, Vera Alexandrovna, I'm longing for the minute when I shall be racing along the high road in a cart. I'm stifling here, I want to get into the open air. I can't tell you how grieved and at the same time light-hearted I feel, like a man setting off on a long journey overseas; he's sad and sick at parting from his friends, yet the sound of the sea is so joyful, the wind is so fresh in his face, that it sets his blood dancing, though his heart may ache. . . . Yes, I'm certainly going. I'll go back to Moscow, to my old companions, I'll set to work. . . .

VERA. You love her, it seems, Alexey Nikolaitch; you love her, yet you are going away.

BELIAYEV. Hush, Vera Alexandrovna, why do you say that? Don't you see that it's all over? It flared up and has gone out like a spark. Let us part friends. It's time. I've come to my senses. Keep well, be happy, we shall see each other again some day. . . . I shall never forget you, Vera Alexandrovna. . . . I'm very fond of you, believe me. . . . [*Presses her hand and adds hurriedly.*] Give this note to Natalya Petrovna for me. . . .

VERA [*glancing at him embarrassed*]. A note?

BELIAYEV. Yes . . . I can't say good-bye to her.

VERA. But are you going at once?

BELIAYEV. This minute. . . . I have not said anything to anybody . . . except Mihail Alexandritch. He approves. I'm going to walk from here to Petrovskoe. There I shall wait for Mihail Alexandritch and we shall drive on to the town together. I'll write from there. My things will be sent on after me. You see it's all settled. But you can read the note. There's only a couple of words in it.

VERA [*taking the note from him*]. And you are really going?

BELIAYEV. Yes, yes. . . . Give her that note and say . . . No, there's no need to say anything. . . . What's the use? [*Listening.*] Here they come. Good-bye. [*Rushes to the door, stops an instant in the doorway, then runs away.* VERA *is left with the note in her hand.* NATALYA PETROVNA *comes in.*]

NATALYA PETROVNA [*going up to* VERA]. Verotchka. . . . [*Glances at her and breaks off.*] What's the matter? [VERA *holds out the note without a word.*] A note? From whom?

VERA [*in a toneless voice*]. Read it.

NATALYA PETROVNA. You frighten me. [*Reads the note in silence and suddenly presses both hands to her face and sinks into an armchair. A long silence.*]

VERA [*approaching her*]. Natalya Petrovna.

NATALYA PETROVNA [*not taking her hands from her face*]. He is gone! . . . He wouldn't even say good-bye to me. . . . Oh, to you he said good-bye, anyway!

VERA [*sadly*]. He doesn't love me. . . .

NATALYA PETROVNA [*taking her hands from her face and standing up*]. But he has no right to go off like this. . . . I will . . . He can't do this. . . . Who told him he might break away so stupidly. . . . It's simply contempt. . . . I . . . how does he know I should never have the courage. . . . [*Sinks into the armchair.*] My God! my God!

VERA. Natalya Petrovna, you told me yourself just now that he must go. . . . Remember.

NATALYA PETROVNA. You are glad now. . . . He is gone. . . . Now we are equal. [*Her voice breaks.*]

VERA. Natalya Petrovna, you said to me just now; these were your very words; instead of tormenting each other hadn't we better think together how to get out of this position, how to save ourselves. . . . We are saved now.

NATALYA PETROVNA [*turning away from her almost with hatred*]. Ah! . . .

VERA. I understand, Natalya Petrovna; don't worry yourself. . . . I shan't burden you with my company long. We can't live together.

NATALYA PETROVNA [*tries to hold out her hand to* VERA *but lets it fall on her lap*]. Why do you say that, Verotchka? . . . Do you too want to leave me? Yes, you are right, we are saved now. All is over . . . everything is settled again. . . .

VERA [*coldly*]. Don't disturb yourself, Natalya Petrovna. [*She looks at* NATALYA PETROVNA *without speaking.* ISLAYEV *comes out of the study.*]

ISLAYEV [*after looking for a moment at* NATALYA PETROVNA, *aside to* VERA]. Does she know that he is going?

VERA [*puzzled*]. Yes . . . she knows.

ISLAYEV [*to himself*]. But why has he been in such a hurry? . . . [*Aloud.*] Natasha. . . . [*He takes her hand. She raises her head.*] It's I, Natasha. [*She tries to smile.*] You're not well, my darling? I should advise you to lie down, really. . . .

NATALYA PETROVNA. I'm quite well, Arkady; it's nothing.

ISLAYEV. But you're pale . . . Come, do as I say . . . Rest a little.

NATALYA PETROVNA. Oh! very well. . . . [*She tries to get up, and cannot.*]

ISLAYEV [*helping her*]. There you see. . . . [*She leans on his arm.*] Shall I help you along?

NATALYA PETROVNA. Oh, I'm not so weak as all that! Come, Vera. [*Goes towards the study.* RAKITIN *comes in from the outer room.* NATALYA PETROVNA *stops.*]

RAKITIN. I have come, Natalya Petrovna, to . . .

ISLAYEV [*interrupting him*]. Ah, Michel, come here! [*Draws him aside—in an undertone with vexation.*] What made you tell her at once like this? Didn't I beg you not to! Why be in such a hurry? . . . I found her here in such a state.

RAKITIN [*perplexed*]. I don't understand.

ISLAYEV. You've told Natasha you are going. . . .

RAKITIN. So you suppose that is what has upset her?

ISLAYEV. Sh! she is looking at us. [*Aloud.*] You're not going to lie down, Natasha?

NATALYA PETROVNA. Yes. . . . I'm going. . . .

RAKITIN. Good-bye, Natalya Petrovna! [NATALYA PETROVNA *takes hold of the door-handle and makes no reply.*]

ISLAYEV [*laying his hand on* RAKITIN'S *shoulder*]. Natasha, do you know this is one of the best of men. . . .

NATALYA PETROVNA [*with sudden vehemence*]. Yes, I know he's a splendid man . . . you're all splendid men . . . all of you, all . . . and yet. . . . [*She hides her face in her hands, pushes the door open with her knee and goes out hurriedly.* VERA *goes out after her.* ISLAYEV *in silence sits down to the table and leans on his elbows.*]

RAKITIN [*looks at him for some time and with a bitter smile shrugs his shoulders.*] Nice position mine! Glorious, it certainly is! Really it's positively refreshing. And what a farewell after four years of love! Excellent, serve the talker right. And thank God, it's all for the best. It was high time to end these sickly, morbid relations. [*Aloud to* ISLAYEV.] Well, Arkady, good-bye.

ISLAYEV [*raises his head. There are tears in his eyes*]. Good-bye, my dear, dear boy. It's . . . not quite easy to bear. I didn't expect it. It's like a storm on a clear day. Well, grind the corn and there'll be flour. But anyway, thank you, thank you. You're a true friend.

RAKITIN [*aside through his teeth*]. This is too much. [*Abruptly.*] Good-bye. [*Is about to go into outer room.* SHPIGELSKY *runs in, meeting him.*]

SHPIGELSKY. What is it? They tell me Natalya Petrovna is ill. . . .

ISLAYEV [*getting up*]. Who told you so?

SHPIGELSKY. The girl . . . her maid. . . .

ISLAYEV. No, it's nothing, Doctor. I think, better not disturb Natasha just now. . . .

SHPIGELSKY. Ah! well, that's all right. [To RAKITIN.] I hear you're going to town?

RAKITIN. Yes, on business.

SHPIGELSKY. Ah! on business! . . . [*At that instant* ANNA SEMYONOVNA, LIZAVETA BOGDANOVNA, KOLYA and SCHAAF *burst in from the outer room, all at once.*]

ANNA SEMYONOVNA. What is it? What's the matter? What's wrong with Natasha?

KOLYA. What's the matter with Mamma? What is it?

ISLAYEV. Nothing's the matter with her. . . . I saw her a minute ago. What's the matter with all of you?

ANNA SEMYONOVNA. Really, Arkasha, we were told Natasha's been taken ill. . . .

ISLAYEV. Well, you shouldn't have believed it.

ANNA SEMYONOVNA. But why are you so cross, Arkasha? Our sympathy's only natural.

ISLAYEV. Of course . . . of course.

RAKITIN. It's time for me to start.

ANNA SEMYONOVNA. You are going away?

RAKITIN. Yes. . . . I am going.

ANNA SEMYONOVNA [*to herself*]. Ah! Well, now I understand.

KOLYA [*to* ISLAYEV]. Papa . . .

ISLAYEV. What do you want?

KOLYA. Why has Alexey Nikolaitch gone out?

ISLAYEV. Where's he gone?

KOLYA. I don't know . . . He kissed me, put on his cap and went out. . . . And it's time for my Russian lesson.

ISLAYEV. I expect he'll be back soon. . . . We can send to look for him, though.

RAKITIN [*aside to* ISLAYEV]. Don't send after him, Arkady, he won't come back. [ANNA SEMYONOVNA *tries to overhear;* SHPIGELSKY *is whispering with* LIZAVETA BOGDANOVNA.]

ISLAYEV. What's the meaning of that?

RAKITIN. He's going away, too.

ISLAYEV. Going away . . . where?

RAKITIN. To Moscow.

ISLAYEV. To Moscow? Why, is everybody going mad to-day, or what?

RAKITIN [*in a still lower voice*]. Well, the fact is . . . Verotchka's fallen in love with him . . . so being an honourable man he decided to go. [ISLAYEV, *flinging up his hands, sinks into an arm-chair.*] You understand now, why. . . .

ISLAYEV [*leaping up*]. Understand? I understand nothing. My head's going round. What is one to make of it? All fluttering off in different directions like a lot of partridges, and all because they're honourable men. . . . And all at once on the same day. . . .

ANNA SEMYONOVNA [*coming up from one side*]. But what's this? Mr. Beliayev, you say . . .

ISLAYEV [*shouts hysterically*]. Never mind, Mamma, never mind! Herr Schaaf, kindly give Kolya his lesson now instead of Mr. Beliayev. Take him away.

SCHAAF. Yes, Sir. [*Takes* KOLYA's *hand.*]

KOLYA. But, Papa . . .

ISLAYEV [*shouting*]. Go along, go along! [SCHAAF *leads* KOLYA *away.*] I'll come part of the way with you, Rakitin. . . . I'll have my horse saddled, and wait for you at the dam. . . . And you, Mamma, meanwhile, for God's sake, don't disturb Natasha, nor you either, Doctor. . . . Matvey! Matvey! [*Goes out hurriedly.* ANNA SEMYONOVNA *sits down with melancholy dignity.* LIZAVETA BOGDANOVNA *takes her stand behind her.* ANNA SEMYONOVNA *turns her eyes upwards, as though disclaiming all connexion with what is going on around her.*]

SHPIGELSKY [*slyly and stealthily to* RAKITIN]. Well, Mihail Alexandritch, may I have the honour of driving you along the high road with my three new horses?

RAKITIN. Why? Have you got the horses already?

SHPIGELSKY [*discreetly*]. I had a little talk with Vera Alexandrovna. . . . So may I?

RAKITIN. By all means! [*Bows to* ANNA SEMYONOVNA.] Anna Semyonovna, I have the honour to . . .

ANNA SEMYONOVNA [*still as majestically, not getting up*]. Good-bye, Mihail Alexandritch. . . . I wish you a successful journey. . . .

RAKITIN. I thank you . . . Lizaveta Bogdanovna. . . . [*Bows to her. She curtsies in reply. He goes into outer room.*]

SHPIGELSKY [*going up to kiss* ANNA SEMYONOVNA's *hand*]. Good-bye, gracious lady. . . .

ANNA SEMYONOVNA [*less majestically but still severely*]. Ah! you are going too, Doctor. . . .

SHPIGELSKY. Yes. My patients, you know, madam. . . . Besides, you see my presence here is not needed. [*As he bows himself out, winks slyly at* LIZAVETA BOGDANOVNA, *who replies with a smile.*] Good-bye for the present. . . . [*Runs off after* RAKITIN.]

ANNA SEMYONOVNA [*lets him disappear, then folding her arms, turns deliberately to* LIZAVETA BOGDANOVNA]. And what do you think of all this, my dear, pray?

LIZAVETA BOGDANOVNA [*sighing*]. I really don't know what to say, Anna Semyonovna.

ANNA SEMYONOVNA. Did you hear, Beliayev too has gone? . . .

LIZAVETA BOGDANOVNA [*sighing again*]. Ah, Anna Semyonovna, perhaps I, too, may not be staying here much longer. . . . I too am going away. [ANNA SEMYONOVNA *stares at her in unutterable amazement.* LIZAVETA BOGDANOVNA *stands before her, without raising her eyes.*]

CURTAIN